The Parmenidean Ascent

The Parmenidean Ascent

MICHAEL DELLA ROCCA

OXFORD
UNIVERSITY PRESS

OXFORD
UNIVERSITY PRESS

Oxford University Press is a department of the University of Oxford. It furthers
the University's objective of excellence in research, scholarship, and education
by publishing worldwide. Oxford is a registered trade mark of Oxford University
Press in the UK and certain other countries.

Published in the United States of America by Oxford University Press
198 Madison Avenue, New York, NY 10016, United States of America.

© Oxford University Press 2020

All rights reserved. No part of this publication may be reproduced, stored in
a retrieval system, or transmitted, in any form or by any means, without the
prior permission in writing of Oxford University Press, or as expressly permitted
by law, by license, or under terms agreed with the appropriate reproduction
rights organization. Inquiries concerning reproduction outside the scope of the
above should be sent to the Rights Department, Oxford University Press, at the
address above.

You must not circulate this work in any other form
and you must impose this same condition on any acquirer.

Library of Congress Cataloging-in-Publication Data
Names: Della Rocca, Michael, author.
Title: The Parmenidean Ascent / Michael Della Rocca.
Description: New York, NY, United States of America : Oxford University Press, 2020. |
Includes bibliographical references and index.
Identifiers: LCCN 2019056873 (print) | LCCN 2019056874 (ebook) |
ISBN 9780197510940 (hardback) | ISBN 9780197510964 (epub) |
ISBN 9780197510957 (UPDF) | ISBN 9780197510971 (Online)
Subjects: LCSH: Parmenides. | Monism.
Classification: LCC B235.P24 D45 2020 (print) | LCC B235.P24 (ebook) |
DDC 147/.3—dc23
LC record available at https://lccn.loc.gov/2019056873
LC ebook record available at https://lccn.loc.gov/2019056874

3 5 7 9 8 6 4 2

Printed by Integrated Books International, United States of America

For My Teachers and My Students

Contents

Acknowledgments   ix
Proem   xiii

1. The Call of Parmenides   1
2. Substance: A Litany of Failure   24
3. Substance: The Underlying Problem   59
4. Action   83
5. Knowledge   112
6. Meaning   145
7. Meaning, the History of Philosophy, and Analytical Philosophy   182
8. Metaphysical Explanation   197
9. Paradox and the Joy of Self-Undermining   219
10. Tamers, Deniers, and Me   226
11. The Taming of Philosophy   260
12. Tractatus Parmenideo-Philosophicus   291
13. The Parmenidean Ascent   292

Bibliography   293
Index   311

Acknowledgments

Parts of several chapters have already appeared elsewhere. I am grateful to the editors and publishers of various volumes or journals for permission to reincorporate this material here. I should note, however, that the parts of earlier papers that are included here have been considerably revised for inclusion in this volume. Part of chapter 3 has already appeared in Eric Schliesser (ed.), *Ten Neglected Classics of Philosophy* (Oxford University Press). Part of chapter 4 has already appeared in "Steps Toward Eleaticism in Spinoza's Philosophy of Action" in Naaman-Zauderer (ed.), *Freedom, Action, and Motivation in Spinoza's Ethics* (Cambridge University Press). Parts of chapters 6 and 7 have already appeared in "Meaning, the History of Philosophy, and Analytical Philosophy," in *Philosophy and the Historical Perspective*, edited by Marcel van Ackeren (British Academy). Part of chapter 8 has appeared in "Razing Structures to the Ground," *Analytical Philosophy* 55. Part of chapter 10 has appeared or will soon appear in a special issue of *Philosophical Studies*, edited by Fatema Amijee. Part of chapter 11 originally appeared in Eric Schliesser, Justin Smith, and Mogens Laerke (eds.), *Philosophy and Its History* (Oxford University Press). Thanks also to Yale University for support during a couple of research leaves when parts of this book were written.

Recently reviewing some of my correspondence and notes from the last few years, I was struck anew by the generosity of the large number of people who have engaged with me and kindly offered comments, criticisms, and encouragement. It is a very positive sign of the health of philosophy itself that views as extreme as mine can be not only tolerated but also constructively engaged with in a spirit of openness. And, in part for this reason, it is a pleasure to express gratitude to the many people who have helped me.

Many thanks to three readers for Oxford University Press for penetrating comments and good suggestions. And I would like to thank Peter Ohlin for guiding this project over the last couple of years.

I would like to thank warmly the many participants at the various conferences and colloquia at which I have presented parts of this project. Such occasions are too numerous to list here, but I would particularly like to acknowledge and thank the organizers of and participants at two events. First,

I am grateful to the department of philosophy at Harvard University for inviting me to give the Whitehead lectures in May of 2014. Those lectures and the memorable discussions that followed were a great impetus for me in embarking on this project. And the encouragement of Alison Simmons and Jeff McDonough was especially appreciated. Second, I would like to thank the department of philosophy at Tel Aviv University for inviting me to give a lecture and to lead a workshop in May 2019 as the book was nearing completion. I am especially grateful to Noa Naaman-Zauderer for proposing the idea of such a workshop, for organizing the visit, for her many insights, and for the warm and unforgettable welcome I received from her and her family and her many devoted students. I am also grateful to Hagi Kenaan for discussions and for encouragement and planning, and to the many faculty members and students at Tel Aviv and elsewhere in Israel who read my work with great care and appreciation. The events in Tel Aviv were uplifting and gave me much needed momentum as I headed into the home stretch.

I am grateful to all of my colleagues—past and present—at Yale who, over many years, have borne with my increasingly extreme ideas. Their patience and insight and sometimes incredulous stares are much appreciated.

The get-right-to-the-heart-of-the-matter challenges from Shelly Kagan have always been welcome to me, even when—especially when—my answers did not satisfy me (or, of course, Shelly).

A special thank you to Brad Inwood for organizing and leading a memorable discussion group on the fragments of Parmenides to which he kindly invited me. More generally, the colleagues and students at Yale in ancient philosophy have been a continuing source of insights both into philosophical topics close to their hearts and mine and into the diversity of ways to approach the history of philosophy.

Ethan Della Rocca offered much appreciated advice about Greek.

I thank Barbara Sattler for her generous support and many wide-ranging and always excellent discussions on topics ancient and contemporary. It was a pleasure to be working on this book at the same time as her monumental work on the concept of motion in ancient thought was taking shape.

I thank Carol Rovane for always giving me good advice, for her many insightful comments on my chapters and papers, and for her skepticism about the PSR. It is a source of surprise and delight that I found my own philosophical views shifting gradually toward positions she has long defended.

I thank Elizabeth Miller for her spirit of genuine questioning and for understanding—and for helping me to understand—the character of the challenge I am trying to raise to standard ways of philosophizing. Her own work also exemplifies, but in a very different way, a similarly radical challenge to the status quo.

Ken Winkler's subtle, generous readings of texts and his great capacity for sympathetic engagement with the work of others always give me something to which I can aspire. It is an honor to work closely with him.

Will Ratoff has, I think, outdone me when it comes to exploring extreme rationalism and its power to take us to unexpected and bracing places. His exemplary commitment to rationalism has frequently served as a model and inspiration for me.

Daniel Moerner's resourceful and generous reactions and his astounding breadth and depth of knowledge have always taught me more than I could incorporate. He never failed to bring to light and develop a wholly unanticipated and extremely valuable perspective on material I thought I had already understood.

Julia Borcherding was among the very first to react to and to help me shape this project. Co-teaching a seminar with her on rationalisms was a great boon for me from which I learned a tremendous amount, and I continue to learn from her unique and challenging perspective on philosophy and its history.

The rationalist joie de vivre that I hope to bring to my work has already been fully manifested in Sam Newlands' work and in the welcome philosophical discussions that he always sparks.

Fatema Amijee's comments are always deeply appreciated. Her abiding love for the PSR rivals my own, and her own dynamic path through rationalism is highly illuminating.

Omri Boehm's many Kantian challenges to my work have shaped it in unmistakable ways, for they were challenges that for a long time I could not answer (and perhaps still can't).

Yitzhak Melamed saw the Parmenidean direction of my thinking perhaps even before I did. And his support has always meant and continues to mean a great deal to me.

I am indebted to Judy Malamut for her appreciation of and insight into my project and for her loyalty in attending so many of my seminars over the last decade.

The students—both undergraduate and graduate—in my many seminars at Yale over the years on topics connected to this book have been simultaneously remarkably challenging and supportive. Almost all of the ideas in this book took shape, in one way or another, in these seminars, and I cannot stress enough how crucial the reactions of the participants in my seminars have always been to me and my work.

Others whom it gives me great pleasure to thank for written comments, philosophical conversations, or both include Harry Alanen, Lilli Alanen, Facundo Alonso, Abraham Anderson, Cole Aronson, Sebastian Bender, John Bengson, Justin Broackes, Sarah Buss, Ulrika Carlsson, Yual Chiek, Andrew Chignell, Luke Ciancarelli, Tim Clarke, Jim Conant, Simon Custer, Jennifer Daigle, Justin D'Ambrosio, Steve Darwall, Isis Davis-Marks, Vincent Descombes, Karen Detlefsen, Bridger Ehli, Sam Elgin, Tom Feeney, Daniel Ferguson, Mark Fiocco, Jeremy Fix, Anton Ford, Dan Garber, Don Garrett, Zach Gartenberg, Rebecca Newberger Goldstein, Dan Greco, John Grey, Emily Grosholz, Jani Hakkarainen, Sungil Han, Scott Harkema, Stephen Harrop, Dai Heide Reier Helle, Paul Hoffman, Des Hogan, Karolina Hübner, Rima Hussein, Robin Jeshion, Antuan Johnson, Julia Jorati, Irad Kimhi, Julie Klein, Dr. Gary Kopf, Ari Koslow, David Kovacs, Jim Kreines, Tony Kronman, Nancy Levene, Yair Levy, Anat Matar, Mark Maxwell, Kris McDaniel, Kelvin McQueen, Louis Menand, Molly Montgomery, Dick Moran, Alexander Mourelatos, Alan Nelson, Michael Nelson, Natalie Nenadic, Karin Nisenbaum, Elliot Paul, Laurie Paul, Dominic Perler, Juan Piñeros Glasscock, John Pittard, Ian Proops, Viorica Ramírez de Santiago, Ursula Renz, Jake Rohde, Bill Salisbury, Tim Scanlon, Jonathan Schaffer, Tamar Schapiro, Anat Schechtman, Eric Schliesser, Jelscha Schmid, Stephan Schmid, Robert Schnepf, Lisa Shapiro, Ted Sider, Alex Silverman, Sophia Sklaviadis, Ernest Sosa, Zoltan Szabo, Peter Thielke, Jonathan Vertanen, Philip Waldner, Eric Watkins, Bruno Whittle, Mary Beth Willard, Tim Williamson, Leslie Wolf, and Jason Yonover. Many apologies to those whose names I have inadvertently omitted.

This book is dedicated to my teachers and my students. Of course, these categories overlap in significant ways. Among my teachers, the late Wallace Matson is one to whom I owe a special debt. Wallace's work in philosophy and Wallace himself—*sub specie aeternitatis*—exemplify the spirit of the Parmenidean Ascent in a way that continues to be an inspiration for me.

Finally, my greatest thanks are to Christine Hayes and to our sons, Ben and Ethan. All three are never-ending sources of being, action, knowledge, meaning, explanation, and love.

Hamden, Connecticut
August 9, 2019

Proem

I have often thought it ironic that the writings of Parmenides—one of the most famous monists in the history of philosophy—are available to us only in the form of fragments. Would that Parmenidean monism had come down to us in the integral form it presumably originally had, a form that would come closer than fragments do to reflecting the monistic world of which he seems to speak!

Perhaps it is because we have only these fragments that most philosophers do not feel the need to address Parmenides' arguments or his insights explicitly. Some do or did feel this demand—most notably, perhaps, Plato and Aristotle both of whom would have had access to more of Parmenides' written words than we do. Indeed, I would say that Plato and Aristotle were, in different ways, practically haunted by Parmenides' arguments and vision. Yet these arguments and this vision are now—if they are discussed at all—more or less relegated to the study of the history of philosophy, a pursuit often seen as, effectively, separate from the pursuit of philosophy itself.

However, whether or not philosophers nowadays actively engage with Parmenides, his thought still hovers like a specter rising above and challenging all subsequent philosophy down to the present day, and it calls for a response. This call of Parmenides arises because his monism embodies a powerful and penetrating philosophical insight which is very difficult to resist legitimately, no matter how much we might try to wish it away or to ignore it. My aim is to counteract such unfortunate evasion of Parmenides by revealing the subversive force of an extreme monism of the Parmenidean variety and by doing so in a clearer, more uncompromising way than has, I believe, been attempted for many a year.

Throughout this book, you will see me engage with Parmenides and other historical figures in significant detail. You will also see me engage in deep explorations of contemporary and recent philosophy. This combination of pursuits may lead you to ask whether this is a book on the history of philosophy or in contemporary philosophy. And my playful but serious answer is: "Yes." In other words, I reject the question, and this is precisely because I see the book as supporting a Parmenidean denial of the distinction between philosophy and the study of its history. In chapter 7, I will argue for this denial explicitly, but the book as a whole is meant to exhibit its truth.

I begin my Parmenidean journey in chapter 1 with what I take to be a strong case for a reading of Parmenides as what I (following others) will call a strict monism. Parmenides is, I contend, a strict monist in the sense that he rejects any kind of distinction or multiplicity whatsoever. On my reading, Parmenides affirms simply the reality of being; he does not affirm the reality of any individual being or beings and does not affirm any distinctions within being. Of course, I freely acknowledge that, as Alexander Mourelatos rightly says in his wonderful book on Parmenides, "Given the paucity of text and the bewildering ambiguities in Parmenides' syntax and vocabulary, it would be interpreter's hubris to claim that any single reading of Parmenides' poem forecloses the possibility of others" (*The Route of Parmenides*, p. xxvi). And, because I am not a specialist in ancient philosophy, I am all the more willing—and indeed happy—to emphasize that my interpretation is neither definitive nor obligatory. However, I am encouraged by the fact that, although this kind of interpretation has recently come under sustained and powerful attack by Mourelatos and many others, it nonetheless enjoys an illustrious pedigree, including interpretations by G. E. L. Owen, Montgomery Furth, Bertrand Russell, and others, and has recently witnessed a kind of renaissance in the interpretive work of Barbara Sattler, Timothy Clarke, and Michael Wedin.[1] It is one of my hopes and aims that my first chapter will contribute to this renaissance, in particular by portraying, with solid textual support, Parmenides' monistic argument as a more thoroughgoing application of a famous rationalist principle than has previously been recognized. The principle I have in mind is the Principle of Sufficient Reason (the PSR), the principle according to which each fact or each thing has an explanation. Others also, as we will see, attribute the PSR to Parmenides, and I am indebted to their work. Where I go beyond them is, perhaps, in seeing the role that the PSR plays in Parmenides' thought as more pervasive and more fundamental.

In advancing this kind of rationalism-infused monism, Parmenides makes what I call the Parmenidean Ascent. Guided by his demand for explanation, he rejects distinctions in general and, in so doing, seeks to capture the reality that we were—by appealing to distinctions—illegitimately trying to capture. In transcending—in making the ascent beyond—distinctions,

---

[1] See Owen, "Eleatic Questions"; Furth, "Elements of Eleatic Ontology"; Russell, *A History of Western Philosophy*, pp. 48–52; Sattler, *The Concept of Motion in Ancient Greek Thought*; Clarke, *Aristotle and the Eleatic One*; and Wedin, *Parmenides' Grand Deduction*.

Parmenides aims to finally see the world aright, as Wittgenstein says in a different but, as I will eventually argue, not entirely dissimilar context.[2] And just as Wittgenstein invokes certain propositions concerning, e.g., logical form, but also transcends them and rejects them as nonsense, so too Parmenides invokes certain distinctions, e.g., between what is and what is not, but also transcends them and rejects them as unthinkable.

My choice of the metaphor of ascent may be seen as alluding to the journey of the youth who narrates Parmenides' poem and who—as recounted in Parmenides' own proem—can be seen as traveling with the daughters of the sun upward to somewhere ethereal (B1.13) and toward the light (B1.10).[3] The trajectory of the youth's journey—up or down or both—is a matter of great dispute in the literature on Parmenides, and I take no stand on this interpretive issue. I merely want to point out that my metaphor of ascent fits in with a natural reading of Parmenides as well as, of course, a natural reading of Wittgenstein, two of the philosophical inspirations for the journey I will take with you in this book.[4]

This journey—my Parmenidean Ascent—is, like the journey of Parmenides' youth, designed to shed light on, and to wreak havoc throughout, philosophy. In the five chapters immediately following the first, I will undertake to argue for Parmenidean Ascents in a number of central philosophical domains. In many ways, these five chapters are the heart of this book. I begin in chapters 2 and 3 with a Parmenidean Ascent with regard to substance or being itself. All or most philosophers should feel—I will argue—considerable pressure to reject as unintelligible distinctions among or within substances or beings. This rejection can be motivated, as is Parmenides' own rejection of distinctions, by the rationalist principle, the PSR. I will offer an analogously structured argument in chapter 4 for a Parmenidean Ascent with regard to action: there are no individuated actions and no distinctions between actions and such items as reasons or beliefs or desires; rather there is simply action

---

[2] Wittgenstein, *Tractatus Logico-Philosophicus* 6.54: "He must transcend these propositions, and then he will see the world aright (*Er musse diese Sätze überwinden, dann sieht er die Welt richtig*)" (McGuiness and Pears translation).

[3] For numbering the fragments of Parmenides' text, I follow the system to be found in Diehls and Kranz, *Die Fragmente der Vorsokratiker*. I mostly follow the translations in Coxon, *The Fragments of Parmenides*. I have also consulted and sometimes drawn on translations by Gallop, *Parmenides of Elea*; Kirk, Raven, and Schofield, *The Presocratic Philosophers*; Laks and Most, *Early Greek Philosophy*, volume V, part 2; and Mourelatos, *The Route of Parmenides*.

[4] For a judicious treatment of the debate on the trajectory of the youth, see Tor, *Mortal and Divine in Early Greek Epistemology*, pp. 347–59. For a strong defense of the reading of the youth's journey as an ascent, see Kahn, *Essays on Being*, pp. 207–17. I am indebted here to Timothy Clarke.

itself. I make similar arguments in chapter 5 with regard to knowledge and in chapter 6 with regard to meaning. In each case, I argue, we have strong reason to make a Parmenidean Ascent with regard to the relevant phenomenon: substance, action, knowledge or meaning.

For each notion, I begin inductively. First, I establish the failure of all or almost all extant theories in the relevant domain to meet a certain explanatory demand that—as all sides seem to agree—structures our understanding of the notion in question. The explanatory demand takes the form: what is it in virtue of which a given substance is a substance? What is it in virtue of which a given action is an action? And similarly natural questions arise with regard to knowledge and meaning. This demand is a seemingly well-placed request for a metaphysical explanation of a certain phenomenon. It is a virtue of the leading theories I discuss that they insist on this demand. I will then conduct a general survey of these leading theories and pinpoint where they fail to meet the explanatory demand that these theories—rightly, it seems—impose on themselves. This widespread and massive failure to meet the relevant explanatory demands indicates—and this is my inductive conclusion—that there is something systematically and fundamentally wrong with the leading approaches in each of these areas.

To identify the source of the difficulty, I will in each of these cases also argue in a complementary *a priori* fashion that all theories of the phenomenon in question that make a certain seemingly harmless assumption—viz. the assumption that we are concerned with differentiated cases of the phenomenon—must fail to meet the explanatory demand relevant in this domain. The crux of the *a priori* argument in each of these cases is a rationalist argument in the spirit of the great British idealist, F. H. Bradley, against the reality of the relevant kind of relation, and hence against the reality of differentiated substance, action, knowledge, or meaning. Though the spirit of my *a priori* argument is Bradleyan—and indeed Parmenidean—its formulation and inner workings are my own.

The upshot (or one upshot) is that, in order to preserve the key notions of substance, action, etc., we must give up the assumption of differentiation or relations in these areas. We must, in other words, make a Parmenidean Ascent in each of these fields and embrace a kind of monism of substance, of action, of knowledge, and of meaning. For example, if we are to retain the notion of substance or being at all, then, instead of individuated, differentiated substances or beings, we should accept only undifferentiated substance or being that stands in no relations of distinction, either internal or external.

There is simply substance or being. Similarly, there is simply action, there is simply knowledge, there is simply meaning. And, of course, there is no distinction between being, action, knowledge, and meaning.

I will lay out this *a priori* argument first and in most detail in chapter 3 in the case of substance. There I will defend my Bradleyan juggernaut against many prominent objections and exhibit the Parmenidean Ascent with regard to substance. Chapter 2 will conduct the inductive argument that leading theories of substance fail to meet their own explanatory demand and that there is something systematically amiss in such theories. The inductive arguments concerning action, knowledge, and meaning occur in chapters 4–6. The *a priori* arguments in these cases have the same form as the *a priori* argument in the case of substance and thus will not require separate chapters.

In the case of action, the Parmenidean Ascent will have shocking and drastic implications for our understanding of free will and also for moral philosophy generally, as I will explain briefly in chapter 4. However, exploring the full impact of the Parmenidean Ascent for matters of moral philosophy will be a project for a future occasion.

In the case of knowledge, the Parmenidean Ascent will lead in chapter 5—despite the pervasiveness of knowledge or the monism of knowledge—to skepticism in the form of a denial that there is knowledge as we ordinarily understand it, and indeed a denial of the coherence of the ordinary concept of knowledge. This will be a denial of the coherence of the claim that there are states of knowledge that are differentiated from each other and from things that are not states of knowledge. I should stress, though, that skeptical implications are not unique to the Parmenidean Ascent with regard to knowledge. In general, the Parmenidean Ascents in this book are skeptical in character: they deny the existence and the coherence of phenomena, including apparent distinctions, to which we are ordinarily committed.

The Parmenidean Ascent with regard to meaning in chapter 6 is especially noteworthy for it is in connection with meaning—perhaps more than in any other area in contemporary and recent philosophy—that philosophers have, perhaps not fully intentionally, advanced arguments that express a form of a Parmenidean Ascent. I have in mind certain arguments in support of a radical holism of meaning in Willard van Orman Quine's "Two Dogmas of Empiricism" (and other writings of Quine's) and in Donald Davidson's "On the Very Idea of a Conceptual Scheme" (and other essays of Davidson's). It is a ray of hope for contemporary philosophy that two of the most consequential arguments in recent philosophy manifest—whether the authors realized this fact or not—a Parmenidean thrust. The Parmenidean Ascent with regard to meaning will also, as we will see, lead to a Parmenidean Ascent with regard to truth: the alleged distinction between a true proposition and the fact that that proposition is about must, like other distinctions, be transcended. The rejection of this distinction amounts to a rejection of realism.

This abandonment of realism is a theme that I pursue further in chapter 7 in which I also advance, on the basis of the Parmenidean Ascent with regard to meaning, a new way of thinking about the distinction between philosophy and the study of its history. Here I urge a Parmenidean Ascent with regard to this distinction too, and in so doing, I also begin the process of challenging some of the foundations—or what I will call the struts—of analytical philosophy itself, a project that I will continue in the remaining chapters of this book. One of these struts is realism, and all of the struts turn upon or presuppose the notion of relations which I challenge throughout the book.

As if the monistic, distinction-less outcomes in the domains taken up in chapters 2–7 are not troubling and provocative enough, I take my Parmenidean chariot in perhaps even more paradoxical and skeptical directions in chapter 8 and beyond. Chapter 8 challenges the notion of metaphysical explanation and the related notion of metaphysical grounding that is prevalent in much of contemporary metaphysics. In this case, however, my challenge proceeds differently from the way I conduct my challenges to accepted notions in the earlier chapters. This is because, in the case of metaphysical explanation, the explanatory demand is not as clearly in place as it is with regard to other central notions. Philosophers are only too happy to treat metaphysical explanation and grounding as primitive, to reject the applicability of the question: in virtue of what is this instance of metaphysical explanation an instance of metaphysical explanation? Nonetheless, in this chapter with the help of a nearly universally beloved principle—Ockham's Razor—I will argue that the notion of metaphysical explanation is incoherent and that employing this notion is irrational. Accordingly, appealing to the notion of metaphysical explanation is not legitimate. The argument in chapter 8 is thus a challenge to the whole edifice of metaphysical explanation and grounding that looms over much contemporary and recent metaphysics (not to mention over much historically prominent metaphysics as well).

And here, as I explain in chapter 9, is where the paradoxical character of my view kicks into even higher gear. For with the rejection of the notion of metaphysical explanation and of the related notion of grounding, we see that there can be no genuine relation of grounding and no genuine metaphysical explanation. However—and this is the paradox—in my earlier arguments I invoke freely and often rely upon the notions of such explanation and of such grounding relations to strike down our ordinary understanding of certain central philosophical notions. In those chapters, I invoke the notion of metaphysical explanation by issuing explanatory demands and asking "in virtue of" questions. There I also praise extant (though misguided) theories of being, knowledge, etc. for their insistence on an explanatory demand, a demand that a given phenomenon be metaphysically explained. But in chapter 8, I reject the very notions of grounding and of metaphysical explanation as incoherent, and so I may seem to undermine my many earlier arguments that are driven by these notions. In the earlier chapters, I deploy these notions with apparent glee in order to mount my arguments against leading accounts of substance, action, knowledge, and meaning. Such accounts fall, I argue in the earlier chapters, because they fail to satisfy the explanatory demand—the demand for a certain kind of metaphysical explanation—that these accounts rightly insist on. But now with the rejection (which I am proposing in chapter 8) of the very notions of grounding and of metaphysical explanation, where do those earlier arguments stand? Indeed, they may seem not to stand at all, but to be instead undermined.

In this light, what are we to do? Can we go back to our original notions of differentiated being, action, etc.? No, because those notions are governed by explanatory demands (and thus by the notion of grounding). These demands, once reinstituted, will eventually lead us again to give up the notions of differentiated substance, etc. But if we then try to defend the undifferentiated notion we get into trouble too, as we are now seeing. We seem, then, to be at another kind of skeptical impasse: there seems to be no way forward for our inquiry.

How then are we to avoid the skeptical, paradoxical instability of self-refutation if we take the explanatory demand seriously, as I do in earlier chapters? We seem to be—just as Parmenides is, as I attempt to show in chapter 1—in a position analogous to Wittgenstein's at the end of his *Tractatus Logico-Philosophicus*. We must recognize that the arguments that have gotten us to this point are illegitimate and also that we cannot return to our original position from which those arguments have purported to deliver us. What step can be taken, then, as Wittgenstein puts it, to see the world aright?

As Wittgenstein counsels, we must *transcend* or *overcome* the problematic propositions on which we have relied; we must, as he puts it, use them as a ladder which we climb and then throw away.[5] That is, in my terminology, we must make a Parmenidean Ascent with regard to the explanatory demand itself. The explanations that I appeal to in the earlier chapters are explanations that are, at least potentially, distinct from the thing explained. They purport to be explanations *of* something *in terms of* something. Such relational explanations—we can now see—are problematic. We must say, instead, that there are no explanations as differentiated from the things explained or from other explanations and that there are no explanations *of* anything or *in terms of* anything, rather there is just explanation, undifferentiated explanation, pure explanation, just as there is pure being, pure action, pure knowing, and pure meaning. Indeed, these phenomena cannot be distinguished from one another, and each is, in effect, explanation itself.

Here on full display is the rationalist character of the Parmenidean view I am espousing in this book: all is simply explanation itself. Reality is not only shot through with intelligibility or explanation, it is simply intelligibility or explanation itself. This theme—all is explanation itself—is one that Parmenides may be articulating in his cryptic pronouncement, "it is the same to think and also to be" (B3). But at the same time that this view is deeply rationalist, it is also deeply skeptical for in portraying reality as pure explanation, being, action, knowledge, and meaning, we are denying the coherence ordinary conceptions of each of these phenomena.

This Parmenidean rationalism—paradoxical and skeptical as it is—certainly seems to be too extreme. Isn't there a way to do justice, as I try to do throughout, to rationalist motivations while at the same time avoiding these Parmenidean precipices, i.e. without taking our chariot so far into uncharted and perhaps unchartable territory? The question here, in effect, is whether there is a way to respect the explanatory demand and to respect the PSR, while limiting the PSR—taming it, as I like to put this point—in some principled way? This strategy of taming the explanatory demand or taming the PSR has been and is a popular and powerful strategy. We find it in some of the less radical interpreters of Parmenides, as I argue in chapter 1, but one can also find, throughout the history of philosophy, other so-called friends of rationalism who also try to limit the PSR. This is what I call a taming strategy, and it is adopted by philosophers as diverse as Kant and contemporary grounding theorists such as Shamik Dasgupta, Kit Fine, and Jonathan Schaffer, and it is

---

[5] I do not advance any particular interpretation of Wittgenstein in this book. I will, though, have a bit more to say by way of situating my position vis-à-vis Wittgenstein's in chapter 9.

one source of potential resistance to the Parmenidean Ascent. I think that this taming strategy should be taken down, and in chapter 10 I take some steps toward doing precisely that. I will attempt to show that the taming strategy is incoherent. I will proceed in that chapter, as I often do in the book, in dialectical fashion by beginning with a critique of one of Leibniz's apparently failed arguments for a strong, untamed version of the PSR. On the basis of this failure, I develop a new way of showing how the limited versions of the PSR on which Kant and others rely invariably turn into a radical monism and an unrestricted PSR that is incompatible with the essence of the strategy of PSR taming. The upshot of that chapter is that the Kantian response to me and, more generally, the response to me that seeks to tame the PSR do not work and that, if one is going to respect explanatory demands at all, one is inevitably led to the kind of skeptical, rationalist monism that I am led to throughout this book. This dialectical argument generates, as I will explain, a positive argument for the PSR, as long as one is willing—as almost all philosophers are—to grant some appeal to the notion of explanation.

With this argument for the PSR, we are not only in a position to claim that if one accepts certain explanatory demands, then one should make various Parmenidean Ascents and accept monism in various domains, but we are also in a position to argue more directly for those explanatory demands and thus for the PSR and for monism in these domains. The earlier, more conditional claims are substantive and provocative in their own right, but the more direct argument in chapter 10 for explanatory demands and for the PSR and for Parmenidean distinction-less monism is truly Parmenideanism run amok.

I am well aware, of course, that you are not likely to embrace the views—or perhaps, the view—I put forth in this book. I expect the resistance to be strong or—worse—the dismissal to be total and peremptory. I know this from long, hard, fascinating, and ultimately uplifting experience. I know that it is overwhelmingly likely that you will not like my conclusions. I am resigned to that, and I expect that. A dear colleague in the profession once said to me—after I expressed one of my Parmenidean conclusions—"I don't like that view." I replied, "You're not supposed to." But even if I do not expect agreement, I want you to take my views seriously, I encourage you to engage with my arguments, and most of all I urge you, as I have said in an epigraph to one of my papers,[6] not to mistake the fact that you don't like my conclusions

---

[6] "The Taming of Philosophy."

for an argument against them. In other words, don't just disagree or dismiss. Show me where I go wrong.

In chapter 11, I will take some further steps toward criticizing and, perhaps, overcoming what I call "The Great Resistance," the inevitable tendency to dismiss my views outright. One source of this tendency to dismiss is the quick way analytical philosophers in particular have of dealing with counterintuitive or implausible views. This high-handedness is a reflection of the method of relying on intuitions—a method that dominates analytical philosophy and forms, as I argue in chapter 7, another one of the struts of analytical philosophy. In chapter 11, I seek to take another step to overcome this resistance to my Parmenidean views by challenging this pervasive method of intuition. My challenge will have two main parts. First, I identify and diagnose several unwelcome features of the method of intuition—its conservatism, its psychologism, and its arbitrary and unprincipled character. Then I will take a different tack and, as I do elsewhere in the book, "go historical" and dig deeper into the early twentieth-century sources of the aversion among analytical philosophers to counterintuitive views. Here, by unmasking one source of this aversion as an ineffectual and, perhaps, question-begging rejection of the PSR, we can see that the method of intuition and indeed much of analytical philosophy itself rests on weak or non-existent grounds.[7] This big reveal may help to overcome some of the opposition or dismissal that will certainly greet the Parmenidean Ascent.

The brief but rich final two chapters embody two modestly proposed, only seemingly different, suggestions for how to proceed in light of my rationalist, Parmenidean Ascent and my rationalist methodological critique of dominant ways of doing philosophy.

An observation for readers of my work on Spinoza: it may seem surprising that in this book I largely refrain from engaging explicitly with Spinoza. I have been tempted to include full-blown discussions of Spinoza in this book because I do think that, in at least one strand of his thinking, Spinoza is drawn to and powerfully articulates a version of the Parmenidean Ascent. But that interpretation is extremely controversial, and it is one that is best entered in separate endeavors devoted to Spinoza.[8] Rest assured, however,

---

[7] For those familiar with U.S. financial law, it is perhaps fitting that the discussion of the bankruptcy of analytical philosophy should occur in chapter 11.
[8] See Della Rocca, "The Elusiveness of the One and the Many," and the forthcoming second edition of my book *Spinoza*.

Spinoza fans: the spirit of Spinoza does hover over much of my thinking in this book in unmistakable ways.

Finally, a general piece of advice for all readers of this book: if you find yourself asking, "What is Della Rocca (MDR) doing?," then it is a good idea to remind yourself that my arguments are probably more rationalist and more skeptical and more Parmenidean than you may suspect. My chariot always aims to outflank you on the rationalist, skeptical, and Parmenidean extreme. But an even more important piece of advice for reading this book is this: ask not what MDR is doing, but ask what you are doing when you are or seem to be doing philosophy. It is, above all else (if there is anything else), this question that I hope that my book inspires you to pursue even more deeply.

1

The Call of Parmenides

I devote this chapter to advancing and defending an interpretation of Parmenides as rejecting any and all distinctions. There are for Parmenides, as I will argue, no divisions in the world, no multiplicity. I will call this position strict monism and will contrast it with other, less strict, more "generous" forms of monism that are often attributed to Parmenides, especially in some prominent recent secondary literature. By uncovering the source within Parmenides of this strict monism, we will be in a position to see how he makes what I called in the proem the Parmenidean Ascent, an explanation-driven rejection of distinctions in general. It is the exploration of and engagement with the reasons for the Parmenidean Ascent as it appears in various domains in philosophy that will constitute the theme of this book. As we will see, the philosophical controversies at work in interpreting Parmenides have been replicated and transformed in many different areas throughout historical and recent and contemporary philosophy

I should stress at the outset that, although in keeping with traditional usage I speak of monism with its suggestion of one-ness, I am not wedded to this term. Although Parmenides does at one point (B 8.6) speak of what-is or being as one (ἕν), it is far from clear whether what-is is one in the same sense that later philosophers have in mind when they express the view that being is one or that there is one thing. When I attribute a strict monism to Parmenides, all I have in mind is the view that there are no distinctions to be found in reality, no multiplicity. I am not necessarily attributing to Parmenides such views as, e.g., that the things in the world can be counted and that the count is one.

I should also stress that in exploring this monistic, no-multiplicity strand in Parmenides' thought, I am, as will soon be obvious, largely leaving to the side many other important interpretive issues, including especially the issue of the relation between thought and reality in Parmenides. Also, I will not discuss in any detail Parmenides' engagement with cosmology. Thus, I am by no means offering a comprehensive interpretation of Parmenides. Rather, my

2 THE PARMENIDEAN ASCENT

inquiry in this chapter is targeted upon the kind of monism that Parmenides may or may not espouse.

Let me give the bare bones of a strict monist reading before exploring some textual objections to this reading and some related philosophical objections to strict monism itself, and before going on to engage with some powerful alternative interpretations.

Parmenides frames his poem around the question of what are and are not legitimate paths of inquiry ("ὁδοί . . . διζήσιός") (B 2.2; see also B 6.3). The first path he considers concerns what-is and what cannot not be ("ἡ μέν ὅπως ἔστιν τε καὶ ὡς οὐκ ἔστι μὴ εἶναι" B 2.3). Parmenides contrasts this path with the way of non-being according to which it is not and it must not be ("ἡ δ' ὡς οὐκ ἔστιν τε καὶ ὡς χρεών ἐστι μὴ εἶναι" B 2.5). For Parmenides, the former path is the "path of persuasion [πειθοῦς . . . κέλευθος]" (B 2.4), and the latter path is a path "wholly without report for you can neither know what is not—for that cannot be accomplished (ἀνυστόν)[1]—nor tell of it" (B 2.6–8). The goddess urges Parmenides to "keep your thought from this way of inquiry [σὺ τῆσδ' ἀφ' ὁδοῦ διζήσιος εἶργε νόημα]" (B 7.2). As the goddess emphasizes, non-being is not (B 6.2).

There has been much controversy over whether Parmenides discusses, in addition, a third way of inquiry "on which mortals with no understanding stray two-headed" (B 6.4–5), the path of those "who believe that to be and not to be are the same and not the same" (B 6.8–9). It is unclear whether this is a separate path or whether it is to be incorporated into one of the other two. We do not need to resolve this matter here.[2] For our purposes, the key point is that the way of being is legitimate and that the way of non-being is not: the invidious treatment of these two ways is enough to enable me to articulate the strict monist reading. On this reading, in rejecting the way of non-being or what-is-not, Parmenides rejects distinctions in general and thus denies the existence of any multiplicity, of any things that are distinct from one another. There are, for Parmenides, on this reading, no true negations, no true negative claims, for to conduct an inquiry via the claim that *x* is not *y* is to inquire into what is not. And this type of inquiry Parmenides disallows.

---

[1] Mourelatos has "cannot be consummated" for reasons that we will see later. This is also a possible translation.

[2] For the record, I favor Nehamas' textual suggestions which support an interpretation according to which there is no such third path distinct from the second, the way of non-being (Nehamas, "On Parmenides' Three Ways of Inquiry"). I differ, though, as we will see from Nehamas, when it comes to the issue of strict monism.

This view is extreme and, perhaps, even paradoxical. To see just how extreme it is, consider this strict monist view in relation to two, by comparison, remarkably tame and mild claims which have recently been portrayed as monistic. Thus, we have the views in contemporary metaphysics known as priority monism and existence monism. Jonathan Schaffer articulates very well the distinction between these views in an important series of papers.[3] According to priority monism, the only fundamental concrete thing—the only concrete thing not explained by other things—is the cosmos itself. Depending on this one fundamental thing is (or may be) a multiplicity of other things, things distinct from the cosmos itself. These dependent things may be parts of or aspects of or modes of the cosmos. This view is monistic because there is only one fundamental (concrete) thing, but it is a *priority* monism because within the one fundamental thing are many parts or aspects or modes to which the cosmos is metaphysically prior.

By contrast, existence monism denies this multiplicity of concrete parts or aspects or modes of the cosmos. For the existence monist, the cosmos itself is the only concrete thing that exists, and there are no distinctions or multiplicity in or within this one concrete object.[4]

Priority monism and existence monism are both controversial, but Parmenides' strict monism is even more extreme in at least two respects. First, both existence monism and priority monism allow for a multiplicity of fundamental, non-concrete objects—e.g., a multiplicity of abstract objects such as, perhaps, abstract universals. Parmenides' strict monism, by contrast, does not invoke or allow any abstract/concrete distinction. There is, for Parmenides, simply what-is, simply being. The rejection of any distinctions in Parmenides' view is more complete than in priority or even existence monism.

Second, both priority monism and existence monism insist that things or the thing can be numbered and that the number of fundamental things is one. By contrast, as I noted, Parmenides is not clearly committed to there being precisely one thing. His view is simply that there are no distinctions within being.

Despite its simplicity and elegance, the strict monist interpretation of Parmenides faces many challenges. First and perhaps most obviously, there

---

[3] For example, Schaffer, "Monism: The Priority of the Whole" and "Monism." The distinction between existence monism and priority monism will prove useful again in chapters 3, 8, and 10.

[4] Horgan and Portç embrace existence monism in their book, *Austere Realism*. Schaffer embraces priority monism.

is the question of how the attribution of a strict monism to Parmenides is compatible with his extensive interest in cosmology. The second part of Parmenides's poem—"Doxa" or "Opinion"—presents various cosmological claims. Parmenides (or the goddess) offers these as "human beliefs" ("δόξας ... βροτείας" B 8.51) and characterizes the verses in which this presentation occurs as "deceptive" ("ἀπατηλόν" B 8.52). Perhaps more positively, he or the goddess also calls these cosmological views "likely" or "plausible" ("ἐοικότα" B 8.60), though this term also conveys the less positive suggestion of being merely apparent or seeming.[5] These opinions are structured around a duality of light and night (φάος and νύξ B 9.1). Given this duality, i.e. given this distinction, it follows that, for a strict monist position which brooks no distinctions, these views are false. But then the obvious challenge to the strict monist reading arises: why does Parmenides spend so much time presenting views that he must regard as false or not true? John Palmer presses this point well, "why should he have bothered to present a fundamentally flawed or 'near-correct' cosmology, founded upon principles that fail to satisfy the very requirements he himself has supposedly specified?"[6]

While supporters of a strict monist reading may find it difficult to explain why Parmenides includes these cosmological passages in the poem,[7] there is much that a strict monist interpreter can do to allay this worry. G. E. L. Owen, e.g., argues that the purpose of the Doxa is "wholly dialectical":

> Parmenides sets himself to give the correct or the most plausible analysis of those presuppositions on which ordinary men, and not just theorists, seem to build their picture of the world.... Whittled down to their simplest and most economical they can be seen still to require the existence of at least two irreducibly different things in a constant process of interaction; and both the plurality and the process have now, on Parmenides' view, been proven absurd. (Owen, "Eleatic Questions," p. 89)

More recently, Sattler nicely develops a similar point, "the cosmology is most fitting as it is as similar as possible to the truth, which is based on one

---

[5] See Mourelatos, *Route*, p. 231.
[6] Palmer, "Parmenides," see also Palmer, *Parmenides and Presocratic Philosophy*, p. 31. Tor also pursues this question in detail in *Mortal and Divine in Early Greek Epistemology*, chapter 4.
[7] See Kirk, Raven, and Schofield, *The Presocratic Philosophers*, p. 262; Guthrie, *A History of Greek Philosophy* vol. 2, pp. 5–6, 52–53.

principle, Being."[8] Andrew Gregory endorses a fairly strict monistic reading while pursuing the interesting suggestion that the two parts of Parmenides' poem are united by Parmenides' overarching interest in the notion of sufficient reason.[9] In general, I think that, while the presence of the cosmology in the poem does put some pressure on the strict monist reading, the issue of the role of the cosmology need not be the make-or-break issue that some may seem to regard it as being.

A potentially more damning challenge comes from the apparently paradoxical nature of the strict monist reading: espousing the strict monist position is often thought to be self-undermining or otherwise incoherent. To argue for—or even just to state—the position that there are no distinctions and no true negations requires the use of distinctions such as the distinction between premise and conclusion in an argument, and requires the distinction between the various parts—the contained concepts or subject and predicate—of any premise. Also, the claim that there are no distinctions requires the use of negation, e.g. in denying that what-is-not exists. As Owen puts the point, "Parmenides can only prove the unintelligibility of οὐκ ἔστιν by himself denying the existence of certain states of affairs."[10] Mourelatos gives expression to a similar worry when he describes a strict monist position and then goes on to say:

> The elaborate structure of B8, the length of the poem, the double account, the epic form, the proem, the imagery—all these become otiose if Parmenides' intention was merely to call our attention to the fact that only (genuinely) positive propositions are possible, and that the universe must have the simplicity of a (genuinely) positive proposition. That, of course, is a *reductio ad absurdum* of philosophy even before Gorgias. Had Parmenides been understood by his contemporaries along the lines of [this] interpretation, philosophy should have moved straight into the paradox-mongering of the Megarians. (Mourelatos, *The Route of Parmenides*, p. 54).

I agree that Parmenides can be seen, on the strict monist view, as employing distinctions and negations in the course of arguing that there are no distinctions or negations, and I agree that his view can thus

---

[8] Sattler, *The Concept of Motion in Ancient Greek Thought*, chapter 2. See also Sedley, "Parmenides and Melissus," and Long, "The Principles of Parmenides' Cosmogony."

[9] Gregory, "Parmenides, Cosmology and Sufficient Reason."

[10] Owen, "Eleatic Questions," p. 100. See also Barnes, *The Presocratic Philosophers*, vol. 1, p. 177.

seem self-undermining. But, I would also argue, this appearance of self-undermining is a feature and not a bug. After all, as strict monist interpreters might say again, Parmenides can be seen as proceeding dialectically. That is, Parmenides can be seen as engaging with an opponent who embraces the way of what-is-not, the way of non-being or negations, that Parmenides seeks to reject. Parmenides invokes distinctions in order to show that this opponent's reliance on distinctions leads to incoherence. Parmenides is using his opponent's own tools—distinctions—against his opponent. Montgomery Furth stresses this aspect of Parmenides's approach, and he notes that Parmenides himself uses the term "ἔλεγχος" in B 7.5 (a word that can mean test or refutation) to describe his approach (Furth, "Elements of Eleatic Ontology," p. 118). In using notions to which—by his own lights—he is not entitled, Parmenides' progress is, as I noted in the proem of this book, in some way like Wittgenstein's in the *Tractatus Logico-Philosophicus*. In that work, one of Wittgenstein's goals is to show that certain apparent statements are nonsensical, devoid of meaning. To reach this result, Wittgenstein makes certain claims that he sees or comes to see as, by his own standards, nonsensical. These nonsensical claims are, as he puts it, a ladder that he must climb and then throw away. In much the same way, Parmenides draws upon distinctions in the course of arguing for the conclusion that there are no distinctions. In a passage part of which I just quoted, Owen—a defender of the strict monist interpretation—invokes this parallel to Wittgenstein, and he also points out that the great skeptic Sextus Empiricus similarly uses the ladder-discarding image:

> Just as Parmenides can only prove the unintelligibility of οὐκ ἔστιν by himself denying the existence of certain states of affairs, so he can only show the vacuousness of temporal and spatial distinctions by a proof which employs them. His argument, to adopt an analogy from Sextus and Wittgenstein, is a ladder which must be thrown away when one has climbed it. (p. 100)[11]

---

[11] The allusion to Sextus is presumably to *Against the Logicians* 8:481 (p. 183 in Bett's edition of *Against the Logicians*). Sextus speaks there of overturning the ladder with one's foot, not of throwing away the ladder as Wittgenstein does. See also Owen, "Plato and Parmenides on the Timeless Present," pp. 321–22. Wedin, *Parmenides' Grand Deduction*, pp. 48–53, offers a non-dialectical approach to the worry about self-defeat. This strategy turns on a distinction between first- and second-order states of affairs and also on a distinction between propositions about first-order states of affairs and propositions about second-order states of affairs. However, these distinctions may seem foreign to Parmenides, and indeed they would have to be foreign to Parmenides if he is to be interpreted as a strict monist. Wedin briefly tries to address this kind of worry on p. 53n74. Wedin (pp. 192–96) directly criticizes Owen's appeal on Parmenides' behalf to Wittgenstein's ladder. This criticism may

Of course, drawing this parallel to Wittgenstein's *Tractatus* and his ladder-throwing display may go only so far in allaying the worry about the incoherence of the strict monist position that I am attributing to Parmenides. After all, Wittgenstein's move here itself may not be coherent. Agreed, but my not entirely glib reply is: if Wittgenstein can do it, why can't Parmenides? The point is that even if (or perhaps because) Wittgenstein's position threatens to be unstable, this position is of great interest and significance. Parmenides' system enjoys, I am claiming, the same kind of interest and significance. I'm not advancing a particular interpretation of Wittgenstein here, nor am I claiming that there is an exact parallel between Parmenides and Wittgenstein. My point is that there may be in Parmenides a willingness to embrace a self-consciously self-undermining argument in something like the way that Wittgenstein sees his own arguments as somehow self-undermining.

The type of dialectic that Parmenides employs will be at work throughout this book: a certain claim or notion espoused by my opponents in a given philosophical domain is or will be used against these opponents. The result in each case is a new and wild and perhaps paradoxical rejection of all distinctions and negations in this domain. Such paradoxicality will be displayed in all its glory (infamy) in chapter 9. And when you see me—as you will indeed see me—making such ladder-throwing, perhaps paradoxical, moves, my again not entirely glib refrain will be: if Wittgenstein and Parmenides can do it, why can't I?

Let's continue with the challenges to the strict monistic reading of Parmenides. Apart from worries about paradox—worries that can, as I just argued, be addressed, if not fully allayed—a powerful objection to this interpretation comes from the venerable principle of charity. One version of this principle specifies that interpreters should not, without compelling reason, attribute implausible or outlandish views to philosophers. Because strict monism is a highly implausible view that, as Palmer puts it, "no serious metaphysician should want to adopt,"[12] the principle of charity dictates that we should not saddle Parmenides with such a position unless a strong argument for strict monism can be found and unless Parmenides can plausibly be seen as sensitive to such an

---

turn too heavily on a controversial reading of Wittgenstein's *Tractatus* as non-paradoxical in a way that Owen's reading and my reading do not.

[12] Palmer, "Parmenides" and *Parmenides and Presocratic Philosophy*, p. 38.

argument.[13] This injunction should be in place especially if there is a less outlandish view that can be attributed to Parmenides instead.

I should say that I'm no fan of the version of the principle of charity invoked here by Palmer and invoked by so many others. This is in part for the reason that I do not regard the implausibility of a philosophical view as a reason for rejecting that view. Chapter 11 will be devoted to the reasons that I stopped worrying about—and learned not to be afraid of—implausibility. In the meantime, let's play along now with this appeal to the principle of charity and let's see where it goes.

Fortunately, from the point of view the principle of charity and of those hostile to—or skeptical of—the strict monist reading, less radical alternative interpretations are available. According to most, if not all, such interpretations, Parmenides rejects not negations or differentiation in general, but rather only a certain kind of negation and differentiation. To articulate more fully and to respond to this complex, further challenge to a strict monist interpretation, I will now offer an outline of this kind of alternative reading and highlight the powerful philosophical and textual grounds that support it. In the process of presenting the best reasons behind this alternative interpretation, I will be laying the groundwork for an articulation of the, perhaps more powerful, philosophical reasons for attributing the strict version of monism to Parmenides. It is by seeing why the more moderate alternative interpretation is or would be, in Parmenides' eyes, ultimately incoherent that we will be able to appreciate the best reasons for attributing the strict monist position to Parmenides.

What, then, is the moderate alternative to a strict monist interpretation? Actually, there are many readings of Parmenides that do not attribute a strict monism to him. I will focus on one of the most clearly articulated and compelling versions of a non-strict monist interpretation: the one offered by Mourelatos in his book *The Route of Parmenides* and in other works. I will, however, also mention several other related non-strict monist accounts. There are important differences among these versions of a non-strict monist reading, but none that materially affects the presentation of the general,

---

[13] In *Parmenides and Presocratic Philosophy*, Palmer describes the strict monist position as "wildly counter-intuitive" (p. 25) and as "extremely counter-intuitive" (p. 189n2). Palmer regards Melissus as holding the strict monist view but deems "Parmenides' monism [to be] something altogether different from the strict monism of the aping Melissus" (p. 223) and urges us to "distinguish the more philosophically serious views of Parmenides from the crude paradoxes of Melissus" (p. 47).

non-strict monist interpretation that I am about to offer or the case against such an interpretation that I will eventually make.

Mourelatos' alternative to a strict monist reading turns on his construal of what Parmenides means when he says that a thing, x, is y (for some feature or thing, y) in a certain distinctive sense of "is." Mourelatos thus addresses the question of what a certain kind of predication amounts to for Parmenides. As Mourelatos puts it, Parmenidean predication is

> a complete exposure of, and insight into, the identity of a thing to such an extent and in such a manner that no further questions with respect to that thing need or may arise. To put it roughly: on the side of the predicate, the subject fully explains itself, and in terms of itself. Predication so understood is at once analysis, explication, and explanation. And it promises to be all these finally and completely. (Mourelatos, *The Route of Parmenides*, p. 57; unless otherwise noted all subsequent references to Mourelatos in this chapter will be to this work)

For Mourelatos, such a full explanatory predication can be expressed as "x is really y" or "x is truly or ultimately y."

> To say . . . that x is y implies that x is really y, or that the reality of x is y, or that x in its reality is y, and so on. (p. 58)

Mourelatos calls such predication "speculative predication," and he also suggests that another way of characterizing this kind of predication is as "explanative predication" (p. 59). He worries, though, that this latter term "suggests rather too strongly and directly a 'Why?' question, whereas the relevant question is of the form, 'What is it?'" (p. 59). However, we will see shortly that Mourelatos' own analysis of Parmenides' argumentation quite naturally highlights the centrality of explanation to Parmenides' line of thought and also highlights Parmenides' engagement with why-questions. Mourelatos goes on to show how the notion of such speculative predication is at work in other thinkers around Parmenides' time such as Xenophanes, Heraclitus, Anaximenes, Anaximander, and Thales (pp. 60–61).[14]

---

[14] Other commentators also appeal to notions like that of Mourelatos' speculative predication, e.g., Curd, *The Legacy of Parmenides*, pp. 39–42, 66; Rapp, "Zeno and the Eleatic Anti-Pluralism," pp. 72–73; and Nehamas, "On Parmenides' Three Ways of Inquiry," pp. 106–7; and "Parmenidean Being/Heraclitean Fire," p. 50.

I have nothing but admiration for the way in which Mourelatos and other scholars establish that Parmenides' notion of "is" is a notion of something like speculative predication. What I do want to challenge, however, is the way in which this notion has been used against a strict monist reading of Parmenides and has been used in the service of what has been called a "generous" monist reading.

We can see how speculative predication is put to this non-strict monist use by looking at how speculative predication interacts with negation or negative statements. In the spirit of Parmenidean speculative predication, to say that x is not F, for some feature F, is to say that x is really not F, is ultimately not F. And when Parmenides rejects the way of non-being, rejects the way of what-is-not, what he rejects is not negation in general, but rather what Mourelatos calls constitutive negation—a negation that purports to specify what x really is, purports to expose the identity of x. In rejecting the path of what-is-not, Parmenides thus eliminates not distinctions in general but rather only distinctions that are purportedly built into the nature of a thing, that fundamentally characterize what a thing is. Mourelatos puts the point this way:

> it is not the word "not," or negative predication in general, which is being rejected, but the view that an unqualified, unrestricted proposition of the form "is really not-F" can ever feature as the last statement (or one of the last) in cosmological inquiry. What is being rejected is constitutive negation; negation which is *in* the world as part of its structure. (pp. 79–80; emphasis in the original)

Mourelatos also says that Parmenides' argument "does not involve a wholesale rejection of negation as such" (p. 90), and he says that "the rejection of the negative route is not a rejection of negative predication in general" (p. 75). Mourelatos later calls the non-constitutive negation that survives Parmenides' attack on the way of what-is-not "supervenient negation."[15] Curd draws a similar distinction between what she calls internal negation and external negation (*The Legacy of Parmenides*, pp. xxi–xxiii, 94–97): internal negation (like constitutive negation) is ruled out, but external negation (like supervenient negation) is not.

---

[15] Mourelatos, pp. 355, 358—originally published in "Some Alternatives in Interpreting Parmenides."

In allowing non-constitutive negation, Mourelatos paves the way for an alternative to a strict monist reading of Parmenides. The fact that constitutive negation is ruled out means that any genuine thing is unified or simple and has no distinctions within it. The fact, as Mourelatos would have it, that non-constitutive negation is allowed, however, means that there can be a multiplicity of such unified, simple things. The resulting view is monist in the sense that each genuine thing is a unified, simple being with no internal negation. But this version of monism is generous (and not strict) because it allows for a multiplicity of such monistic beings.

This is an appealing interpretation, not least because it attempts to capture much of the reasoning behind a strict monist interpretation, but also because it at the same time seeks to avoid the most outlandish results of that interpretation. As we will see, many of the arguments advanced by strict monist interpreters can be advanced as well by generous monist interpreters, and, as Mourelatos emphasizes, his interpretation "seeks to preserve as many of the attractive features of [a strict monist interpretation] as possible" (p. 356). However, the position of the "generous" monist fails on its own terms, as I will now argue.

The key difference between the non-strict monist and the strict monist, viz. whether Parmenides rejects negation in general or only constitutive negation, is also the point at which the generous monist interpretation is at its weakest. And this is because, as I will now argue, the non-strict monist fails to see that and how the reasons Mourelatos and others rightly give for rejecting constitutive negation in Parmenides are at once reasons for rejecting negations in Parmenides in general. Thus, as I will argue, the distinction between kinds of negation that is essential to the generous monist interpretation is undermined.

To see how this challenge to a generous monist interpretation arises, let's consider carefully the reasons non-strict monist interpreters offer for rejecting constitutive negation, for denying that what a thing really is can contain some negations or distinctions. Here again I focus on the reasons offered by Mourelatos.

What then, according to Mourelatos, is wrong with constitutive negation? As I mentioned earlier, Parmenides engages in a search or quest or inquiry. Mourelatos considers what Parmenides regards as illegitimate about an inquiry into what-is-not, and he contends that Parmenides rejects such a search because it "cannot be successfully completed; and it cannot even get started" (p. 75). Mourelatos cites in this connection B 2.7: "This is a path from which

12   THE PARMENIDEAN ASCENT

no tidings ever come. For you could neither come to know the thing itself which is not, for it cannot be consummated (*οὐ γαρ ἀνυστόν*) nor could you point it out." Here I use Mourelatos' translation of "*ἀνυστόν*" as "consummated" (p. 333). As I mentioned, this term can also mean "accomplished."

But why can't there be any consummation of the search or of the object of the search? Ultimately, for Mourelatos, it's a matter of vagueness—literally, of wandering aimlessly:

> The incompleteness of what-is-not is the incompleteness, for example, of "the so-and-so which is really not-bright," or alternately "the real not-brightness of so-and-so." If "the bright" is something, then "the not-bright" is not a second thing parallel and equal in rank to it, but something wholly indeterminate and vague: anything and everything outside it. So, if we consider a journey to "what is really not-F" ..., clearly this is a journey that could never be brought to completion. For we have no criterion for recognizing the goal ... if we should chance to come upon it. (p. 76; see also p. 80)

As Mourelatos also puts the point:

> if we apply the negative particle to an expression that does no more than single out a thing, the resulting negative expression will be utterly vague. It would simply point away from a thing and toward that inexhaustible and uncharted space that lies outside the thing. (p. 327)

See also:

> ... the goddess' express objection to negative statements is not that they fail to refer, but rather that they are uninformative, specifically because they are evasive, vague, and open-ended. (p. 338)

Mourelatos ties Parmenides' emphasis on vagueness or incompleteness to the Homeric motif of wandering or journeying (pp. 17–25). Perhaps more relevantly for our purposes he also ties Parmenides' concern to avoid the wandering incompleteness of the way of negation to the Principle of Sufficient Reason, the PSR: after pointing out correctly that Parmenides' argument against the generation of being turns on "what later came to be known as the principle of sufficient reason," he notes that "[w]e have here still another clue that predication carried for him the force of final and complete explanation" (p. 100). One way to see the connection to the PSR is this: for us to follow the way of non-being and to have a determinate negative thought, we would have to end our wandering by settling on a determinate object of thought. But we could only do so arbitrarily or brutely. Given the PSR's rejection of brute facts, our wandering would thus never come to an end, and we would thus not succeed in having a determinate negative thought. By contrast, the positive way of being does not suffer from such arbitrariness: there is no worry here about wandering and struggling to settle on a particular object of thought. Rather, with the way of being there is no attempt to move from what is not to what is (or what is to what is not). Without negation, there is no movement away, no wandering, no threat of arbitrariness, or of the violations of the PSR that afflict the way of non-being.

To bolster this reading of the PSR-based rejection of the way of non-being, I would like to explore the role of the PSR throughout Parmenides's poem, particularly in the crucial fragment 8. Thus, what follows are a number of ways in which the PSR can be seen to be at work in this fragment. Many of these appearances of the PSR have been noted and stressed by other commentators, including by non-strict monist interpreters; some of these appearances are, as far as I know, newly noted here. All of them indicate the deeply rationalist character of Parmenides' thought, a character that is or can be recognized by both strict monist interpreters and by generous monist interpreters. I invoke these passages in which the PSR is at work, not only to show what may motivate Parmenides' rejection of the way of non-being, but also to lay the groundwork for the ultimate, PSR-driven rejection of a non-strict monist reading of Parmenides.

(1) Consider B 8.5–6: "it never was nor will be, since it is now all together, one, indivisible. For what parentage will you seek for it? [οὐδέ ποτ' ἦν οὐδ' ἔσται, ἐπεὶ νῦν ἐστιν ὁμοῦ πᾶν, ἕν, συνεχές. τίνα γὰρ γένναν διζήσεαι αὐτοῦ]."

What-is or being (ἐόν) never was or will be because (γὰρ) there can be no origin of what-is or being, no coming into being of ἐόν. With his rhetorical question, Parmenides seems to be reasoning in the following way: because there can be nothing that explains the coming into being of being itself, it follows that there is no such coming into being of being itself. Such coming into being would be a brute fact, and so there is no such coming into being.[16]

---

[16] Sattler, *The Concept of Motion in Ancient Greek Thought*, p. 14, also sees the PSR at work in the rhetorical question "what origin will you seek for it?"

(2) Immediately thereafter in B 8.7–10, Parmenides continues the theme of the alleged origination of what-is:

> How and whence grown? I shall not let you say or conceive, "from Not-being," for it cannot be said or conceived that anything is not; and then what necessity in fact could have urged it to begin and spring up later or before from Nothing? Thus it must either be entirely or not be at all. (B 8.7–10)

Here Parmenides seems to be arguing that if being comes to be, it would have to come to be at a specific time (now or later). But there could be no need or requirement (no χρέος) for its beginning at one time rather than another. So Parmenides concludes that there is no coming into being of what-is. This is the passage most frequently regarded as containing some kind of commitment on Parmenides' part to the PSR.[17]

(3) Parmenides' famous analogy of the well-rounded sphere in B 8.42–49 also expresses the role of the PSR in his thought.

> Since now its limit is ultimate, Being is in a state of perfection from every viewpoint, like the expanse of a well-rounded sphere, and equally poised in every direction, from its center. For it must not be either at all greater or at all smaller in one regard than in another. For neither has not-Being any being which could halt [παύοι] the coming together of Being, nor is Being capable of being more than Being in one regard and less in another, since it is all inviolate [ἄσυλον]. For it is equal with itself from every view and encounters determination all alike. (B 8.42–49)

Here Parmenides stresses that being is "equally poised in every direction [ἰσοπαλὲς πάντῃ]"(B 8.44) and is "inviolate [ἄσυλον]" (B 8. 48). The reason Parmenides gives is that nothing can halt or stop (παύοι B 8.46) the coming together of being. Parmenides thus seems to say that there could be no cause, no reason, for any discontinuity, for any halting or disruption in being itself.

---

[17] See Mourelatos, pp. xxix, 100; see also Barnes, *The Presocratic Philosophers*, vol. 1, pp. 187–88; Sattler, *The Concept of Motion in Ancient Greek Thought*, chapter 2; Kirk, Raven, and Schofield, *The Presocratic Philosophers*, p. 250; Wedin, *Parmenides' Grand Deduction*, pp. 89–91; Curd, *The Legacy of Parmenides*, pp. 31n20, 76n31, 77; Owen, "Plato and Parmenides on the Timeless Present," pp. 325–26; Gregory, "Parmenides, Cosmology and Sufficient Reason," p. 29; Sedley, "Parmenides and Melissus," p. 118; Mourelatos and Pulpito, "Parmenides and the Principle of Sufficient Reason."

There is no such halting because there is no cause—no reason—for such disruption. Again, the PSR seems to be at work.[18]

(4) Consider B 8.19-21:

And how [πῶς] could what becomes have being, how [πῶς] come into being, seeing that, if it came to be, it is not, nor is it, if at some time it is going to be? Thus becoming has been extinguished and perishing is unheard of.

Parmenides first asks *how* could what becomes have being and come into being? And he indicates that there is no such "how," no way to explain the coming into being of that which becomes. He concludes that there is no such becoming. Here the PSR-revealing word is "πῶς," "how." Because there is no "how"—no sufficient reason—for becoming, it follows that there is no becoming. Or, equivalently, invoking the contrapositive: if there is becoming, this becoming has a sufficient reason. Here again the PSR is at work. We will see in later chapters and in varied contexts how "how" is a sign of the PSR, a sign of a rationalist commitment.

(5) In B 8.23, Parmenides argues that what-is is indivisible: "nor is it divisible, since it is all alike and not any more in degree in some respect, which might keep it from (εἴργοι) uniting [or being continuous] (συνέχεσθαι)." Notice that because nothing could prevent it from being continuous—i.e. there could be no reason for discontinuity—it follows that what-is is continuous, united, and hence indivisible. Here again the PSR seems to be at work: nothing could explain the divisibility of what-is, so it is not divisible. Or, equivalently, invoking the contrapositive again: if what-is is divisible, then something could explain the divisibility of what-is.[19]

(6) Similarly, Parmenides says in B 8.32 that it is not lawful ("οὐκ ... θέμις") that being should be incomplete (ἀτελεύτητον). In light of what Parmenides says in B 8.23 about there being no source for discontinuity in being, we can see this claim about the law that being not be incomplete as pointing out that there could be nothing in virtue of which being is incomplete, and so being is complete.

---

[18] Gregory, "Parmenides, Cosmology and Sufficient Reason," p. 36; and Mourelatos and Pulpito, "Parmenides and the Principle of Sufficient Reason," pp. 134–38; also read the sphere passage as invoking sufficient reason considerations.
[19] Sattler, *The Concept of Motion in Ancient Greek Thought*, chapter 2, also sees the PSR at work in B 8.23. See also Furth, "Elements of Eleatic Ontology," pp. 128–29.

16 THE PARMENIDEAN ASCENT

All of these uses—implicit or not—of the PSR in these passages from the crucial fragment 8 suggest that when Parmenides says in B 6.2 that "μηδὲν δ' οὐκ ἔστιν" ("non-being is not"), he makes this claim because of the PSR. As we have seen, discontinuity, division, emptiness, and incompleteness—all of which can be seen as kinds of non-being—fail to be because they could have no explanation. In the same way, the most general of these phenomena— non-being itself—also fails to be because it can have no explanation.

One might think that, although the PSR may be at work in fragment 8, it is not the primary reason that Parmenides rejects non-being and distinctions and discontinuity. It might be thought that, instead of the PSR, the driving force behind the rejection of non-being is Parmenides' view that non-being cannot be thought.[20]

In response, I have two things to say. First, it is enough for me that the PSR is playing some role—even if only a subsidiary one—in Parmenides' rejection of non-being (and distinctions). As we will see, it is Parmenides' commitment to the PSR in this stretch of text that makes a generous, less than strict, monist interpretation untenable.

Second, I grant, of course, that it is important to Parmenides' overall argument that he deny the thinkability of non-being. But, I contend, this denial is, in the end, due to Parmenides' commitment to the PSR. Because, as the implicit or explicit invocation of the PSR throughout fragment 8 shows, for Parmenides non-being cannot be explained, non-being is not intelligible and cannot be coherently conceived. We have, then, a PSR-inspired account of why non-being not only cannot be, but also cannot be thought or spoken of (B 2.7-8): "for you can neither know what is not—for that cannot be accomplished [consummated]—nor tell of it [οὔτε γὰρ ἂν γνοίης τό γε μὴ ἐόν, οὐ γὰρ ἀνυστόν, οὔτε φράσαις]." Because non-being is not explainable, one cannot coherently conceive of or think non-being.

Indeed, Mourelatos similarly ties Parmenides' claim that non-being cannot be said to the PSR. On p. 76, he notes that the inability to think or, as Mourelatos puts it, to single out non-being is a function of the vagueness of what-is-not. And, as I pointed out earlier, Mourelatos ties the injunction against vagueness to the PSR (p. 100). Thus, we can see that, for Mourelatos too, the inability to think non-being is a function of strictures laid down by the PSR.

---

[20] Timothy Clarke, Brad Inwood, and Alexander Mourelatos each stressed this point in response to the line I take here.

This exploration of PSR-infused passages in Parmenides' poem has been, in part, in the service of showing exactly how defenders of a moderate or non-strict monist reading of Parmenides see him as arguing when he rejects constitutive negation, i.e. negation or differentiation that is built into the nature of a thing. Parmenides rules out constitutive negation because of his commitment to the PSR. And we've seen that this PSR-based understanding of Parmenides' reasons for rejecting constitutive negation can be and, at least in some cases, has been embraced by generous monist interpreters.

But it is striking here that, as we will soon see, each of these interpretive moves on behalf of a non-strict monist interpretation can be embraced also by a strict monist interpretation. That is, the same explanatory, PSR-driven considerations that a non-strict monist can appeal to support the claim that non-being is not and cannot be thought can also be advanced by a strict monist.

OK, but where then do the non-strict monist and the strict monist interpreters differ when it comes to the rationalist underpinnings of their divergent interpretations? As I noted, the key difference between these two interpretations lies in the kind of negation that is ruled out. The non-strict monist interpreter sees Parmenides as excluding only constitutive negation, not negation in general, whereas the strict monist interpreter sees Parmenides as rejecting negation in general. It is the non-strict monist interpreters' more limited rejection of negation that enables them to make room for multiplicity: non-constitutive or supervenient or external negation makes possible the multiplicity that non-strict monist interpreters are eager to preserve.

However, given the shared commitment to seeing Parmenides as guided by explanation and by the PSR, this multiplicity championed by non-strict monism is in a very precarious position. The non-strict monist interpreter, I will argue, is not able to justify the restriction on negation to constitutive negation. Indeed, such an interpreter's rejection of only constitutive negation is, I will argue, incoherent. By contrast, the strict monist interpreter's blanket rejection of negation does not suffer from the incoherence of the more limited rejection of negation. I thus want to argue that the PSR—which is endorsed in one way or another on all sides on Parmenides' behalf—puts significant pressure on an interpreter to reject not only so-called constitutive negation, but also negation in general.

How does the PSR lead to the rejection of negation in general? Let's take an example of a purported constitutive negation that is rejected—for reasons stemming from the PSR—by a generous monist interpreter:

x (really) originates at t_1 and *not* at t_2.

The "really" in parentheses is meant to specify that this is a case of constitutive predication of the kind that Mourelatos and non-strict monist interpreters are interested in. The presence of the "not" is one of the things that makes this predication a negation: it appeals to differences at least of times. As we've seen, Mourelatos and others reject such constitutive negation because of the PSR and because of the brute fact that really originating at t1 rather than at t2 would involve.

But now take a case of purported non-constitutive negation (or external negation or supervenient negation), the kind of negation that would be acceptable to a non-strict monist interpreter. To see an example of such a purported non-constitutive negation, just remove the "(really)" from the above sentence. Thus, we have:

x originates at t_1 and *not* at t_2.

The predication here is not constitutive, does not specify the nature of x or its identity in the way that Mourelatos and other interpreters stipulate that speculative predication does. The predication here is also clearly a negation, and so we have a purported case of non-constitutive negation.

Now take this sentence, apply the PSR—which, as we have seen, all sides attribute to Parmenides—and let's see what happens. Given the PSR, we can ask: why is it the case that x (non-constitutively) originates at t_1 rather than at t_2? Originating at t_1 rather than at t_2 seems just as arbitrary and brute in the non-constitutive case as in the previous, constitutive case. A similar PSR argument could also be deployed in other cases of purported non-constitutive negation. So, given Parmenides' commitment to the PSR, he would seem to be also committed to rejecting non-constitutive negation, just as he is committed to rejecting constitutive negation.

But wait! Perhaps there is a reason that x (non-constitutively) originates at t_1 and not at t_2 and so there is no violation of the PSR here: perhaps x originates at t_1 because of the action of some distinct thing y which acted at t_0. But here we have to ask: why did y act at t_0 instead of some other time?

Perhaps we can at this point appeal to something else, z, which acted at some earlier time, t_{-1} (t-negative-1). But, of course, another invocation of the PSR is relevant here too, and we seem to be off on an infinite regress. We seem to be at sea again, in search of a resting place but unable to find one. Recall Parmenides' emphasis on incompleteness and on what is ἀνυστόν, being unconsummated (B 2.6).

Perhaps one might say that this regress is not troubling because there is a being outside the chain of dependent beings (y, z, etc.) that leads to x's origination at t1. That is, perhaps there is a being outside the series, a being like the God of the cosmological argument who shows up in the works of philosophers much later than Parmenides, such as Leibniz. This being would stand outside the series of dependencies that link beings such as x, y, and z.

It's not clear whether it's appropriate to consider something like the God of the cosmological argument in connection with Parmenides, but in any event, it's also far from clear than an appeal to such a being would address the explanatory questions that have arisen because of Parmenides' commitment to the PSR. For we can ask: in virtue of what are the God-like being and the series of dependent beings distinct? The PSR demands an answer here, but what would the answer be? If you say that the distinction between the God-like being and the dependent beings is part of the nature of one or the other of God and the dependent beings, then we have a case of constitutive negation, a phenomenon that the generous monist interpreter has already ruled out. If the distinction is not part of the nature of either God or the dependent beings, then why does this distinction obtain instead of not obtain? Again, the PSR demands an answer here, and it's not clear what the reason could be. The distinction between God and the dependent beings—if non-constitutive—seems arbitrary and brute.

So non-constitutive negation—as well as constitutive negation—seems to be ruled out by the PSR. This puts non-strict monist interpreters in a quandary: they endorse attributing the PSR to Parmenides and yet also want to allow non-constitutive negation and to allow, therefore, multiplicity. But it seems that they cannot have both. PSR and multiplicity, one but not the other.

All of this maneuvering against a generous monist reading may seem too quick. Perhaps I wasn't nuanced enough in the way I invoked the PSR to rule out non-constitutive negation. In particular, perhaps my formulation of the PSR was not subtle enough. I was, in effect, invoking a version of the PSR along these lines:

Each fact or predication is explainable.

But perhaps, in light of the non-strict monist's distinction between constitutive and non-constitutive negation, we should reformulate the version of the PSR that Parmenides endorses in this way:

Each constitutive fact or predication is explainable.

According to this version of the PSR, anything's being constitutively F is explainable, but it need not be the case that something's being non-constitutively F is explainable. In light of this nuanced version of the PSR, the claim that x (non-constitutively) originates at t_1 and not at t_2 need not be explained. This non-constitutive fact may be arbitrary and brute and unexplained, but that's OK as far as the more nuanced version of the PSR is concerned. So perhaps the non-strict monist interpreter—by appealing to the nuanced version of the PSR—can avoid the challenge I have raised.

However, even if we adopt the nuanced PSR, a version of the key question still arises. Given that (as the non-strict monist interpreter insists and as the nuanced PSR states) all constitutive predication must be explained, why isn't it the case that non-constitutive predication needs to be explained as well? If bruteness and arbitrariness and being-at-sea-ness is a worry with constitutive negation, then why is it not equally a worry with non-constitutive negation? If we're concerned about bruteness and arbitrariness and being-at-sea-ness, then we're concerned about bruteness and arbitrariness and being-at-sea-ness. Why should it matter whether the bruteness and arbitrariness and being-at-sea-ness occurs in so-called constitutive contexts or not?

Perhaps a "generous" monist interpreter could just stipulate that constitutive predication requires explanation and non-constitutive predication does not. But this move is hardly illuminating. It still leaves us in the dark as to why constitutive predications require explanation but non-constitutive predications do not. This move is, ultimately, question-begging against the proponent of the non-nuanced version of the PSR and is thus not a welcome position with which to saddle Parmenides. And so there is, again, pressure on the non-strict monist to regard both constitutive and non-constitutive negations as requiring explanation and thus there is pressure on the non-strict monist to adopt a non-nuanced version of the PSR and thus to adopt a strict form of monism. And this is the ultimately incoherent position with which the non-strict monist interpreter is faced.

In effect, the problem for the non-strict monist interpreter lies in trying to limit the PSR, lies in saying that the PSR applies to some facts and not others. We will see this sad and, perhaps, tragic dynamic again and again in what follows: an admirable concern for intelligibility and for sufficient reason is curtailed, cut down in its prime, just when this rationalist drive threatens (or promises) to lead to a position which it seems "no serious metaphysician should want to adopt."[21] But by pulling up one's horses at this crucial moment, incoherence is the unfortunate and unintended result.

This challenge to the generous monist interpreter and to the proponent of the nuanced PSR is dialectical. Generous monist interpreters employ a style of argumentation that threatens to carry them off on a journey into a region—the region of strict monism—that they (really!) want to avoid. But they may have no means of resisting such a journey. And in this way, the generous monist interpreter is threatened with incoherence.

We will see, however, that a strict monism may face its own threat of incoherence. But that is a topic for much later (chapter 9), after we have considered and subject to destruction a number of other standard, generous, non-strict positions in a wide range of philosophical areas. For now, the problem for the generous monist interpreter is this: given the acceptance of some form of the PSR, there is considerable pressure on such an interpreter to go all the way and to reject not just constitutive negation, but also negation in general. (And, indeed, one can be forgiven for suspecting at this point that it makes no sense to distinguish constitutive negation and negation in general.) Thus, there is pressure on such an interpreter to attribute a strict, non-generous form of monism to Parmenides. By contrast, given the PSR, there is no comparable pressure on the strict monist interpreter to adopt a non-strict monist reading.

Parmenides, as I understand him, argues from the PSR—or from considerations grounded in the PSR—to strict monism and to a general rejection of distinctions. The non-strict monist position may seem superficially more plausible, but the strict monist position seems to be more in keeping with the rationalist principle that guides Parmenides' thought.

In moving from the PSR to a strict form of monism—perhaps stronger than even existence monism and certainly stronger than priority monism—Parmenides is anticipating certain later thinkers who also, in my opinion, appreciate the link between the PSR and a strong form of monism. Although

---

[21] Palmer, "Parmenides," and *Parmenides and Presocratic Philosophy*, p. 38.

I won't dwell on their views in this book, I would like to point out that Spinoza and Hume agree (surprisingly, perhaps) that the PSR entails a strong form of monism. In Hume's case, the focus may actually be on the contrapositive: the denial of monism entails the denial of the PSR. Hume wants to avoid monism, and so he rejects the PSR which entails monism. By contrast, Spinoza embraces the PSR and so he happily endorses monism.[22] Exactly what strength Spinoza's monism has is a delicate matter of considerable debate. But I have argued that his version of monism is akin to the strict version of monism that I have attributed to Parmenides.[23] Further, as I will argue in chapter 3, F. H. Bradley very much appreciates this link between the PSR and a strong version of monism. It is Bradley's argument for this conclusion—or an argument like Bradley's—that will drive much of the progress of this book. And, as I will discuss in chapter 11, Russell plays the role in relation to Bradley that Hume plays in relation to Spinoza. Russell too sees how the PSR entails monism and, like Hume, Russell avoids monism by denying the PSR. We'll return to the debate between Bradley and Russell in due course, but for now we can see that the original version of the move from the PSR to a strong form of monism may be found in Parmenides. And we can see that Parmenides' argument calls us from across the ages and can serve as a model of a powerful, uncompromisingly rationalist approach that has infused much philosophy in the past and that promises to inspire us even today.

In making the move from the PSR to a strict version of monism and to a denial of distinctions, we can see Parmenides as leaving behind the everyday world—or the world as ordinarily understood, the world as rife with distinctions such as the duality of night and day, distinctions on which he or the goddess dwells in the second half of the poem, the Doxa. In making this move, Parmenides is not—on my strict monist interpretation—leaving anything real or intelligible behind, and this is because nothing that is permeated by distinctions and thus by non-being is real, genuinely exists. Indeed, no such thing is genuinely thinkable. For Parmenides, the reality that we were imperfectly trying to capture when we were on the path of non-being

---

[22] For this kind of pairing of Spinoza and Hume, see Della Rocca, "Playing with Fire." I will return to this Spinoza-Hume connection in chapter 10.

[23] See Della Rocca, "Rationalism, Idealism, Monism, and Beyond," and "The Elusiveness of the One and the Many in Spinoza: Substance, Attribute, and Mode." For reasons to resist this Parmenidean reading of Spinoza, see Melamed, "The Sirens of Elea." Spinoza also endorses Mourelatos' Parmenidean view that an essence cannot contain any negation. However, Spinoza does not, on my interpretation, go on to allow that there are legitimate non-essential negations. See Della Rocca, "Perseverance, Power, and Eternity: Purely Positive Essence in Spinoza."

is better captured by our talk of being without distinction. With this abandonment of any distinctions, Parmenides makes what I call in his honor, the Parmenidean Ascent: he rejects distinctions as unintelligible or even non-thinkable, and he advances to a view that does not posit any distinctions. There is no loss of reality—no failure to explain something real—when Parmenides makes the Parmenidean Ascent. Indeed, there is a gain because with this ascent Parmenides sees the world aright. Parmenides' extreme monistic view is thus far richer than we might have thought, for, by getting rid of distinctions, Parmenides is no longer encumbered by unintelligibility or is, at least, less encumbered.

One can imagine more limited versions of the Parmenidean Ascent, ones in which not distinctions in general are rejected, but rather a certain distinction between two phenomena or, to speak redundantly perhaps, two apparent phenomena is rejected. The less general Parmenidean move would be to regard this particular distinction as unintelligible, and the move would also be, therefore, to rise above one thing as distinct from another. In so ascending, the aim is to capture the reality that we were hoping to capture with a distinction by instead eliding the distinction and appealing to some being—or, better perhaps, simply to being—without the distinction. In making this move, we would thus be led to reconceptualize the phenomenon under discussion. I will be making such apparently relatively limited versions of the Parmenidean Ascent in a number of the chapters to follow, and I will be endorsing the general Parmenidean Ascent as well. We will also see signs on a few occasions of relatively limited Parmenidean moves by more recent philosophers, instances that are some of the most prominent arguments in recent philosophy.

But, despite these bright spots of late, recent and contemporary philosophers almost without exception do not, as I have mentioned, engage explicitly with the strict monism of Parmenides, and they are not keen to make any form of the Parmenidean Ascent.[24] Philosophers, of late at least, tend to be, in other words, afraid of heights.

To understand and explore this acrophobia and to take some steps towards a cure, I want to examine a number of central topics in philosophy through a Parmenidean lens. And so we have the project of this book.

---

[24] For an excellent and refreshing endeavor against this overwhelming tide in recent philosophy, see Matson, *Grand Theories and Everyday Beliefs*.

2
Substance

A Litany of Failure

The first example of the pressure to make and of the failure to make the Parmenidean Ascent concerns substance or being. (In the spirit of Aristotle, I will use the terms "substance" and "being" interchangeably.) This version of the Parmenidean Ascent may seem to be the most fundamental or the most general or the most pervasive of the Parmenidean Ascents that we will consider and make in this book. Being seems to be, after all, a more general, more fundamental, more pervasive notion than the notions of action, knowledge, meaning, and other related phenomena with regard to which I will be taking a Parmenidean path. And you can go on thinking that the notion of being is special in this way, except for the fact that you can't, at least not if my arguments later in the book succeed. But this is to jump the gun. For now, let's just talk of being and see what the movement toward a Parmenidean Ascent might look like here. A "comparison" with "other" Parmenidean Ascents can wait.

In this chapter, I will closely examine a number of historically prominent accounts of substance and, briefly, one contemporary account as well. This—to speak redundantly perhaps—jaunty expedition reveals that these accounts in general fail on their own terms: they fail to meet a certain explanatory demand that these accounts themselves embrace and insist on. This survey constitutes what I regard as an inductive argument for the conclusion that there is something deeply and systematically problematic about ordinary philosophical conceptions of substance or being. In the next chapter, through a more or less *a priori* argument, I seek to identify the source of this problem, and the results will be surprisingly and characteristically Parmenidean. In these two chapters, and indeed throughout the book, I regard these kinds of arguments—both inductive and *a priori*—as mutually supporting and as non-redundant. The conclusions about mainstream philosophical views that I am trying to reach are so counterintuitive and, indeed, in some respects rebarbative that it will be enormously useful to have different ways of reaching them.

I will begin by critically examining some of Aristotle's views on substance or being before moving on to equally negative conclusions about Descartes', Leibniz's, and Locke's theories. I will also address briefly Jonathan Lowe's account. If you're keeping score at home, you might be interested in the observation that this chapter is probably the most "history heavy" chapter in the book—apart from chapter 1 on Parmenides. But if you're keeping score at home, don't. Or perhaps don't try to do that. It is important not to focus on whether the approach in this or other chapters is historical or contemporary. Indeed, as I will eventually argue, it may be that it is not really even *possible* to be interested in such tallying. But this is, again, to jump the gun. I am merely noting now, from a point of view that will eventually be transcended, that this chapter is perhaps more history-laden than subsequent chapters.

Aristotle

Let's begin then with Aristotle, for so many later theories of substance develop from Aristotle's theory or theories. As with my interpretation of Parmenides, I do not aim here—nor am I expert enough in ancient philosophy—to offer a full-blown account of Aristotle on substance. Instead, by means of a kind of rationalist surgical strike, I aim to identify a certain strand in Aristotle's thought that will provide an illuminating perspective on theories of substance in general.[1]

In the *Categories*, Aristotle characterizes substance or *ousia*—literally being—in negative terms as "that which is neither predicated of [or said of] a subject nor present in a subject" (*Categories* I:5, 2a12–13).[2] There is much controversy over the interpretation of these technical terms, but, roughly, for something to be predicated of or said of a subject is for it to be an essential feature of that subject. For something to be present in a subject is for it to be an accidental feature of that subject. Aristotle's examples illustrate these points: a particular color is in a body and is a contingent feature of a body. By contrast, man is said of, or predicated of, an individual man, and

---

[1] For a good overview of some of the problems and for insightful ways of defending the notion of substance, I would particularly recommend, Broackes, "Substance."

[2] Here and elsewhere I follow (with some minor modifications) the translations in Aristotle, *The Basic Works of Aristotle*, Richard McKeon (ed.). For Aristotle's Greek texts, I have relied on the online resource, *Thesaurus Linguae Graecae: A Digital Library of Greek Literature*.

being a man is an essential feature of any man.[3] To specify what is said of a thing or to specify its essence is to say, as Shields puts it, what a thing is in "a deeply explanatory way."[4] This notion of what a thing is or what is said of a thing is thus broadly similar to the characterization in the previous chapter of Parmenides' "is" as signifying what a thing is really or fundamentally.

A substance somehow brings together or unifies properties in such a way that all these properties are properties of *it*, of the substance. Aristotle stresses that this unification is exhibited not only at a single time but also over time. Indeed, it is an essential part of Aristotle's characterization of substance that a substance is the type of thing that can have contrary properties at different times. The very same substance, Socrates, can go from being bent (when he is sitting) to being straight (when he is standing) even though being bent and being straight are contrary properties and cannot be had by the same object at the same time.

However, Aristotle saw or came to see the characterization of substance that he offers in the *Categories* as importantly incomplete.[5] In the *Metaphysics* (7:3) after reiterating the account of substance as "that which is not predicated of a stratum, but of which all else is predicated," he goes on to note, "But we must not merely state the matter thus; for this is not enough [οὐ γὰρ ἱκανόν]" (1029a9). What then is missing?

One gap is this: Aristotle's account in the *Categories* does not answer the question, "In virtue of what is there a substance present?" It's all well and good for Aristotle to specify in the *Categories* that a substance is an ultimate subject of predication, but that insight does not reveal what it is for a thing to be such a subject, what enables a thing to be such a subject, what makes it the case that a thing is such a subject. As Aristotle specifies in the final chapter of book 7 of the *Metaphysics* (chapter 17), a philosopher must take up the question: in virtue of what is one thing predicated of another: "We are," he says, "inquiring . . . why [διὰ τί] something is predicated of something" (1041a23). Aristotle goes on to give an illustration of the explanatory character of his inquiry:

> the inquiry is about the predication of one thing of another. And why [διὰ τί] are these things, i.e. bricks and stones, a house? Plainly we are seeking the cause. (1041a26–28)

---

[3] See *Categories* 1a20–1b9; Shields, *Aristotle*, pp. 181–82.
[4] Shields, *Aristotle*, p. 186.
[5] The *Categories* is usually regarded as earlier than the *Metaphysics*. On the dating of the *Categories*, see Shields, pp. 32–34.

A little later, he is still riffing on the same example:

> clearly the question is why [διὰ τί] the matter is some definite thing, e.g. why [διὰ τί] are these materials a house? Because that which was the essence of a house is present. And why is this individual thing, or this body having this form, a man? Therefore what we seek is the cause [τὸ αἴτιον], i.e. the form, by reason of which the matter is some definite thing; and this is the substance of the thing. (1041b5-9)

At the very end of chapter 17 of book 7, Aristotle states the object of his inquiry is that of identifying the "substance of a thing (for this is the primary cause of its being) [οὐσία δὲ ἑκάστου μὲν τοῦτο (τοῦτο γὰρ αἴτιον πρῶτον τοῦ εἶναι] (1041b27-28).

Earlier—in book 4—after identifying substance as the primary thing and that on which other things depend, Aristotle says that, because substance is thus primary, "it will be of substances that the philosopher must grasp the principles [ἀρχὰς] and the causes [αἰτίας]" (1003b18-19).

Wedin characterizes well the kind of explanatory project Aristotle is here engaged in:

> he is preoccupied with a *specific* explanatory project, namely, identifying the nature of that in virtue of which a c-substance [the kind of substance invoked in the *Categories*] is the sort of thing it is and has the chief characteristics it has. (*Aristotle's Theory of Substance*, p. 425)

> [H]is concern with substance is a concern with the substance-of c-substances and . . . this is motivated by an interest in explaining the nature of c-substances, in particular, explaining certain of their central features— features mentioned in but not explained by the *Categories*. (*Aristotle's Theory of Substance*, p. 171)

In other words, for Aristotle, we seek to explain what makes a substance a substance; we seek to articulate a structural fact about the way the world is or things are.

The explanatory focus of Aristotle's thought here is evident in his criticism of what he sees as a Platonic way of accounting for one thing being predicable of something. Plato appeals to forms that individual things participate in or share in. But Aristotle rejects such an attempted explanation:

> all other things cannot come from the Forms in any of the usual senses of "from." And to say that they are patterns and the other things share in them is to use empty words and poetical metaphors. For what is it that works, looking to the Ideas? (991a19–23)[6]

However, in criticizing the vacuity of Platonic explanation of predication, Aristotle may be in pot-calling-the-kettle-black territory, as we'll soon see.

In addressing the explanatory question that he takes up in book 7 of the *Metaphysics*, Aristotle asks a crucial kind of question that the account in the *Categories* does not address or attempt to address, viz. the question, "what is it in virtue of which a substance is a substance?" All the account in the *Categories* tells us is that something that is a substance unifies certain properties without itself being predicated of anything. "OK, but *how*," we are inclined to say, echoing the "how" of Parmenides, "how does it unify all these properties, making them properties of the same thing, without itself being predicated of anything else?" The account in the *Categories* does not answer or seek to answer the question of how a thing gets to be a substance, and so—from this point of view—the substantiality of a substance remains unexplained. S. Mark Cohen articulates something like this gap:

> The negative criterion ("neither in a subject nor said of a subject") of the *Categories* tells us only which things are substances. But even if we know *that* something is a substance, we must still say what *makes* it a substance—what the cause is of its being a substance. ("Aristotle's Metaphysics," §5)

Christopher Shields similarly calls attention to this unanswered question,

> When Aristotle foregrounds features such as these [which he emphasizes in the *Categories*], he seems to be highlighting characteristic features of substances rather than offering an implicit definition of what it is to be a substance. (*Aristotle*, p. 204)

---

[6] For more on the explanatory inadequacies of Platonic appeals to participation, see *Metaphysics* 8.6 (1045a14–20).

Thus, as far as the *Categories* is concerned, the substantiality of a substance remains, as Cohen says, a "brute fact," something unexplained (see "Aristotle's Metaphysics," §6). And, as Wedin puts it, "From the point of view of the *Categories*, primary substances . . . are taken as unanalyzed primitives" (*Aristotle's Theory of Substance*, p. 4). However, it is the demand for an account of such substances that Aristotle is—rightly, in my opinion—sensitive to in the *Metaphysics*.[7]

It is noteworthy that, as he is articulating his aims in this stretch of the *Metaphysics*, Aristotle, like Parmenides, focuses on *how*: his inquiry is an inquiry into (inter alia) "*how* [πῶς] sensible substances exist, and whether there is a substance capable of separate existence (and if so, why and *how* [πῶς])" (1028b29–30; my emphasis). As Wedin puts it, "*Metaphysics* Z asks in virtue of what are c-substances the sorts of things they are, that is, in virtue of what do they have the central features mentioned in, but not explained by, the *Categories*?" (p. 5; see also p. 452). As we'll soon see, this demand comes back to bite Aristotle.

In seeking to address this demand, Aristotle seeks to show how it is that, e.g., a house or a human being is one thing and not just a collection of stones and bricks or a collection of flesh and bones. That is, he seeks to show how it is that in that house or that human being all these elements are unified. With this explanatory demand, Aristotle takes what can be seen as a perfectly natural, rationalist step. But I would like to emphasize that to be committed to this demand—as Aristotle is—is not necessarily by itself to be committed to the full-blown PSR which is, in effect, a demand for the explanation of any and all facts. What is sought in demanding an explanation of the substantiality of a substance is an explanation of a particular fact or a particular kind of fact: the fact of the substantiality of a given substance. To make this explanatory demand is a natural and—it may seem—plausible constraint to put on one's conception of substance, a constraint that one can, perhaps, embrace without endorsing the PSR in full generality.

---

[7] I am here taking no stand on the question of whether the account of substance in the *Categories* is consistent with the account in the *Metaphysics*, although I am inclined to think that they are compatible for the kind of reasons Wedin gives. All I am saying—and all I need to say—is that the account in the *Categories* leaves an explanatory question unanswered and the account in the *Metaphysics* is an attempt to answer that question.

How then is this marvelous feat of unification which Aristotle demands performed? To answer this question, Aristotle draws a distinction between form and matter. A substance—a concrete substance at least—is present just in case some otherwise non-unified matter, such as stones and bricks, flesh and bones, is unified by something over and above such matter. This unifying something is what Aristotle (in a passage I quoted earlier) calls the form: "what we seek is the cause, i.e. the form, by reason of which the matter is some definite thing; and this is the substance of the thing" (*Metaphysics* 1041b7–9).

So why is a substance of a certain kind present here? Answer: because some matter is unified by a certain form—a form that makes it the case that there is a substance of certain type here. This substance-making form is called, by later philosophers, a substantial form. It is this unification of matter by form that provides Aristotle with his answer to the explanatory question that he himself raises, and it is this unification that provides him with his response to the demand for the principles and causes of substance. Aristotle explains the substantiality of a substance by appealing to this unifying role that form plays with regard to matter. As Wedin sums up this view: "The form of a thing (of a given kind) explains why certain matter constitutes a thing of that kind."[8]

In focusing on the explanatory demand in Aristotle, there is, of course, much in his theory of substance that I am inevitably not discussing. My purposes in the treatment of Aristotle here are met by calling attention to the fact that he invokes the explanatory demand with regard to substance, viz. the demand to explain the unity that substance exhibits, and by calling attention to the fact that he seeks to meet this demand in part by appealing to the relation between—the distinction between—form and matter.

Leibniz's and Descartes' Criticisms of the Aristotelian Account

Let's move forward many hundreds of years—emboldened perhaps by Spinoza's dictum: "It is of the nature of reason to perceive things under a certain aspect of eternity"[9]—a precept that we are only imperfectly abiding by here and that we will have occasion to invoke again in chapter 7. I would

---

[8] *Aristotle's Theory of Substance*, p. 7.
[9] "*De natura rationis est res sub quadam aeternitatis specie percipere*" (*Ethics*, Part 2, Proposition 44, Corollary 2).

like to turn to Descartes' (and other mechanists') criticism and to Leibniz's criticism of an Aristotelian account of substance. The main worry that these philosophers raise is that Aristotle's substantial forms are completely mysterious and unsuited to do explanatory work. Yes, it is good that Aristotle in the *Metaphysics* seeks to explain the unity of substance, and yes, Aristotle does indicate that a substantial form performs a unifying role that results in a determinate being. But merely to offer such an "account" is not to explain *how* the substantial form carries out this remarkable task; it is merely to label the problem without providing any illumination. All that is offered is the mere shell of an explanation of substancehood and not the genuine article. As Leibniz says,

> That is where the Scholastics failed, as did the physicians of the past who followed their example, believing that they could account for the properties of bodies by talking about forms and qualities without taking the trouble to examine their manner of operation [*la manière de l'operation*]. (*Discourse on Metaphysics* §10, Gerhardt IV 434, AG 42)

> To appeal to forms or qualities here [in offering an account of what it is to be a substance] is to say nothing [*ce n'est rien dire que d'y alleguer les formes ou les qualités*]. (Correspondence with Arnauld, July 14, 1686, Gerhardt II 58, Loemker 338; translation altered)

Similarly, Leibniz says in *A New System of Nature* (1695) that he "rightly despised the method of those who use only forms or faculties, from which one can learn nothing [*je méprisois avec raison la methode de ceux qui n'employent que des formes ou des facultés dont on n'apprend rien*]" (Gerhardt IV 478, AG 139).

> Descartes derides the defenders of substantial forms in this way:
> no natural action can at all can be explained by these substantial forms, since their defenders admit that they are occult and that they do not understand them themselves [*nullius planè actionis naturalis ratio reddi potest per illas formas substantiales*]. (Descartes to Regius, January 1642, AT III 506, CSMK 208)

He also speaks ill of the explanations that proceed by

> inventing all sorts of strange objects which have no resemblance to what is perceived by the senses such as "prime matter," "substantial forms" and the

whole range of qualities that people habitually introduce, all of which are harder to understand than the things they are supposed to explain [*expliquer*]. (*Principles* IV 201, French version)

See also *Principles* IV 198:

We can in no way understand [*intelligere*] how [*quo pacto*], by these same attributes (viz. size, shape, and motion), something of a nature quite different is produced. (My translation)

See also: "the substantial form of the sun, in so far as it differs from the qualities to be found in its matter, is an altogether philosophical entity, which is unknown to me" (Descartes to Morin, September 12, 1638, AT II 367 CSMK 122).[10]

See also:

"[In the philosophy of the School], one does not explain matter well insofar as one makes it pure potentiality and one adds to it substantial forms and real qualities which are only chimeras" [*on n'explique pas bien cette Matiere, en ce qu'on la fait puram potentiam, & qu'on luy adjoute des forms substantielles, & des qualitez réelles, qui ne sont que des chimeres*]. (Descartes to Mersenne, October 28, 1640, AT III 212; my translation)

In the same vein:

My principal reason for rejecting these real qualities is that I do not see that the human mind has any notion, or particular idea, to conceive them by; so that when we talk about them and assert their existence, we are asserting something we do not conceive and do not ourselves understand. (Descartes to Mersenne, April 26, 1643, AT III 649, CSMK 216)

Although there are many aspects to the early modern critique of substantial forms,[11] one common theme, as the above passages from Leibniz

---

[10] Similar criticisms can be found in many other philosophers. See Clarke, *Descartes's Theory of Mind*, pp. 18–23.

[11] For other aspects, see Gilson's classic account, "De la critique des forms substantielles au doute méthodique," in *Études sur le Rôle de la Pensée Médiévale dans la Formation du Système Cartésien*, pp. 141–90; Hutchison, "Dormitive Virtues, Scholastic Qualities, and the New Philosophies"; and Ott, *Causation and Laws of Nature in Early Modern Philosophy*, pp. 39–44.

and Descartes indicate, is that the appeal to substantial forms fails to offer a satisfactory explanation of how substantial forms work—how they do what they are said to do. This aspect of the criticism of substantial forms as offering unilluminating, non-explanatory "explanations" is on display in Molière's famous lampooning of Aristotelian explanation in terms of substantial forms and powers with his *virtus dormitiva* (dormitive virtue) explanation.[12] To be told that opium puts one to sleep because it has a *virtus dormitiva* is unilluminating because we are not told *how* the drug works, *how* it does this wonderful deed. We are none the wiser after this so-called explanation than we were before it. Similarly, to say that something is a *substance* because it has a certain *substantial form* that *somehow* performs a unifying role to make it the case that there is a substance is not illuminating. We have merely been told that a thing is a particular substance because it has a substantial form that imposes unity on matter in a substance-making kind of way. How does the substantial form pull this off? Here again, we are none the wiser. Even if we appeal to the other types of Aristotelian causes besides the formal cause that may be relevant to substance—viz. the efficient, material, and final causes—the account of there being a substance here still depends crucially on a particular *substantial* form, and thus the worries about circularity and unilluminatingness would still arise. Malebranche expresses this kind of sentiment in *The Search after Truth*:

> Aristotle presents and resolves all things through the use of these lovely words: *genus, species, act, potency, nature, form, faculties, qualities, cause in itself,* and *accidental cause*. His followers have trouble understanding that these words signify nothing, and that they are no more learned than before just because they are heard to say that fire dissolves metals because it has a dissolving faculty; and the man does not digest because he has a weak stomach or because his *digestive* faculty is not performing its functions well. (p. 443)

If we have learned one thing from the early modern critique of Aristotelian explanations, it is that a mere appeal to the nature of a thing without saying *how* this nature does what it does is an explanation that is indeed empty and

---

[12] From *The Imaginary Invalid*.

unilluminating. And so Aristotle and his followers undergo here what I will call a Molière moment: an unilluminating appeal to the nature of a thing in a failed attempt to explain a certain phenomenon.

Another, perhaps even more general way to characterize the fundamental worry here and to caricature Aristotelian explanation by substantial forms anew is to invoke—of all personages—the figure of John Wayne. The emptiness or unilluminatingness that Aristotelian explanations by substantial forms are alleged to have is perhaps like a kind of emptiness or unilluminatingness that is also found, perhaps in the iconic statement—problematic in so many ways—sometimes attributed to John Wayne and often repeated as a kind of parody: "A man's gotta do what a man's gotta do."[13] This statement is most likely not intended, of course, as an account or explanation of any kind. In saying what he does, Wayne (or the Wayne character or the parody of the Wayne character) may be attempting to demonstrate what a man's gotta do or to embody in his laconic directness what a man's gotta do. But, if intended as an account of what a man's gotta do, this statement would be empty, uninformative, and unilluminating. Similarly, on the simple account of being or substance just offered, substance has gotta be what substance has gotta be. Adopting such a circular, uninformative account is what I call a John Wayne moment. And it would be extremely disappointing, I would think, for a philosopher to propose such an "account" when the stated, shared goal in this area—the philosophy of being—is to provide illumination as to the nature of being or substance. Yet this is precisely what happens time and time again: as we'll see, all or most prominent accounts of substance amount to John Wayne moments in philosophy as well as to Molière moments.[14]

Defenders of Aristotle, of course, have attempted and do attempt in various ways to rebut the accusation that he succumbs to Molière moments or John Wayne moments. Before I examine one such response on behalf of Aristotle, it may go some distance toward mollifying his supporters if I point out that I will be equally critical—and for the same kinds of reasons—of

---

[13] Actually, Wayne may not have said precisely this sentence in any movie, though he said things that were close. Oddly enough, one of the first uses of the phrase in this precise wording comes from the character George Jetson in the animated television show, *The Jetsons*.

[14] For the record, John Wayne moments and Molière moments are closely connected. Both kinds of infelicity involve unilluminating "explanations" of a given phenomenon. The phrase "John Wayne moment" alludes to the failure to explain in general. The phrase "Molière moment" alludes more specifically to a case in which the non-illumination is due to an empty appeal to a thing's nature.

Aristotle's early modern critics when it comes to *their* attempts to explain the substantiality of substance.

Defenders of Aristotelian explanation may claim that to seek the kind of explanation Leibniz or Descartes (or I) insist on here—one whereby it is explained how it is that substantial forms operate—is misplaced. Thus, for example, Wedin says that once we explain substantiality by appealing to the relation between form and matter, we (Aristotle) have discharged the explanatory burden. We have reached "explanatory bedrock" here when we get to substantial forms, and no further demand for explanation is in place. Wedin says:

> the fact that form's realization in material parts is not mediated by anything else appears to leave little room to wonder about the fit between form and the material parts themselves. (*Aristotle's Theory of Substance*, p. 438)

He goes on to say:

> the form of a c-substance just is the primary cause of its being the sort of thing it is and, so, this form ought to constitute explanatory bedrock. (*Aristotle's Theory of Substance*, p. 438; see also similar appeals to "explanatory bedrock" on p. 7 and p. 8.)

But here—siding for the moment with Leibniz and Descartes and other early moderns—I would like to push back against such a dismissal of the need for explanation. The demand for an account of how forms play the unifying role they play is of a piece with the demand—made by Aristotle himself—that the kind of account offered in the *Categories* is not enough (1029a9). For Aristotle, we must dig deeper than the *Categories* goes or Plato goes in trying to explain how properties are united in a substance. We must, for Aristotle, not merely put a label on the problem or use "empty words or poetical metaphors." In the same way and by his own standards, we are faced with a demand to go deeper in explaining the substantiality of a substance than simply appealing to forms which somehow—in John Wayne fashion—get the job done. Merely to label something bedrock or primitive does not get us (or Aristotle) off the explanatory hook—it does not absolve us of the burden of "how," a burden that Aristotle is sometimes—and following Parmenides—only too happy to invoke. I will offer a similar pushback in chapters 10 and 11 against contemporary and recent attempts to take the easy way out and discharge explanatory burdens by invoking explanatory primitives. There I will also explore the possibly skeptical implications of this line of thought.

Leibniz Criticizes Descartes' Account

Leibniz goes on to point out that, despite Descartes' dispute with the Aristotelians, Descartes is to be tarred with the same brush (at least when it comes to corporeal substances) and—to mix a metaphor—just as the explanatory demand came back to bite Aristotle, it comes back to bite Descartes. Descartes fails to heed the basic explanatory demand that the notion of substance places on a theorist.

This failure arises because Descartes strips corporeal substance of Aristotelian substantial forms.[15] Descartes proposes instead that corporeal substance simply consists in matter—infinitely divisible extension—without any substantial forms.[16] Substances are to be accounted for and individuated simply in terms of matter and motion.

Leibniz, though, challenges Descartes by saying that such a thin basis for corporeal substance couldn't provide the unity required for a substance and consequently couldn't individuate one substance from another. For Leibniz, parts are prior to the whole of which they are parts. Indeed, a whole with parts is merely a manner of being of those parts: "what constitutes the essence of a being by aggregation is only a mode [*manière d'être*] of the things of which it is composed. For example, what constitutes the essence of an army is only a mode of the men who compose it" (Leibniz to Arnauld, April 30, 1687, Gerhardt II 97, AG 86).[17]

But in that case, the unity of a complex, divisible substance would have to be explained by its parts. And if those parts themselves are complex unities with parts—as Descartes holds—then the reality and unity of these parts of the parts would have to be explained by the unity of *their* parts and so on all the way down in a spiral of fragmentation. We would be attempting to

---

[15] Descartes is more open to substantial forms in the case of the human soul which he sometimes sees as the substantial form of the human being; see AT 7:355, CSM 2:246; AT 3:503, 505, CSMK 207, 208; AT 4:346, CSMK 279 (where he says that the form of a man is the soul).

[16] See Descartes, *Principles* II 64; Garber, *Descartes's Metaphysical Physics*, chapters 3 and 4.

[17] See Phemister, *Leibniz and the Natural World*, pp. 106–9. Descartes also holds that parts are prior to wholes, see Descartes to Mesland, February 9, 1645, AT IV 166, CSMK 243: "if any particle of the matter were changed, we would at once think that the body is not entirely the same or the same in number." For discussion, see, Schmaltz, "Descartes on the Metaphysics of the Material World," p. 20; and Schmaltz, *The Metaphysics of the Material World: Suárez, Descartes, Spinoza*, chapter 5.

explain what it is for one thing to be a substance in terms of other substances in an endless regress. Thus, Leibniz says (sometime during 1678–1681):

> For since we have said that body is actually divided into parts, each of which is agitated with a different motion, and since for the same reason each part is again divided, then certainly if we consider matter alone, no point will be assignable that will remain together with another, nor a moment at which a body will remain identical with itself; and there will never be a reason for saying that a body is a unity over and above a point, and the same for longer than a moment. (Leibniz, *Labyrinth*, p. 245)

Similarly, Leibniz writes to Arnauld in 1686:

> One will never find a body of which one can say that it is truly a substance. It will always be an aggregate of many. Or rather, it will never be a real being, since the parts that compose it are subject to the same difficulty, and so one never arrives at real being, beings by aggregation having only as much reality as there is in their ingredients [*on ne trouvera jamais un corps dont on puisse dire que c'est véritablement une substance. Ce sera tousjours un aggregé de plusieurs. Ou plustost ce ne sera pas un estre reel, puisque les parties qui le composent sont sujettes à la même difficulté, et qu'on ne vient jamais à aucun estre reel, les estres par aggregation n'ayant qu'autant de realité qu'il y en a dans leur ingrediens*]; (Gerhardt II 72. I am indebted to Levey, "On Unity: Leibniz-Arnauld Revisited," pp. 249–50, for calling this passage to my attention. I have modified Levey's translation of this passage here.)
>
> [E]very part of matter is actually divided into other parts . . . and since this always continues in this way, one will never arrive at a thing of which it may be said, "Here really is an entity," except when one finds animate machines whose soul or substantial form creates substantial unity independent of the external union of contiguity [*toute partie de la matiere est actuellement divisée en d'autres parties . . . et cela allant tousjours ainsi, on ne viendra jamais à quelque chose dont on puisse dire: voila veritablement un estre, que lorsqu'on trouve des machines animées dont l'ame ou forme substantielle fait l'unité substantielle independante de l'union exterieure de l'attouchement*]; (Gerhardt II 77. I am indebted to Garber, *Leibniz: Body, Substance, Monad*, p. 79, for calling this passage to my attention. I have modified Garber's translation here.)

For Leibniz, the explanatory question—"in virtue of what is this substance a substance?"—would thus never be satisfactorily answered on a Cartesian account.

Notice here that Leibniz's worry about Descartes' views has a decidedly Parmenidean cast: just as Parmenides was worried about regress and endlessly being unsettled and at sea, so too Leibniz, in criticizing Descartes, seeks to avoid the incessantly shifting sands of Cartesian corporeal substance.

Leibniz sees the regress in Descartes' case as vicious: in order to explain the substantiality of a Cartesian extended substance one must *first* explain how its parts are substances, and in order to explain how those parts are substances one must *first* explain how their parts are substances, etc. The regress is vicious because the explanatory task can never be completed or even really get started.[18] This problem undermines the unity of a corporeal substance at a time, and, since, as Leibniz acknowledges in the correspondence with Arnauld,[19] the unity of a substance over time presupposes the unity of a substance at a time, unity over time is undermined as well.[20] Further, since the unity of a substance is not explained and since such unity is to make possible the individuation of one substance and another, the individuality of the purported substance and its distinctness from other substances is undermined on a Cartesian picture. Indeed, for Leibniz, on a Cartesian conception of corporeal substance, there is no principled individuation of one substance and another. In Leibniz's assessment, Descartes leaves the key explanatory questions—that Descartes himself insists on—unanswered, as does Aristotle. From this point of view, the empty Cartesian account of corporeal substance is just another John Wayne moment.

Of course, hypothetically, it is open to a Cartesian to say that the unity of a substance is primitive. Perhaps, this infinitely divisible aggregate just is—primitively—a substance and there is nothing in virtue of which there is a substance here. That would seem to be a coherent thing to say, were it not for the explanatory demand that Descartes and Aristotle and Leibniz insist on. Such an appeal to unexplained, primitive individuation would be a desperate move in light of the explanatory demand and would really be no better in

---

[18] Cf. Mourelatos on Parmenides: inquiry "which goes after what-is-not cannot be successfully completed; and it cannot even get started," p. 75.

[19] Gerhardt II 43, AG 79.

[20] See again Leibniz, *Labyrinth*, p. 245; also *Discourse on Metaphysics*, section 12: "if there were no other principle of identity in body other than the one just mentioned [viz. extension], a body could not subsist for more than a moment," Gerhardt II 436, AG 44; and see Sleigh, *Leibniz and Arnauld*, p. 124.

Descartes' eyes than the Aristotelian appeal to substantial forms, no better than another John Wayne moment.

Thus, we can see how, for Leibniz, not only Aristotle, but also Descartes falls prey to—fails to meet—the explanatory demand that they themselves recognize and insist on. However, as one might expect, Leibniz himself suffers a similar fate as we will soon see.

A Different Cartesian Account of Substance

Descartes also explains substance more generally—not just corporeal substance—in terms of independence: a substance is a being dependent on no other being (except perhaps God).[21] Among contemporary philosophers, E. J. Lowe has a view of this type.[22] But does this appeal to independence help? Does it provide us with an account of substance that meets the explanatory demand?

Recall that Aristotle, after saying that substance is that which has predicates but is not predicated of anything else, observed that this account was not enough for him: he and we have to ask the further question, "In virtue of what is something a substance in the sense just described?" And Aristotle then gives his ultimately unsatisfactory answer in terms of matter and form. Still even though he does not answer the question well, he is absolutely right to raise it.

In the same way, Descartes says that substance is independent of everything else (except perhaps God). But we now want to know *how* it is independent, *in virtue of what* is it independent (just as we wanted to know in virtue of what is Aristotle's substance not predicated of anything). And what can Descartes say at this point? If Descartes says in speaking of substance, S, that it is just (part of) S's nature to be independent and that's the end of the story, then we have yet another John Wayne moment and another Molière moment. We were looking for an explanation, and we received a mere restatement of what it is we were looking for. Or, we could try to specify *how* S is independent by invoking another feature, F. But then we inevitably ask "how?" again, "how is it that F makes S independent of everything else?" And

---

[21] *Principles* I 51.
[22] Lowe, *The Possibility of Metaphysics*.

we're off on a troubling infinite regress of explanation as we were before with the regress brought on by infinitely divisible corporeal substances.

A similar problem arises for Lowe's account—indeed, definition—of substance. His ultimate definition in *The Possibility of Metaphysics* is

> x is a substance $=_{df.}$ x is a particular and there is no particular y such that y is not identical to x, and x depends for its existence upon y. (p. 140)

Here the question—unanswered by Lowe and yet very naturally following from the explanatory drive at work in the theory of substance—is: what is it in virtue of which a substance is independent of all other things? Given the explanatory questions we have been asking all along, this is not the place to shrug one's shoulders and say that independence is an explanatory primitive. And if one attempts to appeal to a feature, F, that explains why the substance is independent, then we quickly ask how and are off on another infinite regress.[23]

Returning to Descartes, we might see him as offering this alternative account proposed by Marleen Rozemond: for Descartes, to be a substance is to exist *per se* and not as a mode of or as inherent in anything else.[24] In other words, to be a substance is to be an irreducible subject of predication. This view, of course, goes back to the account in the *Categories*. And, again, we ask (as Aristotle himself does): in virtue of what is this thing an irreducible subject of predication? This is the question to which substantial forms were meant to provide the answer, but to no avail, as we have seen. And here we are back at the original Aristotelian difficulty which Descartes has not helped us to avoid.

Leibniz's Positive Account of Substance

Sensitive to these explanatory demands, but mindful of the failures of Aristotle and Descartes to meet them, Leibniz offers his own characteristically

---

[23] Hoffman and Rosenkrantz also offer a definition of substance in terms of independence (see Hoffman and Rosenkrantz, *Substance: Its Nature and Existence*, pp. 50–53). This account faces a similar problem.

[24] Rozemond, *Descartes's Dualism*, p. 8. For Rozemond's more recent defense of her position, see "Real Distinction, Separability, and Corporeal Substance in Descartes." For a sophisticated account of Descartes' views on substance, see Schechtman, "Substance and Independence in Descartes," pp. 176–80.

complex response. To understand this response, it is helpful to stress at the outset how similar Leibniz's way of approaching this matter is to Aristotle's.

First of all, Leibniz agrees with Aristotle that a substance is an irreducible subject of predication, roughly, something that has properties but is not itself a property of another thing. Thus, Leibniz says,

> when several predicates are attributed to a single subject and this subject is attributed to no other, it is called an individual substance [*lorsque plusieurs predicats s'attribuent à un même sujet, et que ce sujet ne s'attribue plus à aucun autre, on l'appelle substance individuelle*]. (*Discourse on Metaphysics* §8, Gerhardt IV 432, AG 40–41)

This is, of course, reminiscent of Aristotle's account of substance.

Second, Leibniz realizes, as Aristotle at least implicitly does, that this characterization of substance doesn't by itself address the question: what is it in virtue of which a substance is a substance? To meet this explanatory demand, Leibniz sees that one must go beyond the kind of claim made in the *Categories* and say what it is that makes something an irreducible subject of predication. Thus, Leibniz says that the Aristotelian characterization "is not sufficient, and such an explanation is merely nominal [*mais cela n'est pas assez, et une telle explication n'est que nominale*]" (*Discourse on Metaphysics*, §8, Gerhardt IV 432–33, AG 41). As Donald Rutherford puts Leibniz's concern: "In characterizing a substance as an ultimate subject of predication, we refer to an essential feature of all substances, but we do not explain what it is to *be* an individual substance."[25]

Third, as in Aristotle, what is needed is to specify what gives the substance unity, what makes it a unified thing. Leibniz makes clear (in a passage from 1678–1681 that in his account of substance, he is seeking "the principle of unity [*principium unitatis*]" (Leibniz, *Labyrinth*, p. 245), and he points out in a passage from 1684–1686 that "in an entity *per se* [*in Ente per se*]"—i.e. a substance—"some real union is required consisting not in the situation and motion of parts, as in a chain, a house, or a ship, but in some unique individual principle and subject of attributes and operations [*realis quaedam unio requiritur consistens non in partium situ et motu ut in catena, domo, navi sed in unico quodam individuo principio et subjecto attributorum et*

---

[25] Rutherford, *Leibniz and the Rational Order of Nature*, p. 123.

operationum]" (*Labyrinth* p. 283; translation modified). I will return to this passage shortly.

Fourth, like Aristotle, Leibniz sees substantial forms as providing this unity: "substantial form, or soul, is the principle of unity" (*Labyrinth*, p. 245). Also: "Matter in some way has its being from form [*Materia quodammodo esse habet a forma*]" (*De Summa Rerum*, p. 45).

But—and here the differences or apparent differences from Aristotle begin—unlike Aristotle, Leibniz attempts to explain *how* it is that the substantial form provides the unity necessary for being a substance. This is the moment that we and Descartes and those many impatient with the alleged emptiness of Aristotelian explanations have been waiting for: an account of *how* substance is unified or, in these Aristotelian terms, an account of *how* a substantial form confers unity on substance. So how do substantial forms do it? Leibniz's answer (or at least his answer around the 1680s) is that substantial forms confer unity by being the ontological correlate of a complete concept. Thus, Leibniz says in 1685 that the true nature of a substance consists in a complete concept: "it is demonstrated elsewhere in what consists the true nature of a substance, namely, in a complete concept."[26] And immediately after articulating what great work a complete concept does, he stresses that he is thereby and surprisingly capturing what is good in the ancient and much decried notion of substantial forms. Indeed, for Leibniz, substantial forms—when properly understood in terms of complete concepts—are something

> whose knowledge is so necessary to metaphysics that ... without it one cannot properly know the first principles or elevate our minds sufficiently well to the knowledge of incorporeal natures and the wonders of God. (*Discourse on Metaphysics* §10, Gerhardt IV 434–35, AG 43)

So let's consider what complete concepts are before asking how exactly they do what they do as far as unifying substance is concerned. For a thing to have a complete concept, according to Leibniz, is for the concept of that thing to be so rich that *all* the properties of the thing—past, present, or future; necessary or contingent—are contained in that concept. Thus, for Leibniz, Caesar is a substance because Caesar has a concept so complete as to contain the concept of each of Caesar's properties. The concept of Caesar thus contains

---

[26] "*alibi ostendi in quo consistat vera natura substantiae, nempe in notione completa*," A VI.4B, 1240. Cited in Rutherford, *Leibniz and the Rational Order of Nature*, p. 132n61.

the concepts of being killed on the Ides of March, of crossing the Rubicon, etc. Leibniz says more generally:

> the nature of an individual substance or of a complete being is to have a notion so complete that it is sufficient to contain and to allow us to deduce from it all the predicates of the subject to which this notion is attributed [*la nature d'une substance individuelle ou d'un estre complet, est d'avoir une notion si accomplie qu'elle soit suffisante à comprendre et à en faire deduire tous les predicats du sujet à qui cette notion est attribuée*]. (*Discourse on Metaphysics* §8, Gerhardt IV 433, AG 41)

By contrast, the concept of an accident "does not include everything that can be attributed to the subject to which the notion is attributed" (*Discourse on Metaphysics* §8, Gerhardt IV 433, AG 41).[27]

This complete concept of a substance is a reflection of the rich nature that is the source and subject of the properties that a substance has. Thus, Leibniz specifies that it is the *nature* of a substance to have a complete concept, and he goes on to say:

> From all time in Alexander's soul there are vestiges of everything that has happened to him and marks of everything that will happen to him and even traces of everything that happens in the universe, even though God alone could recognize them all. (*Discourse on Metaphysics* §8, Gerhardt IV 433, AG 41)

This nature is what Leibniz calls the substantial form and sometimes calls, as in the passage just quoted, a soul. (Aristotle, of course, also calls a substantial form a soul in the case of living things). See also:

> The substance of a body, if bodies have one, must be indivisible; whether it is called soul or form does not concern me. (Leibniz to Arnauld, October 21/31, 1686, G II 72. I follow Garber's translation here in Garber, *Leibniz: Body, Substance, Monad*, p. 76.)

---

[27] See also Leibniz to Arnauld, May 1686, Gerhardt II 39, AG 70; *Labyrinth*, pp. 282–85. See also the references in Rutherford, *Leibniz and the Rational Order of Nature*, p. 131n53.

Because the substantial form or soul is the ontological ground of all that is true of the substance, including the properties whereby it stands in relations to all other things, the substantial form can be said to *express* all other things and their states. These expressions are the vestiges or traces in a substance of not only all that ever happens to the substance but also of all that ever happens *simpliciter*. As Rutherford puts it, "a substance expresses everything in its world because it has been endowed with a concept which entails that its states are correlated in a lawlike way with those of every other substance" (*Leibniz and the Rational Order of Nature*, p. 146).

Leibniz further spells out this conception of soul or substantial form by pointing out that although each soul or substantial form expresses the entire universe, each does so from the perspective, as it were, of its body. Thus, my soul expresses the states of other substances by means of expressing the states of my body. In fact, the only thing that differentiates one soul from another is not what it expresses, but the perspective from which it expresses things together with the degree of confusion with which it expresses things.

Fascinating though it is, the mechanism, as it were, of a soul's perspective need not concern us here. For our purposes, the key point is that, for Leibniz, what it is to be a substance—what the substantiality of a thing consists in—is the substance's having a nature or substantial form rich enough to make it the case that the substance expresses each thing in the universe.

But exactly how does this count as an explanation of what it is for something to be a substance? Leibniz seems to be thinking along the following lines: something is a substance because it has a substantial form, i.e. because it has a nature so rich that from this nature follow all the properties that belong to that substance and thus a nature so rich that it expresses the entire universe. That is, that thing is a substance because it has a nature into which are built or from which follow all the properties of which that thing is the subject. This is the point Leibniz makes in a passage part of which I quoted earlier:

> An entity (unity) in itself is, for instance, a man: an accidental entity (unity)—for instance a woodpile, a machine—is what is only a unity by aggregation.... But in an entity in itself some real union is required, consisting

not in the situation and motion of parts, as in a chain, a house, or a ship, but in some *unique* (*unico*) individual principle and subject of attributes and operations, which is called a soul, and in every body a substantial form. (*Labyrinth*, p. 283, my emphasis)

Leibniz goes on after this passage to stress that the substance thus has a complete concept.

Leibniz similarly regards the substantiality of a persisting substance as consisting in its nature—which corresponds to a complete concept—that makes it the subject of all of its properties at different times. Thus, for Leibniz there is one—unified—substance over time because the concepts of these successive states are all built into the concept of *the same* substance. That is, unity—sameness—over time is provided by the fact that certain states are states of the *same* substance. As Leibniz says to Arnauld,

It is true that my internal experience convinces me *a posteriori* of this identity [between the I who was in Paris and who is now in Germany], but there must also be an a priori reason. Now, it is not possible to find any reason but the fact that both my attributes in the preceding time and state and my attributes in the succeeding time and state are predicates *of the same subject*, they are in the same subject. [*Il est vray que mon experience interieure m'a convaincu a posteriori de cette identicité, mais il faut qu'il y en ait une aussi a priori. Or il n'est pas possible de trouver une autre, si non que tant mes attributs du temps et estat precedant, que mes attributs du temps et estat suivant sont des predicats d'un même sujet, insunt eidem subjecto*]. (Leibniz to Arnauld, May 1686, Gerhardt II 43, AG 73; my emphasis)

See also Leibniz's claim nearly twenty years later to de Volder:

For me nothing is permanent in those things except the very law that involves the continued succession, which in individual things corresponds to the law that is in the whole universe. . . . The fact that there a certain law persists which involves the future states of that which *we conceive to be the same*—this is the very fact, I say, that constitutes the same substance. [*Nec mihi aliud in eis est permanens quam lex ipsa quae involvit continuatam successionem, in singulis consentiens ei quae est in toto universo . . . Legem quandam esse persistentem, (id) quae involvat futuros ejus quod ut idem concipimus status, id ipsum est quod substantiam eandem constituere dico*]. (Leibniz to de Volder, January 21, 1704, Gerhardt II 263, 264, Loemker 534, 535; my emphasis)

Here Leibniz accounts for the identity over time of a substance by appealing to the future states of what we conceive to be the same thing.[28]

See also this passage from *General Notation* (1683–1686):

> The same thing can remain, even if it changes, if it follows from its own nature that *the same thing* [*idem*] must have successive diverse states. Certainly, I am said to be the same [*idem*] who existed before because my [*mea*] substance involves all *my* [*meos*] states, past, present, and future. (Leibniz, *Textes Inédits*, p. 323, translation modified from Sleigh, *Leibniz and Arnauld*, p. 129; my emphasis.)

Here the sameness over time depends on the nature of a thing, a nature that specifies that the same thing has diverse states over time.

See also this passage from a letter to Electress Sophie in March 1706:

> the nature of created substance rightly consists in this connection, which brings it about that these different states belong to one subject [*la nature de la substance creée consiste proprement dans cette liaison qui fait que ces differens estats appartiennent à un même sujet*]. (*Die Werke von Leibniz*, p. 173; quoted in Rutherford, *Leibniz and the Rational Order of Nature*, p. 166n12.)

Here Leibniz says that the substantiality of a created substance consists in a connection between states. And what is that connection? Leibniz seems to have no other way to specify what this connection is other than as the connection that makes the states states of the same subject.

Consider two more passages; first, one from the *New Essays*:

> to require of this "pure subject in general" anything beyond what is needed for the conception of "the same thing" [*la même chose*]—e.g. it is the same

---

[28] Here Leibniz says that the law of a series of states persists. This suggests that Leibniz is opening up the possibility that what persists is not the particular substance but rather the law itself. I am not pursuing this intriguing suggestion here, but for a thorough exploration of it, see Leisinger, "Leibniz's Response to Primitive Persistence."

thing which understands and wills, which imagines and reasons—is to demand the impossible. (*New Essays* 2.23.2)

Second, consider this passage from Leibniz's middle period: "the nature of an individual substance is such that it has a complete concept, in which all the predicates of *the same subject* [*ejusdem subjecti*] are involved" ("A Specimen of Discoveries about Marvellous Secrets of a General Nature," Gerhardt VII 316, Leibniz, *Philosophical Writings*, p. 84; translation from Adams, *Leibniz*, p. 78; my emphasis).

This kind of story in these passages about substantiality (in general and over time) is nice, but it is really quite empty as an explanation: it explains the fact that something is one thing that has properties and is a substance and persists simply by appealing to the very fact that there is one thing that has properties, is a substance, and persists. In all these passages, it is the *uniqueness* or *sameness* of the subject of a variety of properties or states that is meant to tell us what it is to be *one* substance or the *same* substance at a time and over time.[29]

Seen this way, Leibniz's "account" does not succeed in meeting the explanatory demand that he himself insists on and that he takes Aristotle and Descartes to task for not meeting. Just as it is unilluminating for Aristotle to say merely that there is a substance here because it is somehow unified by a substantial form, just as it would be unilluminating for Descartes to say that the aggregate of corporeal substances is primitively unified, and just as it is unilluminating to say that substance is independent without saying in virtue of what it is independent, so too it is unilluminating for Leibniz to say that there is *one substance* here because it follows from its nature that there are states that are properties of *one substance*. Leibniz has failed to meet the explanatory demand on which he himself so elegantly insisted. Leibniz too has his John Wayne moment. And since this is a case of an unilluminating appeal to natures, Leibniz also has a Molière moment here.

Perhaps one could say, in defense of Leibniz, that there is one substance here because there is a maximal set of consistent properties here. Such an

---

[29] Leibniz's thinking on persistence is thus a reflection of the general claim—which I have argued for elsewhere—that three-dimensionalist accounts of persistence are committed to seeing persistence as primitive. To the extent that Leibniz allows for temporal distinctions at all, Leibniz would be a three-dimensionalist because he would view the persisting substance as prior to any spatial or temporal parts it may have. For the three-dimensionalist commitment to primitive persistence, see my "Primitive Persistence and the Impasse between Three-Dimensionalism and Four-Dimensionalism."

48 THE PARMENIDEAN ASCENT

appeal to a maximal set of properties does not seem to involve a question-begging appeal to the notion of the same substance.[30] But at this point one is naturally led to ask the question: in virtue of what are these properties consistent? And the answer would have to be, I believe, that these properties are consistent because a *single* thing can have them all. Thus, the appeal to consistency seems to presuppose the very notion of singleness or unity that we are trying to explain.

A similar line of response helps me to address another important way of trying to defend Leibniz from my objection. This potential line of defense comes from Rutherford who interprets some of the above passages in a way that seems not to commit Leibniz to an unilluminating explanation of substantiality in terms of substantiality. Rutherford suggests that—to take the case of persistence over time—Leibniz's view is simply that "any two properties are properties of the same subject at different times just in case they are products of the same nature or form" (*Leibniz and the Rational Order of Nature*, p. 140).[31] Rutherford places much weight on the following passage from the Leibniz-Arnauld correspondence in 1686: "these predicates were laws included in the subject or in my complete notion, which constitutes what is called I, which is the foundation of the connection of all my different states" (Gerhardt II 43, AG 73). This interpretation is correct as far as it goes, and it does not seem to import any circular explanation of substantiality in terms of substantiality. Sameness of subject or substance over time seems, on this account, to be explained in terms of the sameness of nature or form. However, the problematic circularity emerges when we ask the obvious and natural question: what is it for the nature or form that produces one property to be the same as the nature or form that produces another property? And here the only answer seems to be that the nature or form in the first case and the nature or form in the second case are the nature or form *of the same substance or subject*. Thus, in the passage from the Leibniz-Arnauld correspondence that Rutherford relies upon, Leibniz identifies the relevant concept which is correlated with the nature or form as *my* concept. Here again we can see that, for Leibniz, sameness or one-ness of substance is in the end "explained" in terms of the sameness or one-ness of that substance itself.

---

[30] I am indebted to Dai Heide for raising this important challenge.
[31] Similarly, according to Adams, "Leibniz seems . . . to have favored a criterion of identity that assigns states to the same individual substance if and only if they are caused by the same individual causal nexus (or the same substantial form, in the favored terminology of his middle years)," Adams, *Leibniz: Determinist, Idealist, Theist*, p. 313, also pp. 77–81.

So the appeal to substantial form understood as corresponding to the complete concept of a substance cannot provide an illuminating explanation of substantial unity. But perhaps Leibniz does not need to rely on complete concepts in this way. Perhaps he needs only to appeal to substantial forms understood as the force a substance exhibits. Or perhaps, he can appeal to substantial form understood as the teleological or end-directed activity of a substance.[32] Perhaps such force or end-directed activity can explain the substantiality or one-ness of a substance. Thus, Rutherford suggests, "Within the *Discourse*, at least, Leibniz's treatment of substance is never completely divorced from its identity as an entelechy or principle of action," (Rutherford, *Leibniz and the Rational Order of Nature*, p. 138). Rutherford also sees "the complete concept theory as emerging against the background of a set of well-entrenched beliefs about what it is to be a substance, including the belief that to be a substance is to be an intrinsic source of action" (p. 138). In this connection, Rutherford cites Leibniz's claim in *A Specimen of Discoveries*: "This principle of actions, or primitive active force, from which a series of various states follows, is the form of the substance" (Gerhardt VII 317, Leibniz, *Philosophical Writings*, 84–85; cited in Rutherford, p. 167n17).

Indeed, as Julia Jorati stresses in an important paper, Leibniz sometimes even goes so far to say that substances just *are* forces.[33] Thus, in the *Theodicy* he speaks of "the Souls, Entelechies, or primitive forces, substantial forms, simple substances, or Monads, whatever name one may apply to them" (Leibniz, *Theodicy*, §396). He says also that the primitive active power of a substance together with its primitive passive power constitutes a substance and that "one without the other is not a complete substance" (Leibniz to Jaquelot, March 22, 1703, Gerhardt III 458; Woolhouse and Francks, *Leibniz's "New System" and Associated Contemporary Texts*, p. 201.) Finally, Leibniz says in "On Body and Force," "primitive active force, which Aristotle calls first entelechy and one commonly calls the form of a substance, is another natural principle which, together with matter or passive force, completes [*absolvit*] a corporeal substance (Gerhardt IV 395, AG 252).

I completely agree with Jorati and Rutherford and others that substance for Leibniz is fundamentally force or activity, and I know that there is a lot more to be said about force and teleology in Leibniz, but I don't believe that these appeals can answer the basic explanatory question that has been

---

[32] For pressing these challenges, I am indebted to Tom Feeney and Stephan Schmid.
[33] Jorati, "Leibniz's Ontology of Force." See also Carriero, "Substance and Ends in Leibniz."

dogging us. If force unifies a substance, makes it one thing, then this is only because it is the force *of that substance* (unindividuated force cannot individuate a substance). Similarly, if the end-directed activity unifies the substance, makes it a substance, then this is only because it is the teleological activity *of that substance* (unindividuated teleological activity cannot individuate a substance). And if, as Jorati stresses, a substance just is force or activity, then we still want to know *how* this force makes the substance what it is, and *how* this force individuates the substance. Merely to say that force is or constitutes a substance does not tell us how force is or constitutes that substance. For force and teleology to serve the explanatory purpose they are invoked to serve, they must presuppose the substantiality that they are invoked to explain. And so the purported explanation isn't really an explanation at all.

Daniel Garber appreciates the explanatory demand in the case of substance, and he offers a rather different and intriguing way of seeing how Leibniz might meet it. Beginning with corporeal substances, Garber offers a good answer in Leibnizian terms to the question of what it is for there to be a unified corporeal substance. Taking the example of a human being in particular, Garber points out that the human soul is, for Leibniz (as for Aristotle and, in a way, even for Descartes) the substantial form of the human body. This soul or form is itself, for Leibniz a unified—indeed indivisible—thing:

> The substance of a body, if bodies have one, must be indivisible; whether it is called soul or form does not concern me. (Leibniz to Arnauld, October 21/31, 1686, Gerhardt II 72; I have used the translation in Garber, *Leibniz: Body, Substance, Monad*, p. 76.)

> Substantial unity requires a thoroughly indivisible and naturally indestructible being . . . which can be found neither in shape nor in motion . . . but which can be found in a soul or substantial form on the model of what one calls "me." (Leibniz to Arnauld, November 28/December 8, 1686; Gerhardt II 76, AG 79)

This substantial form or soul confers unity on the states and parts that constitute the body. Thus, Leibniz says,

> man . . . is an entity endowed with a genuine unity conferred on him by his soul, notwithstanding the fact that the mass of his body is divided into organs, vessels, humors, spirits. (Leibniz to Arnauld, September 10, 1687,

G II 120; I have used the translation in Garber, *Leibniz: Body, Substance, Monad*, p. 78.)

The soul or substantial form is thus, as Garber puts it, "a kind of incorporeal glue that unites the different parts of the body and makes them all belong to one genuine individual, one genuine substance," (Garber, *Leibniz: Body, Substance, Monad*, p. 78).

But *how* does the soul pull off this remarkable unifying feat? *How* does the incorporeal glue work? As Garber points out in the case of the human body, the union is a function of something we saw before, viz. the relation between the soul and the body whereby the soul expresses the universe through expressing the body. Thus, Leibniz says to Arnauld,

> The soul ... is nevertheless the form of its body because it is an expression of the phenomena of all other bodies in accordance with the relationship to its own. (Leibniz to Arnauld, June 1686, G II 58; I have used the translation in Garber, *Leibniz: Body, Substance, Monad*, p. 80.)

This relation of expression Leibniz characterizes as a kind of harmony: "Expression occurs everywhere, because every substance is in harmony with every other." And this harmony amounts to the union Leibniz seeks between the soul and the human body. For Leibniz, the union of soul and body that makes the human body into a substance is simply due to this relation of expression or harmony.[34] And, as we saw earlier, that a substance expresses things and the way in which it expresses things is a function of its complete concept.

As Garber indicates (*Leibniz: Body, Substance, Monad*, p. 81), it is natural to see Leibniz's point that the human body counts as a corporeal substance by virtue of its harmony with the soul or substantial form as holding more generally. Thus, the relation between bodies in general and their souls or substantial forms is one of harmony.

Garber's account goes a long way toward showing how, for Leibniz, a substantial form or soul may provide the necessary unity for a corporeal substance. However, even if this account is an explanation of how corporeal substance is a kind of unity, this account is merely a stopgap as far as the explanatory demand concerning the unity of substance in general is

---

[34] See Leibniz to de Volder, January 19, 1706; Gerhardt II 281, Loemker 538–39.

concerned. Consider: Garber's Leibniz explains the unity of a corporeal substance by appealing to its substantial form. But what is a substantial form for Leibniz? It is a soul which is a "complete individual" entity; the soul is itself a substance or substance-like entity. Thus, the explanation that Garber's Leibniz provides only pushes the demand one step back, for now we are inevitably led to ask: what does the substantiality—the oneness, the unity—of this soul or incorporeal substance consist in? And to *this* question, Garber's Leibniz seems to have no answer. So, while Leibniz may indeed, as Garber suggests, explain the unity of corporeal substance by appeal to souls or substantial forms, Garber's Leibniz still does not have an answer to the more fundamental question of what the unity of substance in general consists in, what makes a substance into a substance.

By merely deferring the question, Garber's Leibniz leaves us short in much the same way that Descartes does in his account of corporeal substance. This is because in responding to the question, "What makes this corporeal substance a substance?," Descartes appeals to another substance (or substances) whose unity is equally in need of explanation. Garber's Leibniz also explains corporeal unity by appealing to something else—in this case by appealing to a single other substance—whose substantiality is equally in need of, and has not received, explanation.

In light of the failures of the interpretations I have discussed to provide Leibniz with a good account of the substantiality of substance, I think that we have good reason to conclude that Leibniz has no legitimate answer to the explanatory demand concerning substance—a demand that he quite rightly insists on and a demand that both Aristotle and Descartes in their own ways likewise insist on and likewise fail to answer satisfactorily. Substantiality, for Leibniz, is despite his best intentions, analogous to Molière's *virtus dormitiva*. Leibniz's account thus disappointingly bottoms out in another John Wayne moment.

Locke

To complete this necessarily incomplete historical investigation of views on substance, I would like to go slightly out of historical order and consider briefly Locke's position. Although his take on substance is—like those of the others—ultimately unsatisfactory and for similar reasons, his sophisticated way of approaching this topic adds important new dimensions to the discussion and his argumentative strategies exhibit problems that will pave the way for my more or less *a priori* critique of standard conceptions of substance in the next chapter.

The first thing to note is that Locke, like the others, makes an explanatory demand when it comes to substance: for a given substance, S, there must be something in virtue of which S is a substance. There must be some thing (or perhaps some fact—the difference is not significant for our inquiry right now) that metaphysically explains S's being a substance. This demand emerges when Locke—in keeping with his "way of ideas" approach—considers the ideas through which we recognize that there is a substance present.[35] We know that there is a substance when we perceive certain qualities—e.g., in the case of a corporeal substance qualities such as size, shape, and color. We observe such sensible qualities that we "find united in the thing called *Horse* or *Stone*" (Locke, *Essay Concerning Human Understanding*, 2.23.4).[36] Locke goes on to say "yet because we cannot conceive, *how* they should subsist alone, nor in one another, we suppose them existing in, and supported by some common subject; *which Support we denote by the name Substance*" (2.23.4; first emphasis mine). Similarly, Locke says to Stillingfleet, "we cannot conceive *how* sensible Qualities should subsist by themselves" (Locke, *Works* IV 445; my emphasis). Locke regards this support—which he also calls "substratum" (e.g., in 2.23.5)—as a *cause* of the union of simple ideas "as makes the whole subsist of itself" (2.23.6).

For Locke, then, sensible qualities must be united and must subsist somehow, there must be some cause or explanation of their union and their subsistence. This substratum which supports and unites qualities helps to explain—metaphysically—why there is a substance present in a given location. There is a substance here, in part, *because* there is a substratum that supports and unites sensible qualities. Locke offers a similar account of spiritual substance which consists in a substratum that somehow supports and unites observable mental qualities such as thinking, reasoning, feeling, etc. In general, for Locke, as he puts it to Stillingfleet, "there must certainly be Substance in the World" (to Stillingfleet, May 4, 1698; Locke, *Works* IV 446).

Locke also stresses, however, that we have no clear idea of what this substance or substratum or support is, or of what it consists in. For Locke, "we

---

[35] As Jonathan Bennett notes, "There is controversy about why Locke writes about qualities in the language of ideas, but not about the fact that he does," "Substratum," p. 198.
[36] Unless otherwise noted, all references to Locke will be to the *Essay Concerning Human Understanding*.

have no clear, or distinct *Idea* of that *thing* we suppose a Support." This epistemic humility is pervasive in Locke's account of substance, and he often expresses it in strong terms indeed: he says that the union and coherence of the parts of a corporeal substance—a union which makes it the case that there is a complex substance here—is "incomprehensible" (2.23.24). This skepticism applies to corporeal and thinking substances alike: "we are no more able to discover, wherein the *Ideas* belonging to Body consist, than those belonging to Spirit" (2.23.29). We are "at a loss" to explain how the parts of a compound substance are united, and he says that when the mind tries to "penetrate" into the causes and manners of production of qualities that we perceive through the senses or through reflection, the mind "discovers nothing but its short-sightedness" (2.23.28; see also 2.23.23).

However, despite our ignorance of what support consists in, Locke still affirms that there is some such support and that "there must certainly be substance in the world." Despite our perhaps irremediable ignorance of how such support takes place or of how it is that there is a union of qualities here, there is for Locke some thing or some feature that makes it the case that there is a substance here. There is, in other words, a metaphysical explanation, even if it is one that we do not and cannot grasp. In this way, Locke insists on the explanatory demand with regard to substance by saying that there is and must be an explanation, even if we cannot understand it or know what it is.

This combination of a commitment to metaphysical explanation of some kind along with skepticism about the character of this explanation is evident when Locke explains to Stillingfleet that the passages in the *Essay* (e.g. 2.13.19) where he seems to make fun of the notion of substance should not be read as denying that there is substance. Rather, those passages were meant to "shew, that though *Substance* did support accidents, yet Philosophers, who had found such a support necessary, had no more clear Idea of what, that support was, than the *Indian* had of that, which supported his Tortoise" (Locke, *Works* IV 448). Edwin McCann sums up the general point here by saying that we should "take the skepticism to concern only the clarity and distinctness of our idea of substance, and not whether there is something answering to this idea. On the latter question, Locke is not skeptic" (McCann, "Locke on Substance," pp. 173–74). I would add only that, for Locke, this something answering to the idea of substance is something that serves as a metaphysical explanation of the unity and subsistence of qualities.

There is much controversy in the considerable literature on Locke as to what this unknown support of sensible qualities is, how it is related to what Locke calls the real essence of a substance, and the precise character of Locke's epistemic humility here.[37] But I would like to rise above these much-contested areas and stress the general point that Locke accepts that there is an explanation of the substantiality of substance, but, with characteristic epistemic humility, he also holds that we don't and perhaps can't grasp what that explanation is. On this general way of seeing Locke, his approach is continuous the concern that Aristotle, Descartes, and Leibniz bring to this issue—viz. a concern with what it is in virtue of which a substance is a substance—even if he ends up with a more skeptical position than theirs.[38]

On the Lockean view, then, there is some*how* some thing (or some fact or whatever) that explains why there is a unified substance here. Even though we may not be able to grasp this explanation, this explanation must, for Locke, have certain features. In particular, Locke would reject a circular explanation of the substantiality of a substance. An explanation of the form, "S is a substance because S is a substance" will not do for Locke (and rightly so). He makes this understandable aversion to such circular explanations of substantiality clear when he ridicules what he takes to be an analogous account of the notion of support in architecture.

> an intelligent *American*, who enquired into the Nature of Things, would scarce take it for a satisfactory Account, if desiring to learn our Architecture, he should be told, That a Pillar was a thing supported by a *Basis*, and a *Basis* something that supported a Pillar. Would he not think himself mocked, instead of taught with such an account as this? . . . But were the Latin words *Inhaerentia* and *Substantia*, put into the plain English ones that answer them, and were called *Sticking on*, and *Under-propping*, they would better discover to us the very great clearness in the Doctrine of *Substance* and *Accidents*. (2.13.20)

This kind of unilluminating, circular account is precisely what Locke objects to in appeals to substantial forms. See especially 2.23.3 and 2.31.6.

---

[37] For some of the opposing lines in the current debate, see Ayers, "The Ideas of Power and Substance in Locke's Philosophy," and *Locke*, chapters 3 and 4; and Bennett, "Substratum." For a judicious treatment of this debate, see McCann, "Locke on Substance."

[38] Thus, Jolley says: "[Locke] regularly invokes the concept of substratum, or substance in general, to address a problem which goes back to Aristotle; it is the issue of giving a philosophical analysis of our concept of a thing, or of a thing of a certain kind, as opposed to a property or even a collection of properties," *Locke: His Philosophical Thought*, p. 73.

Another reason to be confident that Locke holds that the explanation of substantiality is not circular is this: if circular metaphysical "explanations" of the form, "S is a substance because S is a substance" were allowable, then Locke would have no good reason to say, as he does, that we cannot grasp such an explanation, for we can certainly grasp the trivial truth of "S is a substance because S is a substance."

So Locke does, like the others we have considered, insist on the explanatory demand when it comes to substance, but where he is most different and perhaps most attractive is in his epistemic humility. Gone, perhaps, is the metaphysical hubris of Aristotle, Descartes, and Leibniz who purport to explain the substantiality of S and not merely to say that there is such an explanation. Has Locke succeeded then in threading the needle? Has he respected the explanatory demand with regard to substantiality and met this demand simply by disavowing knowledge of the explanation while affirming that there is an explanation? Perhaps here—as in life in general—a little humility goes a long way. Unfortunately, however, no matter how well-founded it may be, Locke's humble style doesn't—for reasons that will have general import as we'll see in the next chapter—succeed in giving him a coherent way of addressing and respecting the explanatory demand.

How is Locke's account incoherent? Why does Locke fail just as the other luminaries do? Let's begin with Locke's own point that there is a substantive, non-circular explanation of substantiality that we cannot grasp. That is, there is a further element or fact beyond the fact that S is a substance that explains why S is a substance and why there is this unity of qualities. Call this further element, E. E is what makes it the case that S is a substance. But recall that the explanatory demand is in place here, so just as we (with Locke's blessing) demanded that there be an explanation of *how* S is a substance (even if we can't know that explanation), so too we demand that there be an explanation of *how* E makes it the case that S is a substance. In virtue of what does E make it the case that S is a substance? Even if we cannot grasp what this explanation is, there must be such an explanation. The demand here is really just a version of the original demand for an explanation of how S is a substance: looking more closely now, we see that this amounts to a demand for an explanation of *how* E does it, *how* E makes it the case that S is a substance.

Even if we cannot grasp this explanation, there are still some constraints on what this explanation must be like. First of all, the explanation cannot be circular (Locke would rightly insist). Locke wants, as do I, substantive explanations. So the explanation of how E makes it the case that S is a substance must appeal to something, some further element beyond E itself. Let's call this further element EE: EE explains how it is that E explains that S is a substance. Of course, now—given the general explanatory demand—we want an explanation of how it is that EE does *its* explanatory work, and this further explanation must itself not be circular, and so we need to appeal to yet a further element, EEE. We are obviously off on an infinite explanatory regress. It seems, then, that the unknown Lockean metaphysical explanation of the substantiality of S—if not outright circular—can never be completed or really ever get started.

Locke, of course, is opposed to infinite regresses of this kind. This is evident in his rejection of Cartesian infinite divisibility of matter (e.g., in 2.23.31). Despite wanting to avoid the dizzying whirlpool of a Cartesian infinite regress of attempted explanation of the substantiality of a given corporeal substance and despite his overall epistemic humility, Locke seems to wind up in such a regress anyway, and so—in much the same way that Descartes does—he faces an infinite regress without explanatory value. That is, of course, unless Locke embraces an explanatory circle—something he is, rightly, equally unwilling to do.

So, despite his remarkable and, perhaps, welcome epistemic humility, Locke joins the ranks of his more epistemically ambitious colleagues—Aristotle, Descartes, and Leibniz—in failing to meet the explanatory demand that he, like these others, insists on. Like the others, Locke succumbs to a John Wayne moment.

Conclusion

We stand then amidst the wreckage of a number of the most important and influential theories of substance in the history of philosophy. There are countless other theories of substance that I have not addressed here. Forgive me if I have not tried specifically to do away with your favorite theory of substance. No offense meant, but there's only so much that I—a mere substance or being, if I'm lucky—can do. However, with these failures of theories, we have seen enough, I believe, to suspect on inductive grounds that most or all theories of substance would meet a similar fate.

But can this really be so? Can it really be that most or all theories that endeavor to explain a given phenomenon—substance—central to philosophy are vitiated by an implicit circularity or emptiness or regress? Can it really be that throughout the history of philosophy, philosophers never really learn the lessons which they accuse other philosophers of failing to heed? Think about this question for just one second. The answer should be clear: *of course*, this litany of failure is possible, and indeed it is not surprising at all. It is eminently plausible to think that philosophers make, over and over again, the same mistake, in different guises, with regard to substance. And the analogous flaws that, as we will see, debilitate theories in other domains only strengthen this sad, inductive case.

These inductive grounds lead us also to suspect that there is something systematically wrong with the notion of substance or at least with the way in which this notion is ordinarily understood in philosophy. So let's try to figure out what is going on here. It is to this task, that of laying bare—on relatively *a priori* grounds—the systematic problem afflicting standard theories of substance, that I turn in the next chapter. And these *a priori* grounds for the demise of the ordinary understanding of substance will be a model for the grounds for similar attacks on ordinary notions in other central philosophical domains in later chapters.

3
Substance
The Underlying Problem

Although I am delighted to criticize Locke's and Leibniz's and Descartes' and Aristotle's and others' views on substance, I don't want to wallow in such negativity. As you might suspect, I'm a positive kind of person. (I will close this chapter by shedding light on why I am so positive.) Still, I must go even more negative before I can be positive again. As I mentioned at the end of the previous chapter, the failures I have identified lead us to suspect on inductive grounds, as it were, that there is a more general problem at work when it comes to the concept of substance or being. I will now proceed on a relatively *a priori* basis to argue that there is indeed a single, powerful source of the difficulties we have encountered: Locke's, Leibniz's, Descartes', and Aristotle's failures are inevitable for any account of substance that makes a certain widespread and seemingly innocuous assumption. Any account of substance that makes this assumption will inevitably rely on objectionable primitives or question-begging notions or explanatory regresses that skirt legitimate explanatory demands and thus prevent us from having an intelligible account of substance.

The apparently harmless assumption of just about any account of substance is that in order for there to be a substance, there must be some relation between the substance, S, and some item or items. In other words, the presupposition of just about any account of substance is that we are trying to understand what it is to be a *related* substance, a substance that stands in relations to some, perhaps other, items. Depending on the account of substance, this relation may be, as in Locke, Leibniz, and Aristotle, one of unification between the substance and its states or properties. Or, the relation may be a relation between S and a certain nature—S's own nature. This would be the case on a theory, such as Aristotle's, that sees substantiality as a function of S's nature alone. Substantiality would then be an internal relation that holds simply in virtue of the nature of S. Alternatively, this relation may be, as in Descartes' account of corporeal substance, a relation of containing other substances as parts. Or alternatively again, this relation may be, as in Lowe's and as in Descartes' general accounts of substance, a relation of independence between S and other actual or possible particulars. But the character of this relation is not relevant for the general argument I am about to give. What is relevant is instead that the account of substance must invoke at some stage a *relation* between the substance and items of some kind or other as part of what it is to be a substance. Each of these possible relations provides a way of answering Aristotle's question: what is it in virtue of which S is a substance? Or, as I put it in the previous chapter: what explains the substantiality of S? What does the substantiality of S consist in? The explaining relation—call it "R"—can thus be seen as the substance-making relation.

The Argument

In seeking to understand the substance-making relation, R, there are four exhaustive and mutually exclusive options.

(1) R is primitive. That is, the relation, R, between S and some items is not grounded in or explained by anything. There is nothing in virtue of which S stands in R to these items.

(2) R is not primitive, but is, rather, ultimately grounded in or explained by or ultimately holds, at least in part, in virtue of a relation to something other than S.

(3) R is not primitive, but is, rather, ultimately grounded in or explained by or ultimately holds in virtue of the nature of S alone. That is, it follows from the nature of S alone that S is a substance. R is thus, in one sense of the term, an internal relation, a relation that stems simply from the nature of a thing.

(4) R is not primitive, but also is not ultimately grounded (as in (2) and (3)); instead, R is grounded in other items in a non-terminating regress or in a circle with a multiplicity of items.

A few notes on these options before beginning the argument proper. First, I say "ultimately grounded" in (2) and (3) in order to contrast such grounding with what might be called intermediate grounding. It may be that something a is grounded in some item b and b is grounded in c. In this case, a would be grounded in b, but not ultimately grounded in b. Instead, a would be intermediately grounded in *b* and ultimately grounded in *c*. This distinction between ultimate and intermediate grounding will soon be important.

Second, falling under option (2) are at least two subsidiary options: the relation in question is grounded in S and some other item, *x, together*, or the relation in question is grounded in *x alone*.[1] For my purposes, it doesn't matter which of these two sub-options under (2) is adopted. The problem I am about to raise would arise on either sub-option.

Finally, I won't discuss option (4) separately because my reasons for rejecting explanatory regresses or circles in connection with option (2) will also suffice to reject option (4).

Let's begin the argument. R—the substance-making relation—must fall into one of the three categories just outlined: (1), (2), or (3). Which option, if any, will be the lucky winner?

The first option can be eliminated in this context in which we are focusing on the demand for an account—an explanation—of what it is to be a substance. To appeal to a primitive relation, R, that makes it the case that S is a substance is really to turn one's back on the commitment to explanation that actuates philosophers in this domain. We saw this kind of issue arise when we considered a hypothetical Cartesian view that makes the unity of particular extended substances primitive. As I pointed out, such a view is in conflict with the explanatory goals of a theory of substance. Thus, R must not be primitive; it must not be a free-floating relation. Instead, it must be grounded in and explained by some thing or things. Hence option (1) is ruled out.

In so ruling out (1), I am committed to a key principle that will in fact drive the rest of the argument: a relation must obtain in virtue of some thing or things. That is, relations are grounded in things that serve as their metaphysical explanation. On this view, relations need to be made intelligible, and they are made so in terms of their grounds.

To say this is not to be committed to a full-blown principle of universal intelligibility or to a full-blown PSR. It is merely to insist that relations, in particular, must somehow depend on other things in order to obtain. Relations cannot be brute; there can be, as it were, no free-floating relations. To rule out (1) is not, by itself, to take a stand on whether other things or facts may be brute.

Let's take option (2) next. According to this option, the substance-making relation is not free-floating but rather is grounded, at least in part, in certain

---

[1] I am indebted here to James Van Cleve.

items other than S. The substance-making relation holds in virtue of things other than S and to which S is related in such a way to render S a substance. The substance-making relation may also be grounded in part in S itself. This grounding is just a manifestation of the general view that relations are ultimately grounded in their relata (or in at least one of their relata). We can find such an account in, e.g., Descartes' actual view on corporeal substance according to which a corporeal substance's being a substance depends on its standing in part-whole relations to other corporeal substances.

However, while the lack of an explanation of R offered by a proponent of option (1) is *immediately* unsatisfactory in this context, an explanation that a proponent of option (2) offers is *ultimately* unsatisfactory. If, e.g., the substance-making relation, R, is, in part, grounded in something other than S and, in part, grounded in S, then the fact that S amounts to a substance holds, in part, because R stands in a relation of partial grounding to S; S partially grounds R. That is, R is, in this case, a substance-making relation only because R stands in a relation of partial grounding to S. (The other relatum or relata of the substance-making relation is also such that R stands in a relation of partial grounding to it.) Thus, not only is R—the substance-making relation—grounded in part in S and in part in the other relatum or relata, it is also grounded in part in a further relation between, e.g., S and R itself. This is a relation of partial grounding between S and R.

To see why the demand for this further relation emerges, note that R—the substance-making relation—and indeed relations in general as such and by their nature, seem to be dependent entities. Relations are not, as I indicated in eliminating option (1), free-floating. Rather, they are, by their nature, dependent at least on their relata. Here the etymology of "relation"—its Latin root—is suggestive: a relation is, literally a bringing or carrying *back*, a *back*-carrying. The "re"—the "back"—points, it seems, to that which is prior to or more fundamental than the relation. Thus, the relation by its nature demands not only that its relata be in place, but—because a relation is by its nature dependent on its relata—the relation also demands that there be a relation of partial grounding between the relation and each relatum individually.[2]

Further, it seems to be generally true that if one thing is built into the nature of another thing, then the second thing depends on the first.[3] In the case

---

[2] Cf. Maurin, "Bradley's Regress": "Relations . . . are there basically to hold things together," p. 803.
[3] For a specific version of this general claim, see Fine, "Senses of Essence," p. 61; "Ontological Dependence," pp. 275, 283–84. For potential counterexamples to Fine's particular way of making this point, see Wilson, "Essence and Dependence."

at hand, because standing in a relation of grounding to one or more of its relata is built into the nature of any relation, it follows that our relation R depends not just on its relata, but also depends on the relation of grounding that it stands in to one or more of its relata. Call this relation of grounding, R'. Thus, R depends not only on its relata, but also on R' (the relation of grounding between R and one of its relata). So R' is the relation of grounding between R and S.

We can fancifully illustrate this point as follows. Let's say that I am relation R and I don't yet exist, but I'm a pushy not-yet-existent relation, and so I demand of God that God create me. (I am, as Leibniz would say, one of the striving possibles.) So God says: "OK, MDR, tell me what you need." And in demanding of God that I come into existence, I demand not only that there first be S (and perhaps another relatum of the relation R), but I also demand the path—the relation R'—between S and me, i.e. between S and R. (I may also demand that there be a path between the other relatum and me.) So the relation, R, depends not only on S, but also on R', the relation of partial grounding between S and R.

It may be that R' comes for free with S and the other relatum, i.e. it may be that the relation R' between S and R comes automatically, as a "free lunch" to use Armstrong's term,[4] as soon as S and the other relatum or relata are in place. In such a case, R may not depend *ultimately* on R'. But, even so, R depends non-ultimately on R': R depends intermediately on the path from S to R. Or, to put the point in yet other terms: R holds at least in part because each of S and the other relatum or relata *do their part* in making it the case that R holds. And, S's part is to partially ground R, to be related to R by R', the relation of partial grounding. So, given the substance theorist's commitment to the grounding of the substance-making relation, R depends on at least S and R' (and also on some other relatum and, perhaps, some relation of partial grounding between that other relatum and R).

Thus, I disagree with Karen Bennett when she says, "Quite generally, when A grounds B, the ground of B is not A plus the grounding relation—the grounds of B are simply A."[5] On the contrary, I say, if standing in a grounding relation is part of the nature of the grounded (as it is in the case of relations and as it would be for items in general), then the grounded is grounded in part in the relation of grounding between the grounded and ground.

---

[4] Armstrong, *A World of States of Affairs*, pp. 12–13.
[5] Bennett, "By Our Bootstraps," p. 31; see also *Making Things Up*, pp. 196–98.

Given that R depends in part on R', in asking what the substance-making relation, R, depends on, we are led to ask: in virtue of what does the relation, R', of partial grounding between R and S hold? Because R' is more fundamental than R, R' is more genuinely the substance-making relation. This point concerns a metaphysical dependence relation between R' and other items. There is also a parallel epistemological point: we cannot be said to have fully understood the substance-making relation, R, until we understand in what it is grounded, and so we cannot understand R until we understand R'. Thus, we cannot fully understand R until we understand on what R' is grounded.

So we ask: on what is R' grounded? Well, R' is a relation (of partial grounding) between S and R and, as such, it depends not only on S and on R but also on a relation of partial grounding between S and R' itself. (R' also depends on a relation of partial grounding between R' and R). Call the relation of partial grounding between R' and S, R"—i.e. R double prime. Notice that in order to metaphysically explain R and thus in order to metaphysically explain R', it now turns out that we must metaphysically explain R", and so on *ad infinitum*. Or to put the point epistemologically, our understanding of what makes S a (differentiated) substance is not complete until we have a grasp of the substance-making relation, R. But we cannot be said to grasp R until we grasp the relation, R', of partial grounding on which R depends. And we cannot be said to grasp R' until we grasp a further relation, R", of partial grounding, and so on *ad infinitum*.

As my presentation of it already indicates, this regress is vicious. The initial relation R *depends* on a further relation, R', which in turn *depends* on a further relation, R". *Before* one can explain R, one must *first* explain R'. But *before* one can explain R', one must *first* explain R", and so on *ad infinitum*. One's explanation of R can thus never be completed and, since the explanatory goal—essential to the theory of substance—demands that we account for the substance-making relation, our explanatory goal cannot be reached, and we must, as Hume would say, inevitably be dissatisfied. This vicious regress is simply a more general form of the kind of regress that a Cartesian account of corporeal substance gets into, according to Leibniz, or a more general form of the kind of regress that a Lockean explanation (ungraspable though it may be by us) ultimately gets into when it comes to the metaphysical explanation of the substantiality of a substance. Indeed, the viciousness here is also in the spirit of the unsettled, regressive state of being at sea when, for Parmenides as we saw in chapter 1, one tries to think what is not. Thus, option (2) is, in the end, incompatible with the explanatory aims that all theorists of (differentiated or, more generally, related) substance embrace. Given this regress, we have an ultimately empty explanation. We have a John Wayne moment

Before moving on to option (3), I would like both to enrich the line of thought I have presented so far and also to address some potential objections; actually, these objections are not merely potential, but re actual objections that I have been greeted with at one time or another.

(a) Many philosophers accept the position that I too adopt: this kind of regress is vicious.[6] But, of course, some disagree.[7] I would like to look at one particular way of advancing the non-vicious-regress strategy. One could argue that my argument conflates Kit Fine's important distinction between constitutive essence and consequential essence.[8] The constitutive essence of a thing includes properties that tell us what a thing is fundamentally. The consequential essence includes properties that logically follow from the properties in the constitutive essence. Fine draws the distinction this way:

> A property belongs to the *constitutive* essence of an object if it is not had in virtue of being a logical consequence of some more basic essential properties; and a property might be said to belong to the *consequential* essence of an object if it is a logical consequence of properties that belong to the constitutive essence. ("Ontological Dependence," p. 276; see also "Senses of Essence," p. 57)

---

[6] For example, Vallicella, "Relations, Monism, and the Vindication of Bradley's Regress"; Lewis, "Tensing the Copula"; and Leibniz (see the discussion in Della Rocca, "Violations of the Principle of Sufficient Reason (in Leibniz and Spinoza)," p. 150).

[7] In addition to the passages from Bennett cited in note 5, see Wollheim, *F. H. Bradley*, p. 114; Quine, "Responses," p. 183; deRosset, "Grounding Explanations," §6.1; Gaskin, *The Unity of the Proposition*, pp. 314–18, 338–48. A few words on Gaskin's sophisticated approach: he says that the "basic point" of his response to the Bradleyan regress is to invoke the view that "the logical copula is that sentential feature which, by virtue of its having reference in a quite special way, captured by the regress, unifies the proposition," p. 345. My brief response: what is this "special way" and *how* does it unify the proposition? It is hard to see how we can have anything other than a dormitive virtue explanation here. Gaskin also says that Bradley's regress arises in an analysis of meaning and that "a regress that arises in the analysis of meaning will be innocent just in case it is a 'metaphysical' regress, in the sense that it places an infinitistic structural condition on what it is to understand; its stages are not epistemically discrete moments, requiring to be processed *seriatim* by the understander, but are rather acquired all at once and in their entirety as an epistemological package," p. 351. My question would be: *how* are these stages acquired all at once? To say that we just do acquire all these stages somehow, in such a way as to make relational thought possible, does not shed light on how such thought is possible. I will have more to say in chapter 6 about the notions of reference and meaning of the kind that Gaskin invokes here.

[8] Jonathan Schaffer, in insightful comments on a presentation of mine, made precisely this charge.

Fine makes clear that an object depends on items built into the constitutive essence, but the object does not or need not depend on items merely built into the consequential essence. The charge against me here is this: R' (the relation of grounding between the relation, R, and the relatum, S) is not built into the constitutive essence of R: R' is merely part of the consequential essence of R. For this reason, we can say—contrary to me—that R does not depend on R'. But, without such a dependence relation, the regress of relations (R, R', R" ...) cannot be vicious.

My primary response to this challenge is—granting, for the moment, the constitutive/consequential distinction, for the sake of argument—to claim that R' is indeed built into the constitutive essence of R. It does seem that it is part of what it is to be a particular relation that the relation is grounded. What a relation is, is, in part, to be tethered to its relata, to be—as I put it—not free-floating. Compare, in this connection, Spinoza's modes of substance: modes are *defined* as that which is in another and is conceived through another (*Ethics*, part 1, definition 5). The in-relation and the conceived-through-relation are, for Spinoza (as is widely agreed) dependence relations. Spinoza indicates in his definition of mode that a mode is, by its nature, dependent on *another*. This relation of dependence on something else is thus built into the nature of a mode. This relation of dependence is not a mere logical consequence of the mode's essence or nature; it is partially constitutive of that nature. Similarly, I am claiming, a relation of dependence on its relata is built into the nature of relation, R. R by (real) definition, stands in a relation of dependence and so this relation of dependence is built into R's nature. The relation of dependence on R' is not a mere logical consequence of R's nature, it is something constitutive of R's nature.

I have a further, and perhaps deeper, response to this objection. The objection presupposes a distinction between constitutive and consequential essences, but I would contend that this distinction itself is arbitrary and impossible to draw in a principled way. Fine himself admits that there is "considerable doubt" as to how to draw the line.[9] And I doubt that there are any robust intuitions about such an esoteric matter as constitutiveness vs. consequentialness that will help us draw this line.[10] The distinction between constitutive and consequential essences can thus seem itself ungrounded and, in this light, a defender of seeing R' as built into the nature of R can well regard

---

[9] "Senses of Essence," p. 58. See also "Ontological Dependence," pp. 275–76.
[10] And, in any event, as we will explore later in this chapter and especially in chapters 7 and 11, I am very much not a fan of the reliance on intuitions in philosophy.

the claim that R' is part of the consequential essence but not part of the constitutive essence as, in effect, question-begging. The opponent of the claim that the regress is vicious is merely claiming, without sufficient grounds, that R' is not part of the constitutive essence when that is precisely the point in question. I will return to the constitutive/consequential distinction in chapter 10 when I argue against attempting to limit the scope of the PSR.

(b) Although I defend the viciousness of the regress, it is important to note that the problem I have isolated does not turn on whether there is a regress here and so doesn't turn on whether that regress is vicious, for there is another way to show that the grounding question we have asked leads to an intolerable problem. So forget about the regress and turn to another old favorite philosophical problem: circularity. For once we ask the grounding question, we can see that in addition to generating a regress (vicious or not), our question also reveals a circle. Thus, as we saw, R is grounded, in part at least, in S and R'. But R' is grounded in (*inter alia*) its relata, and so R' is grounded, in part, in S and R. Putting these two grounding claims together and given the transitivity of grounding, we reach the result that R is grounded in part in R itself.[11] This is because R is grounded, in part, in R' which is grounded in part in R. Thus, R is grounded, in part, in R, and so we have a circle. This is a problem.

Whatever one thinks of the regress in this case, it seems that in this context, the grounding of R—the metaphysical explanation of R—in terms of R itself is unacceptable. Thus R—which stands for any relation here—can only be circularly grounded and cannot be metaphysically explained and thus cannot be made intelligible.[12]

(c) It is also important to note that this argument doesn't turn on treating relations as objects in their own right. Bradley who, as will soon see, purveys something like the kind of argument I have just made is sometimes criticized because, in generating the regress, he invokes (e.g., *Appearance and Reality*, p. 126n1) relations as *things* that require other *things* to be related to them.

---

[11] For a challenge to the transitivity of grounding, see Schaffer, "Grounding, Transitivity, and Contrastivity." For a good defense, see Litland, "On Some Counterexamples to the Transitivity of Grounding." See also Raven, "Is Ground a Strict Partial Order?"

[12] In rejecting explanatory regresses or circles as I have done here in connection with option (2), I am also rejecting option (4) which similarly involves regresses or circles and which, as I mentioned, I will not discuss separately.

One might argue that the above argument just misses the point that relations are precisely not things, and so the regress (or circle) cannot even get going.[13]

However, this argument does not depend on treating relations as things. For one way to see why this is so, let's focus not on things as grounds and grounded, but on facts as grounds and grounded. So, ask not: what thing or things does relation R depend on?; ask: on what fact or facts does the fact—call it F—that S is related to other items depend on? In asking this question, we do not presuppose that there are things that are relations. Just as a relation depends by its very nature on its relata, so too the relational fact, F, depends at least in part on the fact that S exists. And just as the relation between S and certain items depends on the relation of partial grounding between S and R, so too the fact that S and certain items are related depends in part on the fact, F', that the fact that S exists partially grounds the fact—F—that S is related to certain items. Figuratively: the pushy fact that S is related to other items demands that there be a path of partial grounding from the fact that S exists to the fact that S is related to other items.

But what fact is this further fact, F', grounded in? F' is grounded in the fact that S exists and the fact—F"—that S exists partially grounds the fact that F' obtains, etc. This result is every bit as viciously regressive or every bit as circular as the result in the previous argument that seemed to treat relations themselves as objects.

(d) An appeal to relational facts as opposed to relations as objects can avert another potential objection to the line of argument I am advancing. If one takes relations as objects, then a question arises: are these objects universals or particulars? It might be thought that if the relations are particulars—something like tropes, for example S's relation to another item—then there may be a problematic regress. But, it might also be thought, if we treat relations as universals, then there may be no problematic regress. For consider the relations of partial grounding that were at work in the regress R', R", R''', etc. If relations are universals, then they can be wholly present in multiple places or at multiple times. Thus, it might seem that the relations of partial grounding are really the same relation that is multiply instantiated, i.e. R' = R" = R''', etc. But if such identities hold, then it's no longer clear that there is any problematic regress or any regress at all.[14]

---

[13] For discussion of this charge, see Hylton, *Russell, Idealism and the Emergence of Analytic Philosophy*, p. 48; Candlish, *The Russell/Bradley Dispute*, p. 168. Russell makes the charge in *Outline of Philosophy*, p. 263.

[14] For this objection, I am indebted to Philip Bricker and others.

Even *if* it is the case that invoking relations as universals would bypass the regress, the regress re-arises once we turn (again) to relational facts instead of relations as objects. For facts are not universals. They are not capable of multiple instantiation, i.e. in this respect, they are more like tropes. Thus, the fact that R is partially grounded in R' and the fact that R' is partially grounded in R" are, though similar, nonetheless distinct facts, and so any regress here would involve a proliferation of distinct entities (the relational facts) with the earlier items in the series dependent on later ones.

(e) A different objection to the argument I have presented so far is that the argument trades in way too many ontological commitments. Instead of treating ground—as I do in my argument—as a relation or as a relational fact, we can appeal to ground in a way that does not carry such ontological baggage. Thus, rather than stating that when a more fundamental thing grounds a less fundamental thing there is (as I have put it) a grounding *relation* between these things or between the fact that the more fundamental thing exists and the fact that the less fundamental thing exists, we should treat "ground" simply as a sentential operator.[15] Thus we can say:

> The less fundamental thing exists *because* the more fundamental thing exists.

Here, in using the sentential operator "because," we do not commit to any grounding relation. In the spirit of Ockham's Razor—"Don't multiply entities beyond necessity"—it might seem best to adopt the ground as sentential operator approach. And once we clean our ontological house in this spirit of austerity, it might seem that no regress or circle of relations could arise because there simply are no relations or relational facts to which we are committed.[16]

I am a big fan of Ockham's Razor and of ontological austerity, and chapter 8 will devote much time to its exploration, interrogation, and defense. But this appeal to austerity is not enough to obviate the problem I have raised for ordinary notions of substance, and this is because regresses or circles of the same kind arise even when one switches to the sentential operator approach as I will now argue.

---

[15] See Fine, "Some Puzzles of Ground," p. 99; Fine, "A Guide to Ground," p. 46; Fine, "The Question of Realism," p. 16.
[16] I am indebted to Ted Sider for raising this objection.

70 THE PARMENIDEAN ASCENT

Start with the claim that A is related to B and ask: why is it the case that A is related to B? My answer is that

A is related to B in part because the relata exist.

Notice here that I use only the sentential operator "because"; I don't invoke (at least not explicitly) any grounding relations.

Continuing the original argument in this new, more austere register, I go on to say that it is *also* true that

A is related to B in part because it is the case that A is related to B because the relata exist.

Perhaps it would help to slap on some brackets here. Thus, we have:

A is related to B in part because [it is the case that A is related to B because the relata exist].

This somewhat cumbersome claim with its nested "because's" corresponds to my claim in the original, ontologically loaded version of the argument that the relation, R, is grounded in part in a grounding relation, R', between R and a relatum.

But, in my new-found ontologically svelte, but linguistically heavy way of talking, I ask:

Why is it the case that A is related to B in part because [it is the case that A is related to B because the relata exist]?

And my answer, of course, is:

A is related to B in part because [[it is the case that A is related to B because the relata exist] because [[it is the case that A is related to B because the relata exist] because the relata exist]].

This beautiful sentence corresponds to the claim in the original, ontologically loaded version of the argument that the relation of grounding between the relation, R, and the relata, A and B, is grounded in part in the further relation, R", of grounding between the grounding relation, R', and the relation, R.

Of course, and you knew this was coming, now we must ask ever so austerely:

Why is it the case that A is related to B in part because [[it is the case that A is related to B because the relata exist] because [[it is the case that A is related to B because the relata exist] because the relata exist]]?

And the annoying answer, of course, is:

A is related to B in part because [[[it is the case that A is related to B because the relata exist] because [[it is the case that A is related to B because the relata exist] because the relata exist]] because the relata exist].

And, of course, we can ask . . . let me know if you've had enough. Obviously, we are embarking on another infinite regress—the only difference is that this time the regress is not one of relations or relational facts but of "because's". This ontologically austere, but linguistically profligate regress is every bit as vicious or circular as the more ontologically robust versions in our original argument. I conclude that the ontological scruples which lead to the sentential operator approach to grounding are no inoculation against the vicious regresses (or circles) that have plagued talk of substance throughout this chapter and the previous one.

Let's turn now to option (3), the only remaining option. On this view, the substance-making relation, R, that S stands in is not primitive, nor does S stand in this relation because of some other thing. Instead, this relation is ultimately grounded in S's nature alone. If we take option (3), R is thus (in one sense of the term) an internal relation instead of an external one. This account is found in Aristotle, in Leibniz, in Locke, and perhaps in Lowe's or Descartes' notion of substance as independent. The independence of an independent item is perhaps not dependent on anything other than the independent item.

It might be thought that the situation would look brighter for option (3) than for option (2) because, with (3), R is grounded in the nature of S *alone*. Here there is no other relatum external to or independent of S, and so we don't have to appeal to any perhaps problematic notion of partial grounding in the way that we had to with option (2).

However, even with option (3), we have to appeal to a further relation in spelling out the grounds of relation R. If we don't appeal to a further relation as a ground of R, if we just say that R is grounded in S's nature and leave things at that, then we will be saying that S stands in the substance-making relation R simply because that is the nature of S. But while such a pronouncement is nice, it is nothing more than another Molière moment, another dormitive virtue explanation, an empty appeal that is the mere shell of the kind of substantive explanation we were seeking. As I said in chapter 2, if we've learned one thing from the early modern critique of Aristotelian explanations, it's that mere appeals to natures are *not* explanatorily illuminating. So if we are to preserve option (3), we need to say not just *that* R is grounded in S's nature alone, but we also need to say *how* it is grounded in S's nature alone.

Let's make this point in connection with particular theories of substance we encountered in the previous chapter. Even if, as on an Aristotelian view, it is part of S's nature to unify states or properties or parts, before we can understand what it is for S to be a substance, we must first understand *how*[17] it is that S plays this unifying role. Otherwise we have been given only the outer shell of an answer to our explanatory demand without being told the manner in which the substance operates so as to unify states or parts. The substantiality of S would still remain a mystery.

Similarly, even if it's part of S's nature to have a complete concept, as on Leibniz's view, we still want and need to know what it is in virtue of which it can have such a concept, a concept that makes reference to all of S's properties. Without an account of how it is possible for a thing to have such a concept, we are again left with a mystery about how S is a substance. How does one thing—and not another such as an accident—get a complete concept? Further, as before, a bare Leibnizian appeal to the force or teleological activity of a substance won't help explain *how* it is that a substance is a substance.

Similarly, even if it is part of S's nature to be independent of all other actual or possible particulars, as on Descartes' general view of substance and as on Lowe's view, we still want and need to know in virtue of what S enjoys such independence. Otherwise, merely to invoke such independence is to place a label on the problem, to offer a placeholder for an account without offering a genuine account.

Similarly, and finally, even if as on the Lockean view, there is some metaphysical explanation of S's substantiality, if we merely say that there is some feature without saying how that feature makes S into a substance, then we merely put a label on the problem without illuminating it.

---

[17] Or, as Parmenides would say, "πῶς."

So we need to specify *how* the substance-making relation R is grounded in S alone. But this "how" points to the fact that we need to specify another relation—call it R*—in virtue of which R is grounded in S alone. In other words, we are now seeking a relation R* which is the relation of grounding between S and R. Since R* is thus more fundamental than R, R* turns out to be—more genuinely than R itself—the substance-making relation. And thus of *this* substance-making relation we are naturally led to ask: what is R* grounded in?

As before, option (1) is incompatible with the explanatory aims of the theory of substance. As before, option (2) leads to a vicious regress. And, as we have just seen, option (3) gets us either an empty shell, dormitive virtue kind of explanation or it leads us to appeal to a further relation—let's call it R**—concerning which we must ask the same explanatory questions which have the same unsatisfying results. And so the same regress would be upon us.[18]

In reaching these negative conclusions about substance, I am not merely raising the tamely skeptical worry that there are or may be no substances; rather, I'm raising the prior and more deeply skeptical worry that ultimately we don't even have a grasp of what it would be for there to be a substance, the worry that ultimately we have no coherent understanding of substance. The worry is that—like Parmenides' non-being—substance cannot be and cannot be thought. As long as we stick to standard theories of substance, we seem to have only empty explanations of substantiality, explanations which are really no explanations at all. And so we are faced with a John Wayne moment.

The Spirit of Bradley

My argument is that standard theories of substance are incoherent: they have no way to make intelligible the notion of relation that is essential to substance as conceived in these theories. This argument, turning as it does on a regress

---

[18] It is by means of this kind of consideration that I would respond to Priest's view that a vicious regress like this one can be "broken" by appealing to unifying "gluons" to which the transitivity of identity does not apply and which both are and are not objects (Priest, *One*, p. 15 and chapter 2). I'm not so much worried about Priest's invocation of the paradox-threatening denial of transitivity. (As we'll see in chapter 9, I embrace perhaps even wilder paradoxes.) Rather, my worry about Priest's gluons is that no account is (or perhaps can be) given of *how* they unify the parts of a complex whole and of how it is that gluons, unlike other things, are not subject to the transitivity of identity. Obviously, Priest's sophisticated views deserve more attention than this note or this chapter can provide. I hope to engage further with Priest's views in subsequent work.

or circle of relations, is unabashedly in the spirit of F. H. Bradley, a seminal figure—in a dark way—for analytical philosophy. I freely acknowledge that, in many respects, my argument derives from Bradley's. Like my argument, Bradley's argument relies on the view that relations cannot be free-floating. In speaking of relations, Bradley says, "There is no absolute 'between' or 'together.'"[19] Earlier—in *The Principles of Logic*—he says, the terms of a relation must always be more than the relation between them" (vol. 1, p. 254). In this vein, Bradley insists, as do I, that relations must be grounded or metaphysically explained. He says that a certain relation "cannot ... possibly be bare chance" (p. 520). And he demands that there be a "how and why" of a particular relation (p. 521). A bit earlier, he specifies:

> any ... irrationality and externality cannot be the last truth about things. Somewhere there must be a reason why this and that appear together. (p. 517)

And he laments the fact (as he sees it) that we are unable to justify relations and render them intelligible (p. 21, see also pp. 25, 27).

I believe that Bradley is committed to the broader PSR—every thing or fact must have an explanation.[20] But strictly, Bradley's argument, like mine, explicitly only calls for the explanation of relations and relational facts, not for the explanation of facts or things in general. Bradley's connection to the PSR proves to be a crucial to the genealogy of analytical philosophy, as we'll see in chapter 11.

To continue with the connections between Bradley's arguments and my own, note that Bradley's argument specifies that any attempt to meet the demand for intelligibility when it comes to relations ends up in a vicious explanatory regress:

> here again we are hurried off into the eddy of a hopeless process, since we are forced to go on finding new relations without end. The links are united by a link, and this bond of union is a link which also has two ends; and these require each a fresh link to connect them with the old. (p. 28)

---

[19] Bradley, *Appearance and Reality*, p. 512. Unless otherwise noted, all references to Bradley will be to this work.
[20] Hylton, *Russell, Idealism, and the Emergence of Analytic Philosophy*, p. 56; Candlish, *The Russell/Bradley Dispute*, pp. 46–48; Campbell, *Scepticism and Construction*, p. 25.

Or, as he says perhaps even more vividly in his posthumous essay on relations:

> [In relational thought] we find ... no rational answer to our inquiry of "how in the end"; but we find there the question forced on us, only to leave us, if we accept relational truth as final, turning hopelessly in a blind maze of unending regress. ("Relations," p. 641)

And Bradley too, like me, is happy to see the problem as one of circularity and not just regress. Thus, he says:

> if you mean that A and B in such a relation are so related, you appear to mean nothing. (p. 17)

> Relation presupposes quality and quality relation ... the vicious circle in which they turn is not the truth about reality. (p. 21)

Further, Bradley, like me, sees the worry about regress as undermining both external and internal relations. He claims that the same dilemma of explicability affects internal relations as well as external relations. Thus, speaking of internal relations—relations "within each term"—Bradley says,

> The diversity between, and the union together, of the "respects" taken within each term raise the old dilemma, still insoluble and still unavoidable if we keep to relational experience. (Bradley, "Relations," p. 644)

So it would not be correct to say, as some have (e.g., Peter van Inwagen in his *Metaphysics*, chapter 2) that Bradley seeks to eliminate or treat as unreal only external relations (whatever they are). Despite some focus on external relations by Bradley,[21] Bradley makes clear that his target is relationality in general—both internal and external relations, if there is a distinction between internal and external relations. Thus, Bradley argues that any distinction between internal and external relations not only "involves us again in contradiction," but also "exhibits once more the discrepancy inseparable from all relational thought."[22]

---

[21] For example, "I do not admit that any relation whatever can be merely external and make no difference to its terms" (p. 513).

[22] "Relations," p. 641. See also Bradley's claim, "Criticism ... which assumes me committed to the ultimate truth of internal relations, all or any of them, is based on a mistake," *Essays on Truth and*

In all these respects—using rationalistic insights to argue by way of regress or circle that relations and distinctions are not real—Bradley's thought points in a Parmenidean direction, toward a monism without distinctions. Bradley and Parmenides have each hit upon what might be seen as a kind of natural kind within philosophy, a style of argument that is a natural resource in philosophy that philosophers can return to again and again.[23] Finally, just as I regard my Parmenidean view as deeply skeptical, so too Bradley regards his view as deeply skeptical. Thus, we find Bradley saying in the preface to *Appearance and Reality*:

> The chief need of English philosophy is, I think, a skeptical study of first principles, and I do not know any work which seems to meet this need sufficiently. By skepticism is not meant doubt about or disbelief in some tenet or tenets. I understand by it an attempt to become aware of and to doubt all preconceptions. Such skepticism is the result only of labour and education, but it is a training which cannot with impunity be neglected. And I know no reason why the English mind, if it would but subject itself to this discipline, should not in our day produce a rational system of first principles. If I have helped forward this result, then, whatever form it may take, my ambition will be satisfied. (p. xii)

Two notes, however, temper my homage here to Bradley. First, central to my argument is the claim a relation is grounded in the relation of grounding between the relation and the relata. I do not see this specific move in Bradley. He does appeal to a regress of relations and does say that relations must be grounded. But it's not clear that he invokes the particular point that a relation is grounded in a relation of grounding between it and the relata.[24] So this crucial aspect of my argument is, perhaps, my own and not Bradley's.

Second, the general style of argument concerning relations that appears in Bradley is not really original to Bradley. It can also be found in Leibniz[25] and

---

Reality, p. 239. Candlish, *The Russell/Bradley Dispute*, chapter 6, has a good treatment of this issue. See also Hylton, *Russell, Idealism, and the Emergence of Analytic Philosophy*, pp. 54–55.

[23] It's a great mystery to me, though, that Bradley seems not to have engaged directly with Parmenides' poem or even to cite Parmenides as a forebear. Perhaps this is the one brute fact that I will accept.

[24] I am indebted here to Jonathan Schaffer.

[25] See Della Rocca, "Violations of the Principle of Sufficient Reason in Leibniz and Spinoza"; Mugnai, "Leibniz and 'Bradley's Regress' "; Mugnai, *Leibniz' Theory of Relations*.

in certain medieval thinkers.[26] I am happy, though, to fly a Bradleyan banner here, and throughout the book I will—despite the reservations in this paragraph and the previous one—call the general argument I employ a Bradleyan argument.

Ascent

So it seems that none of the three available options for trying to appeal to a relation in order to account for what it is for S to be a substance works. This is a failure that mirrors the massive and general failure of the historically prominent theories of substance that we surveyed in the previous chapter, a failure to meet the same explanatory demand. We seem then to be in the grips of a version of the ancient Agrippan Trilemma: in attempting to give an account of substance either we make a dogmatic claim (this would be option (1) where we treat the substance-making relation as primitive), or we are faced with an vicious regress (option (2)), or we are faced with an unilluminating explanatory circle (option (3)).[27]

What are we to do in light of this pervasive and, as we can now see, inevitable failure of extant attempts to answer the explanatory question: what is it to be a substance? Must we say that substance—like Parmenides' non-being—cannot be and cannot be thought? The worry is that we have no coherent understanding of substance or being.

However, as I said, I am a positive person, so amidst all this skepticism about the very notion of substance, I ask: do we have to abandon all talk of substance? Or is there some way to redeem the notion? Perhaps the answer to this latter question is: there is. (As we'll see, "there is" is, in a way, the answer to all the questions that I raise in this book, the answer to any question whatsoever.)

The notion of substance that I have rejected as incoherent is the notion common to Aristotle, Descartes, Leibniz, Locke, Lowe, and many others. It is the notion of a substance as distinct somehow from other items, substance as differentiated either from its states or parts (if any) or from other actual or

---

[26] See Henninger, *Relations: Medieval Theories 1250-1325*, pp. 9-10, 110, 155-56; Weinberg, *Abstraction, Relation, Induction*, chapter 2, esp. pp. 90, 93, 95, 106; and Gaskin, *The Unity of the Proposition*, p. 314. Normore ("Buridan's Ontology," pp. 197-200) sees Buridan as grappling with a Bradleyan regress in his account of inherence.

[27] For more on the Agrippan Trilemma, see Franks, *All or Nothing*.

possible substances. Or it is at least the notion of substance as related to some thing or things. Or, again, it is the notion of a substance that stands in an internal relation to its nature.

In giving up this notion of substance as differentiated or related, it doesn't follow that we should give up the view that there are somehow undifferentiated or unrelated substances or—better yet, so as not to be committed to any problematic distinction among substances—it doesn't follow that we should give up the view that there is undifferentiated substance. Equivalently, it doesn't follow that we should give up the view that there is *undifferentiated* or *unrelated* being.

So on this view, there is no multiplicity of substances or beings. Should we say, then, that there is just one substance or being? If, as I have argued, relations are to be rejected as unintelligible, then counting in general is to be rejected as unintelligible for counting presupposes relations among (at least) numbers. And if counting in general is to be rejected, then it is unintelligible even when the count in question is one. To count substance or being as one is to presuppose the intelligibility of counting and thus of relations.

Thus, on this view, not only is there no multiplicity of substances or beings, there is not even one being. But even if there are no differentiated beings or no being differentiated from its states or parts, no being that stands in relations, there may still be undifferentiated, unrelated being.

In this way, the term "being" is something like a mass noun, not a count noun. However, I hasten to point out this important disanalogy: Often with mass terms, we can speak specific quantities or portions of the relevant mass. But with regard to being on my Parmenidean view, it does not make sense to speak of quantities or portions of being. Any such quantities or portions would imply that there are relations. And that we cannot have.

The reality that Aristotle, Descartes, Leibniz, and others were trying unsuccessfully to capture is, perhaps, better captured by a view that rejects relations and the distinctions within and among things altogether. This move would be what I called earlier a Parmenidean Ascent: a rejection of a certain kind of distinction and by transcending this distinction, an attempt to capture the reality that was only imperfectly expressed by appealing to such a distinction.[28]

---

[28] In rejecting, in my Parmenidean spirit, differentiated beings or being, I am also rejecting any differentiation among ways of being in the sense of "ways of being" profitably explored by McDaniel in *The Fragmentation of Being*.

The resulting position—substance without substances and substance without differentiation, or being without beings and being without differentiation—is an extreme form of an extreme form of monism. To see how this is so, let's place this view on Schaffer's spectrum of monistic positions, a spectrum I discussed in chapter 1. Thus, there is a relatively weak form of monism—priority monism—which recognizes a multiplicity of concrete objects such as dogs, and cats, and chairs, but only one fundamental concrete object, viz. the whole cosmos. The kind of multiplicity in priority monism is to be distinguished from the multiplicity in non-monistic views. Such views—which Schaffer calls versions of pluralism—recognize a multiplicity of fundamental concrete objects. A more extreme form of monism, for Schaffer, is existence monism which recognizes only one concrete object, the cosmos itself and which does not recognize other concrete objects such as dogs, cats, and chairs at all even if these other objects would be nonfundamental. However, even according to existence monism, as Schaffer defines it, there may be a multiplicity of (perhaps) fundamental, *non-concrete* items, viz. the fundamental features of the one thing, and there is a distinction between the one fundamental thing and these features.[29]

The view I have just outlined—the result of a Parmenidean Ascent with regard to substance—is certainly not as weak as priority monism which requires a multiplicity of distinct things that stand in relations. But it is also not as weak as existence monism, as defined by Schaffer, for existence monism allows a distinction between a thing—the one concrete thing—and its properties or features. The general argument I gave aims to show that even such a distinction between a thing and its features is unintelligible. So the view I have argued for not only rejects a multiplicity of objects, but it also rejects even one object where that object is differentiated from its properties. And, of course, this view is incompatible with pluralism, as Schaffer defines it, which espouses a multiplicity of fundamental concrete objects. Thus, the view I propose is an extreme view that "goes beyond" both pluralism and monism (both in the form of priority monism and existence monism). If there is to be substance, we cannot intelligibly place substance or substances *within* reality in a place differentiated from other places.

These radical results all follow from the explanatory demand, the demand for an account of what it is to be a substance. If—in the spirit of Aristotle,

---

[29] Schaffer, "Monism: The Priority of the Whole." As I noted, Horgan and Portç (*Austere Realism*) adopt a form of existence of monism.

Descartes, Leibniz, and Locke—we take this demand completely seriously, then, as I have argued, we are led to make a Parmenidean Ascent in this area. In rising above the distinction among and within things, we are not losing anything intelligible. Rather, we now have a better view of the reality we were misguidedly trying to capture with our talk of distinctions. In other words, without distinction among or within things, we finally see the world aright.

Of course, most, if not all, of you might think that to reject distinctions in general is, contrary to what I have said, to see the world awrong and that we can see that this view is wrong because it is so contrary to common sense and goes against so many of our most deeply held intuitions.[30] In fact, you might be inclined to say—and so let me save you the trouble—that the conclusion that there is no differentiated being or substance is quite simply a *reductio* of my overall approach. The costs of my view—in the form of counterintuitive results—are just too high and the benefits too weak or even non-existent for this view to be taken seriously.

I understand this reaction, and I share it sometimes, but the propriety of this response turns on the propriety of the appeal to common sense and to intuition and of the cost-benefit analysis as a method of doing philosophy. I have much to say about and against this approach to philosophy as a kind of cramped bookkeeping, as we'll see in chapters 7 and 11. But here I will limit myself to pointing out that the appeal to common sense or intuition is, in this context, at once question-begging and deeply conservative.

First question-begging: I have argued in this chapter and the previous one drawing on much historical detail that there is an explanatory demand at the heart of the notion of substance or being. I have also argued that when we (and many great philosophers) try to meet this demand, we see and have reason to see that we don't and can't meet it. In the face of this problem, to appeal to intuition or to common sense is not helpful. As is widely recognized, intuitions are fallible[31] and common sense is not sacrosanct. In light of this fallibility, to reject my conclusions because they go against intuitions is just question-begging. Why should we trust our fallible intuitions in this case unless we are already presupposing that my Parmenidean conclusions are wrong?

---

[30] I recognize that the appeal to common sense and the appeal to intuitions are significantly different. I thus don't equate them here, but I am merely pointing out that these are two ways of resisting the conclusions I have drawn. More on this distinction in chapter 11.

[31] As I will again have occasion to note, Descartes and Spinoza (and other historical figures) are important exceptions who regard intuitions as infallible. Thus, the charges I make here against the method of relying on intuitions may not apply to them.

Look at it this way: my argument is self-consciously an argument for counterintuitive conclusions. My opponent points out that my conclusions are counterintuitive. Well, tell me something I don't already know. In particular, tell me where my argument goes wrong. Merely invoking intuition or common sense just tells me that you (and perhaps I) don't like where my argument goes. OK, but why should what you and I *like* matter? Indeed, isn't a large part of the appeal of philosophy that it encourages us to be open to—and promises to lead us to—places that we might not have anticipated going to and might not have antecedently been drawn to?

This leads to the point about the conservatism of the model of the philosopher as bookkeeper. By insisting on intuition and common sense, this approach shuts us off from views that depart too much or too radically from what we already believe, and it does so without good reason. This approach to philosophy thus enforces a kind of conservatism in philosophy. Again, I will develop these methodological points in chapters 7 and 11.

Because of the question-beggingness and conservatism of appeals to intuition and common sense in this context, I am not moved by the charge of a potential *reductio* of my argument for the Parmenidean Ascent. Unless we can identify a place where this argument goes wrong—and not merely point out that it leads to conclusions we don't like—then I would say that we have every reason to take the Parmenidean Ascent seriously.

"But wait," I can hear the objection run, "the most you've shown (and I'm not even granting you this, you irrational rationalist, but I'm willing to play along) the most you've shown is that there cannot be differentiated being or substance. But even if one grants this conclusion, then there are still two different ways to go: either everything is substance or being (this would be something like a monism of substance) or everything is non-substance or non-being. (This would be something like a monism of non-being). Why"—you might say in closing this objection—"do you favor the more happy view that all is substance rather than the darker view that all is non-being?"

The reason I favor something like a monism of being over a monism of non-being is that non-being is inherently relational and as such, for the reasons I have given, incoherent. However, there is, perhaps, no similar incoherence in undifferentiated being or substance. Given the explanatory demand which leads to the rejection of differentiation and relations in general, there's pressure on one who accepts differentiation to reject differentiation. But there may be no analogous pressure on one who rejects differentiation to accept differentiation.[32] In particular, undifferentiated being seems to bring with it none of the problematic relations that have plagued us. In other words, we are looking at a kind of pure being. Undifferentiated being—unlike non-being—is purely positive and not at all relational and, as such it is free from the paradoxes of relationality. And because I thus favor being over non-being, we can see some of the reasons why I referred to myself at the beginning of this chapter as a positive kind of person.

In making this Parmenidean Ascent—in eliding the distinctions and relations traditionally associated with the notion of being and advancing to a view of being without relations—one adopts a view of reality that is, in some ways, analogous to Aquinas' view of God. For Aquinas, God is subsistent being itself,[33] being without any internal distinctions, purely simple being. Being or substance, as I invoke it here, is like God, as Aquinas sees God. However, it is important for Aquinas that God, as perfectly simple, is distinct from the created world of finite, composite, substances. By contrast, on my view, there is no such distinction between God or pure being and a world of other beings. There is just being. When we make the Parmenidean Ascent with regard to substance, we do not lose the finite, related things we know and love, for those things could never coherently be conceived anyway. Rather, again, we finally see the world aright.

Of course, as I said, philosophers are afraid of heights, and so they tend to resist the Parmenidean Ascent in the case of substance or being. But it's hard to see how a philosopher can legitimately resist and not take seriously and not be motivated by the explanatory questions: What is a substance? What is it for a substance to exist? And if we do take these questions seriously and address them in true Parmenidean spirit, we will in making this ascent realize that Locke, Leibniz, Descartes, Aristotle, and many others are wrong: there are no differentiated beings and there are thus no beings and not even one being. There is, simply, being.

---

[32] Recall an analogous point I made in chapter 1 with regard to Parmenides: there is no pressure on strict monists to adopt "generous" monism.

[33] "*Deus sit ipsum esse subsistens*," *Summa Theologiae* 1.4.2; see also 1.14.9: "God is being itself" (*Deus sit ipsum esse*). See Gilson, *The Philosophy of St. Thomas Aquinas*, chapter 6.

4
Action

At the end of the previous chapter, we reached the result that all is being and that there are no relations and no differentiation in the world. While it may be true, in light of chapter 3's denouement that it's all being, it's also true that it's all over, for there is now nothing more to say.[1] In particular, there is no need to explore domains besides or "besides" being, such as meaning, knowledge, and, in this chapter, action. This conclusion is, of course, right: it is, in a way, all over. So why then do I go on? Why does any of us go on? What is it to go on anyway? These are good questions, and I will have something to offer in response to them much later in the book. But, before we get to that point and can appreciate it, I want to strengthen the drastic conclusions I have already reached, for I'm well aware that, given their extremely counter-intuitive character, they are in need of as much support as they can get. And so I will argue in this and subsequent chapters for a similar—and ultimately the same—conclusion in very different or apparently very different domains in philosophy. The convergence of a number of different perspectives on the same radical conclusion lends considerable support to that conclusion, and, further, as I've already indicated, the fact that in each domain I reach the same conclusion by both inductive and *a priori* means is yet further support for the radical rejection of relations. It is one of the ironies—let us politely say—of this book that I seek support for my rejection of multiplicity from an exploration of what might seem to be a multiplicity of different domains through a multiplicity of different means.

Davidson and the Explanatory Demand

To begin our journey into action, I want to highlight—as I did in the case of substance—a certain explanatory demand. The demand drives, I believe, much recent and not-so-recent work in the philosophy of action.

---

[1] And I will attempt to not say it in chapter 12.

The Parmenidean Ascent. Michael Della Rocca, Oxford University Press (2020).
© Oxford University Press.
DOI: 10.1093/oso/9780197510940.001.0001

As Anton Ford puts the explanatory demand, "the presumptive task of the philosopher of action is to answer the question: what is action?" ("Action and Generality," p. 95). David Velleman sees this aim as guiding the philosophy of action: "The difference between mere occurrences and actions is what the philosophy of action seeks to explain" ("Introduction," p. 1). Kieran Setiya sees the guiding question as, "What do intentional actions have in common in virtue of which they are intentional?" (*Reasons without Rationalism*, p. 24n8). In this vein, we might ask: what is it to be an action? Or: what is it in virtue of which an action is an action? Here we seek, as in the case of substance, to articulate a structural fact about the way the world is.

Let's begin with a matter that has so often framed the discussion in the philosophy of action: what is the basis of the distinction between actions such as my raising my arm or my running downhill and mere events or processes or non-actions such as the ball's rolling downhill or my arm's going up (e.g., when it is moved by a strong wind)? That is, what makes it the case that a certain event is an action and other events, distinct from the first event, are not? As we will see, the explanatory demand also takes the form of an investigation of the nature of the relation between an action and distinct events or states such as beliefs and desires which may be reasons for the action, or between an action and other actions which may also be reasons for the action, or the relation may be an internal relation between the action and its own nature. I call attention here to the fact that these in-virtue-of questions that guide the philosophy of action presuppose—apparently harmlessly—that there are differentiated actions: actions as differentiated from mere events, and actions as differentiated from their reasons and from other actions. More generally, the presupposition of all these in-virtue-of questions is that actions stand in relations of some kind or other. After our experience with the notion of substance in the previous two chapters, you can well imagine that I will regard this assumption of differentiated or related actions as far from harmless.

In approaching the question of the nature of actions, both Donald Davidson and G. E. M. Anscombe—perhaps the two central figures in the philosophy of action in the latter half of the previous century—insist that actions are typically done for a reason. Actions can, as Davidson says, be rationalized. And, as Anscombe puts it, a certain sense of the question "why?" applies to actions: "the sense is of course that in which the answer, if positive, gives a reason for acting" (*Intention*, p. 9). Two pages later, she indicates that she is investigating "what it is to act for reasons,"

Davidson and Anscombe typically invoke different kinds of reasons for action.[2] An Anscombian reason for an action is, very often, another action. Davidson, who attempts to account for action in terms other than action itself, appeals to beliefs and desires—and not to actions—as reasons. This difference between Anscombe and Davidson with regard to reasons for action is a reflection of the fundamental difference between these two, as we shall see, equally unsuccessful accounts of the nature of action.

To begin to see how these accounts of action and of their reasons are meant to work, let's begin with an example of a Davidsonian reason for action: my reason for flipping the switch might be that I want to turn on the light, and I believe that by flipping the switch I would turn on the light. The belief-desire pair, for Davidson, constitutes my so-called primary reason for the action. Or, to use an Anscombian reason for acting: I might be crossing the street because I'm avoiding an unpleasant person. My avoiding this person provides a reason for my crossing the street.

However, if we focus on beliefs and desires as reasons for action, we can see, as Davidson points out, that the mere presence of reasons that would rationalize an action is not enough to make something an action. I may have the belief and desire in question, but the fact that I do is not enough by itself for that reason to be the reason upon which I act. Perhaps I inadvertently flip the switch while lunging—as I am wont to do—for what I think is a candy bar. The relevant belief and desire are present: I want there to be light or I want to do something that will illuminate the room, and I believe that by flipping the switch I will illuminate the room, and I do flip the switch. However, in this case, that belief and that desire do not rationalize my flipping of the switch; they are not reasons on which I am acting. In general, I might have the belief and desire in question but not be acting on these reasons when I bring about a certain event that somehow fits the reasons. Thus, simply appealing to the presence of such reasons is not enough to meet the explanatory demand. To fill this gap, Davidson says, we need to nail down the force of the "because" or the "for" when we say that someone performed an action *because* of that

---

[2] See Thompson, *Life and Action*, chapter 5.

reason or *for* that reason. We can do this, Davidson claims, only by specifying that the rationalizing reason *causes* the action. In his classic paper, "Actions, Reasons, and Causes," Davidson introduces the central point this way:

> In order to turn the first "and" to "because" in "He exercised *and* he wanted to reduce and thought exercise would do it," we must, as the basic move, augment condition C1 [which states that a reason consists of a relevant belief-desire pair] with:
> C2. A primary reason for an action is its cause. ("Actions, Reasons, and Causes," pp. 11–12)

Davidson thus invokes the notion of causation in order to answer the explanatory question: an event is an action only if it is *caused* by a belief-desire pair, by reasons. In giving this answer, Davidson takes a stand against theories of action that do not regard an action as an action in virtue of a causal relation between the action and its reasons. While Anscombe may allow that the action is caused by reasons that are like the reasons that Davidson appeals to,[3] Anscombe nevertheless does not make causation central to her account of action. She does not say—as Davidson seems to say—that an action is an action *in virtue of* a causal relation between the reason and the action. Indeed, Anscombe holds that "something I do is not made into an intentional action by being caused by a belief and a desire, even if the descriptions fit" ("Practical Inference," p. 111). More generally, Anscombe rejects the view that there is a "feature in virtue of which [an event] is an intentional action" (*Intention*, p. 28). For Davidson, those who, like Anscombe, do not rest their account of action on causation have no good way to meet the explanatory demand at the heart of the theory of action because, according to Davidson, they leave the force of the "because" in claims such as "He did A because he wanted to do B" a mystery. I will return shortly to the question of whether Anscombe is left without a way of addressing the explanatory demand.

However, as many philosophers—even including, as we will see, Davidson himself—point out, the appeal he makes to causation is not enough: causation does not by itself provide an explanation of what action is, and it does not by itself provide an illuminating sufficient condition for an event's being an action. There

---

[3] Thus, Anscombe agrees with Aquinas when she says, "Practical knowledge is 'the cause of what it understands,'" *Intention*, p. 87. See the discussion in Thompson, *Life and Action*, pp. 95–96n14.

can always be counterexamples to a causal theory that aims to provide such a sufficient condition. The problem is that for a causal theory there is merely an *external* relation between belief and desire, i.e. reasons, on the one hand, and action, on the other, and so there is always room for an unanticipated or uncontrolled causal intermediary that is not taken into account in one's practical reasoning.[4] Harry Frankfurt gives this example (similar examples abound in the literature):

> [A] man at a party intends to spill what is in his glass because he wants to signal to his confederates to begin a robbery and he believes, in virtue of their prearrangements, that spilling what is in his glass will accomplish that; but all this leads the man to be very anxious, his anxiety makes his hands tremble, and so his glass spills. ("The Problem of Action," p. 70)

For Frankfurt, the causal theory of action—by relying crucially on external relations—fails to unify reason and the caused bodily movement: these two items are thus, for the causal theorist, always in danger of fragmenting, of falling apart in such a way that the event which occurs as a result of the reason is not rationalized by that reason. And no matter what causal intermediaries are inserted, no matter how fine the casual story gets, there would still be a possible rationalization gap between the reason and the alleged action. Thus, no causal relation is sufficient for the occurrence of an intentional action, and no causal relation can by itself provide a good, illuminating explanation of intentional action.

Yet is Frankfurt right that Davidson's account is unilluminating? Yes, he is—and Davidson would, in a way, be the first to agree. This is apparent if we consider some textual upheaval surrounding the passage I recently quoted from "Actions, Reasons, and Causes," In the original version of the paper (published in 1963), Davidson believed that a sufficient (as well as necessary) causal condition for a movement to be an intentional action could be provided. In the midst of the passage I just quoted from this article, Davidson included an optimistic footnote that pointed to such an account. Here is what the footnote said in 1963:

> I say "as the basic move" to cancel the suggestion that C1 and C2 are jointly *sufficient* to define the relation of reasons to the actions they explain. I believe C2 can be strengthened to make C1 and C2 sufficient as well as

---

[4] Frankfurt characterizes the relation between reason and action, on Davidson's view, as an extrinsic relation, "The Problem of Action," p. 70. See Lavin: "Rational purposiveness is to be understood in terms of [material processes such as bodily movements] standing in external relations to something else," "Must There Be Basic Action?," p. 277.

necessary conditions, but here I am concerned only with the claim that both are, as they stand, necessary. (1963 version of "Actions, Reasons, and Causes," p. 693n5)

However, as Davidson acknowledges in the introduction to his collection, *Essays on Actions and Events*, published in 1980, he came to abandon this aim of providing a sufficient condition and, as he notes (p. xiii), the hopeful 1963 footnote was made less hopeful, and any suggestion that C2 could be strengthened was deleted. In fact, Davidson eventually comes to "despair of spelling out . . . the way in which attitudes must cause actions if they are to rationalize the action," and he comes to view the problems for offering an illuminating account of how reason must cause action as "insurmountable" ("Freedom to Act," p. 79).

So Davidson abandons the attempt to give a sufficient causal condition for intentional action. In pointing out that Davidson's causal theory was unable to provide such a sufficient condition, Frankfurt wasn't saying anything that Davidson hadn't already realized. Frankfurt may have been misled here because when he published his article on the topic in 1978, the revised footnote in "Actions, Reasons, and Causes" hadn't yet appeared.

Davidson can be seen as—both earlier and later—trying to give what might be called a *building block* account of action. He attempts to explain action by appealing to elements—beliefs, desires, causal relations—that are not themselves actions. Early on, he offered his optimistic, sufficient condition approach in which he aspired to specify building blocks that were sufficient for an event's being an action. Later, his goal was to illuminate action through an incomplete list of necessary conditions that may not fully nail down what it is to be an action, but nonetheless—with the help of an appeal to the right kind of causal relation—goes some distance toward explaining what constitutes an action. In other words, despite the insurmountable problem of deviant causal chains that Davidson acknowledges, he does not abandon the causal theory.[5] He is willing to appeal to a primitive, un-analyzed notion of "the right way" in order to maintain some form of a causal theory.

Of course, Davidson is as entitled as anyone else to appeal to a primitive notion at this point.[6] But is such an appeal any better than the mystery he accused the non-causal theorists of propagating? It's hard to see how. In the

---

[5] See Davidson, "Problems in the Explanation of Action," p. 106.
[6] And, by my lights, that would mean, of course, the he is not entitled at all! But that is not a point I am pressing now.

absence of a causal theory, the "because" in "he flipped the switch because he wanted to turn on the light" was, according to Davidson, a mystery because it left unspecified *how* the action came about. Davidson enters the scene and claims, at first, that he has cleared up the mystery with his causal theory. But he comes to realize that even with his much-vaunted appeal to causation, he needs to make—in order to specify *how* the action came about—an additional appeal to the right way of causing the action, a way he is unable to unpack without begging the question. Thus, Davidson comes to recognize that his account faces a mystery and, indeed, as he thinks, an insoluble one. Despite his efforts, Davidson is still unable to specify *how* reasons are connected to actions and so, with his appeal to a primitive, we are still in the dark. Davidson has still not met the explanatory demand in this area.

It may seem that Davidson nonetheless takes an important step since he has at least specified a component of the answer to the explanatory question. He can explain, at least in all non-deviant cases, why an action is intentional, but a non-causal theorist offers no satisfactory explanation in any case of action. Yet this rosy assessment cannot be right. Without an account of the right way, Davidson cannot explain how action occurs even in the non-deviant cases because even in the normal case the action is intentional not simply because it was caused by reasons, but because it was caused by reasons in the right way. Yes, it might seem as if there is some progress because Davidson has specified a feature that may be necessary for intentional action.[7] However, there are two things to be said at this point. First, without the other components of an illuminating sufficient condition for intentional action it's not clear that we are on the right track in specifying that the relation is causal. Second, even if the question that Davidson leaves unanswered—"what is the right way?"—is not the same as the question about the force of the "because" that his opponents may leave unanswered, it is a question of relevantly the same kind. In each case, we are seeking to explain *how* reason and action are connected and in each case the answer offered is not illuminating. In each case, the same general explanatory demand goes unmet despite the fact that, as we saw, it's this drive for explanation that propels us into this region of the philosophy of action.

Here's another way to see this point: even if he doesn't offer an illuminating sufficient condition, Davidson is happy—in his building-block manner—to

---

[7] This is what Smith says in his exchange with Hornsby, "The Standard Story of Action: An Exchange," p. 52.

stack together necessary conditions for an event's being an action: an event must, as it were, match the content of a belief and a desire, and it must be caused by the belief and desire, and it must be caused by them in the right way. This may be a fine list of necessary conditions, but there is no indication as to how these necessary conditions hang together, i.e. how they follow from—or better, perhaps, flow from—the nature of action, and thus there is no indication as to how the components invoked in the account (the beliefs, desires, and the causal relations) are integrally connected with one another. The various components are thus, as it were, externally related to each other and to the action itself that they are meant to help generate. Because it is not clear *how* the components Davidson appeals to flow from the nature of action itself, his necessary conditions do not illuminate what it is to be an action.

This failure to provide an illuminating account of action is Davidson's John Wayne moment—actually it is *one* of Davidson's John Wayne moments. As we'll see in chapter 6, Davidson also lapses into empty explanations when it comes to meaning. We will also see, however, in the same chapter that Davidson is one of the few recent, analytical philosophers who comes close to making a version of the Parmenidean Ascent.

Other Causal Theories and Their Travails

In light of this failure by Davidson, let's look at several insightful and sophisticated attempts to solve the problem of deviant causal chains within the framework of a causal theory. These attempts are all unsatisfactory and instructive in their unsatisfactoriness.

First, let's consider one of the earliest responses, viz. what might be called the counterfactual strategy introduced by Christopher Peacocke and developed by Michael Smith, John Bishop, and others.[8] According to this strategy, in the deviant cases, what's missing is "differential sensitivity." The requirement that Peacocke and others insist on is this: if the agent's intention had been ever so slightly different and he successfully carried out the intention, then he would have behaved in an appropriately different manner. Thus, in the spilled drink case: if the plan had been different—e.g., if the plan had been that the agent would signal the beginning of the operation by scratching his

---

[8] See Peacocke, "Deviant Causal Chains," and *Holistic Explanation*, chapter 2; Smith, "Four Objections to the Standard Story of Action (and Four Replies)," pp. 397–400; Bishop, *Natural Agency*, chapter 5.

nose instead of by spilling the drink—and if the agent successfully carried out this plan, then he would have scratched his nose. But in this case, if the plan had been different in this way, then—given his nervousness—it seems that he would still have spilled his drink. The nervous agent's behavior is thus not differentially sensitive to his plan, and that's why the behavior doesn't count as intentional. It is such an appeal to differential sensitivity that provides for Peacocke and others following him a way to differentiate the deviant from the non-deviant case.

However, this account faces the following problem: Peacocke and friends ask us to consider what the agent would have *done*, how he would have *acted* in similar cases. But such an appeal invokes the very notion of acting we are seeking to illuminate.

More subtly, the worry arises in this way: perhaps we can say that Peacocke need not appeal to the notion of action. He can ask merely what would have occurred had the intention been different. This might be OK, but then we need to make sure that what would have occurred is not anomalous or deviant in some way. After all, if the scratching of the nose in the alternative situation were due to the wind, etc., then that would not be a way of satisfying the differential sensitivity requirement. So we need to appeal to what would have happened *non-deviantly*. But to make this appeal either is just to appeal to what genuine action would have occurred or requires some account of action which has not yet been given. Either way, there is again a problem of circularity or lack of illumination.

Another way to see this point is the following: Peacocke and the others appeal—in keeping with standard accounts of counterfactuals—to what would have happened in *nearby* possible worlds. But the problem here is to specify what worlds are nearby in this kind of case. It's hard to see how one could single out the nearby worlds except by stipulating that the nearby worlds are the ones in which nothing deviant happens, i.e. ones in which nothing happens that would undermine the claim that the agent's spilling of his drink is an action. In this way, the appeal to nearness of worlds already presupposes the notions of non-deviance and of action. Thus this appeal cannot be used to illuminate the notion of action itself.[9]

The notion of *what the agent would have done in nearby worlds* and the notion of *non-deviance* are loaded with precisely what it is we are trying to understand, viz. the notion of action itself. These notions, therefore,

---

[9] For discussion of Peacocke's strategy, I am indebted to Michael Nelson.

cannot provide us with genuine illumination about the notion of action unless they are unpacked. But it seems impossible to do so in a non-circular or non-question-begging way. We will see similar difficulties in the next chapter for theories of knowledge that appeal to the similar notion of *relevant alternatives*.

I now want to turn to Frankfurt's own response to the deviant causal chain worry and to a series of alternatives in a Frankfurtian spirit for addressing this problem. Each of these responses, as we will see, suffers from the same kind of inadequacy that besets Davidson's original account.

In his initial response, Frankfurt appeals to the notion of guidance. He is interested in the question, "whether or not the movements as they occur are *under the person's guidance*" ("The Problem of Action," p. 72; emphasis in original). In the same vein, Frankfurt says, "What counts is that he was prepared to intervene if necessary, and that he was in a position to do so more or less effectively" (p. 75). It is the relation that certain bodily movements bear to the agent's readiness to intervene if necessary that turns what would otherwise be a mere event into an intentional action. This relation, for Frankfurt, is thus what might be called the action-making relation.

But to make this appeal is merely to push the explanatory issue back one step; it is not to resolve it. Frankfurt tries to explain why a movement is an intentional action by appealing to the agent's guidance and what she is prepared to do. But the notions of guidance and of being prepared to do something presuppose the notion of intentional action or at least a notion as much in need of illumination as that of intentional action is. Thus, at best, Frankfurt has explained why something—a movement, perhaps—is an intentional action by invoking other, related actual or possible intentional actions or guidings. The intentionalness of these other actions or these guidings also would need to be explained, and so we can see that Frankfurt is, like Davidson, in the case of action, well on his way to a troubling regress or a troubling circle. Frankfurt's own account thus seems no more illuminating than Davidson's.[10]

In other papers, Frankfurt focuses on what it is for an event to be a full-blooded or robust action. Here the contrast is not only with mere events, but also with mere bits of behavior such as my drumming my fingers on the table[11] or any ungoverned or non-autonomous activity such as slips of the tongue. To say what it is for an event to be a full-blooded action, Frankfurt appeals

---

[10] Sehon makes a similar point against Mele in "Deviant Causal Chains and the Irreducibility of Teleological Explanation," p. 203, and *Teleological Realism*, p. 99.
[11] Frankfurt, "Identification and Externality," p. 58.

not just to an agent's readiness to guide behavior, but also to his wholehearted identification with the values that help generate the action and to the agent's thus "being fully satisfied that [these psychic elements] . . . should be among the causes and considerations that determine his cognitive, affective, attitudinal, and behavioral processes" ("The Faintest Passion," p. 103). Notice two things here: First, the satisfaction is satisfaction concerning the causation of the agent's affects and behavior. This causation must not be mere causation of behavior, but must also be causation of the right kind so that the resulting behavior is an action or a full-blooded action. Here the problems associated with the "right way" re-emerge. Second, the satisfaction that Frankfurt crucially appeals to in his account of wholeheartedness consists in "absence of any tendency to alter its condition" ("The Faintest Passion," p. 104; see also "Identification and Externality," and "Identification and Wholeheartedness"). Here Frankfurt appears to appeal to an agential notion—tending to alter—in the account of wholeheartedness and satisfaction by which he attempts to elucidate what it is to be a full-blooded action. But this notion of altering is as much in need of illumination as the notion of action in general that Frankfurt has set out to illuminate. That is, the altering in question must be non-deviant, and with this appeal to non-deviance we are faced with the same threat of unilluminating explanation.

Velleman appreciates this kind of *tu quoque* charge against Frankfurt.[12] To put an end to these worries, Velleman appeals to a desire or constitutive aim that not only guides one's action, but also is such that one cannot be alienated from it without undermining one's own status as an agent ("What Happens When Someone Acts?," p. 142). For Velleman, this constitutive aim is the aim of knowing what one is doing, of being able to make sense of one's behavior. Thus, as Velleman specifies, an event is an action in the full-blown sense just in case it is regulated by the aim of knowing what one is doing ("Introduction," pp. 22, 27, and "What Happens When Someone Acts?," pp. 140–41). Similarly, in chapter 5 of *How We Get Along*, Velleman speaks of the aim of self-understanding as constitutive of agency. And in chapter 1 of that book, he speaks of an action of crying as manifesting "that emotion under the guidance of one's conception of crying" ("Introduction," p. 26). He also describes our activity as pursued "in a manner regulated for intelligibility" ("Introduction," p. 28). If an event is not regulated by the aim of

---

[12] Velleman, "Introduction," pp. 12–13. See also Velleman, "What Happens When Someone Acts?" pp. 135–37.

knowing what one is doing, then the event is not an action in the full-blown sense, and the event is not fully one's own, autonomous action. It is the *relation* between certain bodily movements or other events and such a constitutive aim that renders what would otherwise be a mere event or a mere bit of behavior a full-blown action. This relation is, for Velleman, the action-making relation.

Velleman's account may be a necessary deepening of Frankfurt's, but ultimately it is, I believe, no more illuminating, for we are now faced with the question of what it is for some behavior to be regulated by the constitutive aim of knowing what one is doing as opposed to that behavior merely being caused—perhaps deviantly—by such an aim. Because causation is not enough, Velleman's account by itself does not tell us *how* an event that is to count as a full-blown action must be regulated by or result from or be guided by the aim of knowing what one is doing. But without an understanding of this *how*, we are no closer to understanding what it is in virtue of which a given event or a given bit of behavior counts as a robust action.

Velleman spells out his story further by characterizing the constitutive aim of knowing what one is doing as sub-agential ("Introduction," p. 21). This characterization is in keeping with Velleman's overall aim of avoiding a problematic circularity whereby agency is "explained" in terms of agency (see p. 18). Velleman thus attempts to say what it is for an event to be an action in non-agential terms—in terms that do not presuppose action. But this appeal to a sub-agential aim does not address the pressing need to understand *how* it is that this aim—constitutive and sub-agential though it may be—performs the magical, unifying feat of turning what would otherwise be at best mere activity into full-blown autonomous action.

In his later book, *How We Get Along*, Velleman may be more open to a circular account here:

> The aim of making sense can itself be justified as making sense, but it cannot be given a noncircular justification, because it sets the ultimate criterion applied to practical reasoning, and so it cannot be justified in relation to any ulterior criterion. Although this aim cannot be justified practically without circularity, its criterion-setting status can be established by noncircular theoretical arguments, which show that it is indeed constitutive of agency. (p. 146)

Despite this this openness to a kind of circularity, the explanatory demand still goes unanswered, for—again—we still need to show *how* the so-called constitutive aim plays its role in making something an action. The constitutive aim must be *applied* somehow and must *guide* one's reasoning somehow, but this application and this guidance must still take place in the right way which has still not been nailed down.[13]

Setiya, I believe, gets into similar difficulties. Like Velleman, he wants to avoid any unilluminating circles in understanding action; in particular, he wants to avoid Davidson's claim that the right way for a reason to cause an action is basic, for "that would make the connection between causation and motivation a mystery" (*Reasons without Rationalism*, p. 31; see also p. 42 on circles). Nonetheless, his own positive, Frankfurtian account appeals to a notion of guidance and of behavior that exhibits "sustained causation of a process toward a goal" (*Reasons without* Rationalism, p. 32). Such sustained causation is in effect, for Setiya, the action-making relation. But now the challenge becomes one of understanding this action-making relation and understanding *how* such purposive and not merely mechanically caused behavior is indeed caused. Unless we can say more than merely that such behavior is guided or aimed at a goal, then we are no closer than before to seeing what it is in virtue of which an event or a bit of behavior counts as a full-blown intentional action. And indeed, Setiya acknowledges that we lack an adequate theory of such sustained causation (p. 32).

Sarah Paul's sophisticated defense of the causal theory of action threatens to be similarly unilluminating. According to her account, intention is "a kind of non-cognitive practical commitment to action" (Paul, "Deviant Formal Causation," p. 18). While valuable in other ways, this account leaves two key questions unanswered. First, what makes it the case that one is so committed or what does this commitment consist in? Paul acknowledges that "It is no simple matter to articulate the nature of this commitment" (p. 18). Second, how does such commitment lead to one's action? Here—in the causal path from this commitment to action—there is still the familiar room for deviance and, as before, it does not seem that this deviance can be eliminated in a perspicuous fashion.

---

[13] Cf. Kripke's Wittgensteinian critique of Platonism in mathematics in Kripke, *Wittgenstein on Rules and Private Language*, p. 54.

Michael Bratman's account of action admirably keeps the explanatory demand concerning action in focus as well as the need to avoid circularity. Thus, Bratman states his goal in this area in these terms:

> What we want to know is whether there is a kind of psychological functioning, a kind we can characterize without presupposing the very idea of agent determination of action, such that agent determination of action consists in such functioning. Can we uncover truths along the lines of
> (A) S is the full-blown agent of X iff X is the issue of psychological functioning of type T. (Bratman, "Two Problems about Human Agency," p. 92)

After criticizing Frankfurt partly on grounds similar to those I have invoked, Bratman goes on to offer the following positive account of agency: "the ground of agential authority involves higher-order intentions, plans, and policies." The intentions, plans, and policies in question are to be seen as ones "whose function includes the constitution and support of the temporal extension of agency" ("Two Problems about Human Agency," p. 99; see also "Reflection, Planning, and Temporally Extended Agency," pp. 50–51).

Note, however, that these intentions, plans, and policies are (in general) intentions, plans, and policies for *acting*. And so the worry arises that Bratman's account of agency presupposes the very notion of agency of which he is attempting to give an account. Bratman is rightly concerned about such circularity and, like Velleman, he attempts to avoid it by appealing to a kind of sub-agential processing. For Bratman, the content of the relevant policies (etc.). need not appeal to a notion of "full-blown agency." Thus, Bratman says:

> Let us say that when a desire for E functions in the cited way [i.e. as figuring in a suitable intention, plan, or policy] it *functions as end-setting for practical reasoning*. Since this functioning may fail to be directed or endorsed by the agent, it need not be an instance of full-blown agency. We can then say that a policy of treating a desired end, E, as a reason in one's motivationally effective deliberation consists, in the basic case of a policy in favor of that desire's functioning, by way of this very policy, as end-setting for practical reasoning. In this way, the explicit content of the self-governing policy need not appeal to a prior notion of full-blown agency. ("Two Problems," p. 103, emphasis in original; see also "Reflection," pp. 45–50; "Hierarchy, Circularity, and Double Reduction," pp. 74–78)

Despite the intricacy of Bratman's approach, the usual challenge forcefully emerges and does so in more than one way. First, Bratman's account of agency in terms of plans (etc.) specifically appeals to practical reasoning—i.e. reasoning about how to *act* or what to *do*. But action and doing are what Bratman was hoping to illuminate. So how can appealing to those very notions in our purported explanation help? Further, this account of agency is in terms of how a desire functions *by way of* a certain policy. The "by way of" here is a causal notion, and the policy explains how a desire helps to cause a specific action. Of course, however, as clever philosophers can easily show, there could be deviant cases in which a policy enables a desire to effect a certain action, but that enabling or that effecting is deviant. To avoid such cases, one would inevitably need to appeal to a "right way," a way that makes the case one of genuine agency. Thus, we would again be presupposing the notion of the very phenomenon of which we are trying to give an account.

Finally, Peter Railton's approach to the problem is in some ways the most attractive of the ones we are considering. One of the great advantages of Railton's approach is that he explicitly offers an account of regulation, the notion on which Velleman's account foundered (see especially Railton, "Normative Guidance"). Another is that he is—perhaps even more than the others—sensitive to problems of regress and circularity. However, the problem with his approach is that the notion of default trust that he appeals to at critical points in his account of action can be characterized only as the kind of trust that makes agency possible ("How to Engage," pp. 193, 197). Similarly, he appeals to beliefs and desires being related in the right way or with the right architecture ("How to Engage," p. 198). But there seems to be no way to spell out the right way without appeal to agency itself.

The same difficulty arises in connection with Railton's account of guidance by a norm:

> Agent A's conduct C is guided by norm N only if C is a manifestation of A's disposition to act in a way conducive to compliance with N, such that N plays a regulative role in A's C-ing, where this involves some disposition on A's part to notice failures to comply with N, and to feel discomfort when this occurs, and to exert effort to establish conformity with N. (p. 10)

The notion of a regulative role of a norm is here spelled out in terms of the agent's dispositions to notice, to feel discomfort, and to exert effort. Two worries here: First, it seems that this notion of regulation—crucial for the account of acting for a reason—is specified at least in part in agential terms such as making an effort. This threatens to render the account circular and unilluminating. Second, to characterize the relevant dispositions here (e.g., the dispositions to notice, to feel discomfort, to exert effort), one must specify that the result toward which one is disposed does not come about in a deviant way. An outcome that occurs in a deviant fashion is not a manifestation of the agent's disposition to reach that outcome. Again, however, it does not seem that one can specify the right or non-deviant way for such states to occur other than in terms of the notion of agency itself, i.e. other than in terms of what is needed in order for the outcome to be a manifestation of the disposition needed to secure the fact that one is acting for a reason. Here yet again we have a problematic circle. Here yet again we have a John Wayne moment: action has gotta be what action has gotta be.

Anscombe to the Rescue?

It might seem that the last best hope for the philosophy of action or really—given the chronology of the philosophy of action over past generation or two—the first best hope lies in returning to some form of an Anscombian view. Anscombe doesn't face a deviant causal chain problem simply because she does not seek to explain what it is to be an action in terms of an external casual relation between reason and action. For Anscombe, the key mistake of Davidson and similar causal theorists is to seek a special feature or element that, by some kind of alchemy, turns a mere event into an intentional action. The mistake lies in thinking that, in order to give an account of action one needs to appeal to something extra, to something beyond the action itself. That is, for causal theorists, one needs to appeal to an external relation and to beliefs and desires or some other attitudes distinct from the action. Instead, Anscombe contends, events that are actions don't need to be pumped up by such external relations: "an action is not called 'intentional' in virtue of any extra feature which exists when it is performed" (*Intention*, p. 28). Similarly, Anscombe rejects the view that being intentional is "a mere *extra* feature of events whose description would otherwise be the same" (p. 88, emphasis in original). For Anscombe, only certain events are actions, and these are actions simply because they are, by their nature, actions and are, by their nature, done for a reason. There is no need to understand—and indeed no possibility of understanding—what it is to be an action in terms that do not appeal to the very notion of action done for a reason. Fred Stoutland expresses these Anscombian points well:

> a bodily movement that is an action is not a movement that happens to have some property additional to any of its neurophysiological properties. Being intentional is an *essential* feature of the bodily movements normal agents make in the normal course of their lives....
>
> [S]ince a normal agent's moving her body and the bodily movements involved are *essentially* intentional, they cannot be so in virtue of factors *external* to her moving her body or to the bodily movements. ("Introduction: Anscombe's *Intention* in Context," pp. 15 and 16; emphasis in original)

See also Hornsby:

> if actions and other movements are of fundamentally different kinds, then an action in its nature is not an event about which it is genuinely an open question whether it is an action or a movement of some other sort ("The Standard Story of Action: An Exchange (2)," p. 61, see also p. 65)

Candace Vogler makes the similar point that, for Anscombe, the action is inherently rational: "there is reason in intentional action" (Vogler, *Reasonably Vicious*, p. 220). And Douglas Lavin in the same vein speaks of "an order of practical reason" that is "internal to what happens, to the progress of the deed itself" ("Must There Be Basic Actions?," p. 274). For Anscombe, the action by its nature is simply a manifestation of our basic capacity for action.[14]

Anscombe can and does acknowledge that there may be cases in which things go awry, but those cases are beside the point; instead, the point is that the basic case is the non-deviant one, the case in which we exercise our natural capacity to do things for a reason (man is, by nature, a rational animal after all). The other, deviant cases can be understood only against this background.

Anscombe thus avoids Davidson's (and others') vain hope of trying to illuminate the notion of action by stringing together necessary conditions for being an action that do not clearly flow from the nature of action itself.

---

[14] See also Paul's characterization of Anscombe as appealing to the formal cause of an action, to the "account of what-it-is-to-be" that action in "Deviant Formal Causation," p. 5.

Instead, she turns directly to the nature of action, to our nature as rational animals. Anscombe can thus be seen as calling causal theorists—such as Davidson, Frankfurt, and Velleman—to task for appealing to external relations between actions and certain other items in order to specify what it is to be an action. And she can be seen as invoking an internal relation between an action and its very nature as intentional in order to illuminate what it is to be an action. For Anscombe, action is not to be understood in terms of things that are not inherently actions and in terms of relations to non-actions such as beliefs and desires. Rather, the constituents of our practical life and their distinction from things that are not parts of our practical life are to be understood only through the notion of action itself. In this respect, Anscombe's approach might be thought to mirror Timothy Williamson's "Knowledge First" approach to knowledge, an approach that will be subjected to my rationalist treatment in the next chapter.[15] However, I'm reluctant to see Anscombe as adopting something like an "Action First" approach, and this is because it's not clear to me that Anscombe seeks to reverse the traditional explanatory structure with regard to action in the way that Williamson seeks to do so with regard to knowledge.[16]

There is much more to be said regarding—and in favor of—Anscombe's subtle approach, but I want to stress here that Anscombe does not offer an answer that will help us say in an illuminating fashion what makes an event an action or why a given event is not an action. Anscombe's answer to the question "in virtue of what is this event an action?" is simply that this event is, by its nature, an action and is a manifestation of our basic capacity to act for a reason. This answer appeals to the notion of action itself, to our capacity to act, and so Anscombe, in the end, explains what it is to be an action in terms of the notion of action. This emerges very clearly in Stoutland's summary of Anscombe's view:

> To act is not to have one's bodily movements caused by one's beliefs and desires: it is to *exercise* the power to move one's body directly and intentionally. (Stoutland, "Introduction," p. 19; my emphasis)

Here action is explained in terms of exercising a power. And, of course, the notion of exercising a power is as much in need of clarification as the notion

---

[15] For a program along these lines, though not one that is offered as an interpretation of Anscombe, see Levy's important paper, "Intentional Action First."

[16] I am indebted here to a comment from James Conant.

of action is. Such an account can thus hardly be seen as an illuminating account of action. It has the earmarks of the kind of empty appeals to the nature of a thing for which, as we've seen, Aristotelian-inspired accounts often come under fire: appeals that may be no more illuminating than "dormitive virtue" explanations. This is Anscombe's Molière moment.[17] To say that an event is an action because it is its nature to be an *action* or because it is a manifestation of our capacity to *act* for a reason is unilluminating because we are not told in an informative way *how* the event enjoys the status of being an action. Because of this non-illumination, it's not clear that Anscombe—any more than Davidson—offers any real progress on the question, "What is action?"

One might, in Anscombe's defense, claim that she doesn't seek to answer the explanatory question that, as I have claimed, guides the philosophy of action, viz. the question "What is action" or "What is it in virtue of which a given event is an action?" But Anscombe's text doesn't seem to allow such a defense. Her book, *Intention*, is filled with claims about how action and mere events are to be distinguished and, further, she is very concerned—and appropriately so—to avoid unilluminating explanatory circles or regresses in the case of action. Thus, she says:

> it is not illuminating to be told that one [a statement concerning the future] is a prediction and the other is the expression of an intention. For we are really asking what each of these is. (p. 2)

> Why is giving a start or gasp not an "action," while sending for a taxi, or crossing the road, is one? The answer cannot be "Because the answer to the question 'why?' may give a *reason* in the latter cases," for the answer may "give a reason" in the former cases too; and we cannot say "Ah, but not a reason for *acting*"; we should be going round in circles. (p. 10; emphasis in original)

> [W]e do not yet know what a proposed action is; we can so far describe it only as an action predicted by the agent, either without his justifying his prediction at all, or with his mentioning in justification a reason for action; and the meaning of the expression "reason for acting" is precisely what we are at present trying to elucidate. (p. 22)

---

[17] Paul similarly criticizes Anscombe for offering "no non-question-begging" account of what it is to do something intentionally or for a reason, "Deviant Formal Causation," p. 14.

In a later paper, in considering the view that the agent makes *something* happen in the endeavor to φ, Anscombe says:

> if the endeavor is *all* that he makes happen, there isn't at any stage an answer to "Namely?" asked about this "something." If the *only* reply is "the endeavor" that is equivalent to having no answer. ("Chisholm on Action," pp. 86–87; emphasis in original)

But, despite Anscombe's laudable attention to the explanatory demand and despite her laudable concern to avoid circularity, Anscombe may nonetheless offer only such empty, circular answers to the guiding explanatory question.

Perhaps, despite these passages, Anscombe can be seen as simply rejecting the explanatory demand, and perhaps this is what a Wittgensteinian explanations-must-come-to-an-end-somewhere approach would lead to. But Anscombe doesn't clearly take this step. In fact, there's clear evidence that she does not take this step; much less does she *argue* that the explanatory demand in the case of action is to be rejected. In the end, as I indicated in the proem, I will, in chapters 8 and 9, be rejecting the explanatory demand with regard to action and in general, but I will do so on the basis of an argument—a decidedly and paradoxically rationalist argument—of a kind that Anscombe does not avail herself of and that she would probably have no sympathy for.

Self-Constituting Agency to the Rescue?

I would like to place within my rationalist sights a prominent, often broadly Kantian account of action or agency that has many affinities with the Anscombian account that I have just considered. According to this general position, the fact that an agent is somehow self-constituting provides an explanation of action or agency. Although many defenders of this kind of position explicitly see it as Kantian, I will not comment here on the extent to which this kind of view is indeed to be found in Kant. (I will engage more directly with Kant in chapter 10, though not on the topic of action in particular.) Kantian versions of the view I will discuss in this section are to be found in the work of Christine Korsgaard and in the work of Tamar Schapiro (and in the work of a number of others). And, although Carol Rovane's view is self-consciously non-Kantian in certain respects (e.g., in its rejection of the Kantian emphasis on the unconditional normative force of moral reasons),

Rovane's invocation of self-constitution is importantly similar to Kantian positions in respects that most concern us here.

First of all, note that the proponent of self-constituting agency seeks to offer some kind of explanation of action or agency. Such a theorist takes up the question of *how* it is that agency is constituted. And the answer is that it is constituted normatively. (We'll begin to see what this might come to shortly.) For example, just as causal accounts do, Korsgaard's account seeks to understand what it is in virtue of which a certain movement is the agent's own. Korsgaard says in this vein, "My question is ... what entitles us to attribute a movement to an agent as her own" (*Self-Constitution*, p. 83). Of course, as we'll soon see, the self-constitutionalist may and does have a distinctive understanding of the character of this kind of explanation of agency, but the aspiration, as in Davidson, is to offer an explanation of some kind.

The self-constitutionalist's explanatory ambitions are on display also in their criticism of alternative accounts of agency—often causal accounts of agency in the broad Davidsonian tradition—as failing to offer a satisfactory account of agency. In fact, self-constitutionalist accounts may well agree with the kinds of criticisms of Davidsonian approaches that I offered earlier in this chapter, as we can see by articulating their positive account.

For the self-constitutionalist, a movement or event counts as an action not because it has a certain kind of cause located in the series of antecedent events. Instead, a certain event counts as an action because I make myself the author of that event. I make it my own because I, as it were, sweep this event up in the net of things that I care about or things that I value. The event is my own, my action, because I have the ability to set ends for myself and to act for the sake of those ends and because I bring about this event in the service of those ends. In thus setting ends and acting for the sake of them, I constitute myself as a free agent. Korsgaard says:

> To act is not just to cause an end, but to *make yourself into* the cause of the end, and so to *make yourself into* the kind of thing that achieves that end. To be an agent is to transform yourself into a certain kind of cause. The activity we exhibit in action is a kind of *self-determined* efficacy. ("The Normative Constitution of Agency," p. 197; emphasis in original)

> action is determining yourself to be the cause of some end.
> (*Self-Constitution*, p. 81)

> To act is to render a change in the world. (*Self-Constitution*, p. 95)

> when an animal acts, she effects a certain change in the world by effecting a change in herself, in a way that is responsive to her conception of her environment. (*Self-Constitution*, p, 96)

Korsgaard's explanation of action is that an action takes place because I have the ability to act freely, to determine myself, to make myself into a certain kind of cause. As Schapiro puts the point, "action is an exercise of authorial causality" ("Three Conceptions of Action in Moral Theory," p. 112).

Rovane similarly attempts to account for agency in terms of self-determination throughout her book, *The Bounds of Agency: An Essay in Revisionary Metaphysics*. See, for example, p. 131 where an agent is characterized in terms of a commitment "to achieving overall rational unity within its rational point of view." Rovane expands on this theme in a later paper:

> agents are not metaphysically given things that are already there, prior to the exercise of effort and will through which they come to be. ("Self-Constitution, Reductionism, and Their Moral Significance")

> it is only through the *actual embrace and pursuit* of such projects, along with whatever rational unity their pursuit requires, that particular agents with particular deliberative points of view come into existence. ("Self-Constitution, Reductionism, and Their Moral Significance"; emphasis in original)

> *any* metaphysical condition can be the site of individual agency *so long as* the requisite unifying intentional activities and commitments can take place. ("Self-Constitution, Reductionism, and Their Moral Significance"; emphasis in original)

Notice that in these passages, Rovane offers an explanation of agency in speaking of what it is *through* which an agent comes into existence or in saying that agency exists *so long as* certain conditions obtain. And, for Rovane, these explaining conditions of agency include *exercises* of effort and the *embrace* of projects.[18]

---

[18] Rovane develops these themes in "What Sets the Boundaries of our Responsibility."

Prima facie (and perhaps even *ultima facie*), the general account of agency as self-constituting may seem circular or unilluminating: agency is to be accounted for in terms of such agency-presupposing notions as freely acting, effecting changes in oneself, self-determination, setting ends, the exercise of authorial causality, rendering, etc. It's not clear how action is to be illuminated in terms of these action-presupposing notions.[19]

Yet the self-constitutionalist has a ready reply at this point. To press this charge against the self-constitutionalist is to presuppose that explanation must be *theoretical* explanation, explanation of an object or phenomenon in the natural world, explanation that is external to the point of view of agency itself. The appeal to free action and end-setting and self-determination is not to a theoretical concept of a natural phenomenon. Rather, the concept of end-setting free action is a practical concept "that does not even purport" to pick out a phenomenon. Freedom and end-setting specify "a form of activity, and a form of achievement, in which we are already engaged and to which we are already committed" (Schapiro, "Kant's Approach to the Theory of Agency").[20]

So for the self-constitutionalist, there is an explanation of action here, but it is a distinctively practical explanation, not a theoretical explanation of the kind that Davidson and friends aim to (and fail to) provide: there is action here, for the self-constitutionalist, *because* I have the capacity to set ends, to determine myself, and this event is an action *because* it forms part of, gets taken up by, my end-setting activity. This *because* is not theoretical; the explanation at work here is a practical explanation made from the perspective of an agent, a perspective in which we are always already engaged. In this light, we can say that the self-constitutionalist (perhaps like the Anscombian) offers an *internal* explanation of action, not the quasi-mechanistic, building-block, *external* explanation found in causal theories.

It is certainly important to see the Kantian (and perhaps Kant) and, more generally, the self-constitutionalist as engaging in this purportedly wholly different kind of explanatory project. And this non-theoretical, practical approach to agency is an attractive aspect of a self-constitutionalist view (just as Anscombe's similarly internal explanation of action is attractive). But

---

[19] Bratman makes this charge against Korsgaard in particular, "Rational and Social Agency: Reflections and Replies," p. 326.

[20] Rovane similarly stresses the distinction between theoretical and practical explanations in giving an account of agency. See, e.g., Rovane, "From a Rational Point of View," p. 215; see also Korsgaard, "Personal Identity and the Unity of Agency."

does this shift to an apparently non-theoretical explanatory project help to allay the worries with regard to unilluminating explanations? I can't see that it does.

I'm going to put aside the rationalist qualms I have about the theoretical/practical distinction on which this self-constitutionalist response turns and which I always find deeply problematic and elusive. Let's grant the distinction between theoretical accounts and practical accounts of agency. My worry here is that the practical account nonetheless lacks genuine explanatory value. An internal, practical explanation is still meant to be an explanation. One who seeks to explain still seeks to shed light on agency somehow, and this explanation is in terms of the notions of freedom, end-setting, self-determination, authorial causality, etc.—each of which is in as much need of illumination as the notion of agency itself. Either the notion of action is in need of illumination or it is not. And if it is—as all sides seem to agree—then how can it be of help to invoke that very notion or a notion that presupposes that very notion? How can it help to say that you already know—from a practical, agential point of view—what agency is.

By contrast, the aim of the causal theorist is, in intention at least, of the right kind: to explain action in other terms, in terms that do not presuppose action. The causal accounts may not succeed (and I have argued that they do not), but their aim is laudable. It's just too bad that this aim hasn't been and perhaps can't be achieved. The self-constitutionalist's aim of practical, internal explanation may be equally laudable, but it's hard to see how a circular explanation can meet our goals in embarking on the philosophy of action.

At this point, it may be helpful to try to address an objection that you've probably been saying under your breath all along throughout this section and the previous one and that I frequently hear in defense of a self-constitutionalist or Anscombian view: "Although little circles may be bad, big circles are just fine and can be illuminating." In this case, we might say, if we put action and agency in its rightful place in a big enough tent of related concepts such as freedom, end-setting, self-determination, valuing, etc., then we will succeed in shedding light—from within—on the notion of agency.

My response to this objection should be clear, but let me make it explicit. If a notion is, indeed, ultimately understood in circular fashion, can we be said to have any insight into it? You might say that there is insight here because there are these connections among the concepts in question. But I say: if these connections are understood only through the notion we are trying to illuminate—in this case, the notion of action—have we really made any progress? I'll offer a similar criticism of certain theories of knowledge in the next chapter where I will also develop more fully this "big circles are good" objection to my critique of circularity and where I will expand accordingly my response to this kind of objection.

I want to make a further point: far from being better than small circles, big circles are, in one respect at least, positively *worse*. With a small circle, only one notion, A, is not well-founded and is not given an illuminating explanation. But with big circles which link notions A, B, C, etc. we now have not one but three or more notions that suffer the fate of being not well-founded, the fate of not being illuminated. In an effort to illuminate one notion, we have succeeded only in failing to shed light on a number of notions. In trying to save one drowning, not well-founded concept, other concepts have futilely jumped into the water only to suffer the same fate. This fate would be the fate of the suite of notions that the self-constitutionalist invokes in order to shed light on the notion of action.

The self-constitutionalist—just like Anscombe, on my interpretation—does not succeed in explaining agency. What these positions do is, it seems, to appeal to our very nature as agents and to the notion of action itself in order to shed light on action. But to appeal to the nature of action and the nature of agents in this way is the kind of move I have been calling a dormitive virtue explanation. Offering such an explanation is yet another Molière moment.

Ascent

We are at the same point with regard to agency that we occupied at the end of chapter 2 with regard to substance: we have witnessed the failure of a wide swath of extant accounts of a phenomenon—perhaps, in this case, a practical and not a theoretical phenomenon—central to philosophy. With these failures of this range of theories, we have seen enough, I believe, to suspect, on inductive grounds, that most or all theories of action would meet a similar fate.

But, as I asked after the equally bleak survey of theories of substance in chapter 2, can this really be? Can it really be that most or all leading accounts of action are vitiated by an implicit (or explicit) circle or emptiness or regress? Can it be that philosophers make the same kind of mistake time and time again? You know what my answer is. Don't make me say it.

And just as we saw in chapter 3, an *a priori* argument is available that not only supports the negative conclusion about theories of actions, but also helps us to pinpoint the source of all these difficulties that Davidsonian and Anscombian and self-constitutionalist theories alike face with regard to explaining action.

Let me begin by pointing out again that most accounts of action proceed upon the seemingly harmless supposition that what it is for a certain event to be an action requires a distinction—a relation—between the action, A, and some items. The action theorist tends to presuppose that we are trying to understand what it is to be a *differentiated* action, an action that is differentiated from other items, perhaps other actions, or at least an action that is *related* to some items. The relation in question may be, as in Davidson's case, an external relation of causation between the action, on the one hand, and beliefs, desires, or reasons, on the other. It may instead be, as in Anscombe's case, an internal relation, i.e. a relation dictated by the nature of A itself. Or, it may be, as in the self-constitutionalist's case, a relation between an event and an agent's end-setting activity. Or, finally and perhaps most simply, it may be simply a relation of distinction between A itself and other actions or other events that are not actions. Thus, on accounts of action in general, A must stand in some relation or other in virtue of which A counts as an action. In each case, the relation in question is at least part of what it is in virtue of which A counts as an action. Thus, the relation, which I will call "R," is the action-making relation.

In seeking to understand the action-making relation, R, there are four exhaustive and mutually exclusive options. These options are precisely parallel to the four options we faced in chapter 3 for understanding the substance-making relation.

(1) R is primitive. That is, the relation, R, between A and some items is not grounded in or explained by anything. There is nothing in virtue of which A stands in R to these items.

(2) R is not primitive, but is, rather, ultimately grounded in or explained by or ultimately holds, at least in part, in virtue of a relation to something other than A.

(3) R is not primitive, but is, rather, ultimately grounded in or explained by or ultimately holds in virtue of the nature of A alone. That is, it follows from the nature of A alone that A is an action. R is thus, in one sense of the term, an internal relation, a relation that stems simply from the nature of a thing.

(4) R is not primitive, but also is not ultimately grounded (as in (2) and (3)); instead, R is grounded in other items in a non-terminating regress or in a circle with a multiplicity of items.

Option (1) (as in the case of option (1) for the substance-making relation) is not viable given the explanatory demand when it comes to action, a demand accepted by all sides.

Option (2) which invokes external relations is represented by Davidson's or Davidsonian causal theoretic approaches to action that are found in Frankfurt, Bratman, Setiya, Railton, Paul, etc.

Option (3) which invokes internal relations is represented by Anscombe's approach and by what I have called accounts of agency as self-constituting.

As in the case of substance, options (2), (3), and (4) do not succeed in offering a good account of R, the action-making relation. I won't here rehearse in all their glory the powerful Bradleyan, rationalist, and ultimately Parmenidean reasons for the failure of these options to provide an illuminating account of what it is to be an action. But I do note that the arguments in the case of action are exactly analogous to the arguments regarding substance in chapter 3. You may be parachuting into this chapter without exposing yourself directly to the power of the detailed arguments I gave in chapter 3. That's OK. Parachuting in is allowed. But just keep in mind that any attempt to deny or resist my arguments in the current chapter is inevitably ineffective without a successful argument against the Bradley-inspired moves I offered and defended in chapter 3 against the intelligibility of relations.

In the light of my multifarious arguments against the notion of relational activity, is there any way to redeem the notion of action? As before, the answer is my usual answer: there is. The problem that we have considered in the case of action arose only on the presupposition, shared by Davidson, Anscombe, Frankfurt, Velleman, Korsgaard, Rovane, Schapiro, and others, that actions stand in relations—internal or external—to things of some kind, or the presupposition that actions are distinct from mere events and from other actions, or, most generally, the presupposition that an action stands in relations to items. It is only on such presuppositions that we faced options (1), (2), (3), and (4) for dealing with the action-making relation, options each of which is unacceptable. But if we get rid of the problematic assumption that there are actions that stand in relations, that is, as one might say, the assumption of differentiated or related action, then we may no longer face the problem of incoherence. For the problem that, as we have seen, related or differentiated action faces cannot arise for unrelated or undifferentiated action. On this view, while there may be no actions as distinct from other actions and from mere events, there may be action. If there is to be action, it cannot occupy a place differentiated from other things or related to things: we cannot intelligibly place action or actions *within* reality in a place differentiated from other places; we cannot intelligibly relate an action to anything. Thus, if there is to be action at all, then all is action. The reality that Anscombe, Davidson, and friends were trying, unsuccessfully, to capture is better captured by a view that rejects relations between actions and things (even internal relations). This move would be a Parmenidean Ascent with regard to action: a rejection of certain kinds of relations involving action and, by transcending these relations, an attempt to capture the reality that was only imperfectly expressed by appealing to such relations. On this view, there is no differentiated or individuated action. Should we then say that all is one action? No, and for the same reasons as before with substance: the notion of *one* presupposes counting, counting presupposes the intelligibility of relations, at least relations between numbers, and relations have been ruled out. There are no actions, not even one action. There is just action. And, as before with the term "being" and with the same reservations, the term "action" can be seen as something like a mass noun, not a count noun. And, as before with being and non-being, I am inclined to say that all is action rather than that all is non-action. This is because non-action is inherently relational since it is defined in terms of what it is not, viz. action. But action can, perhaps, be regarded in purely positive terms.

As before, I'm well aware that the Parmenidean Ascent is counterintuitive and implausible, and perhaps even paradoxical. And, again as before, I place very little stock in such appeals to intuition and plausibility, for reasons that I gestured toward at the end of chapter 3 and that I will explore in more detail later in the book.

Also, as before, an appeal to Aquinas might help (or, of course, might not help) to shed light on what is going on with this Parmenidean Ascent. Just as Aquinas thinks that God is subsistent being itself, so too—in keeping with Aquinas' commitment to divine simplicity—God is *actus purus*, pure act, pure actuality.[21] For me, the world itself is pure act. There is nothing but action and all is action, just as, as we saw in chapter 3, all is being. And just as,

---

[21] "God has no admixture of potency, but is pure act [[*Deus*] *nullam habet potentiam admixtam, sed est actus purus*]," *Summa Contra Gentiles* 1.16; see also Gilson, *The Philosophy of St. Thomas Aquinas*, pp. 100–1.

for Aquinas, given the simplicity of God, being itself—*ipsum esse*—is also pure act, for me too being itself is pure act. The key difference in this respect, though, between Aquinas and me is that, for Aquinas, God or pure act or being itself is distinct from the world of created beings that have their own activity. For me, there is no such distinction between pure act and a world of other beings or agents or actions. There is simply action.

Despite (or, perhaps, because of) this quasi-Thomistic flourish, the Parmenidean Ascent with regard to action is vastly skeptical in the sense that it denies that we can coherently conceive of the differentiated actions and agents that we hold dear. As with substance or being, this is not merely a skeptical doubt about whether or not there are any (differentiated) actions. Rather, this is a skeptical denial of the very coherence of the concept of differentiated actions.

To display this skeptical denial, I want to point to, and—skirting paradox again—*make my own*, two implications of this skepticism about the ordinary notion of action. First, in this skeptical light, the problem of free will takes on an entirely new dimension. Thus, consider this problem and the constellation of perennial issues in its orbit, e.g., the issue of whether an agent's freedom or an agent's responsibility is compatible with determinism. Discussions of the nature of freedom and responsibility, at least when it comes to human agents and human actions, focus on individuated—i.e. differentiated, related—acts or agents. But once the notions of individuated agents and acts are rejected as incoherent in light of the Parmenidean Ascent, we can see that compatibilists and incompatibilists alike make the mistake of thinking that we can legitimately deal with individuated action.

The second implication I want to make my own here is this: with the rejection of individuated action, most standard moral theories are also undermined to the extent that such theories as consequentialism, deontological theories, and virtue ethical accounts focus on individuated actions or individuated agents. If these theories have such a focus—and it's difficult to see how they don't—then they trade in incoherent relational notions.

I will not attempt a full-blown Parmenidean Ascent with regard to moral notions (beyond the notion of action) in this book. I will, though, take up the issue of normativity in other (i.e. "other") domains when I turn to the notions of knowledge and meaning in the next two chapters. A more fully worked out treatment of freedom and moral normativity in my Parmenidean light will be a topic for future work. For now, the relatively modest conclusion that all is action will have to suffice.

5
Knowledge

Knowledge and the Explanatory Demand

A widespread explanatory demand seems to inspire many of the pilgrims who make their way through contemporary epistemology. Expressed in one way, the demand is the question: what is it in virtue of which an individual knows that a particular state of affairs obtains or that a particular proposition is true? Or: what is it in virtue of which a given state that a knower is in amounts to a state of knowledge? Or, more grandly, what is the being of knowledge? Or, most simply: what is knowledge? A fundamental task—perhaps *the* fundamental task—of epistemology is to illuminate what it is to be a state of knowledge, what makes something a state of knowledge, and what it is in virtue of which that state differs from any state of non-knowledge.

Epistemologists of very different stripes seem to embrace something like this explanatory demand. Thus, near the beginning of her excellent introductory work on epistemology, Jennifer Nagel asks the question, "What is knowledge?," and she later restates her guiding theme as, "What is it for you to know something, rather than merely believe it?"[1]

Barry Stroud, always deeply attuned to crucial methodological issues, sees his task and the task of epistemologists in general as one of "understanding human knowledge." He elaborates this explanatory aim by saying, "What has come to be called 'epistemology' is the attempt to explain how we know the things we know."[2] Elsewhere he continues in the same vein: in epistemology, "we want . . . some kind of *explanation* of our knowledge—some account of how it is possible."[3] Finally, consider this general question that Stroud raises: "What exactly is knowledge, and how do human beings know the sorts of things they have to know in order to live the kind of lives they lead?"[4]

---

[1] Nagel, *Knowledge: A Very Short Introduction*, pp. 1, 4.
[2] Stroud, "Introduction," p. ix.
[3] "Scepticism and the Possibility of Knowledge," p. 4; emphasis in the original.
[4] "Epistemological Reflection on Knowledge of the External World," p. 123.

Similarly, Robert Nozick asks, "How is knowledge possible?" and announces that "we seek a hypothesis to explain how, even given the skeptic's possibilities, knowledge is possible."[5]

Or consider Jason Stanley's clear statement:

> A central part of epistemology, as traditionally conceived, consists of the study of the factors in virtue of which someone's true belief is an instance of knowledge.[6]

In the preface, he says that his book's thesis concerns "what *makes* someone's true belief a case of knowledge" (p. v; my emphasis). Stanley issues a call to epistemologists to meet the explanatory demand.

Even Timothy Williamson, whose revolutionary views stand opposed in many respects to those of the theorists I have just quoted and who regards the notion of knowledge as primitive and unanalyzable, seeks to explain knowledge. He says that he aims to offer "a modest positive account of the concept" of knowledge and that a "reflective understanding of knowledge is possible,"[7] though not an analysis.[8] Williamson's account is meant to illuminate knowledge, to help us see what it is, and, in this way, he also feels the pull of the explanatory demand. Rationalist that I am, "explanation" is not too strong a term for me, but perhaps it is too strong a term for Williamson or for you. No matter. I'm not going to fight about the word. It's enough to say this: Williamson certainly seeks to give an account of—to illuminate—knowledge and so, from this point of view we can speak of Williamson, and of the others that I have quoted, as motivated by what we might call an illuminative demand with regard to knowledge, the demand that knowledge should somehow be illuminated.

Much work in epistemology does not, of course, focus on the explanatory demand, but that does not mean that the epistemologists who take up these other topics are not committed to there being an answer to this demand. Thus, e.g., contextualists as such focus on giving an account of the circumstances in which one may ascribe knowledge truly, and they do not

---

[5] Nozick, *Philosophical Explanations*, pp. 167, 169. Notice that both Stroud and Nozick use the magic Parmenidean word "how."

[6] Stanley, *Knowledge and Practical Interests*, p. 1.

[7] Williamson, *Knowledge and Its Limits*, p. 33. All references to Williamson in this chapter will be to this work.

[8] In a different context, Lewis draws a similar contrast between an account and an analysis in "New Work for a Theory of Universals," p. 20.

thereby give an account of what knowledge is. Nevertheless, contextualists invariably see their contextualist accounts as meshing with views about the nature of knowledge in a way that resolves epistemological issues, such as the proper response to skepticism. This is exactly how Keith DeRose sees his work on contextualism as interacting with substantive, independent views on the nature of knowledge. DeRose writes that he seeks to "utilize a very partial but still substantive proto-theory of what knowledge is, together with contextualist semantics, to address a central problem of skepticism" (*The Case for Contextualism*, p. 19). DeRose is committed to there being an answer to the explanatory demand, and he combines that answer with his contextualism in order to make progress in epistemology.

Countless other epistemologists give expression to the explanatory or illuminative demand. Each of them realizes that answering this demand enables an epistemologist to grasp the difference between knowledge and non-knowledge. Or at least that's the goal.

In this chapter, I examine a number of leading contemporary theories of knowledge and show how they all—while embracing the explanatory demand—fail to meet it in subtle and not so subtle ways. We've acted out such a tragedy in the case of both standard accounts of substance and standard accounts of action. Now it is the turn of standard accounts of knowledge to meet the same fate. These proceedings may thus take on an air of inevitability, but, I claim, they are no less fascinating for all that, in much the same way that the tragic hero's steps toward his foreseen end are fascinating. And, in any event, the destructive conclusion has to be earned anew in each case, and that is what I propose to do here, as in the other cases, with my detailed probing of theories. I will, in fact, eventually show that *any* theory of knowledge which makes a certain seemingly harmless assumption—as all, or nearly all, theories of knowledge do—inexorably fails to meet the explanatory demand, fails, in a way contrary to its stated aim, to illuminate knowledge. The assumption in question is that a state of knowledge is differentiated, that it somehow stands in relations.

From the conclusion that all or most standard theories of knowledge inevitably fail to meet the explanatory demand, we will be able to arrive at something like a monism of knowledge, i.e. something like the view that there are no states of knowledge differentiated from other things, rather—instead of differentiated knowledge—there is simply knowledge. To put it roughly, all is knowledge. Or perhaps even better: knowledge is.

To begin this examination of the failure of standard theories, I want to focus on more or less contemporary epistemological views and divide them into two broad categories: what I will call "building-block" theories and "knowledge-first" theories. We saw earlier a similar division in theories of substance and in theories of action. As should become clear, this distinction cuts across other, perhaps more familiar distinctions among epistemological theories, such as the internalism/externalism distinction and the foundationalism/coherentism distinction. I do not claim that my division between building-block and knowledge-first theories is exhaustive, but the distinction does cover at least a large swath of contemporary epistemology. Indeed, the positive, monistic view of knowledge that I will ultimately gesture toward is not a version of either a building-block view or a knowledge-first theory, but here I'm getting ahead of myself.

Building-block views seek to shed light on knowledge—to explain what it is to be knowledge—in terms of such conditions as truth, belief, and justification, and perhaps some further condition. These conditions are the building blocks of knowledge, as it were. This is the approach of the long-suffering (and long suffered!) project of analyzing the concept of knowledge that has dominated so much of analytic epistemology. But it's not the case that building-block views are committed to there being an analysis of knowledge. For example, Stanley holds a building-block view and is explicitly not committed to knowledge being analyzable (*Knowledge and Practical Interests*, p. 88). More generally, one can even reject the analytic/synthetic distinction and with it the notion of conceptual analysis, yet still—in building-block fashion—believe that knowledge is dependent on features such as truth, belief, justification (and more) that do not presuppose the notion of knowledge. All that one needs for a building-block account is the dependence of knowledge on other features. One does not need an analysis of the concept of knowledge.

The—or an—alternative to a building-block view is a knowledge-first view. Such a view does not seek to illuminate knowledge by appeal to features such as belief, truth, and justification (and more) that are regarded as somehow prior to knowledge. On a knowledge-first view, knowledge is primitive or basic and not dependent on those other features. This approach seeks instead to account for other epistemic notions in terms of knowledge. Thus, the nature of belief, justification, and assertion, for example, can all be accounted for in terms of knowledge (instead of vice versa). In taking this tack, the aim is to reveal important structural connections, e.g., in the case of

Williamson's version of a knowledge-first view, externalism, anti-luminosity, the denial of the KK principle (the principle that knowing requires knowing that one knows), and the thesis that one's evidence is one's knowledge. These connections serve to illuminate knowledge without analyzing it. Through charting these connections involving knowledge, we gain the illumination of knowledge that Williamson seeks. This is Williamson's way of seeking to meet the explanatory demand—not through an analysis of knowledge, but rather through a "reflective understanding" of knowledge.

Williamson's view need not be the only version of a knowledge-first strategy. For example, we can say that knowledge comes prior to belief but, unlike Williamson, have an internalist conception of belief and also insist that knowing requires knowing that one knows. Whether such an alternative version of a knowledge-first view can be developed is an interesting question. Williamson's version, however, is remarkably well worked out, and my point here is that it provides a useful contrast to building-block views even though in the end, as I will argue, the contrast is not as significant as Williamson takes it to be.

Building-Block Views

Building-block views tend to take it for granted that, for a given state to be one of knowledge, that state must be a belief that is true. The question for building-block theorists has generally concerned what conditions, if any, must be added to these two in order for the state to amount to knowledge.[9] The challenge here is to spell out the way the belief must be related to the truth in order for the belief to count as knowledge.

For some time now, the relation in question has been thought to be a justificatory relation, the relation whereby the belief is connected to the truth in such a way that the belief is justified. And so we have the justified true belief account of knowledge. But then—with one of the most consequential and frequently cited papers in recent philosophy—along came G . . . , along came Ge . . . , along came Get . . . —I can't bring myself to say the name.[10] Suffice it to say that devastating counterexamples to the justified true belief account were introduced, and philosophers went back to the ranch to try to

---

[9] See again the quote from Stanley, *Knowledge and Practical Interests*, p. 1.
[10] But consult the bibliography of this book, under the "G's," if you must see the one billionth reference to this paper.

assemble the building blocks of knowledge once again, to try to articulate the way in which a true belief must be related to the truth in order to count as knowledge.

Let me consider a potential response to these counterexamples that shall remain nameless. In these counterexamples, the belief is justified, but somehow the justification is not of the right kind for the belief to count as knowledge. This suggests the following potential response: knowledge is not justified true belief, but rather is true belief that is justified *in the right way*. This may not be a response that anyone has actually given to the problem of explaining what knowledge is.[11] And the inadequacies in this account should be obvious—or, if not, they will soon be. Nonetheless, these inadequacies will be instructive. Without specifying what the right way is, we can say only that this way is right because it is the kind of justification needed for the subject to have knowledge. Thus, the account would be:

S knows just in case S's true belief is justified in the way that is needed for that belief to amount to knowledge.

This would be a circular account of knowledge. Knowledge would be explained in terms of knowledge, and that can hardly be a satisfactory answer to the explanatory demand.[12]

Such a charge—that certain accounts of knowledge illegitimately and circularly appeal to knowledge itself was perhaps first made by Plato in the *Theaetetus*. The last proposed definition of knowledge in that dialogue is "correct judgment together with an account" (Plato, *Theaetetus* 208b; "account" here translates Plato's "*logos*"). Plato spells out "account" as "being able to tell some mark by which the object you are asked about differs from all other things" (208c). Plato quickly shows (or seems to show) that being able to tell such a differentiating mark means that "we are required to get to *know* the differentness" (209e). And so the proposed definition of knowledge is really: "Correct judgment accompanied by *knowledge* of the differentness" (210a). As Plato rightly points out, "it is surely just silly to tell us, when we are

---

[11] Though, as we'll see, Goldman's initial response comes pretty darn close to this one.
[12] Many building block theorists acknowledge that these theories must avoid such circles. Thus, e.g., Sosa agrees that a satisfactory theory of knowledge must specify conditions in which no epistemic status plays any role at all (Sosa, *Reflective Knowledge*, pp. 175–76).

trying to discover what knowledge is, that it is correct judgment accompanied by knowledge" (210a).[13]

We can also portray the problem here as one of a vicious regress. As we have stipulated, the account is that in order to be knowledge, S's state of true belief must be justified in the right way. In order to avoid the problem of circularity, let's specify the way not as "the right way" but in terms that do not presuppose the notion of knowledge (as does "the right way" in this context). So let's specify the way here simply as "way 1." Since way 1, so specified, does not presuppose that the belief amounts to knowledge, it's still an open question as to whether the belief amounts to knowledge. So we must further specify that way 1 is a feature that the belief comes to have in the right way. But, again, we want to avoid knowledge-presupposing notions, so we are led to specify this way in which the belief is justified in way 1, "way 2." But this specification still leaves an open question whether the belief amounts to knowledge, so we must further specify that this way of being a way of being justified must itself attach to the belief in the right way. Call this way of being a way of being a way in which a belief is justified "way 3." And so on. We seem to have here a regress of ways of a belief's being justified in order for that belief to amount to knowledge. Unless the right way is cashed out or the regress stopped, we have an unsatisfactory account, one that either circularly invokes the notion of knowledge in order to explain what knowledge is or one that—because of an infinite regress of ways in which a justified belief is connected to the truth—never succeeds in spelling out and nailing down this connection to the truth that a justified belief must have in order to amount to knowledge.

Such a circular or regress-laden account is evidence of a kind of emptiness or unilluminatingness that I have characterized as a John Wayne moment in philosophy. Here, the worry is that the building-block account of knowledge simply amounts to the unsatisfactory claim: knowledge has gotta be what knowledge has gotta be. It would be extremely disappointing, I would think, for a philosopher to propose such an "account" when the stated, shared goal of epistemology is to provide illumination as to the nature of knowledge. (In the same way, I argued that in the case of the causal theory of action, bare appeals to the right way in which an event is caused are most unhelpful.) Yet this is precisely what happens time and time again: as we'll see, all or

---

[13] I am indebted to Jennifer Nagel for reminding me of the Platonic roots of the considerations I raise here.

most prominent theories of knowledge amount to John Wayne moments in philosophy.

Before we proceed, it is important to note that the concern here with circularity is *not* another concern that often comes up in epistemology in, e.g., discussions of the so-called Cartesian Circle. As the legend of the Cartesian Circle goes, Descartes illegitimately helps himself to claims of a kind that he previously called into doubt. He relies on a faculty—clear and distinct perception—that he has just been impugning and has not yet validated. But the kind of circle at work in the John Wayne moments in epistemology is not a circular attempt to show that we have knowledge in the face of particular doubts about whether we have that knowledge. No, the circle here comes at an earlier stage—not one of wondering whether we have knowledge, but, as I stated at the beginning, one of wondering what knowledge, whether or not we have it, consists in. The circle I am concerned with and that I regard as clearly unacceptable is one according to which we explain what it is to have knowledge in terms of knowledge itself. Even if the "Cartesian" circle can be avoided or rendered unproblematic,[14] this would go no distance toward showing it to be acceptable to try to illuminate or explain knowledge in terms of knowledge itself. In other words, the explanatory demand demands a non-circular response.

Other building-block views are more sophisticated than the skeletal view I have used as an illustration. But most or even all of them fail in the way that my sample view does: they invoke the notion of knowledge itself in an account of knowledge (or they get into a regress), and they wind up experiencing John Wayne moments. My argument for the general conclusion will, in the first instance, be inductive: by looking at a variety of examples of prominent building-block views and showing how they shatter upon precisely this rock of circularity, I will offer an inductive basis for thinking that building-block views of knowledge in general succumb to this problem. I will follow this up with a more or less *a priori* argument for precisely the same conclusion, an argument that, moreover, identifies the underlying source of this problem of circularity (or regresses). You might say that given the latter, *a priori* argument, the former, inductive argument is not needed. But, as was the case with the complementary *a priori* and inductive arguments with regard to

---

[14] As, e.g., Sosa thinks it can be; see *Reflective Knowledge*, chapter 8, esp. p. 176, and chapter 9. See also Della Rocca, "Descartes, the Cartesian Circle, and Epistemology without God," where I argue that the legend is just a legend.

substance and action, I see the pair of arguments in this case as mutually supporting. Each of the arguments is controversial, and so each can use the support that a separate argument for the same conclusion provides.

Most building-block views, when they get into circles of the kind that I'm interested in, do so in subtle ways. But, in some, the circularity is right there on the surface, brazenly hanging out. This is the case with one of the earliest responses to the original counterexamples that come from Edmund L. What's-his-name. Thus, consider the response found in Alvin Goldman's causal theory of knowing which is remarkably similar to the toy account just presented. Goldman says that S knows that p just in case "the fact that p is causally connected in an 'appropriate' way with S's believing p" ("A Causal Theory of Knowing," p. 369). Goldman characterizes the appropriate way in terms of perception and memory both of which are, of course, ways of knowing and thus in as much need of illumination as knowledge itself is. In this early paper, Goldman has, at best, merely pushed the problem back one step and not resolved the question of what it is to be knowledge. It seems, then, that Goldman (at this stage) has no non-circular way of characterizing knowledge, and so we have a John Wayne moment in the early literature on the analysis of knowledge.[15]

Many other building-block views take a different approach and rely crucially on the notion of relevant alternatives. As I will now argue, these views also get into circularity problems. To see the difficulties that the notion of relevant alternatives poses, it will be helpful to split up building-block accounts of knowledge into contextualist and invariantist accounts. On contextualist views, whether it is true to say that S knows a given proposition p depends on the standards for knowledge that are in force in the context in which the word "knows" is being used, the context of the person (who may be S herself) who attributes knowledge or the lack of knowledge to S. It is a key feature of contextualist views of knowledge that the standards for knowledge—i.e. what is required for S to know—may shift from one context of use of the word "knows" to another. Often the semantical mechanism of such shifts is regarded as a function of the allegedly indexical nature of the verb "knows."

By contrast, an invariantist epistemologist regards the standards for knowledge as remaining constant across different contexts of use. Whether it is

---

[15] For this kind of criticism of the causal theory, see Nagel, *Knowledge: A Very Short Introduction*, p. 52.

true to say that S knows depends not on the context of use or attribution, but rather simply on such factors as the situation of S herself.

A relativist or assessment-sensitive semantics for "knows" distinguishes more finely than do standard contextualist views between the context of use of the term "knows" and the context of assessment of knowledge claims. Context of assessment may, on this view, diverge from context of use. In this way, a proponent of an assessment-sensitive semantics is neither a standard contextualist who focuses on context of use nor an invariantist because, for the relativist, whether S knows does vary from one context (of assessment) to another. I will not separately discuss this perhaps more sophisticated form of contextualism about knowledge, for this account relies crucially upon the notion of relevant alternatives and of those possibilities that "may properly be ignored." The worries that I am about to raise about how to draw the line between relevant alternatives and irrelevant alternatives would apply equally to such relativist or assessment-sensitive views.[16]

Building-block views can be either contextualist or invariantist. An invariantist building-block theorist would hold that whether S knows p depends on facts such as whether p is true, S believes p, and how the belief is related to the truth that p. In a given situation, whether S knows does not depend on the context in which knowledge is being attributed to S. According to a contextualist building-block view, whether it's true to say that S knows depends on the belief, the connection between it and truth, and *also* on the context of use of the term "knows." Different kinds of connection to the truth may be required in different contexts of use in order for S to count as knowing p.

Let's turn to the problems that the notion of relevant alternatives creates for building-block views. I will begin with invariantist building-block views.

Some early versions of a relevant alternatives view were invariantist.[17] On such accounts, S's knowledge that p requires not just the true belief that p but also that S be in a position to eliminate alternative situations in which p is false.[18] Specifically, S is required to eliminate not all alternatives to p, but only

---

[16] For such an approach see MacFarlane, *Assessment Sensitivity*, chapter 8, and for the reliance on the notion of relevant alternatives, see pp. 188–89.

[17] Dretske and Nozick would be examples of invariantist building-block folks.

[18] Or alternatives to knowing that p. I won't continue to make the qualification about alternatives to knowing that p, a qualification important in some contexts, though not here. Also: the language of elimination or ruling out may problematically presuppose knowledge in a way that would render the account circular. It might be thought that an alternative is eliminated only because one *knows* it not to obtain. Lewis characterizes "elimination" in a way that may not presuppose knowledge, see Lewis, "Elusive Knowledge," p. 424. Alternatively, one can avoid any problematic talk of elimination entirely by appealing simply to whether in nearby possible situations S has false beliefs as to whether or not

those that are relevant in some way. Thus, consider an example of a kind famously offered by Fred Dretske. Marion visits the zoo and sees what he thinks to be a zebra before him. Does Marion know that there is a zebra there? On a relevant alternatives view, in order to know in this situation, Marion must be in a position to eliminate certain alternatives to p, to the claim that a zebra is present, e.g., the alternative that what's before him is not a zebra but a giraffe (or an elephant, gazelle, etc.). However, some alternatives to being a zebra are typically not—so the account goes—relevant, e.g., the alternative that the animal before Marion is a mule cleverly disguised to look like a zebra, or the possibility that there is no zebra at all before Marion and his experiences as of a zebra are, in fact, deceptively generated in Marion who is merely a brain in a vat.

The problem I want to focus on arises when we consider just what it is for an alternative to be relevant on an invariantist building-block view. Relevant alternatives views are motivated to invoke this notion in part because they seek a way of handling skepticism. A building-block theory would collapse into skepticism if *all* alternatives—even the painted mule alternative or the brain in a vat alternative—were deemed relevant and if they needed to be ruled out in order for one to know p.[19] After all, the painted mule possibility and the brain in a vat possibility are designed to be difficult or even impossible to rule out. The account of knowledge offered by an invariantist relevant alternatives theorist is thus this:

S knows that p just in case S truly believes p and S is able to eliminate all relevant alternatives to p.

For invariantist relevant alternative theorists, safeguarding the knowledge of p in this way may come at the cost of denying the deductive closure of knowledge, and, in particular, at the cost of denying that one knows that the skeptical possibilities don't obtain. That may seem implausible, but Nozick and Dretske go to great lengths (unsuccessfully, in my view and in the view of many others) to defend the denial of closure. In any event, the difficulties

---

a given proposition is true. This is DeRose's preferred, "double safety" approach, *The Appearance of Ignorance: Knowledge, Skepticism, and Context*, pp. 211–14.

[19] Dretske makes this point in "The Pragmatic Dimension of Knowledge," where he says (p. 372) that for the skeptic the set of relevant alternatives is identical to the set of alternatives, or, in his terminology, the relevancy set = the contrasting set.

associated with the denial of closure aren't my main objection to invariantist relevant alternative views. I am focusing on a deeper worry.

And this is the worry expressed in the question: how does the relevant alternatives theorist specify which alternatives are relevant? Until that is done, the account of knowledge is not complete, the explanatory demand is not met. We haven't fully explained what knowledge consists in.

Sometimes, relevant alternatives theories appeal to counterfactuals. The giraffe counterpossibility is relevant because if p were false, something like the giraffe possibility (or the elephant possibility, etc.) would be the case. But the painted mule possibility or the brain in a vat possibility is not what would be the case if p were false. It's not that the painted mule and brain in a vat situations are impossible. They are, let's stipulate, possible. Rather, the point is that such possibilities are not what would obtain were p to be false. Such possibilities are—to use a metaphor from theories of possible worlds—too remote from the actual world to be relevant, whereas the giraffe possibility is not too remote. The world where a giraffe is in front of Marion is a nearby possible world, but the painted mule and brain in a vat situations obtain only in remote worlds. Compare here Peacocke and co.'s appeal to counterfactual possibilities in their attempt to avoid the deviant causal chain problem in the philosophy of action. We will see presently that epistemologists who appeal to counterfactuals to cash out the notion of relevance face problems analogous to action-theorists like Peacocke.

Fair enough, but what makes it the case that the brain in a vat or painted mule possibilities are too remote, and the giraffe possibility is not too remote? The answer seems to be that the brain in a vat and painted mule possibilities are too remote because if we had to rule them out in order to know, then we would not know p, and some form of skepticism would be true; whereas the giraffe possibility is not too remote because requiring that it be ruled out wouldn't lead to skepticism. Thus, the relevance of an alternative or the nearness or remoteness of a possibility is to be characterized in terms of what is required for avoiding skepticism. In other words, a relevant alternative is an alternative the ruling out of which is relevant for securing *knowledge* of p. And an irrelevant alternative is an alternative that does not need to be ruled out in order to know p. The relevance of an alternative is characterized in terms of knowledge.

This is explicit in many statements of the relevant alternatives view. Thus, Dretske says:

> its being an eagle, a Mallard, or a Loon *are* members of the relevancy set since if the bird watcher could not eliminate these possibilities (sufficient

unto knowing that it was not an eagle, a Mallard, or a loon) on the basis of the bird's appearance and behavior, then he would not know that it was a Gadwall. ("Pragmatic Dimension," p. 371)

Here the relevance of an alternative is characterized in terms of knowledge ("sufficient unto knowing"). Notice also that the alternative is relevant *since* (as Dretske says) if one did not eliminate it one would not *know*. An alternative is thus relevant *because* of the connection between knowing *p* and ruling out that alternative. Similarly, Dretske indicates that an alternative is irrelevant because one need not rule it out in order to know

> *for purposes of assessing someone's knowledge* that this is a table, certain alternative possibilities are simply not relevant. ("Pragmatic Dimension," p. 368; my emphasis)

Similarly, DeRose characterizes a general notion of relevance of alternatives in terms of knowledge:

> this raising of epistemic standards consists in expanding the range of relevant alternatives to what one believes, that is, the range of alternatives that one must be in a position to eliminate in order to count as knowing. ("Solving the Skeptical Problem," p. 8n11)

Notice that the notion of relevance is glossed here in terms of knowing.[20]

Goldman's reliabilism—which he sees as a successor to his earlier causal theory—also invokes relevant alternatives. In "Discrimination and Perceptual Knowledge," Goldman articulates an early version of the contextualist/invariantist distinction (pp. 775–776) and says that he is "officially neutral" between these views, although he is "attracted by" contextualism (p. 777). Thus, Goldman's discussion is meant to apply to invariantist versions of a relevant alternatives view (as well as to contextualist versions). Like Dretske and DeRose, he too cashes out his notion of relevance in knowledge-presupposing ways. As Goldman specifies, the relevance of an alternative is a

---

[20] DeRose does not endorse this account of relevance here because it is expressed in terms of the notion eliminating possibilities, a notion of which, as I indicated in note 18, DeRose is rightly suspicious. However, for DeRose, whether one knows does still turn on what one believes as to whether a given proposition is true in nearby worlds, and, as we will see, for DeRose, which worlds count as nearby is a function, in part, of what it takes for a subject to know.

function of whether the alternative is unusual enough to count as relevant *for a non-skeptic* (p. 787). And there are shades in Goldman's reliabilism of his earlier problematic appeal to *appropriate* causal relations when he specifies that S's propensity to form a belief must have an appropriate genesis, where the appropriateness of a genesis turns on whether it is "enough to support knowledge" (p. 789). The apple of reliabilism doesn't fall far from the tree of the causal theory.

There may be another way that reliabilism faces a problem of circularity stemming from the notion of relevance. This is the generality problem. There are very many types under which a particular process leading to the formation of a particular belief falls. Only some of these types are reliable. Thus, consider my belief that Paul McCartney was born in 1942. I acquired this belief because Sally—a well-known Beatles expert who was standing next to me—told me that Paul was born in 1942. Is my belief justified? For the reliabilist, the question is: is the type of belief-forming process under which the formation of my belief falls reliable? The problem is that my belief-forming process falls under many types. Which process type is relevant to determining whether my particular belief is justified? If the relevant process type is: "believe whatever a Beatles expert tells me about the Beatles," then, great, my belief-forming process is reliable. But if the relevant process type is "believe whatever anyone standing next to me says," then my belief-forming process is, perhaps, not reliable. Obviously, we need a way to specify which belief-forming process type is relevant in this case. But it's difficult to see how to do so in a principled way, i.e. in a way other than a way that amounts to saying that this process type is relevant because it yields the intuitive verdict that the belief in this case is justified.[21]

One might think that the appeal to relevance can be saved from circularity by characterizing relevance not in terms of knowledge (as Dretske, DeRose, and others do), but merely in terms of the similarity of possible worlds to the actual world, or in terms of the nearness of possible worlds to the actual world. On this way of talking, skeptical possibilities are relatively

---

[21] For a good statement of the generality problem and its difficulty, see Conee and Feldman, "The Generality Problem for Reliabilism." For some good arguments that this problem of relevance affects not just reliabilism, but also theories of justification in general, see Comesaña, "A Well-Founded Solution to the Generality Problem," and Bishop, "Why the Generality Problem is Everybody's Problem." For an illuminatingly different agency-focused approach to the problem, see Miracchi, "Epistemic Agency and the Generality Problem." Brewer, *Perception and Reason* (pp. 92–98) offers an excellent account of the kinds of problems of circularity faced by the reliabilist. I am indebted here again to Jennifer Nagel.

unlike, and distant from, the actual world, and non-skeptical alternatives are relatively similar to or close to the actual world. And it is because of these differences in terms of similarity and closeness—and not because of considerations turning on knowledge itself—that the distinction between relevant and irrelevant alternatives is introduced. However, it's not at all clear that these claims about similarity and closeness are true. After all, the skeptical painted mule and brain in a vat possibilities are more like the actual situation than is the non-skeptical giraffe possibility in at least one respect: in the painted mule possibility and the brain in a vat possibility, as well as in the actual world, Marion believes that there is a zebra before him. But that is not the case in the giraffe possibility. Why isn't this respect of similarity between the actual situation and the skeptical possibilities significant enough to make it the case that the skeptical scenarios are more similar to actuality than the giraffe scenario? I don't see how one can answer this question without appealing to what is required for Marion to know that there is a zebra before him.[22] (A similar point was reached in the previous chapter in discussing problems for accounts of action that invoked certain counterfactual possibilities concerning the way in which the agent would have acted.)

There is one further invariantist building-block view that I would like to consider and critique, viz. subject-sensitive invariantism. But, because subject-sensitive invariantism is, in some ways, built upon (yet divergent from) contextualist approaches, it will be easier to discuss this view after we have taken up contextualist views. We can already see, however, that many invariantist views that rely on a distinction between relevant and irrelevant alternatives invoke the notion of knowledge itself in their accounts of knowing. They say, in effect,

> S knows that p in part in virtue of the fact that S is able to rule out those alternatives to p that S needs to rule out in order to know that p.

These accounts that invoke relevant alternatives, just like Goldman's original causal theory and just like my toy example that appeals to being justified in the right way, all say, in effect, that S knows because S does what S needs

---

[22] More needs to be said here, of course, about just why, in this situation, an account of similarity that does not appeal to what is required for Marion to know is not available, but it is worth noting that Lewis, the great deployer of the notion of similarity among possible worlds, in effect reaches a similar conclusion concerning similarity in his contextualist account, as we will see shortly.

to do in order to know. Such an account clearly does not meet the explanatory demand. It amounts to what I have called a John Wayne moment in philosophy.

So things do not look good for invariantist building-block theories of knowledge in general. Do contextualist building-block accounts meet with more success? Most such views—like many of their invariantist counterparts—rely on some form of the distinction between relevant and irrelevant alternatives. One knows just in case one rules out the contextually relevant alternatives. Such a view can in a way be friendly to skepticism because it allows that in some contexts skeptical possibilities are relevant and that, therefore, it is true to say in those contexts that we don't have knowledge. But in other, more ordinary contexts, only some alternatives are relevant and other alternatives may, to use David Lewis' terminology, be "properly ignored." We may in these contexts truly say that we (or others) have knowledge.

The problem for the contextualist—at least the problem that I want to focus on—is that the distinction between relevant and irrelevant alternatives is characterized in a way that presupposes knowledge. Thus, as we saw already, DeRose characterizes relevance for relevant alternatives theorists in general in terms of knowledge ("Solving the Skeptical Puzzle," p. 8n11). Later in the same wonderful paper, DeRose specifies what it takes to "count as knowing" (p. 36) according to his own contextualist account:

> Context... determines how strong an epistemic position one must be in to count as knowing. Picture this requirement as a contextually determined sphere of possible worlds, centered on the actual world, within which a subject's belief as to whether P is true must match the fact of the matter in order for the subject to count as knowing. (p. 36)

Similarly, in an influential early contextualist paper, Stewart Cohen says:

> We need to say more about the criteria of relevance. Whether S knows q will depend on whether any alternatives to q are relevant—whether the conditions are such that S's epistemic position with respect to any alternatives precludes knowledge of q. Thus the criteria of relevance should reflect our intuitions concerning under what conditions S does know q. (Cohen, "How to Be a Fallibilist," pp. 101–02)

In these passages, DeRose and Cohen explicitly characterize relevance in terms of knowledge.

Similarly, in a seminal contextualist paper, Gail Stine suggests that a certain alternative is irrelevant because, if it were relevant, we would be prevented from giving a certain answer to the skeptic:

> To allow it [a certain alternative] as relevant seems to me to preclude the kind of answer to the skeptic which I sketched in the opening paragraph of this section. (Stine, "Skepticism, Relevant Alternatives, and Deductive Closure," p. 253)

Here, the relevance or irrelevance of an alternative seems to be a function of what we know or don't know.

Finally, Lewis, in a classic paper that DeRose labels "a prominent contextualist manifesto" (DeRose, *The Case for Contextualism*, p. 29), explicitly says that his "Rule of Resemblance" by which he determines which alternatives are relevant is ad hoc (or, more precisely, has an ad hoc exception), and he does not know how to fix this situation. This is because, as he recognizes, there is no way to characterize the resemblance that is relevant to knowledge other than in terms of knowledge itself. For Lewis, what it is to know p is to eliminate all possibilities in which p is false that must be eliminated in order to secure knowledge of p. This is the account that, Lewis says, must be given in order to avoid "capitulation to skepticism," and it "makes good sense in view of the function of attributions of knowledge (Lewis, "Elusive Knowledge," p. 430). Lewis laments the ad hoc nature of his account: "What would be better, though, would be to find a way to reformulate the Rule so as to get the needed exception without the *ad hoc*ery. I do not know how to do this" (p. 430). But apparently he does not lament the *ad hoc*ery enough to reject this account and try some other approach.[23]

A contextualist's appeal to nearness of possible worlds to the actual world and to the similarity of possible worlds to the actual world is similarly ad hoc. A defender of contextualism might say that the skeptical scenarios describe possible worlds that are less similar to the actual world than are non-skeptical alternatives, and thus, because of this similarity, the former alternatives are

---

[23] For some more detailed criticism of the ad hoc-ness of Lewis' account, see Vogel, "The New Relevant Alternatives Theory."

irrelevant and the latter relevant. But, as I said before, it's not at all clear that these claims about similarity and closeness are true, and I suspect that one cannot justify such claims independently of appealing to what is required for knowledge of *p*. Indeed, this point is precisely what Lewis' lament about his ad hoc exception amounts to.

Jonathan Schaffer offers a distinctive form of contextualism called "constrastivism" which, despite its virtues, also offers no non-circular way to characterize the alternatives that are relevant in a given situation. For Schaffer, as for standard contextualists, the truth of simple knowledge ascriptions of the form "S knows that *p*" depends on context. But for contrastivism, the mechanism of the context dependence is different from the mechanism at work in standard epistemic contextualist theories. For the latter theories, the truth of knowledge ascriptions is, as I mentioned, often regarded as a function of the indexical nature of terms such as "knows" which are indexed to specific epistemic standards by contextual features. By contrast (!), for a contrastivist the context-dependence of "S knows that *p*" is a function of an implicit contrast condition which is supplied by context. Context thus determines that the content of the attribution is really something like "S knows that *p* rather than *q*," e.g., "Marion knows that there is a zebra before him rather than a mule." So the mechanism of the context-dependence of the truth of knowledge attributions is different from the mechanism in standard contextualism, but there is still context-dependence and thus contrastivism counts as a form of contextualism.

Given this context-dependence, the truth of "S knows that *p*" depends on S being able to rule out certain possibilities that contrast with *p*, but does not require that one be able to rule out other such possibilities. What makes a possibility one that S needs to rule out in order to know *p*? That is, what makes a contrasting possibility one that S needs to rule out? Schaffer claims that, unlike Lewis's way, his own way of handling the difference between relevant and irrelevant alternatives is not ad hoc. Perhaps, then, Schaffer may avoid the dreaded circularity that other contextualist views face. But this is not the case: for Schaffer specifies which alternatives need to be addressed by appealing to "the role of knowledge in inquiry" ("Contrastive Knowledge," p. 267). Here Schaffer says, in effect, that to know *p*, one need not rule out the painted mule possibility because needing to do so would conflict with the way we employ knowledge. For Schaffer, it is "unnatural and unaccommodating" to invoke certain possibilities in certain contexts (p. 263) because doing so would undermine our knowledge and be incompatible with the role of knowledge in inquiry. Here again, we have the same kind of circularity that besets other contextualist views.

All these contextualist views rely upon a notion of relevance of alternatives that—as these views sometimes acknowledge—cannot be characterized other than in terms of knowledge. This result shows that these accounts of knowledge amount to something like this:

> In a given context of attribution, S knows that p in part in virtue of the fact that S is able to rule out those alternatives to p that S needs in that context to rule out in order for S to know that p.

In other words, in a given context of attribution, S knows because S does what she needs to do in order to know. That is, S knows because S knows. And all I can say in response is: well, sure, but such an account is hardly illuminating. We have again the failure to meet the explanatory demand. We have again a John Wayne moment in philosophy.

In light of this discussion of contextualist views, we can turn to a remaining invariantist view which can best be understood in terms of its contrast with contextualism (indeed this invariantist view appeared on the scene in the aftermath of contextualist accounts of knowledge). Stanley who defends this form of invariantism—subject-sensitive invariantism—attempts to meet the explanatory demand with regard to knowledge by specifying that a true belief is a case of knowledge in virtue of facts concerning the practical interests of the putative knower.[24] On this view, whether an individual knows does not vary with standards at play in the context of attribution: the same standards for knowledge are in play regardless of changes in such contexts. (Hence this view is invariantist.) However, among the facts that do affect whether an individual knows is the individual's own practical situation, the practical importance of the matter that is a candidate to be known. Thus, on this view, one individual can know p and another can fail to know p simply because of a difference in their practical situations. Whether it's true to say that an individual knows varies with the situation of the subject (hence the "subject-sensitive" in "subject-sensitive invariantism") and not with the context of attribution (as in contextualism). It is the subject's practical interests that enable us to identify certain alternatives as alternatives that may not properly be

---

[24] See Hawthorne, *Knowledge and Lotteries*, chapter 4, and Fantl and McGrath, "Evidence, Pragmatics, and Justification," for other subtle treatments of subject-sensitive invariantism.

ignored and that must be ruled out. Other possibilities lie outside the sphere of the individual's practical concerns, and the ignoring of them by the subject does not undermine her knowledge. As Stanley puts it, "Given that we are not ideal rational agents, there will be a range of alternatives that it will be legitimate to ignore" (*Knowledge and Practical Interests*, p. 92).

The question that naturally arises at this point is: which alternatives exactly is it proper (for the subject) to ignore? Stanley makes clear that for him skeptical scenarios—like the brain in a vat and painted mule cases—"are not serious practical questions . . . " (*Knowledge and Practical Interests*, p. 125) and may be properly ignored. But why may they be properly ignored? For Stanley, such scenarios are put on the may-be-ignored list because if it were not legitimate to ignore these possibilities, then—because the scenarios cannot be ruled out (they are skeptical scenarios, after all, and are designed to be difficult or impossible to rule out)—we would be led into skepticism. This line of thought is implicit in the passage just quoted (from p. 92) about our not being ideal rational agents. Also, this invocation of the need to avoid skepticism as providing a basis for the line between relevant and irrelevant alternatives emerges from Stanley's reliance on Lewis' notion of what alternatives may properly be ignored. As we have seen, Lewis, explicitly specifies that in order to avoid "capitulation to skepticism" ("Elusive Knowledge," p. 430), certain alternatives must be deemed irrelevant. Lewis makes this point in connection with his contextualist theory of knowledge. Stanley adopts this point and incorporates it in his own, invariantist account:

> Since Lewis is a contextualist, he interprets proper ignoring in contextualist terms; it is a matter of the possibilities properly ignored by the knowledge attributor. But insofar as the interest-relative invariantist is attracted to Lewis's response to skepticism, she can appropriate the resources he has developed. For example, she can construe Lewis's notion of *proper ignoring* in terms of what the subject of the knowledge attribution may properly ignore, rather than the attributor. (*Knowledge and Practical Interests*, p. 130)

The upshot is that, for Stanley (as for Lewis), whether it's true to say that one knows depends on whether one has ruled out the alternatives that one needs to rule out in order to avoid skepticism and have knowledge.[25] Such

---

[25] Cf. Fantl and McGrath, "Evidence, Pragmatics, and Justification": "A subject is justified in believing something just in case she has evidence that is good enough for her to know," p. 88.

an account is problematically circular in just the way that the other accounts we have examined so far are. We have another John Wayne moment in philosophy.

Of course, one general strategy—open, perhaps, to contextualists and non-contextualists alike—for drawing the line between relevant and irrelevant alternatives would be to appeal simply to our intuitions about what possibilities are relevant to knowledge and need to be ruled out in order to know. However, it's hard to see how the appeal to intuitions *about knowledge* wouldn't embroil us in the kind of circularity that I have been inveighing against. But, bracketing that worry, I would also direct the reader to the general reasons I develop in chapter 7 and, especially, 11 against the reliance on such intuitions in philosophy.[26]

A Knowledge-First Account

This critical survey of a good sample of building-block views of knowledge amounts, I believe, to a strong inductive case against such building-block views as failing to meet the explanatory demand. I haven't (yet) shown that all building-block views *must* fail to meet the explanatory demand because of such problems with circularity (or regresses), but one can suspect on inductive grounds that there is an underlying problem that makes such failures inevitable for building-block views of knowledge.[27] I will later give a more or less *a priori* argument for just this conclusion, but at this point, given the poor track record of building-block views, we may, in an effort to meet the explanatory demand, be led to take seriously alternatives to a building-block approach to knowledge. Perhaps the most prominent such alternative is Williamson's knowledge-first approach.

A knowledge-first strategy characterizes a possible family of views all of which place knowledge first in a sense that I will specify. Williamson's own view is, in principle, only an example of such a view. Nonetheless, I will, for the most part focus on Williamson's version of a knowledge-first view.

---

[26] I am indebted here to David Kovacs.

[27] Others note—for reasons different from mine—that there is an inductive case against building-block views of knowledge. See Williamson pp. 30, 63, 91. And see Cassam who quotes Willamson while making a similar point, "Given that attempts to analyse the concept of knowledge have succumbed to a 'pattern of counterexamples epicycles'..., it is not unreasonable to conclude that all such attempts suffer from a common underlying defect" (Cassam, "Can the Concept of Knowledge be Analysed?," p. 21).

As I noted at the outset of this chapter, Williamson, like most or all other epistemologists, seeks to meet the explanatory demand. He seeks to give some kind of account of knowledge which at least illuminates the notion of knowledge and enables us to distinguish knowledge from ignorance and from non-knowledge generally. But the way in which Williamson endeavors to meet the explanatory demand exhibits considerable—dare I say, true—grit: it undertakes a reversal of the procedure found in building-block approaches. Instead of understanding knowledge in terms of other epistemic notions such as belief and justification, we are, for Williamson, to understand other epistemic notions in terms of knowledge. The idea is that, in so doing, we illuminate knowledge itself even while treating knowledge as a primitive. In Williamson's version, this illumination comes in the form of a characterization of knowledge as the most general factive, or truth-entailing, mental state. This account is explicitly not an analysis (p. 36). For Williamson, the notion of knowledge is prior to the notion of a factive mental state or at least the notion of a factive mental state is best understood in terms of knowledge (see p. 39 where, as I will discuss presently, the notion of a factive mental state operator [FMSO] is understood in terms of knowledge.) But we can see how knowledge is connected to other mental states, and thus we shed light on knowledge. Not only is knowledge characterized as the most general factive mental state, but there is also the illuminating outline of structural connections or the lack of structural connections with other notions. Among such connections or non-connections are the denial of the KK principle, the denial of luminosity, and the claim that one's evidence is identical to one's knowledge. What is important, for Williamson, is that these connections somehow follow from the nature of knowledge. Thus, for Williamson, much light can be shed on knowledge once we give up the analytic project and begin our account with knowledge treated as basic.

How successful is Williamson at meeting the explanatory demand? Let's look more closely at what he takes to be the factors that, apparently, illuminate knowledge, and let's focus first on the connection between knowledge and being the most general factive mental state. Williamson recognizes that, in the end, this way of meeting the explanatory demand is circular. For him, being a factive mental state is best understood in a way that is not independent of knowledge itself. If being a factive mental state could be understood independently of knowledge, then Williamson's characterization would not only be illuminating but would also threaten to be an analysis of knowledge after all, an outcome Williamson would not welcome. So it must be the case that, for Williamson, the notion of a factive mental state is best understood through the notion of knowledge itself. Williamson indicates as much when he summarizes what it is for an operator to be a factive mental state operator (FMSO). He offers "three principles":

(18) If Phi is an FMSO, from 'S Phi's that A' one may infer 'A'.
(19) 'Know' is an FMSO.
(20) If Phi is an FMSO, from 'S phi's that A' one may infer 'S knows that A'.
(p. 39; Williamson's numbering)

Here Williamson indicates that being a factive mental state is to be understood in part in terms of the notion of knowledge. He makes a similar claim when he says,

> If we could isolate a core of states which constituted 'pure mind' by being mental in some more thoroughgoing way than knowing is, then the term 'mental' might be extended to knowing as a mere courtesy title. On the conception defended here, there is no such core of mental states exclusive of knowing. (p. 6)

For Williamson, knowledge is a core state in terms of which we can best understand the notion of the mental.

In this light, we can see that Williamson's characterization is ultimately circular: the notion of knowledge is illuminated through—explained in terms of—its connection to the notion of being a factive mental state, but this notion in turn is illuminated through the notion of knowledge. How is this roundabout performance illuminating? In the end, this seems to be just another John Wayne moment in epistemology. Knowledge has gotta be what knowledge has gotta be.

Similarly, the other purportedly illuminating connections Williamson draws between knowledge and other structural epistemic features, such as the denial of the KK principle and the identification of evidence and knowledge, also presuppose or are understood through the notion of knowledge itself. So once again we are faced with a circle of dubious value as far as illumination is concerned.

Here's another way to make what is essentially the same point. Although for Williamson knowledge is a primitive notion and has no analysis, he nonetheless claims to be able to draw connections between the nature of knowledge and features such as being a general factive mental state, etc. Since knowledge is thus primitive, how can we find the hooks in it, as it were, which enable us to make these connections between the nature of knowledge and these other features? The question we must ask—and that Williamson does not and cannot answer—is this: *how* is it that these purportedly illuminating connections hold? Without specifying this "how"—this er πῶς—we do not have an informative account of knowledge. All we know—or apparently know—is that the nature of knowledge *somehow* dictates that knowledge is the most general factive mental state and *somehow* dictates that knowledge has the other structural connections Williamson outlines. But without insight into these "how's," no genuine advance in understanding knowledge has been achieved.

One might think that this charge of emptiness is unfair to Williamson. After all, Williamson is merely attempting to shed light on knowledge through the explanatory role it plays or can play. This approach, one might say, is a specific version of a perfectly legitimate attempt to clarify a phenomenon by outlining its theoretical role or connection to other phenomena, something we do, e.g., whenever we Ramsify in our theory building.[28] Thus, in a functionalist philosophy of mind, for example, we might elucidate belief as that mental state which, together with certain desires and other beliefs, leads to certain actions. And we might understand desires as those mental states that, together with beliefs and other desires, lead to action, etc. Here belief is understood in terms of its connection to desire which is understood in terms of belief. Yes, one might argue, this account of belief may be circular at some level, but it's still illuminating as long as the circle is large enough. Similarly, one might say, knowledge, on Williamson's view, is understood in terms of its connection to (in particular, its priority over) belief and justification (etc.) which are understood in terms of knowledge. In this case too, there is circularity, but the circularity is OK, and there is illumination as long as the circle is large enough.

However, I think that in each of these cases the circularity is problematic and, indeed, undermining of any genuine illumination.[29] In the belief case, if we are in the dark as to what belief is and if we seek illumination, then being told that belief is understood in terms of desire which is understood in terms of belief is not going to help us with our illumination deficit.

---

[28] See Lewis, "How to Define Theoretical Terms."
[29] Yes, I'm doubling down.

How can we make use of these connections for the purpose of illuminating belief if these connections can, in the end, be understood only in terms of the very notion—viz. belief—that we are trying to illuminate? Similarly, in the case of Williamson's appeal to the theoretical role that knowledge plays in an economy of other notions: if the connections to other phenomena—such as justification, luminosity, etc.—can, in the end, be understood only in terms of knowledge itself, then how can these alleged connections relieve us of our illumination deficit when it comes to knowledge? We gain illumination here only if we already understand what knowledge is, but, of course, we do not already understand what knowledge is—otherwise why would we be embarked on this inquiry at all?

Drawing out the dialectic further than Williamson does in this context, you might say in response to me that we do indeed already have some understanding of what knowledge is—at least a rudimentary or preliminary understanding—and that is why, building on this initial understanding, we can invoke the connection between knowledge and other notions, such as justification and luminosity, etc., in order to achieve even greater insight into knowledge (even if not a full-blown definition of knowledge). (Obviously, the analogous dialectic with regard to the philosophy of substance and of action in the previous chapters could be elaborated in similar fashion.)

And, continuing the dialectic even further, I respond: sure, but what does this initial, rudimentary understanding of what knowledge consist in? If we appeal here again to the connection between knowledge and such notions as justification and luminosity, then we are clearly going in a circle: we understand what knowledge is rudimentarily because we appreciate the connections between knowledge and notions such as justification and luminosity. And we are then able to build on this understanding of knowledge in order to achieve the further insight that knowledge is connected to notions such as justification and luminosity. It's hard to see how this performance can be anything other than viciously circular.

Perhaps we can appeal to some other known fact about knowledge—besides the fact that knowledge is connected to such notions as justification and luminosity. But the question would then be: in virtue of what do we come to know these other facts? Perhaps in order to explain how we come to know these other facts, we can appeal to yet further known facts about knowledge. But how would these yet further facts be known? It's clear that we have merely pushed the problem back one step and that an infinite regress looms.

KNOWLEDGE 137

The only alternative at this point seems to be that we just do—brutely—have a rudimentary grasp of knowledge on which we can build. But if one is willing to settle for a kind of brute understanding of knowledge, then why do we need any explanation or illumination of knowledge at all? Why don't we just give up the explanatory or illuminative demand altogether? An appeal to brute knowledge thus seems in tension with accepting the explanatory or illuminative demand when it comes to knowledge.

Thus, given the acceptance of the explanatory or illuminative demand, appealing to this rudimentary grasp is unacceptable—either because of the circularity or regress at work or because this rudimentary grasp would be brute. Notice that we are, in effect, invoking again a version of the Agrippan Trilemma: when we try to explain knowledge, we wind up in a circle or in a regress, or we dogmatically appeal to a primitive. It appears then that Williamson has no good way to meet the explanatory or illuminative demand on which he insists.

What Williamson offers here is what I have called a dormitive virtue response to the explanatory or illuminative demand. A dormitive virtue explanation is unilluminating because it purports to shed light on the power of a thing simply by appealing to the nature of that thing. What's missing in such an explanation of, e.g., opium's power is a way of indicating *how* the opium has this power. Williamson's account is, obviously, much more sophisticated, as we can see from the complicated dialectic I have just been carrying out, but at bottom the purportedly illuminating step is one in which he seeks to shed light on knowledge through knowledge itself. Without spelling out, in independent terms, *how* it is that a given state gets to be a factive mental state (let alone the most general such state), we don't really have an understanding of what it is to be knowledge, just as without spelling out in independent terms *how* opium has the power to put one to sleep, we don't really have an explanation of why opium puts one to sleep. More generally, although there may be the connections Williamson alludes to, if all we know or think we know is *that* there are these connections without seeing, in independent terms, *how* they follow from the nature of knowledge, then we do not understand what knowledge is. We have no more insight into knowledge than Molière's characters have into the workings of opium.[30]

---

[30] In a similar way, Cassam criticizes Williamson's minimalism as leaving knowledge ultimately unexplained ("Can the Concept of Knowledge be Analysed?," p. 30).

So not only is Williamson's account—because of its circularity—yet another disappointing John Wayne moment and a failure to meet the explanatory or illuminative demand, it is also—because it rests on a brute appeal to the nature of knowledge as acting or being a certain way we know not how—an unilluminating Molière moment in philosophy.[31]

Finally, let me return to the kind of objection I raised in chapter 4 to the Molière charge. There, in connection with Anscombian and self-constitutionalist accounts of action, I considered the thought that while little circles might be bad, big circles can be illuminating. My response is the same as before. In this context in which we are trying to meet an explanatory or illuminative demand, a circle is bad no matter how big. Further, far from being better than small circles, big circles are, in one respect at least, positively *worse*. Again, in a headlong rush to save a drowning concept, other concepts have futilely jumped in only to suffer the same watery fate. As in the previous chapter where this fate met the group of notions that the self-constitutionalist with regard to action invokes, the same fate now befalls the suite of notions connected to knowledge that Williamson seeks to shed light on. The same fate also undermines, I would argue, circular attempts to understand belief and desire and action in terms of one another. And thus so much the worse also for typical functionalist accounts in the philosophy of mind.[32]

A More or Less A Priori Argument

The knowledge-first and building-block approaches are—for all their differences—in the same boat: each of them (or the examples of these approaches that we have examined), though in different ways, fails to meet the explanatory demand that drives contemporary epistemology. And because these views insist on a demand which they themselves do not meet, these views also suffer from a kind of internal incoherence. For these theories,

---

[31] In the same way, I would respond to Samuel Elgin's important suggestion—not Williamson's—that knowledge, though it lacks a full analysis, has a partial analysis (say, in terms of justification, truth, and belief). See Elgin, "Merely Partial Definition and the Analysis of Knowledge." Issues of unacceptable circularity arise here if the notion of justification can be understood only in terms of knowledge. Further, given that knowledge has no full analysis, it's not clear that we can be confident that the nature of knowledge as a whole dictates that knowledge requires justification. As before, we need to see not only *that* this connection holds but also *how* it holds. But, given the lack of a full analysis, this connection remains opaque. Once again, the account seems not to provide the insight that we seek and seems not to meet the explanatory demand.

[32] I'm doubling down again. Perhaps then I'm quadrupling down.

there is no illuminating account of knowledge, and, ultimately or even *ab initio*, what knowledge has gotta be just is what knowledge has gotta be. The Duke would be proud.

In the same way that there was an inductive case against most ordinary theories of substance and of action, there is thus an inductive case now not only against building-block views of knowledge, but also against knowledge-first views. Thus, we see the failure of most ordinary theories of knowledge. But, as I've mentioned, there could be, for all I've said so far, building-block or knowledge-first views—other than the ones I've discussed—that do meet the explanatory demand. So it's not clear that this kind of problem is inevitable. Further, and more importantly, it's not clear what the mechanism of the problem that building-block and knowledge-first views face is, what the source of this problem is. I would like to outline now a more or less *a priori* argument, analogous to the *a priori* arguments about substance and action in the previous two chapters, that simultaneously addresses both of the issues I just raised. First, the argument shows that building-block views and knowledge-first views in general—and indeed any view that, like these, makes a certain seemingly innocent assumption—inevitably fail to meet the explanatory demand. Given that ordinary views, as we have seen, insist on the explanatory demand, this failure—this inevitable failure—is damning indeed. Second, this more or less *a priori* argument has the virtue of isolating the common culprit behind the failures of building-block and knowledge-first views. Appropriately enough—since all the views which I am about to undermine trade on the explanatory demand—my argument, as before, will turn on the notion of explanation.

By making the explanatory demand or by insisting that knowledge be illuminated, epistemologists tend to search for what might be called the knowledge-making relation. They ask, in effect, what is the relation between the state that is in fact a state of knowledge—call the state "K"—and some item or items that make K a state of knowledge. Different theories of knowledge have different proposals as to what the knowledge-making relation is. On many accounts, the relevant relation is a relation between K and other items such as other states that make it the case that the knower's beliefs are justified in the right way or, more generally, connected to the truth in the right way. (This would be the approach of building-block theories of knowledge.) Or, the relation may be a relation between K and a certain nature—K's own nature—which is that in virtue of which K is a state of knowledge. In this case, the relation would be a kind of internal relation. (This would be the approach of knowledge-first theories.) More simply and more generally, the relevant relation may be a relation of distinction between K and states of non-knowledge, and the epistemological work in this vein seeks to shed light on what differentiates K from states of non-knowledge in general.

In this light, we can see that most accounts of knowledge proceed upon the seemingly harmless presupposition that what it is for something to be a state of knowledge requires a distinction—a relation—between the state of knowledge, K, and some items. The epistemologist thus tends to presuppose that we are trying to understand what it is to be a *differentiated* state of knowledge, a state of knowledge that somehow stands in relations. This focus on differentiated or relational knowledge is, of course, crucial.

Here, then, is my *a priori* argument concerning knowledge, the structure of which should, by now, be familiar. In identifying the knowledge-making relation, R, there are four exhaustive and mutually exclusive options, options that mirror the options in the previous two chapters concerning the substance-making relation and the action-making relation:

(1) R is primitive. That is, the relation, R, between K and some items is not grounded in or explained by anything. There is nothing in virtue of which K stands in R to these items.
(2) R is not primitive, but is, rather, ultimately grounded in or explained by or ultimately holds, at least in part, in virtue of a relation to something other than K.
(3) R is not primitive, but is, rather, ultimately fully grounded in or explained by or ultimately holds in virtue of the nature of K alone. That is, it follows from the nature of K alone that K is a state of knowledge. R is thus, in one sense of the term, an internal relation, a relation that stems simply from the nature of a thing.
(4) R is not primitive, but also is not ultimately grounded (as in (2) and (3)); instead, R is grounded in other items in a non-terminating regress or in a circle with a multiplicity of items.

As before, option (1) is not really an option given the explanatory demand with regard to knowledge, a version of which is accepted by all parties to the debate over knowledge. Option (2), which concerns external relations, is represented by proponents of a building-block approach to knowledge, such as Dretske, DeRose, Goldman, Stanley, etc. Option (3) is embraced by knowledge-first accounts such as Williamson's.

As with options (2), (3), and (4) in the case of substance and action, these options with regard to knowledge fail to provide a good account of the knowledge-making relation. Again, for the structure of the arguments against options (2), (3), and (4) consult chapter 3 where I spell out these wonderfully powerful arguments against these options in the case of substance. The arguments against options (2), (3), and (4) in the case of knowledge work in exactly the same way. And, as before, any attempt to resist my arguments in this chapter without a successful challenge to my Bradleyan arguments is powerless.

I note here that the demise of option (2) in the case of knowledge signals the demise of the project of analyzing knowledge and the demise of the building-block project in epistemology more generally. Thus, I agree with Williamson's conclusion that this project fails. However, Williamson's reasons for welcoming this demise are different from mine. Williamson's argument, as we've seen, is largely an account of what he sees as the theoretical advantages of adopting his knowledge-first approach which rejects such an analysis.[33] By contrast, my reasons for ushering the building-block project out the door do not stem from any purported advantages of Williamson's knowledge-first approach. Indeed, as I've argued for the case of Williamson's approach, and as I'm arguing for the case of knowledge-first views in general, I deny that there are any such advantages of the knowledge-first account at least insofar as satisfying the explanatory aim is concerned.

And with regard to option (3), the challenge facing Williamson's view is to spell out the knowledge-making relation by specifying *how* it is that a certain mental state is a factive mental state. Williamson acknowledges the need to spell out how R is grounded in K: "Of course, something needs to be said about the nature and significance of this matching [between mind and world]" (p. 40). However, to unpack this "how," we need to specify another relation—R*—in virtue of which R is grounded in K alone. But since R* is now the knowledge-making relation, we are led to ask the same Bradleyan question—"What is R* grounded in?"—and we face the same Bradleyan challenges as before. Turning once again to the specific content of Williamson's view, we can see that Williamson fails to meet the Bradleyan challenge by failing to explain how K is a general factive mental state. Williamson leaves it a mystery how K is state of knowledge.[34]

---

[33] See Ichikawa and Steup, "The Analysis of Knowledge," section 11.

[34] In the same way, I would argue that Anscombe's view of action and the self-constitutionalist's view of action leave it a mystery how an action is an action. And, in the same way, I would argue that Lockean or Aristotelian or Leibnizian views of substance leave it a mystery how a substance is a substance.

142 THE PARMENIDEAN ASCENT

This Bradleyan argument which eliminates options (1)–(4) is a more or less *a priori* argument for the negative result that our survey of leading theories of knowledge had given us inductive reason to suspect was the case.

Ascent

The problem that we are now facing has arisen only on the presupposition, shared by Williamson, Goldman, DeRose, Stanley, and all or most other epistemologists, that states of knowledge stand in relations. In other words, the difficulty arises on the assumption that the knowledge we are trying (and failing) to understand is differentiated knowledge, i.e. a state of knowledge that is distinct from cases of non-knowledge or distinct from items such as justifications or mere beliefs or causes of states of knowledge, or, again, a state of knowledge that stands in an internal relation to its own nature. It is only on such a presupposition that we faced the exhaustive options (1)–(4) for dealing with the knowledge-making relation, options each of which is unacceptable. Indeed, I contend that it is the alleged relationality of knowledge that is the culprit responsible for the problems of circularity and regress to which each of the leading theories of knowledge have fallen prey.

But if, for this reason, we get rid of the problematic assumption that there are states of knowledge that stand in relations, that is, the assumption that there is relational knowledge, then we no longer face these problems. For these problems arise only on the assumption of the relationality of knowledge. For the proponent of non-relational, undifferentiated knowledge, although there are no states of knowledge as distinct from other states of knowledge or as related to things, there may simply be knowledge. Just as we saw with regard to substance and action, if there is to be knowledge at all, it cannot occupy a place differentiated from and related to things: we cannot intelligibly place knowledge *within* reality in a place differentiated from other places. Thus, if there is to be knowledge at all, then, as we might put it, all is knowledge. The reality that epistemologists have been trying—unsuccessfully— to capture with their building-block theories and knowledge-first theories which appeal to relational, differentiated knowledge is better captured by a view that rejects relations (even internal relations) between states of knowledge and things. This is a move that I am calling a Parmenidean Ascent: a rejection of a certain kind of distinction and, by transcending this distinction, an attempt to capture the reality that was only imperfectly expressed by appealing to such a distinction.

This view, according to which there is simply knowledge, there is simply relationless, structureless knowledge, can be seen as a monism of knowledge, a version of monism that would be much more extreme than either priority monism or even existence monism, in the sense outlined by Schaffer. (See my earlier discussions of priority monism and existence monism.) Also, I would prefer the view that all is knowledge to the view that all is non-knowledge for reasons analogous to the reasons I gave in chapter 3 for preferring the view that all is being to the view that all is non-being.

Actually, I'm a bit reluctant to call this view a kind of monism of knowledge at all, because it may be that to number a thing as *one* (as monism seems to do) presupposes that that thing stands in relations. It may be that there cannot be one thing without there being some kind of relation involving that thing. Thus, because this thing that is knowledge is non-relational—as I have just argued—it may not be proper to call it "one" (or—as I just tried to do—to refer to it as "this thing"). And so monism may not be the correct label for my view after all. But regardless of this worry concerning one and relationality, the view I have offered is like a monism of knowledge in that it affirms that there is knowledge while denying that there is differentiated knowledge. There is thus simply pure, relationless, structureless knowledge. Here, as in the case of "being and "action," the term "knowledge" may, in some way, be best seen as a mass noun.

As before, I am happy to appeal to Aquinas in order to get a handle on this extreme and extremely counterintuitive view. I have already argued that reality itself—not a transcendent God—is simply being and simply action, just as for Aquinas, God is subsistent being itself and *actus purus*. In this chapter, I have argued that reality is also simply knowing. In the same way, Aquinas argues that God is knowing itself. Thus, Aquinas says that God's "act of understanding is his essence [*suum intelligere sit sua essentia*]" (Aquinas, *Summa Contra Gentiles* I 45).[35] The simplicity of being, act, and knowing that Aquinas accords to God, I accord to reality itself.

---

[35] See also, Aquinas, *Summa Theologiae* 1.14.4,"When God is said to be understanding [*Deus dicitur intelligens*], no kind of multiplicity is attached to his substance." See Kenny, *Aquinas on Being*, p. 145.

In making this sort-of Thomistic move with regard to knowledge, the extreme skepticism of my view is, again, apparent. This is a skepticism about knowledge, but it is nothing so tame as a skepticism about whether we have knowledge. Rather, the skepticism here is a denial of the coherence of our ordinary conceptions of knowledge. The skeptical challenge I'm raising is that we cannot coherently conceive of the differentiated states of knowledge and differentiated knowers to which we are ordinarily deeply committed. There is, instead, simply knowledge.

6
Meaning

The drill should be familiar by now. I start by showing that the philosophical investigation of a key phenomenon is driven by an explanatory demand: what is it in virtue of which instances of this phenomenon are instances of this phenomenon? Then—in order to show that I'm not making this up—I support my claim about the prevalence of the explanatory demand with regard to this phenomenon by highlighting some pithy and telling quotes from leading theorists. I then show that representative theories in this field all fail to meet—perhaps inevitably fail to meet—this explanatory demand which they impose on themselves or at least to which they are committed. Finally, after we are shaken by the ubiquity of this failure, I try to seal the case against leading theories by trotting out my sort-of Bradleyan, sort-of *a priori* argument that shows that all theories in this domain must fail to meet the explanatory demand. From these bracing skeptical depths, I encourage us to ascend to Parmenidean heights and, in doing so, to embrace an undifferentiated, no-relations version of the phenomenon in question. We have gone through this drill in the cases of substance, action, and knowledge. Actually, however, this hasn't been a drill, for in both the destructive and positive phases of my argument, quite literally our very being—as differentiated things—is at stake, our very status as agents and knowers is at stake. From this point of view, we can see that nothing can be more consequential than these "drills," nothing can have more significance or meaning. And, given this significance of our approach so far, can a similar treatment of the notion of significance or the notion of meaning itself be far behind? Indeed, it is not far behind, for it is upon us at this very moment with the latest Parmenidean Ascent that I now embark on. And so—like the good not-really-a drill sergeant that I am—I ask in virtue of what does an expression, sentence, thought, or text mean what it does or is about or signifies what it is about or signifies? And in virtue of what are such meaningful items distinct from other items (such as, perhaps, a rock) that may lack meaning or aboutness of the kind that expressions, sentences, thoughts, and texts enjoy?

As this formulation indicates, I express this explanatory demand with regard to meaning or aboutness in the most general terms. This generality is intended.[1] I seek an account of what it is for representation or aboutness or meaning to be present in general or at all. Some of the philosophers I will discuss express an interest in the apparently narrower question of what it is in virtue of which linguistic items—words, sentences, texts, or speakers' uses of such items—mean what they do. But other philosophers take up the question in full generality. In any event, despite the particular focus they may have, leading theorists in this area are committed to addressing the more general question about representation or aboutness or meaning as well as the specific, narrower question—which is of the same form—concerning, for example, linguistic meaning. If the particular question is legitimate, then it's hard to see how the general question wouldn't be as well.

The Explanatory Demand with Regard to Meaning

As promised, here are some examples of leading theorists expressing one form or another of the explanatory demand with regard to meaning or aboutness. Thus, Paul Horwich expresses such an explanatory demand when he asks:

> What is meaning? Why are some sounds imbued with it and others not? How, for example, does it come about that the word "dog" means precisely what it does? How is it possible for those intrinsically inert ink-marks (or some associated state of the brain) to reach out into the world and latch on to a definite portion of reality: namely, the dogs? (*Meaning*, p. 1).

He later says that the

> primary purpose [of his own theory] is to specify the underlying non-semantic properties of expressions in virtue of which they possess their particular meanings. (p. 52)

---

[1] Pun intended.
    [note on this note: Pun intended.]
    [note on this note on this note: Pun intended.] . . .

These expressions of the explanatory demand specifically concern linguistic meaning, but, as Horwich makes clear (pp. 4, 44, 94), the notion of meaning he operates with—and presumably for which the explanatory demand is relevant—is more general than merely linguistic meaning. He stresses that the meanings he is interested in are to be identified with concepts which he takes "to be abstract objects of belief, desire, etc., and components of such objects (i.e. propositions and their constituents)" (p. 4).

Jeff Speaks articulates the explanatory demand well when he says:

> foundational theories of meaning . . . are attempts to specify the facts in virtue of which expressions of natural languages come to have the semantic properties that they have. ("Theories of Meaning," section 3; see also section 1)

Michael Devitt and Kim Sterelny likewise say that a central problem in the study of language

> is to describe and explain these meanings: to say what they are and what makes it the case that something has one. (*Language and Reality*, p. 4)

They go on to say that one problem

> is to describe and explain the properties of symbols in virtue of which they play the central role they do in our lives; we call this the problem of explaining meaning. (p. 8)

Scott Soames expresses a version of the explanatory demand focused on representation in general:

> Surely, beliefs, assertions, hypotheses, and conjectures *are* representational. Hence, there should be an answer to the question of what makes them so. (*What Is Meaning?*, p. 64; emphasis in original)

To return to an explanatory demand focused on language, consider John Searle's pronouncement in the preface to his book, *Intentionality*: the capacity of sentences "to represent is not intrinsic but is derived from the Intentionality of the mind." Searle goes on to say that "the Intentionality of mental states, on the other hand, is not derived from some more prior forms of Intentionality but is intrinsic to the states themselves" (p. vii).

Finally and perhaps most simply, Donald Davidson begins his important volume, *Inquiries into Truth and Interpretation* with the question: "What is it for words to mean what they do?" (p. xiii). Given Davidson's views on the connection between linguistic meaning and the contents of thoughts, views according to which thoughts are by their nature expressible in language, in answering the question of what it is for words to mean what they do, he would also be answering the question of what it is for thoughts to mean or be about the things they mean or are about. That is, in addressing this in-virtue-of question concerning the meanings of words, Davidson can equally be seen as addressing the in-virtue-of question concerning the representationality of thoughts in general.

Failing to Meet the Explanatory Demand

In keeping with the predetermined path I must follow, I now endeavor to show that leading theories of meaning or representation do not meet the general versions of the explanatory demand in this domain. I will focus first on theories that seek to locate the source of the aboutness of an item such as a term, thought, or text—call it "T"—in something, other than T, that also exhibits meaning or aboutness. I will later move on to representatives of theories that locate the source of aboutness in other things that do not exhibit aboutness. In between, I will discuss views—those of Vincent Descombes and Horwich—that are more difficult to characterize along this spectrum.

I should stress that, as in previous chapters, I can't hope to cover in my survey all, or even most, important theories of meaning. But I do hope and believe that I engage with a sample of views that is fairly representative of the options that have been put forward often with wonderful ingenuity. And please don't be put out if I do not discuss your favorite view here. Just keep in mind that if you feel a gap in my survey, a gap that takes the shape of an important theory that I omit, there's no need to worry, for the *a priori* argument I outline later in this chapter will take care of any omitted theories.

I will begin with three accounts that seek to explain one kind of meaning in terms of the meanings of other items, i.e. in terms of other items that also exhibit meaning or aboutness.

Grice

Let's turn first to Paul Grice who isolates what he calls "non-natural" meaning which is the kind of meaning to be found in linguistic expressions (and is to be contrasted with natural meaning which we invoke when we say, e.g., "Smoke means fire"). Grice sets himself the task of "trying to give an explanation of" this non-natural meaning ("Meaning," p. 379) and characterizes himself as employing the notion of intention "to explicate the notion of meaning" ("Meaning Revisited," p. 283). More specifically, Grice seeks to account for the *linguistic meaning* of certain terms or expressions or sentences in terms of *speaker meaning*, i.e. what a speaker means in uttering the linguistic expression. Grice goes on to account for speaker meaning in terms of the speaker's intentions and beliefs. Here is how Speaks articulates the basic structure of this last stage of Grice's enormously influential account:

a means *p* by uttering *x* iff *a* intends in uttering *x* that
1. his audience comes to believe *p*,
2. his audience recognize this intention, and
3. (1) occur on the basis of (2). (Speaks, "Theories of Meaning," section 3.1.1)

For all the merits of this approach, it doesn't meet the explanatory demand with regard to meaning or aboutness in its full generality. It merely offers an account of linguistic meaning ultimately in terms of the content of—the aboutness of—mental states such as beliefs and intentions. And, of course, as Grice realizes (as we'll see momentarily), the question of how beliefs and intentions come to have the content they do is every bit as urgent as the question of how linguistic expressions come to have the meaning they do. From this point of view, Grice's account simply pushes the main problem one step back from the problem of explaining the meaning of linguistic items to the problem of explaining the meaning or aboutness or representational content of thoughts. Pushing the problem back in this way may represent progress of a kind, but only if an answer to the general explanatory question with regard to meaning or aboutness is on the horizon.

And, indeed, Grice's work on linguistic meaning may be able to be supplemented by an account of the content of mental states such as beliefs and intentions. With this supplementation we would then have the prospect of an answer to the explanatory demand in its full generality. Grice accounts for the content of mental states in broadly functionalist terms ("Method in Philosophical Psychology"). According to such an account, the content of a mental state is a function of the functional role that that state plays in an economy of mental states in the thinker's mental life. Thus, an intention of a certain kind can be seen as, by its nature, a state that typically has certain causes (including beliefs, desires, and other intentions) and effects (including intentional actions). A particular, token intention thus has the content it does in virtue of its having certain characteristic causes and effects. Similarly, a (token) belief has the content it does in virtue of its causal relations to other items, including causal relations to other mental states (such as desires, intentions, and other beliefs) and to actions.[2] This kind of functionalist account would be an instance of a kind of account of the meaning or aboutness of an item in terms of other items that also exhibit meaning or aboutness.

All of this is lovely (really), and this kind of research program has been very productive in a certain way, but I have a significant worry that I have already expressed in one form or another.

One way to express the worry about this kind of research program is via my critique (at the end of the section "A Knowledge-First Account" of chapter 5) of functionalist accounts in philosophy of mind and of Ramsification in general as ultimately empty and unable to tell us in an illuminating fashion what a given phenomenon is.

Another way to express my worry about this kind of research program concerns the always problematic role of causation. I will focus on this version of the worry here. Thus, consider what the functionalist research program says about the causation of, for example, an intention by beliefs and desires in such a way as to make it the case that the intention is an intention with a certain content. On this view, this causal relation cannot be just any old causal relation. Certain unusual or deviant cases of causation must be ruled out in ways that are familiar to us from the discussion, in chapter 4, of deviant causal chains in the philosophy of action. Thus, if a given mental state, M, is caused by a desire to raise one's arm and, in turn, causes my arm to go up, but

---

[2] For an example of an account of mental states in terms of their functional or causal role, see Lewis, "Mad Pain and Martian Pain," p. 124: "Our view is that the concept of pain, or indeed of any other experience or mental state, is the concept of a state that occupies a certain causal role, a state with certain typical causes and effects. It is the concept . . . of a state apt for being caused in certain ways by stimuli plus other mental states and apt for combining with certain other mental states to jointly cause certain behavior. It is the concept of a member of a system of states that together more or less realize the pattern of causal generalizations set forth in commonsense psychology."

the causal path from the desire to M includes the intervention of a mad scientist manipulating my brain in dastardly way, then M would not count as an intention to raise my arm, even if it may have, in some respects, the kind of causal role we were looking for. We need, of course, to specify that the causal relation here *is of the right kind*. But what is the right kind? For reasons that emerged in the case of deviant causal chains involving action, the prospects of specifying the right way in an informative manner are not good. It seems likely that the account will ultimately be of the form: M is an intention of a certain kind when it is caused *in the right way* by a certain belief and desire and when it causes *in the right way* a certain bodily movement, i.e. in the ways required for M to be a certain intention. Thus, not only does this kind of functionalist account specify the content of a given mental state in terms of the contents of other mental states, but it also seems to have no way to specify the requisite causal relation other than in terms of the contents of the very mental state we were trying to express.[3] Thus the problem of deviant causal chains haunts functionalist accounts of mental states in general as much as it does causal theories of action.

You can also see this problem facing Grice's account of perception in his classic paper, "The Causal Theory of Perception." Grice accounts for perception in causal terms. His causal theory of perception specifies that perception is of a certain object if it is caused by that object in the right kind of way. Thus, Grice says:

> for an object to be perceived by X, it is sufficient that it should be causally involved in the generation of some sense-impression by X in the kind of way in which, for example, when I look at my hand in a good light, my hand is causally responsible for its looking to me as if there were a hand before me, or in which ... (and so on), *whatever that kind of way may be*. ("The Causal Theory of Perception," pp. 143–44; emphasis in original)

Grice later says:

> X perceives M if, and only if, some present-tense sense-datum statement is true of X which reports a state of affairs for which M, in a way to be indicated by example, is causally responsible. (p. 151)

---

[3] Fodor (at the end of "Fodor's Guide to Mental Representation") raises this kind of worry about functionalist accounts of mental content.

152 THE PARMENIDEAN ASCENT

It's hard to see how this account of perceptual content can spell out the right causal way other than in terms of the relevant content that is in question.

Soames

Like Grice's, Soames' account of aboutness primarily concerns linguistic meaning as turning on the representational content of certain mental states. Thus, Soames says, "the representational content of sentences is due to our cognitive attitudes toward them" (*What Is Meaning?*, p. 80). Soames makes similar claims concerning propositions (which themselves make linguistic representation possible):

> if the formal structures with which we might identify propositions aren't intrinsically representational, they can play a useful role in our theories only if their representational properties are somehow *derived from* the cognitive relations we bear to them. (p. 56; my emphasis)

He says further that propositions

> are representational *because* of their intrinsic connection to the inherently representational cognitive events in which agents predicate some things of other things. (p. 107, emphasis in original; see also p. 88)

Notice that Soames sees the representational state which makes linguistic meaning possible as "inherently" representational. This talk suggests that, for Soames, the representationality of the state in question is primitive and not susceptible to further explanation. But such inherent representationality of certain mental states is as much in need of clarification as the representationality of propositions or the meaning of sentences is. Soames is happy to say that mental representation takes place via acts of predication and that, as he insouciantly affirms, such mental predication must be taken as primitive. Thus, Soames says:

> One might ask what we mean by 'predication'—what, in effect, the *analysis* of predication is. Although it is unclear that an informative answer can be

given to this question, it is equally unclear that this is anything to worry about. Some logical and semantic notions—like negation—are primitive. (*What Is Meaning?*, p. 29; see also, p. 81)

"[T]he explanation of what is predicated of what in the proposition bottoms out in predication as a cognitive activity of agents" ("Truth and Meaning: In Perspective," p. 19)

Soames' account invokes a kind of primitive mental representation, and thus, by his own lights, doesn't need to meet the general explanatory demand. Indeed, he seems to think that the lack of an explanation here—the primitiveness of predication—should not "provoke hand-wringing" (*What Is Meaning?*, p. 29).

Searle

John Searle's treatment of meaning and aboutness is, in some respects, very different from Soames', but Searle, like Soames, sees linguistic representation as turning on mental representation and sees the representationality of the relevant mental state as inherent or, to use Searle's term, intrinsic. Thus, Searle says:

Since sentences—the sounds that come out of one's mouth or the marks that one makes on paper—are, considered in one way, just objects in the world like any other objects, their capacity to represent is not intrinsic but is derived from the Intentionality of the mind. The Intentionality of mental states, on the other hand, is not derived from some more prior forms of Intentionality but is intrinsic to the states themselves.... [B]eliefs and desires and other Intentional states are not, as such, syntactical objects... and their representational capacities are not imposed but are intrinsic. (*Intentionality*, pp. vii–viii)

Searle does go on to elaborate his account by stressing that the representationality of mental states is a biological phenomenon (*Intentionality*, chapter 10). Searle also highlights the primitiveness of intentionality in *The Rediscovery of the Mind*:

> You cannot reduce intentional content (or pains or "qualia") to something else, because if you could they would be something else, and they are not something else. (p. 51)

And Searle stresses in that work too that intentionality is a biological phenomenon and that mental phenomena "are themselves features of the brain" (*Rediscovery*, p. 1). But in the end—even though biological—these phenomena cannot be explained in non-mental terms. Here again our explanatory ambitions are curtailed.

Descombes

Descombes offers an extremely rich theory that sometimes seems to account for the meaning of certain items via the meaning of other items. What it is for an individual to have a mind and to mean certain things by her words or thoughts is for there to be an "*objective mind* of institutions [that] precedes and makes possible the *subjective mind* of particular persons" (*The Institutions of Meaning*, p. 9). For Descombes

> the subject, in order to acquire a mind, must be situated within a milieu that would have been described in classical French as "moral" or in German as "spiritual" [*geistig*]. This moral milieu is formed by institutions as providers of meanings that individual subjects can make their own. (*The Institutions of Meaning*, p. 9)

At times, Descombes may seem to say that the institutions of the objective mind themselves exhibit content or aboutness. Thus, he says that these institutions are "'ways of thinking and acting' that individuals, in coming to the world and acting within it, find already established and already defined" (*The Institutions of Meaning*, p. xxix). These ways of thinking "have been established outside of the individual and serve as models to guide her in her conduct" (p. xxv). In his book, *Le Complément de Sujet*, he speaks of the rule—which is the objective basis of my meaning what I do—in terms which indicate that the rule itself exhibits meaning or aboutness: "If you ask me why I act as I do, I can only say one thing in response: it is the rule that wants this, it is the rule that demands that one acts thus."[4] Descombes thus seems to account for one kind of meaning—the meaning deployed by individual persons—by appealing to a prior kind of meaning, the meaning of an objective mind or practice.

However, elsewhere it becomes clear that Descombes' position is actually that, although the practices or objective mind determine that we mean what we do, they do not have an intentional content of their own. If we think otherwise, we would, as Descombes recognizes, be forced to raise a question concerning the practices or objective mind analogous to the question that we raised concerning our use of words or language: what is it in virtue of which they or it mean what they do? And we would be embarked on a vicious circle or regress. Raising such a question of the objective mind would thus be, for Descombes, extremely problematic. In this vein, Descombes stresses that the initial acquisition of meaning by us proceeds, not from definitions which themselves have aboutness, but rather from a kind of teaching by example (*Le Complément de Sujet*, p. 463). Thus, for Descombes, although the practices impart meaning, they don't themselves have meaning; the practice or objective mind doesn't speak, we speak. But we do so in virtue of the practices' endowing what we say and do with meaning.[5]

This account in the end, unlike Soames' and Searle's, doesn't seek to explain the meaning of our terms by appealing to something else with meaning. The account just appeals to the way in which not-inherently contentful practices determine the meaning of my utterances. But now the question that arises is my familiar Parmenidean query: how? *How* do the practices or the objective mind contribute meaning? We have not explained the meaning of our terms until we can specify how it is that the practices or objective mind determine this meaning. And this Descombes does not clearly do.

Perhaps Descombes would appeal to the essence of the practices.[6] Such an appeal to essences may be good, but it's not clear if this invocation of essences sheds any light on how the institution of meaning takes place, for now—or still—we want to know: in virtue of what does something with the essence these practices are alleged to have operate? How do these practices do what they (essentially) do? As we've seen a number of times already in previous

---

[4] "*Si vous me demandez pourquoi j'agis comme le fais, je ne peux vous répondre qu'une chose: c'est la règle qui le veut, c'est elle qui réclame qu'on agisse ainsi,*" Descombes, *Le Complément de Sujet*, p. 447.
[5] I am indebted here to Vincent Descombes for clarifying his position for me.
[6] This is indicated by Descombes' favorable quotation of Charles Taylor's appeal to the essence of practices (*The Institutions of Meaning*, p. 299).

chapters, a mere appeal to essences or natures does not in cases such as these satisfy the explanatory demand, at least not the explanatory demand in its full generality. So, in the end, Descombes' account also seems to fail to meet the explanatory demand with regard to meaning.

Horwich

Let's turn briefly to Horwich's sophisticated Wittgensteinian view that meaning is use.[7] Horwich begins by considering the meanings of words. A word's meaning or the concept that it expresses "is constituted by its having a certain basic acceptance property (or, in other words, by its conforming to the regularity, 'All uses of *w* stem from such-and-such acceptance property')" (*Meaning*, p. 46). The relevant acceptance property of a word accounts for the acceptance of sentences containing the word (p. 45). Thus, on this theory, the meaning of a word is constituted by its use, and its use is constituted by the word's possession of a certain acceptance property which "designates the circumstances in which certain specified sentences containing the word are accepted" (p. 45). Because Horwich holds that the meaning of sentences and longer expressions derives from the meanings of the constituents of those sentences or longer expressions—i.e. because he has a compositional theory of meaning—Horwich builds up his theory of meaning in general out of his use theory of the meanings of individual words or expressions. As Speaks puts it,

> Horwich's core idea is that our acceptance of sentences is governed by certain laws, and, in the case of non-ambiguous expressions, there is a single "acceptance regularity" which explains all of our uses of the expression. (Speaks, "Theories of Meaning," section 3.2.4)

Despite its intricacy, Horwich's account, like others we have examined so far, merely pushes the explanatory issue one step back and fails to meet the explanatory demand in its full generality. This is because, although this account may appear to shed some light on meaning by adverting to use, the kind of use Horwich has in mind essentially involves regularities in

---

[7] Field adopts a different and also sophisticated view along these lines. See his "Deflationist Views of Meaning and Content."

MEANING 157

the *acceptance* of certain sentences. But what it is to *accept* a sentence is as much in need of clarification as the notion of the sentence's meaning. Indeed, it seems most natural to say that a sentence is accepted in virtue of what it means. One accepts a certain sentence because of what it means, because it is about a specific state of affairs.⁸ Thus, the account of meaning as use seems merely to shuffle things in need of explanation around—merely to rearrange deck chairs on the *Titanic*—and not to provide an answer to the explanatory demand in its full generality.

In response to this kind of objection, Horwich does not claim that he is *not* seeking to meet the explanatory demand in its full generality; rather, he claims that acceptance is not a semantic notion (and so does not presuppose the notion of meaning). To make this point, Horwich correctly notes that although to accept a sentence "goes hand in hand with accepting its *truth*," it is equally the case that other attitudes to sentences go hand in hand with accepting their truth. Thus,

> *supposing* something goes hand in hand with supposing its *truth*, *doubting* something goes hand in hand with doubting its *truth*, and so on. (*Meaning*, p. 95)

Horwich concludes:

> [the] relationship [of acceptance] to truth is not what distinguishes acceptance from other attitudes (such as doubting, conjecturing, etc.) and does not help to constitute its nature. Thus the relevant concept of acceptance does not presuppose the notion of truth. (*Meaning*, p. 95)

However, even if acceptance is not distinctive in its relation to truth and thus is not distinctively semantic, it still is related to truth and is still a semantic notion. In other words, all these attitudes—acceptance, supposing, conjecturing, etc.—are concerned with certain states of affairs and thus seem to turn on the *meaning* of the sentences to which the attitudes are directed. Horwich's way of generalizing the relationship to truth that acceptance manifests does not eliminate its dependence on meaning.⁹

---

⁸ Speaks ("Theories of Meaning," section 3.2.4) raises a similar concern: "One might worry that his use of the sentential attitude of acceptance entails a lapse into mentalism, if acceptance either just is, or is analyzed in terms of, beliefs."

⁹ At an analogous point in his similar theory of meaning. Field helps himself to a believes-that or desires-that relation to sentences that does not presuppose a notion of content or meaning: "the

Because Horwich's acceptance—despite his intentions—does offer an explanation of aboutness in one case in terms of aboutness in another case (that of acceptance), his account, like Grice's, Soames', and Searle's, explains the representationality of some items in terms of the representationality of other items.

Causal Theories

I would now like to turn to theories that are in a way more austere than the ones we have examined so far, for they clearly appeal solely to non-representational items in order to explain representationality in general. I will argue that each of the theories of this type that I am about to examine fails to meet the explanatory demand with regard to meaning.

First, consider an enormously influential family of theories that stem from the work of Saul Kripke and Hilary Putnam. These theories tie the meaning of a term to the causal origins of our use of the term.[10] On this view, the meaning of an expression as used by me is given by a relation—usually thought of as a causal relation—between my use of the expression and some object or objects distinct from the expression and my use of it. Thus, in my use of "Aristotle" or "water," those terms mean a certain individual (Aristotle) or a certain natural kind (H_2O), things that are the ultimate and dominant cause of my use of those terms.

Notice that according to such accounts, the heavy lifting as far as explaining meaning is concerned is performed by a causal relation to an object. This relation and this object are (in typical cases) not constituted by meaning-properties. This kind of account is, unlike Grice's, Soames', Searle's, and perhaps others' theories in that it does not explain the meaning of a certain item by appealing to other items that exhibit meaning.

---

assumption is that we can speak of a language-user as believing and desiring sentences in his or her own language—or at least, as believing and desiring internal analogs of them in which some or all of the ambiguities may have been removed—and that this relation can be made sense of without a prior notion of content for the belief or desire states or of meaning for the sentences," "Deflationist Views," p. 254. Field calls this assumption "harmless," but I can't see that it is harmless in the context of a theory with the deflationist ambitions of Field's. He does, however, sketch a justification of this assumption on p. 254n7.

[10] Kripke, *Naming and Necessity*, Putnam, "The Meaning of 'Meaning,'" and countless others.

MEANING 159

Although such accounts, as Kripke's and Putnam's, have been developed with increasing resourcefulness over the last half-century, they still fail to meet the explanatory demand with regard to meaning. For these accounts, my use of a term has a certain meaning in virtue of standing in a certain relation, R (a kind of causal relation), to certain objects. But this explanation is necessarily incomplete until we understand what it is about relation R, in particular, that *suits* it to be a meaning-determining relation. After all, there are many other relations, R', R", etc., between my use of a term and other items. For example, there is the relation between my use of "Aristotle" and the brother of the dominant cause of my use of "Aristotle" or between my use of the term "water" and the complement of the natural kind that causes my use of the term "water." Why should R get to be the meaning-making relation and not one of these other perfectly respectable relations?

Perhaps one can appeal here to an alleged conceptual truth: the concept of meaning just is the concept of a feature of the use of a term that stands in relation R (causation of a certain kind) to other items. That answer may be correct as far as it goes, but it doesn't go very far for, again, it doesn't show us what *suits* R to be the core of the concept of meaning instead of some other relation R' or R". From this point of view, that R is built into the concept of meaning, instead of R' or R" is arbitrary. We need to understand—to return to my favorite Parmenidean word—*how* it is that R (and not R', etc.) is central to the concept of meaning.[11] We still have not fully explained why the meaning of a given term is what it is and what distinguishes meaningful items from things that lack meaning.

One may—in defense of the causal view—appeal to the intuitive plausibility of such a view and of the cases used to illustrate it. This is, in effect, how Kripke and Putnam argue, both of whom are (in this stretch of their work) staunch defenders of relying in this way on intuition or appeals to common sense. I'm willing to grant the intuitive plausibility of Kripke's and Putnam's treatments of the examples they invoke (and thus I will spare you the millionth discussion of Twin Earth or Gödel's nemesis, Schmidt). The general point I want to make is that it's difficult to see what relevance the appeal to intuition or common sense has in this matter. Merely to say that such cases are intuitively plausible is to tell us what we already know; it is not to offer an explanation, an explanation of why a term means what it does. And to build

---

[11] For more on explaining why concepts have the features they do, see Della Rocca, "The Identity of Indiscernibles and the Articulability of Concepts."

an account of these intuitions—an account that codifies them—may be interesting but doing so does not by itself explain why one's use of a certain term has one meaning rather than another. If the "theory" thus developed cannot answer the basic explanatory question that is essential to the debate about meaning, then what is the point of such codification? In this context, one's account counts as a genuine theory of meaning only if it provides a satisfactory answer to the explanatory question, and causal "theories" fail to provide such an answer. No matter how much we may systematize our intuitions on these matters, no matter how good we feel after we elegantly devise—in stodgy, reflective equilibrium fashion—a "theory" which "captures" these intuitions, it remains the case that if the basic explanatory question goes unanswered, if we cannot in an illuminating fashion say why it is that one's use of a term has one meaning rather than another, then, we simply have no account of meaning. Here the Kripkean and Putnamian approach—insofar as it appeals to intuitions and common sense—is also merely rearranging deck chairs on the *Titanic* without shedding any genuine light on the question that brings us to the theory of meaning. I will have much more to say about the pervasive reliance on what I call the method of intuition in chapters 7 and 11.

Another possible problem, at least with the Kripkean view, is that it seems to rely essentially on the intentions that the user of the word has. Thus, my meaning Aristotle by "Aristotle" depends on my intending to use the term with the same reference as did the person from whom I ultimately learned the term (*Naming and Necessity*, p. 96). Because intentions are specified in terms of their content and, as we have seen, such content is as much in need of illumination as linguistic meaning is, the Kripkean account, in this respect, at best succeeds only in pushing the debate one step back. Again, it leaves the original explanatory question basically untouched. Here is a respect, then, in which at least Kripke's account doesn't live up to the austere standard of explaining meaning in terms that do not presuppose meaning or content.

Causal accounts of meaning in general thus fail to illuminate the difference between meaningful items and other items. Like the other accounts, they fail to meet the explanatory demand.

Reference Magnetism

The general line of thought that I just raised according to which there is no good reason to think that reference and meaning are fixed by causal relations rather than by some other equally respectable relation is in the spirit of the kinds of reasoning behind the skeptical attacks on meaning itself to be found in other parts of Kripke's and Putnam's works beside those in which they propose a causal theory of meaning.[12] These arguments purport to show that there is a thoroughgoing indeterminacy when it comes to meaning for there are in every, or almost every, case indefinitely many ways to make our sentences come out as true, and there are indefinitely many objects—often gerrymandered or otherwise arbitrary—to see as the referents of our terms.

David Lewis argues that we can avoid this kind of indeterminacy if we specify that our terms cannot refer indiscriminately to any arbitrary object or pseudo-object. Rather, only certain elite things "are carved at the joints" and are "eligible to serve as referents" ("Putnam's Paradox," p. 65). Such elite objects are so-called reference magnets. As Lewis stresses, such eligibility is not a function of our theorizing, but an objective, real feature of the world itself and of the so-called natural properties that the elite items exhibit. These natural properties are typically non-semantic properties, and so Lewis' account is austere in that it does not explain the meaning of one item in terms of the meanings of other items. In seeing reference as constrained by naturalness, Lewis believes he is able to avoid the counterintuitive results of Putnam and Kripke which reject *any* determinacy of meaning. Thus, Lewis says, "if the natural properties are sparse, then there is no reason to expect any overabundance of intended interpretations" ("New Work for a Theory of Universals," p. 48).[13]

Without going further into Lewis' appeal to naturalness or examining the elaborate ways in which philosophers have developed the theoretical uses of naturalness,[14] we can already see that the main problem with the reference magnet strategy as a theory of meaning is that no answer is given to the question: in virtue of what is a certain item a reference magnet? What suits one thing to be an eligible referent while another is not an eligible referent? Or, in other words, what is it in virtue of which one property is natural (and thus makes an item with that property eligible for reference) and another property is not natural? The notion of naturalness at work here is left as a

---

[12] I have in mind here especially Putnam, "Models and Reality," and Kripke, *Wittgenstein on Rules and Private Language*.
[13] Millikan in her account of content in terms of evolutionary function makes a similar appeal to a "metaphysical distinction between natural properties and kinds and artificially synthesized grue-like properties and kinds," "Truth, Hoverflies, and the Kripke-Wittgenstein Paradox," p. 334.
[14] For example, Sider, *Writing the Book of the World*.

primitive,[15] and once again this leaves us bereft of the illumination we were hoping to achieve. To say that a term means one thing rather than another because a certain object is an eligible referent is not illuminating unless we can say what it is to be an eligible referent. The account appeals to "objective joints in nature," but what are objective joints? Can we say anything about them other than that they are the features that make our terms refer to and mean what they refer to and mean? If this is the case, then in appealing to this primitive, what Lewis (and his followers) have done is to leave the notion of meaning unexplained or, at best, to explain meaning in terms ultimately of what is needed to explain meaning. Again, this is correct as far as it goes, but it doesn't go far at all, and it doesn't meet the explanatory demand.

Of course, one can appeal at this point, as before, to common sense or intuitions: treating properties as natural is justified because in doing so we are able to preserve very many intuitions about what our ordinary terms mean and refer to.[16] And, again, I want to discount this reliance on intuition or common sense as of no use in the absence of an answer to the explanatory demand. A foot-stamping invocation of brute naturalness is no substitute for a genuine explanation of how it is that certain items are endowed with meaning. Again, I will have a lot more to say on intuition and common sense in chapters 7 and 11.

Davidson (the Negative Story)

Instead of enlisting causal relations between a speaker's utterances and objects or states of affairs as causal theories and, in a different way, the accounts that appeal to naturalness do, Davidson's ambitiously austere research program appeals merely to the truth-conditions of those utterances, i.e. to the relations between the utterances and the conditions under which they would be true. For Davidson, these truth-conditions can be specified using the simple resources of a Tarskian-style, extensional theory of truth.[17] According to such a theory, in specifying the truth-conditions of a sentence of a speaker's language, we specify the meaning of that sentence.

---

[15] See Lewis, "New Work for a Theory of Universals," p. 14; Lewis and Langton, "Defining Intrinsicness," p. 119; Lewis, "Against Structural Universals," p. 79.
[16] This seems to be Lewis' method in general. See Lewis, "Introduction," p. x.
[17] See Davidson, "Truth and Meaning" and many other papers.

Thus, individual theorems of the theory of truth (which serves as a theory of meaning) will take the form:

"Snow is white" is true in language L1 iff snow is white.
"Schnee ist weiss" is true in language L2 iff snow is white.

And so on. One of the crucial virtues Davidson sees in this kind of account is that it can meet the explanatory demand, which as we saw Davidson accepts, simply by appealing to the notion of truth—an extensional notion—without "smuggling into the foundations of the theory concepts too closely allied to the concepts of meaning" ("Introduction," p. xiii).

Another crucial virtue of tying meaning to truth in this way is, for Davidson, that appealing merely to truth-conditions shows how meanings—our own and others'—are knowable. To know the meaning of a speaker's utterance, one merely has to grasp a theory of truth for that speaker's language. By not appealing to mysterious intensional entities such as meanings, Davidson makes both the meaning of a speaker's utterance *and* our knowledge of that meaning unproblematic. For Davidson, a theory of meaning for a speaker's language is at the same time a theory of interpretation for that speaker, a theory of how one comes to know the meaning of a speaker's utterances.

However, as Davidson realizes, the austerity of the appeal merely to truth-conditions runs into immediate difficulties, for not just *any* conditions under which an utterance is true can plausibly be seen as giving the meaning of that utterance. Thus, for example, my utterance of "Snow is white" is true if and only if snow is white.[18] Equally, however, "Snow is white" is true if and only if grass is green. And this latter biconditional can hardly be seen as giving the meaning of "Snow is white" even though this biconditional, like the previous biconditional, simply and accurately states truth-conditions.

A similar difficulty turns on the truth of the following biconditional:

"Snow is white" is true iff snow is white and not-(q and not-q).

---

[18] I am bracketing here considerations of tense and context, etc.

q here is any arbitrary proposition. But again this biconditional cannot be said to give the meaning of "Snow is white." What does "not-(q and not-q)" have to do with the meaning of our wintry sentence?[19]

Davidson thus needs to put some constraints on his theory of truth/theory of meaning that will preclude the kind of problematic biconditional from playing a role in the theory. In other words, he must specify a way to distinguish truth theories in general from *translational* truth theories in which the right-hand side of the relevant biconditionals translates—captures the meaning of—the sentence mentioned on the left-hand side.

But such an appeal to *translational* biconditionals is deeply problematic given Davidson's aims for a theory of meaning. First, it is far from clear that one can specify the constraints on formulating a theory of truth that will guarantee that the relevant biconditionals are translational without invoking the notion of meaning or of (as Davidson puts it) "allied" concepts. Further, in order for the truth-theory for a speaker to generate knowledge of the meaning of the speaker's sentences, one must know not only that the relevant biconditionals are true but also that they are translational. That is, the theory of truth provides knowledge of the meanings only if one already knows a crucial meaning-related fact, viz. that the relevant biconditionals capture the meanings of the speaker's utterances.

Thus, when Davidson's account is modified to avoid the problems brought on by the "grass is green" and "not-(q and not-q)" examples, it becomes clear that his account cannot succeed in explaining meaning in the austere truth-theoretical way he had hoped. Can Davidson nonetheless be said to meet the explanatory demand by appealing to the notion of meaning itself in the way that he does in spelling out his account of meaning? It's hard to see how. Explaining the *meaning* of a speaker's utterances by appealing to a theory of truth whose theorems are specified as capturing the *meanings* of those utterances is, of course, hardly explanatory of the meanings. This is another John Wayne moment in philosophy for Davidson. In relying on meaning to explain meaning, Davidson, like the others we have discussed, treats meaningful items as, in effect, primitively distinct from other items. For this reason, Davidson, like all the other theorists of meaning I have discussed, fails to meet the explanatory demand. Of course, Davidson, like Grice and

---

[19] For discussion of these problems, see Foster, "Meaning and Truth Theory"; Davidson, "Reply to Foster"; Speaks, "Truth Theories, Translation Manuals, and Theories of Meaning"; Soames, "Truth and Meaning: In Perspective."

others, may succeed in explaining something about communication, but even so he still leaves meaning itself unexplained.

A Relatively A Priori Argument

There is, of course, much more to be said about the accounts of meaning I have discussed, and there are certainly many other kinds of theory of meaning. However, I think that one can see from the survey that I have offered that there are, as it were, inductive grounds for thinking that theories of meaning in general fail to meet the explanatory demand at the heart of our philosophical concern with meaning. And the pattern behind the failures that we have seen puts us, I believe, in a position to appreciate an, as it were, *a priori* argument that the failure of theories of meaning in general is inevitable—at least the failure of theories of meaning that make a certain seemingly harmless assumption.

In responding to the explanatory demand, the theories that we have examined—and indeed almost all theories of meaning—take it for granted that the meaning we are seeking to explain is *differentiated* meaning, the kind of meaning that some things have as opposed to other things that lack this kind of meaning, and the kind of meaning that things enjoy in virtue of some kind of relation that the meaningful items bear to certain things. These theories are thus looking to articulate and understand the meaning-making relation, the relation that explains the difference between things with meaning and things without meaning, and the relation that explains why this meaningful item has the particular meaning that it has instead of another meaning. The theories thus presuppose that the meaning-making relation is somehow grounded. Without appealing to such a ground, there would not be a satisfying account of meaning; there would be a failure to meet the explanatory demand.

What, then, are the options for articulating and understanding this meaning-making relation (call it "R") that explains what it is in virtue of which a term, expression, sentence, thought, or text (call it "T") has meaning and has the meaning it does? There are the following familiar exhaustive and mutually exclusive options.

(1) R is primitive. That is, the relation, R, between T and some items is not grounded in or explained by anything. There is nothing in virtue of which T stands in R to these items.

(2) R is not primitive, but is, rather, ultimately grounded in or explained by or ultimately holds in virtue of a relation to something other than T.
(3) R is not primitive, but is, rather, ultimately fully grounded in or explained by or ultimately holds in virtue of the nature of T alone. That is, it follows from the nature of T alone that T has meaning and has the meaning it does. R is thus, in one sense of the term, an internal relation, a relation that stems simply from the nature of a thing.
(4) R is not primitive, but also is not ultimately grounded (as in (2) and (3)); instead, R is grounded in other items in a non-terminating regress or in a circle with a multiplicity of items.

As before, I won't discuss option (4) separately because my arguments against explanatory regresses or circles in connection with option (2) will also suffice to reject option (4).

All the views discussed so far—as well as any other theories of meaning—must, in one way or another, fall under these options. As we have seen in the case of analogous relations in previous chapters, option (1) can be eliminated right away in light of the explanatory demand that philosophers in this area tend to accept. However, exactly how to characterize the views discussed so far with regard to the other options is complicated by the fact that some of these theories give a bifurcated account of meaning. To see this, note first that certain accounts we have examined more or less straightforwardly fall under option (2). Thus, the causal theories of Kripke and Putnam, the reference magnetist views of Lewis and others, and the truth-conditional approach of Davidson and his cronies all see the meaning of T as a function of items distinct from T. The causal theory ties the meaning of a term to its relation to items, such as natural kinds or rocks or animals, etc., distinct from T that are causally related to the speaker's deployment of T. Lewis's theory links the meaning of a term to items that are distinguished by exhibiting Lewisian natural properties. And on the Davidsonian theory, the meaning of linguistic items is a function of the relation of those items to their truth-conditions. Descombes can also be seen in this general light for he ties individual meaning—the meaning of an individual's utterances or thoughts—to distinct practices that themselves are not bearers of meaning even though they determine individual meaning.

In their accounts of linguistic meaning, Grice, Soames, Searle, and Horwich also fall under option (2): this stretch of these theories ties the meaning of a linguistic term to other things (typically other things that exhibit meaning or aboutness). Thus, Grice ties the meaning of linguistic items to the content of certain intentions or belief of the speaker. Soames and Searle (in different ways) see linguistic meaning as function of inherently representational mental states. Horwich ties the linguistic meaning of T to certain acceptance properties that one's use of T manifests. All of these theories, in appealing to things other than T in accounting for linguistic meaning, fall under option (2).

However, in the case of the more fundamental bearer of meaning, some of these theories fall under option (3). Thus, for Searle and Soames, the relevant representational states that ground linguistic meaning are inherently or intrinsically representational. Searle and Soames thus see the meaning of this item—the representational state—as a function of the nature of that state alone. Grice differs from Searle and Soames here because he offers a functionalist account of the content of the mental states that undergird linguistic meaning. Such a functionalist account ties the content of our mental state to the content of other intentional states. So in this stretch of his overall account, Grice falls under option (2).

In previous chapters, we did not deal with bifurcated theories—theories that, when it comes to some instances of the relevant phenomenon (substance, action, knowledge), fall under option (2) and, in other instances fall under option (3). The way in which my options (1)–(4) played out in those earlier chapters was simpler because in those cases, unlike in the case of meaning, we did not have, on the one hand, some substances, actions, or instances of knowledge that were explained in terms of things other than the relevant substance, action, or instance of knowledge and, on the other hand, other items that had the relevant status in virtue of their own nature. In other words, such theories were not bifurcated in the way that theories of meaning are sometimes bifurcated.

However, just as in previous chapters, both option (2) and option (3)—popular options as far as theories of meaning are concerned—fail to meet the explanatory demand with regard to meaning. Thus, consider option (2): the meaning of T turns on T's relation, R, to some item distinct from T. Call this other item, "X." In order for relation R to illuminate meaning it must be the case that R itself is capable of being grounded or explained. If there is no such explanation of R, then, in attempting to explain the meaning of T by appealing to an unexplained relation R, we would merely be moving the original difficulty one step back. We would merely replace one mystery (concerning what explains why in wielding T, one means X rather than, say,

Y) by another (concerning what explains why R which relates T to X, instead of, say, R' which relates T to Y, determines meaning). The alternative relation R' would be some alternative to a causal relation in Kripke's case or some alternative to a relation to a Lewisian reference magnet or some alternative to a Davidsonian truth-condition (e.g., a relation to a non-translational truth-condition). Indeed, these two mysteries—why does T mean X and why does R determine meaning—are at bottom the same: the challenge is, in each case, to explain why one object should receive preferential treatment over another when it comes to meaning relations. By merely pushing the problem back in this way, we lose our grip on why X—which stands in R to T—should be the item meant. If there is equally good reason to see Y—which stands in R' to T—as the item meant instead, then the meaning of T will remain fundamentally unexplained, and so the explanatory demand will not be met.

How, then, in the case of option (2) can the meaning-making relation, R, be explained? We are looking, in other words, for the ground of relation R, according to option (2). And here again I invoke my old friend, the Bradleyan regress argument as re-imagined by me, which I have deployed at crucial moments in each of the previous three chapters and which I defended most extensively in chapter 3. This argument shows that (2)-like explanations are ultimately empty and unilluminating. They thus offer nothing more than what I have called John Wayne moments in philosophy.[20]

Turn, then, to option (3) which sees the meaning of T as grounded in T's nature. This option, as the previous versions of option (3), is ruled out because, an appeal to the nature of the item in question as explaining its meaning (or its status as a substance, action, or state of knowledge) is, in the terms that I have used in this book, a Molière moment in philosophy, another unilluminating appeal to the nature of a thing.

With the rejection of each of (1)–(4), we have eliminated any hope of trying to meet the explanatory demand when it comes to meaning, on the assumption that the kind of meaning we are seeking to explain is differentiated meaning. This result is not merely the relatively tame skeptical worry that there are or may be no meanings. Rather, as in the previous three chapters, my claim here is the more deeply skeptical claim that, as long as we remain with standard accounts of meaning, we have no coherent understanding of meaning.

---

[20] For similar reasons, option (4) can be eliminated.

Ascent

One's focus at this point inevitably turns to a presupposition of all the unsuccessful theories of meaning that we have considered. This is the presupposition that the kind of meaning we are dealing with is, in each case, *differentiated* meaning: meaning as enjoyed only by some things and not by others. According to this presupposition, the meaning of one item, T, is very often also distinct from the meanings of other items. Further, on this pervasive view, things that exhibit meaning do so in virtue of a relation to other things (with or without meaning) or in virtue of an internal relation to T's own nature. Thus, we've seen cases in which the meaning of T is a function of a relation to something distinct from T (its cause, etc.) or in which the meaning is a function of a relation between T and its own nature (as in the case of Searle's and Soames' treatments of mental representations), things that are intrinsically, by their nature, endowed with meaning properties. Meaning on all these views is a function of a relation that the thing endowed with meaning stands in to certain things.

But what if we were to give up this assumption of the differentiation of meaning, just as we gave up analogous assumptions in the cases of substance, action, and knowledge? Doing so may be our only hope for understanding meaning, for meeting the explanatory demand with regard to meaning.

The problem that arose for differentiated meaning cannot arise for undifferentiated meaning. If we reject differentiated meaning, then, if there is to be meaning at all, this meaning cannot occupy a place differentiated from and related to things. We cannot place meaningful things in a differentiated place. Instead, if there is to be meaning at all, then all is meaning. As before, the reality that philosophers of meaning have tried—and failed—to capture with their theories of differentiated meaning is better captured by a view that rejects relations (even internal relations) between meaning and certain things. This is the latest version of the Parmenidean Ascent: this version is a rejection of certain kinds of relations involving meaning, and, by transcending these relations, an attempt to capture the reality that was only imperfectly expressed by appealing to such relations. On this view of meaning as undifferentiated, meanings are not housed in, as it were, discrete nuggets or chunks within the world, meaning does not occupy a differentiated place within the world. We cannot even say that there is one meaning because (as we have seen) to *count* meaning (or being or action or knowledge) as one is to presuppose the intelligibility of relations of some kind (at least among numbers). And such relations have already been ruled out. There are, thus, no meanings, not even one meaning, rather there is meaning. The world is imbued with meaning.

According to this Parmenides-inspired view and as in the case of the terms "being," "action," and "knowledge," the term "meaning" is something like a mass term. "Meaning" cannot be a count noun because, as I've just indicated, counting or numbering presupposes relations, but such relations are ruled out, for our usual Bradleyan reasons. So "meaning" can only be something like a mass term. But, as I've indicated, the analogy to a mass term is not exact for it might be thought that the notion of a mass term, even if it doesn't presuppose distinct meanings (or substances or actions or states of knowledge) does presuppose the notion of *quantity*. This notion may import some notion of differentiation or relation, for quantities are precisely such as to be divided or increased or, at least, measured, and such actions presuppose relations. Nonetheless, regarding "meaning" as a mass term does suggest, perhaps not perfectly, the kind of Parmenidean position which I'm embracing.

In Lieu of Aquinas: Quine and Davidson

This is the point at which, in previous chapters, I invoked a surprising parallel between my Parmenidean Ascent in a particular domain and Aquinas' position concerning God's simplicity: in much the same way that God, for Aquinas, is undifferentiated being, action, and knowledge, reality itself for me—*qua* follower of Parmenides—is undifferentiated being, action, and knowledge. Unfortunately, I don't have a ready Thomistic parallel when it comes to meaning. Although some theologians are happy to say, perhaps, that God is meaning (undifferentiated meaning, I imagine), I don't see that Aquinas says such a thing, though perhaps some enterprising Aquinas scholar will find such a parallel. However, I have some good news for the parallel-hungry: I am ready to trade in a Parmenidean parallel to *one* medieval philosopher for a Parmenidean parallel to *two* twentieth-century philosophers. It's a deal I am happy to make, and I hope that you will be too. (We will return to our Thomistic parallels later in this chapter.)

Thus, to begin this twentieth-century swap, note that, perhaps surprisingly, W. V. Quine takes some steps toward what might be seen as a Parmenidean view of meaning. The first step in this direction is Quine's argument for the rejection of the analytic-synthetic distinction, or, perhaps I should say, his best argument against that distinction: his argument from the holism of confirmation near the end of his classic essay, "Two Dogmas of Empiricism." The arguments in earlier sections of "Two Dogmas" are perhaps less successful,[21] though it's not entirely clear how to see the connection between those arguments and the argument from confirmation.

One way to regard this argument is as follows. For Quine, any statement may be held onto "come what may" ("Two Dogmas," p. 43) in the face of apparent counterevidence as long as one is willing to make appropriate adjustments in the web of other statements one accepts. Similarly, no statement is immune to revision as long as one is willing, again, to make necessary adjustments. Quine concludes from this holism that there is no meaningful distinction between, on the one hand, analytic statements whose truth is dependent solely on meanings and not on the way the world happens to be, and, on the other hand, synthetic statements whose truth is dependent on the way of the world. As Quine says, "[W]e at present lack any tenable general suggestion, either rough and practical or remotely theoretic, as to what it is to be an analytic sentence" ("Carnap and Logical Truth," p. 129). Also: "It is not clear wherein an adoption of the conventions, antecedently to their formulation, consists" ("Truth by Convention," p. 105). I regard Quine as making a rationalist move in so rejecting the analytic/synthetic distinction: that distinction is to be rejected because there is no principled way to draw it, no reason for drawing the distinction here rather than there. Of course, Quine—great empiricist that he is—would never, ever characterize his basis for rejecting the distinction in these rationalist terms—*except for the fact that he does*. As I have mentioned elsewhere,[22] in Quine's paper "Carnap and Logical Truth," which discusses the kind of move concerning the holistic nature of the structure of theories that Quine favors, he says explicitly that "the law of sufficient reason" licenses the rejection of distinctions like the analytic/synthetic distinction ("Carnap and Logical Truth," p. 114).[23]

What interests me primarily here is a claim Quine makes in "Two Dogmas" after rejecting the analytic/synthetic distinction on these holistic grounds. One might think that without any such distinction one cannot speak meaningfully about meaning. If no statement is true simply by virtue

---

[21] See Williamson, *The Philosophy of Philosophy*, p. 50.

[22] Della Rocca, "The Taming of Philosophy," p. 196.

[23] It's interesting that in this paper, as well as in the earlier classic, "Truth by Convention," Quine expresses some sympathy for Carroll's regress argument concerning logical inference. The connection among Bradley's regress concerning relations, Carroll's regress concerning logical inference, and a strict Parmenidean monism are rich and well worth exploring further.

of the meanings of its contained terms as opposed to being true in part by virtue of the way the world is, then there is no way to speak meaningfully of *the* meaning of the terms or statement. One might think that, if terms generally do have meaning, then there is always the possibility that terms can be combined in such a way that the resulting statement is analytically true, i.e. true simply by virtue of these meanings. But if there are no analytic statements and no analytic-synthetic distinction, then it seems that terms and statements do not genuinely have meaning. In rejecting the analytic/synthetic distinction, Quine may thus seem to give up on the notion of meaning in general.

But this is not the conclusion Quine draws in "Two Dogmas." He recognizes that we can—in light of his arguments—no longer locate meanings in terms or statements taken individually. But meaning is not thereby lost; instead meaning finds its proper home in language as a whole. As Quine says—in my favorite all-time sentence from Quine—"the unit of empirical significance is the whole of science" (p. 42). Here Quine is making something like a Parmenidean Ascent. He rejects differentiated meaning on largely rationalist grounds but preserves and indeed rescues the notion of meaning by appealing to undifferentiated meaning. The unit of significance is science as a whole. The phenomenon of meaning that we were trying to capture by distinguishing between meanings of individual terms and statements is better captured—from this Quinean perspective—by rejecting differentiated meaning and embracing undifferentiated meaning. For Quine, there are, one might say, no meanings and not even one meaning, but there is meaning. The phenomenon that we were trying to capture by our talk of meanings differentiated from one another is better captured by speaking simply of meaning without such differentiation. Davidson interprets Quine in these (heroic) Parmenidean terms: "erasing the line between the analytic and the synthetic saved philosophy of language as a serious subject by showing how it could be pursued without what there cannot be: determinate meanings."[24]

This kind of reading of Quine is also offered by Michael Dummett and Descombes. The latter interprets Quine's semantic holism as committing him to "an *undifferentiated block, a collection devoid of internal structure*" (*The Institutions of Meaning*, p. 115, emphasis in original). Dummett also says that

---

[24] Davidson, "A Coherence Theory of Truth and Knowledge," p. 313. In this vein, it is interesting to note that, at one point at least, Quine makes the suggestion that I invoked in the previous section that "meaning" is a mass term. Thus, see (and hear) a videotaped interview with Quine, available on YouTube: https://www.youtube.com/watch?v=cR_7QRknNtQ. The claim that "meaning" is a mass term occurs at 10:04. I am indebted here to Carl Posy for this reference.

"total theory," for Quine, confronts "experience as a single undifferentiated block" (*Frege: Philosophy of Language*, p. 597). However, while Descombes and Dummett offer this reading in criticism of Quine, I, of course, view the position attributed to Quine here as his finest hour, for this position is an instance of the Parmenidean Ascent exhibited in all its glory in one of the most consequential philosophical arguments of the last century. As Darth Vader might say of Quine, "The Parmenidean Force is strong with this one."

But perhaps not strong enough: for Quine, unfortunately, later climbs down from his Parmenidean heights. He steps away from the radical holism of "Two Dogmas" and instead sees my favorite Quinean claim only as "true enough in a legalistic sort of way" ("Two Dogmas in Retrospect," p. 268) and as expressing "an uninteresting legalism" ("Five Milestones," p. 71). Instead, Quine comes to prefer to see language as divided into "chunks" which "may be ascribed their independent empirical meaning, nearly enough" ("Five Milestones," p. 71; see also *Pursuit of Truth*, pp. 14–16, and "Three Indeterminacies," pp. 10–12). And, indeed, even at the time of "Two Dogmas," Quine was only imperfectly Parmenidean, for at that point and later, Quine allowed for entire conceptual schemes that are differentiated from one another, and so he allowed for differentiated loci of meaning.[25] And it's on precisely this point that Davidson, as we will now see, attacks Quine most deeply.

Despite the fact that in his account of actions as differentiated from mere events, Davidson falls short of the Parmenidean ideal (as we saw in chapter 4), and despite the fact that (as we saw earlier in this chapter), Davidson again fails to reach the Parmenidean pinnacle when he articulates his Tarskian theory of truth as a theory of meaning, he like Quine—and perhaps more than Quine—sometimes seems to wax Parmenidean. I regard Davidson's rejection of the distinction between conceptual scheme and content as approaching a version of the Parmenidean Ascent. The scheme/content distinction, relied on heavily by Quine, is intended to be a distinction between one's framework for thinking about things, on the one hand, and those things themselves which are to be captured within this framework, on the other. The things captured are variously thought of as the world or as things-in-themselves or as experience (see "On the Very Idea of a Conceptual Scheme," p. 192). For the proponent of the scheme/content distinction, all such items are meant to be not dependent on or even necessarily connected with the

---

[25] I am indebted here to Daniel Moerner.

concepts we may employ to understand those items. In other words, bound up with the scheme/content distinction is the idea that, although the world can be captured or conceptualized by our conceptual scheme, the world could equally well be captured by a completely different conceptual scheme, one that has nothing in common with our own. Thus, the scheme/content distinction presupposes the intelligibility of there being radically different or "incommensurable" conceptual schemes. One way Davidson attacks the scheme/content distinction is by attacking the idea that there can be different schemes in this sense.

Davidson can be seen as mounting this charge by making an "in virtue of" claim. Take a purported case in which some other individual has a different conceptual scheme from our own. Davidson asks, in effect, what could make it the case that this individual is operating with a different conceptual scheme as opposed to using the same—or some of the same—concepts as we do, though perhaps expressing these shared concepts in words different from our own words? Any concept-user's language can be translated into our own language and can thus be made sense of using our concepts as long as we can make suitable adjustments in the range of beliefs and other attitudes attributed to this other individual. What guarantees that we are always able to make such adjustments is the radical holism that Davidson adopts from Quine together with the rationalist underpinnings Quine provides for his holism. Davidson invokes holism in precisely this way when he says:

> Given the underlying methodology of interpretation, we could not be in a position to judge that others had concepts or beliefs radically different from our own. ("On the Very Idea of a Conceptual Scheme," p. 197)

If, because of the holism of the conceptual, another agent's behavior can always be made sense of using our concepts, then there will never be any ground for the purported fact that the other agent is operating with a conceptual scheme wholly different from our own. Thus, the holism of the conceptual generates what can be seen as the imperialism of our concepts. Anyone's conceptually laden behavior can always be understood in terms of *our* concepts or otherwise it wouldn't be explicable as—and wouldn't be—conceptually laden behavior at all.

So, for Davidson, the idea that there are radically different conceptual schemes is unintelligible: given the holism of the conceptual, nothing could ground any such distinction among schemes. And because a scheme/content distinction presupposes such a distinction among schemes, it follows that the scheme/content distinction is to be rejected as unintelligible too.

One might think that, in rejecting the scheme/content distinction and in rejecting any distinction between conceptual schemes, Davidson is committed to eliminating the conceptual altogether, for it might be thought that the conceptual presupposes such distinctions. But Davidson rejects this presupposition. We can retain our commitment to the conceptual as long as we give up any commitment to the conceptual as differentiated from the world or from the things conceptualized and as long as we give up any commitment to one conceptual scheme as differentiated from another. Just as Davidson's and Quine's holism requires us to give up determinate or differentiated meanings, Davidson's holism also requires us to give up determinate conceptual schemes, i.e. conceptual schemes differentiated from the world and differentiated from one another. For Davidson, then, there are no conceptual schemes and not even one conceptual scheme. As Davidson says, "if we cannot intelligibly say that schemes are different, neither can we intelligibly say that they are one" ("On the Very Idea of a Conceptual Scheme," p. 198). Instead, for Davidson, there is simply reality which can be conceived.

Of course, all these steps in Davidson's argument are very controversial, and I cannot hope to defend them here. And, in fact, we will return in chapter 9 to worries about the intelligibility of the kind of position that Davidson takes up here and that I am embracing even more broadly than Davidson does. My point is simply to note that this enormously influential argument is an instance of the Parmenidean Ascent. Davidson rejects certain distinctions on explanatory grounds: these distinctions cannot be explained, are unintelligible, and so are to be rejected. But we can better capture the phenomenon we were trying to capture—in this case the phenomenon of the conceptual—by rejecting the determinate or differentiated version of the phenomenon and invoking instead the phenomenon as undifferentiated. That is the Parmenidean place Davidson regards himself as arriving at when he says:

> In giving up the dualism of scheme and world, we do not give up the world, but re-establish unmediated touch with the familiar objects whose antics make our sentences and opinions true and false. ("On the Very Idea of a Conceptual Scheme," p. 198)

176 THE PARMENIDEAN ASCENT

Perhaps, even more so than with Quine, the Parmenidean Force is strong with Davidson.

Of course, however, like Quine, Davidson loses his rationalist nerve and so fails (at points already noted) to make the Parmenidean Ascent in its full generality. Nonetheless, Davidson, like Quine, makes the Parmenidean move, and they both do so prominently. My aim in this section has been to show how these great philosophers yielded—in perhaps their most significant arguments—to the Parmenidean impulse. In seeing this, my hope is that we might come to feel less resistance to the general Parmenidean move I have promoted throughout this book so far. We will turn to other strategies in chapters 10 and 11 for overcoming the resistance to the Parmenidean Ascent.

Truth

In this final section of the chapter, I will argue that in light of the Parmenidean Ascent with regard to meaning or aboutness, we are now in a position to make a Parmenidean Ascent with regard to (to use Davidson's term) the closely allied notion of truth. The path to this Parmenidean Ascent will not follow that pattern I've deployed in previous chapters and earlier in this chapter with regard to substance, action, knowledge, and meaning. In those other cases, as you know (or should know if you're not parachuting in), I started off with a widely accepted explanatory demand and then used that point of agreement against standard theories in the relevant domain. However, I don't intend to—and, indeed, I can't—follow that procedure with regard to truth. This is because the explanatory demand with regard to truth—what is it in virtue of which a given proposition, sentence, statement, belief, etc. is true?—is not as widely accepted as analogous explanatory demands are in other cases. To be sure, versions of the correspondence theory of truth that offer a *definition* of truth in terms of correspondence would accept the explanatory demand here and try to meet it by appealing to the notion of correspondence to the facts. Yet many other philosophers who discuss truth regard the explanatory demand as out of place. I have in mind, in particular, deflationists about truth. According to many deflationists about truth, truth is indefinable and there is nothing interesting to say about its nature.[26] So I will not

---

[26] See Stoljar and Damnjanovic, "Deflationary Theories of Truth." Horwich explicitly rejects the explanatory demand with regard to truth. See Horwich, *Truth*, pp. 12–13.

proceed to my Parmenidean Ascent in this case through an explanatory demand with regard to truth.

My path will be more indirect. Building on the Parmenidean Ascent with regard to meaning defended earlier in this chapter, I will make the case for a Parmenidean Ascent with regard to truth. More specifically, given the explanatory considerations that lead to a commitment to undifferentiated meaning, we also have to accept a Parmenidean Ascent with regard to truth. Although an explanatory demand with regard to truth doesn't drive this ascent, the explanatory considerations that propel us along a Parmenidean path with regard to meaning also drive the Parmenidean Ascent with regard to truth. So the Parmenidean Ascent with regard to truth has, indirectly at least, an explanatory pedigree, as do all other versions of the Parmenidean Ascent we have discussed so far. We will see in chapter 8 that my Parmenidean Ascent with regard to metaphysical explanation will also proceed along a somewhat indirect path because the explanatory demand with regard to metaphysical explanation is also not pervasively accepted.

Let me briefly sketch three traditional theories of truth before showing how each of them is committed to a Parmenidean Ascent. And I should point out right away that I have no commitment as to what the bearers of truth are. On some views, truth-bearers are sentences. On other views, statements; on yet other views, propositions; on yet other views, beliefs or other mental states. These distinctions between such truth-bearers won't matter for my purposes here.

Perhaps the oldest and most venerable theory of truth is the correspondence theory which can be formulated as the claim that a proposition (say) is true just in case it corresponds to a certain fact. Or, to use Aquinas' phrase which is often thought to express a version of the correspondence theory: truth is the conformity of idea and thing. Indeed, these are the terms in which for Aquinas truth is *defined*.[27] On a coherence theory, truth is a matter of the coherence among certain statements or beliefs. More specifically, as Ralph Walker helpfully states the position: "For a proposition to be true is for it to cohere with a certain system of beliefs" (*The Coherence Theory of Truth*, p. 2). Finally, on a deflationary theory of truth, all we can say about truth is that a proposition or sentence or statement "*p*" is true if and

---

[27] "*Per conformitatem intellectus et rei veritas definitur,*" *Summa Theologiae* 1.16.2; see also Aquinas, *De Veritate* 1.1.

only if *p*. There is no nature to truth beyond such biconditionals. Stoljar and Damnjanovic state the theory this way:

> To say that "snow is white" is true, or that it is true that snow is white, is equivalent to saying simply that snow is white and this, according to the deflationary theory, is all that can be said significantly about the truth of "snow is white." ("Deflationary Theories of Truth")

There are, of course, other kinds of theory of truth (e.g., the pragmatist theory and the identity theory of truth, etc. See Glanzberg, "Theories of Truth"). I won't discuss these other theories here, but I believe that the argument I am about to give would apply to these theories as well.

So how does the argument for a Parmenidean Ascent with regard to truth go? The key steps are four:

(1) On standard theories of truth, items with a truth-value—sentences, beliefs, statements, propositions, etc.—have meaning, content, or aboutness.
(2) The meaning (etc.) that these items exhibit is, on standard theories of truth, differentiated meaning or aboutness or content.
(3) Since differentiated meaning (etc.) has been rejected earlier in this chapter, there can be no truth as standard theories conceive it, for truth, so conceived, presupposes differentiated meaning (etc.).
(4) In light of the preceding steps, we can preserve the or a notion of truth by appealing to undifferentiated truth.

I will now unpack these steps.

(1) On standard theories of truth, the items with a truth-value—a proposition, sentence, statement, or belief—all exhibit aboutness, have meaning or content. On the correspondence theory, each of these items, if true, corresponds to a certain state of affairs that obtains, i.e. to a certain fact. The truth-bearer is *about* this state of affairs that it corresponds to. On the coherence theory, a true belief coheres with other beliefs because—or in virtue of—these contents, because these beliefs are about what they are about. Even on a deflationary theory of truth— a theory that avoids the metaphysical machinery of correspondence to facts or relations to certain states of affairs—a true statement has

meaning even if its being true and having this meaning is not a matter of the sentence standing in a relation to a certain state of affairs. Thus, e.g., Horwich, a deflationist with regard to truth, sees true sentences as having a meaning which is simply a matter of the way in which the terms in the sentence are used. (We can see here again that Horwich accepts the explanatory demand with regard to meaning, even if he does not accept an explanatory demand with regard to truth.) The key point here is that even for a deflationist, truth-bearers have meaning or content.

(2) On all standard theories, the meaning that truth-bearers exhibit is differentiated meaning. This is, in the first instance, because the truth-bearers on all these theories are multiple. There are, typically, many statements, sentences, propositions, or beliefs with a meaning, and these meanings are very often different from one another. The differentiated meaning of truth-bearers on some standard theories emerges in other ways too. For example, on the correspondence theory, truth consists in a relation of correspondence to a state of affairs that is, typically, distinct from the truth-bearer that exhibits meaning.

(3) However, differentiated meaning is, for the reasons I have advanced earlier in this chapter, to be rejected. So standard theories of truth—correspondence, coherence, and deflationist—presuppose something that is bad: differentiated meaning. And thus because of this taint, these standard theories are unsustainable.

(4) In order to offer an alternative theory of truth that is free of these problems, we need to avoid any commitment to differentiated meaning. This can be done by and only by embracing undifferentiated truth. If we have a theory of truth that avoids differentiated meaning, the truth that we invoke must be undifferentiated truth.

To see what a theory of truth that gives up differentiated meaning would look like, consider the connection between there being no differentiated meaning and there being no differentiated truth. If there is no differentiated meaning, then if there is to be truth at all, it cannot be differentiated truth. The bearers of differentiated truth would have meaning which would be differentiated from other meanings and from non-meaningful things.

Similarly, if there is no differentiated truth, then there cannot be differentiated meaning. If there were differentiated meaning, then there would be a bearer or bearers of this differentiated meaning, and these bearers would thus, if true, exhibit differentiated truth.

So if there is no differentiated truth, there is no differentiated meaning, and if there is no differentiated meaning, there is no differentiated truth. Commitment to undifferentiated meaning is equivalent to commitment to undifferentiated truth. Thus, if we are going to have a notion of truth at all, then—given the commitment to undifferentiated meaning—that truth must be undifferentiated truth.

Of course, to be committed to undifferentiated truth is just to make a Parmenidean Ascent with regard to truth. By transcending the distinctions that we typically associate with truth, i.e. by embracing undifferentiated truth, we finally see truth aright. This Parmenidean Ascent is based crucially on the rejection of differentiated meaning that I've already argued for, on the Parmenidean Ascent with regard to meaning. And it is a Parmenidean Ascent because it stems from an explanatory demand, as all the other Parmenidean Ascents discussed so far—dating back to Parmenides himself—do. As I've mentioned, the unusual aspect of this Parmenidean Ascent is that it is not derived from an explanatory demand with regard to the target notion—truth—but stems from the Parmenidean Ascent with regard to meaning which, in turn, stems from the explanatory demand with regard to meaning.

And, just as with previous Parmenidean Ascents, the claim that there is undifferentiated truth amounts to the claim that there are no *truths*, there is no multiplicity of truths. Also, there is not even one truth because, as we have seen, to count—even to count to one—presupposes relations of some kind, at least with regard to numbers. Because my argument here turns on a general Bradleyan denial of relations, and because there can thus be no relations of counting, there cannot be even *one* truth. There is, then, simply truth. On this view, as in the previous cases and with the usual qualifications, "truth" is something like a mass term.

I'm happy to announce at this point that I can return here to my customary practice of drawing parallels between versions of the Parmenidean Ascent and Aquinas' notion of God. As we've seen, Aquinas embraces the view that God is subsistent being, God is pure act, and God is understanding itself. Similarly, for Aquinas, God is truth. In *Summa Theologiae* 1.16.5, Aquinas asks whether God is truth, and he answers in the affirmative, citing the New Testament: "Our Lord says, I am the way, the truth, and the life" (John 14:6). Drawing a connection between being, understanding and truth, Aquinas says, "He himself is his own existence and act of understanding. Whence it follows not only that truth is in him, but that he is truth itself, and the sovereign and first truth [*ipse sit ipsa summa et prima veritas*]" (*Summa Theologiae* 1.16.5; see also *Summa Contra Gentiles* 1.60, *De Veritate* 1.7).

Of course, for Aquinas, the truth that is God is in some way differentiated from other things, including God's creatures and other truths (that is why Aquinas says that God is the *sovereign* and *first* [*summa et prima*] truth). And it is in this important respect that Aquinas' view differs from mine, for on my view reality itself—and not a transcendent God—is truth, just as reality itself is being, action, knowledge, and meaning. Here, again, my Parmenidean Ascent is something like an affirmation of Aquinas' God. But what it affirms is more like a Thomistic God minus the transcendence, the relation to creation. And, as I've argued throughout, to be *minus* such relations, to be without such relations, is not really to lose anything at all for relations are not real.[28]

Further, we can, at this point also stop feeling bad about not having a clear Thomistic parallel to my Parmenidean Ascent with regard to meaning, something I seemed to lament earlier in this chapter. Given the widely accepted tight connection between meaning and truth, the fact that Aquinas does believe that God is truth may be enough to show that—even if Aquinas does not explicitly say that God is meaning—he may be committed to such a position.

---

[28] For a very helpful treatment of Aquinas' view that God is truth, see Wood, "Thomas Aquinas on the Claim that God is Truth."

7
Meaning, the History of Philosophy, and Analytical Philosophy

At various points in this book, I have engaged in the interpretation of historical texts in philosophy. Thus, in chapters 1 and 2, I was explicitly concerned to draw out the meaning of certain classic works with regard to monism and the nature of substance. And later chapters will see me again engaging with historical figures and historical texts, in particular in chapters 10 and 11. How—in light of the Parmenidean Ascent with regard to meaning that I just promulgated in chapter 6—are we to understand this enterprise of mining historical texts for their meaning? A minimal concern with consistency and a minimal tendency to reflect forces this question upon us. And so in this chapter, I will consider the implications of the Parmenidean Ascent with regard to meaning for the interpretation of historical texts in philosophy. More broadly, I will explore the implications of this Parmenidean Ascent for the distinction between philosophy itself and the study of its history—a distinction of which, as you might imagine given my general hostility to distinctions, I am skeptical.

With regard to the alleged contrast between philosophy and the study of its history, I will concentrate on so-called analytical philosophy because I think that here the problem of the relation of philosophy to the study of its history arises in a distinctive, illuminating, and rather acute way. I choose this emphasis despite the fact that the distinction between analytical and non-analytical philosophy is another distinction of which I am (unsurprisingly) skeptical. Indeed, this distinction comes into even greater doubt in the course of this chapter. The phenomenon that I seek to understand better is what I see as analytical philosophy's apparently widespread indifference to, neglect of, or disdain for the history of philosophy and the study of the history of philosophy. My worry is that, in many quarters of analytical philosophy, the study of the history of philosophy is merely tolerated. It is, perhaps, required, but only as a background to the real action in philosophy, and, from this contemporary perspective, the study of the history of philosophy has, at best, only a second-class status. With the help of the Parmenidean Ascent with regard to meaning, I will challenge this attitude toward the study of the history of philosophy. In so doing, I will, in effect, be making yet another Parmenidean Ascent, this time with regard to the distinction between philosophy and the study of its history.

Three Struts of Analytical Philosophy

I believe that several key features of analytical philosophy help to generate and support this prevalent, negative, or at least indifferent, attitude toward the study of the history of philosophy. Obviously, some analytical philosophers notably do not accept some of the features I will be outlining. For example, Quine—who has already played an important role in our proceedings and who will do so again—is certainly one of the outliers among analytical philosophers, as well as Davidson and Michael Dummett. And I do not claim to provide an exhaustive list of important general features in analytical philosophy. There are, of course, many other plausible candidate features around which one can offer a compelling general account of the nature of analytical philosophy. Nevertheless, I think that the features I will call attention to are, indeed, structural features of much of analytical philosophy, and I think that they also help to illuminate why analytical philosophy has been, in important respects, anti- or non-historical. As we will see, these pillars of analytical philosophy point to problems that threaten to undermine the kind of support analytical philosophy enjoys.

The features I have in mind are three:

(a) *Realism*: The world is, in general, not dependent on our ways of thinking about it. Rather, the world is the way it is prior to—or independently of—our beliefs about the world. We strive to capture the features of the world that are there *anyway* or "out there," independently of our beliefs. Thus, Bernard Williams speaks of "the absolute conception of reality," of an "adequate conception of the reality which is there 'anyway'" (*Descartes: The Project of Pure Enquiry*, p. 65). Theodore Sider memorably expresses his commitment to realism in the following terms:

> A certain "knee-jerk realism" is an unargued presupposition of this book. Knee-jerk realism is a vague picture rather than a precise thesis. According to the picture, the point of human inquiry—or a very large

chunk of it anyway, a chunk that includes physics—is to *conform* itself to the world, rather than to *make* the world. The world is "out there," and our job is to wrap our minds around it. This picture is perhaps my deepest philosophical conviction. I've never questioned it; giving it up would require a reboot too extreme to contemplate; and I have no idea how I'd try to convince someone who didn't share it. (*Writing the Book of the World*, p. 18)

Of course, such characterizations of realism do not, by themselves, enable us to settle the question of whether certain philosophers are realists. For example, Kant is a realist of a certain kind (a so-called empirical realist), even if he is non-realist of another kind (a so-called transcendental idealist). Exactly how to understand Kant in relation to the kind of realism described by Williams and Sider is a difficult question in Kant scholarship. Some of what I say about Kant in chapter 10 will bear on this issue.

(b) *The Method of Intuition*: Analytical philosophers characteristically invoke common sense and so-called intuitions as ways of trying to advance or settle philosophical disputes. According to this method, one is entitled to reject a philosophical thesis if it goes against what is seen to be common sense or is somehow contrary to our intuitions. This method has been prominent throughout philosophy but has taken on a new and awesome and, I would say, strange importance with the rise of analytical philosophy. In chapter 11, I will explore the issue of *why* this method became so important in the analytical era. But for now, I simply want to call attention to the prevalence of this method in analytical philosophy. Thus, here are three of my favorite analytical philosophers speaking out strongly on behalf of this method. First, Kit Fine:

> I'm firmly of the opinion that real progress in philosophy can only come from taking common sense seriously. A departure from common sense is usually an indication that a mistake has been made. If you like, common sense is the data of philosophy and a philosopher should no more ignore common sense than a scientist should ignore the results of observation. A good example concerns ontology. Many philosophers have wanted to deny that there are chairs or numbers or the like. This strikes me as crazy and is an indication that they have not had a proper understanding of what is at issue. By recognizing that these things are crazy we can then come to

a better understanding of what is at issue and of how the questions of ontology are to be resolved.[1]

And here's Judith Jarvis Thomson in a similar vein:

I came to think that the main, central problems consist in efforts to explain what makes certain pre-philosophical, or nonphilosophical, beliefs true. Which beliefs? Philosophers differ in their interests, but the ones that have interested philosophers, generally, in generation after generation, are those that we rely on in ordinary life. Not surprisingly, it was Moore, not Wittgenstein, who struck me as the leader. (I suspect that I could have said Aristotle instead of Moore.) I still think that way of understanding what philosophy is roughly right.[2]

Finally, we find David Lewis saying in an oft-quoted passage:

One comes to philosophy already endowed with a stock of opinions. It is not the business of philosophy either to undermine or justify these pre-existing opinions to any great extent, but only to try to discover ways of expanding them into an orderly system. (*Counterfactuals*, p. 88)

Fine, Thomson, and Lewis here invoke common sense and pre-theoretical beliefs or opinions. Other philosophers, as Lewis himself sometimes also does, speak in terms of "intuition."[3] Some of these philosophers see intuitions as including commonsense beliefs—perhaps Lewis falls into this category; others—e.g., George Bealer and John Bengson—distinguish intuition from commonsense beliefs.[4] On this latter view, intuitions may be a matter of an intellectual seeming, a kind of rational insight or presentation that we might have, e.g., when seeing how a certain geometrical argument works. (Here the quasi-perceptual terms are intentional.) Both the appeal to common sense

---

[1] Kit Fine, Interview with *3:AM Magazine*. See also Fine, "The Question of Realism," p. 1.
[2] Thomson, "How It Was," p. 54. For calling my attention to this passage from Thomson as well as the interview with Fine, I am indebted to Brian Leiter's philosophy blog.
[3] Lewis, "Introduction," p. x.
[4] Bealer, "Intuition and the Autonomy of Philosophy," and "Modal Epistemology and the Rationalist Renaissance"; Bengson, "The Intellectual Given." See also Jenkins, "Intuition, 'Intuition,' Concepts, and the A Priori," and Symons, "Intuition and Philosophical Methodology," p. 86.

and the appeal to intuition in the sense of intellectual seeming involve a kind of direct mental access to—and passive reception of—important truths. I will, somewhat inaccurately, call the general methodology at work here by the term "the method of intuition."[5]

There are many domains in which this method holds sway in philosophy, from epistemology to moral philosophy to philosophy of language to metaphysics. Readers of philosophy are asked to consult their magical faculty of intuition or magical faculty of common sense in order to reach certain conclusions. Of course, as is agreed on almost all sides nowadays, appeals to common sense or intuitions are fallible.[6] (This apparent fallibility of intuition invoked in contemporary and recent philosophy will form the basis of one of my challenges to the method of intuition in chapter 11.) Despite this apparent fallibility, such appeals to intuition or common sense are, as it were, the gold standard in analytical philosophy. As Kripke puts it in an oft-quoted passage, "I think it [having intuitive content] is very heavy evidence in favor of anything, myself. I really don't know, in a way, what more conclusive evidence one can have about anything, ultimately speaking" (*Naming and Necessity*, p. 42). Goldman similarly claims that "[t]he evidential weight accorded to intuition is often very high, in both philosophical practice and philosophical reflection."[7]

In his recent book, *Philosophy Without Intuitions*, Herman Cappelen offers an intricate and provocative rebuttal of the view of Goldman and others that philosophers rely on intuitions as a kind of evidence. Cappelen is certainly

---

[5] For an illuminating, historically informed discussion of some of the different things that might be meant by "intuition" and "common sense," see Dutilh Novaes and Geerdink, "The Dissonant Origins of Analytic Philosophy: Common Sense in Philosophical Methodology." Bengson regards presentations (of which his intuitions are a variety) as passive and non-voluntary ("The Intellectual Given," p. 721).

[6] For discussions of the fallibility of intuitions, see Parsons, "Platonism and Mathematical Intuition in Kurt Gödel's Thought," pp. 56, 59; Bengson, "The Intellectual Given," p. 715; Cappelen, *Philosophy Without Intuitions*, p. 12; Bealer, "The Incoherence of Empiricism," pp. 102, 104, "Modal Intuition and the Rationalist Renaissance," p. 202; Weatherson, "What Good Are Counterexamples?," pp. 3–5; Weinberg, "How to Challenge Intuitions Empirically Without Risking Skepticism," pp. 320–21; Jenkins, "Intuition, 'Intuition,' Concepts and the A Priori"; and Kornblith, "Naturalism and Intuitions," pp. 36–37. Lewis says of intuition, "It's not that common sense speaks with the voice of some infallible faculty of 'intuition,'" (*On the Plurality of Worlds*, p. 134). Weinberg, Crowley, Gonnerman, and Vandewalker in "Intuition and Calibration," offer a lively presentation of many important ways in which intuition may be fallible. By contrast, Ludwig regards intuitions as expressing conceptual competence and thus, for him, "their reliability is guaranteed" ("The Epistemology of Thought Experiments: First Person versus Third Person Approaches," p. 137n20). Of course, in the history of philosophy, intuitions were often regarded as infallible. See, e.g., Descartes, *Rules*, rule 3 and Spinoza, *Ethics*, especially the second scholium of part II, proposition 40.

[7] Goldman, "Philosophical Intuitions: Their Target, Their Source, and Their Epistemic Status," p. 1. See also Kelly, "Common Sense as Evidence," pp. 53–78.

right to point out that analytical philosophers do not use the term "intuition" in any precise way and that they employ the term with "undisciplined variability" (p. 86). At the same time that he downplays intuition, however, Cappelen is happy to see analytical philosophers relying on "pre-theoretical claims" and appealing to a "common ground" of beliefs or claims taken for granted.[8] Such reliance—whether or not it is an explicit appeal to something called "intuition"—plays much the same role that the reliance on intuition or common sense plays in much of analytical philosophy and in the self-understanding of many analytical philosophers. So, in the end, Cappelen doesn't depart very much from the general phenomenon that I am calling the method of intuition but that I am equally happy to call the method of relying on common sense or on pre-theoretical claims or on a common ground.

I will have more to say about the method of intuition in chapter 11, but for our purposes in this chapter, it is enough to point out that the method of intuition which appeals to our direct access to important truths goes hand in hand with the realism that is characteristic of analytical philosophy. Intuition and common sense put us in touch with facts that are out there anyway, and these facts are facts about the world and not, primarily, about us or about our way of thinking of the world. If, as realism contends, the world is independent of our beliefs, and if we are to have knowledge of the way the world is, then—so the reasoning behind the method of intuition goes—there must be some means by which we can receive or come to know facts about the world. In many cases, the passive faculties that allow us to have such knowledge are our senses, but in other cases, the relevant passive faculty is not sense, but rather common sense or intuition. This reliance on common sense or intuition is coherent only if one presupposes that there is a world out there independent of our beliefs, i.e. only if one presupposes that some form of realism is true.

(c) *Discreteness*: Prevalent in analytical philosophy—though perhaps less so than either realism or the method of intuition—is the view that the world is full of independent things or facts with no metaphysically necessary connections among them. Such discreteness is evident in the independence between belief and world that is at work in realism and in the method of intuition which presupposes realism. This discreteness is also at work in such views as Humean supervenience (to be found in the work of David Lewis and his followers), in Russellian logical atomism,

---

[8] See *Philosophy Without Intuitions*, pp. 137, 147, 165, 167n19, 172, 178, 184n29, 187.

and, perhaps, in Wittgenstein's *Tractatus Logico-Philosophicus*. I call the general position here by the less usual term "discreteness" since this term is more general than the more common term "atomism." Discreteness may not require, as atomism does, that the items are metaphysical simples or atoms. Of particular interest to us, given our topic in this chapter, will be the way in which the *meanings* of expressions, sentences, thoughts, and texts are often presumed, in many stretches of analytical philosophy, to be discrete and to be independent of the meanings of other expressions, sentences, thoughts, and texts, and, in general, the way in which the meaningfulness of meaningful items is presumed to be independent of the non-meaningfulness of non-meaningful items.

Because it will be important when we turn to the study of the history of philosophy, I want to highlight a key feature of each of the three struts of analytical philosophy, viz. that each of these three themes trades upon a commitment to bare, external relations among some things. Thus, realism evinces external relations between the state of the world and our beliefs about the world. The world is the way it is independently of those beliefs. Given this independence, it is a challenge to secure the matching of these beliefs with the world. This is a version of the problem of skepticism, and it arises because of the independence that realism entails. Realists who want to maintain their realism must (and do) resort to Moorean or other more or less desperate maneuvers in order to head off skepticism, and so we have a major strand in the contemporary field of epistemology. Some of these maneuvers—such as the appeal to a marvelous faculty of intuition—may seek to re-establish some kind of connection between beliefs and the world, but still the question "in virtue of what does this special relation hold?" seems to remain unanswered. A brute connection is posited, and thus again—as with realism—we have a bare, external relation between beliefs and the world.

With regard to the method of intuition, we can see in another way a commitment to such relations. To employ the method of intuition is to privilege certain attitudes (the intuitive or commonsensical ones) over others despite the fallibility of those intuitions. I would argue that, given such fallibility, there is no good reason to privilege certain attitudes, and thus the distinction between—and thus the relation between—beliefs that we privilege and those that we do not must remain arbitrary and unprincipled. I will return to and develop this point in chapter 11.

The commitment to brute relations is even more evident with regard to discreteness. According to discreteness, things or facts of various kinds are fundamentally loose and separate, and it is this looseness that makes whatever relation these things or facts happen to enjoy arbitrary and ungrounded. Such a commitment by proponents of discreteness to ungrounded relations is evident in the widespread denial of the Principle of the Identity of Indiscernibles and in the consequent affirmation of the possibility of things that are distinct *solo numero*, i.e. things whose non-identity is a brute fact.[9]

The Three Struts and the Study of the History of Philosophy

Each of the three features of analytical philosophy—realism, the method of intuition, and discreteness—together with the bare, external relations that these features bring along help generate the distinctive neglect of or disdain for the study of the history of philosophy that we find in much of analytical philosophy.

Thus if, as with realism, the way the world is, is independent of our thoughts about the world, then, in our attempts to understand the world, why should we dwell on what philosophers have thought about the world? From this perspective, it is urgent to get on with the business of getting at the world itself, and luckily we have the means to do so.

For a proponent of the method of intuition, we have a faculty that gives us access to mind-independent facts relevant to philosophy. Given this blessed gift, why do we philosophers—it might be thought—need to expend the effort required to study the history of philosophy which is, for the most part, riddled with counterintuitive or non-commonsensical and ultimately confused views?[10] Such historical study may be useful and may provide good background for our philosophical endeavors, but it is hardly central to

---

[9] For critical discussion by analytical philosophers of the Principle of the Identity of Indiscernibles, see Black, "The Identity of Indiscernibles," and Adams, "Primitive Thisness and Primitive Identity." For defenses of the Principle, see Della Rocca, "Two Spheres," and "Primitive Persistence."

[10] Of course, one may wonder why it is the case that—as on the prevailing view—we contemporary philosophers are so much better at making use of intuitions than earlier philosophers were.

philosophy, the main business of which, again, is, as Fine suggests, the judicious deployment of intuitions or commonsense beliefs in order to get at the world as it really is.

Finally, given the discreteness of things in general, the significance of our views today is independent of past philosophical views. Thus, it is unclear what bearing, if any, historical views have on our philosophical endeavors today. In light of this independence, it can seem better, insofar as we are doing philosophy, just to do philosophy and not to focus on trying to understand historical views. Again, our views can be advanced without appeal to—or study of—earlier, invariably misguided, views.

This disdain for, or marginalization of, or disregard of, the history of philosophy on the part of some analytical philosophers has given rise to a kind of frozen-ness or suspended animation or artificial atemporality of analytical philosophy. With analytical philosophy often comes the sense of a totally new beginning in philosophy, a beginning in which—with the transcending contributions of the likes of Frege, Russell, and Moore—we have made a decisive break with the past. Our task now is to accommodate, internalize, and unpack the meaning of their unprecedented insights. Frege and Russell and Moore are now timelessly our eternal conversation partners for they advanced (or, speaking timelessly, "advance") philosophy to a new plane. It is *their* projects we need to pursue. Later luminaries may be great, but they in one way or another merely carry out the marching orders given, in some cases, more than a century ago by Frege and Co. who are in a strange way our contemporaries in a kind of specious present of philosophy. Their works thus have the appearance of both transcending time and of being absurdly present to us. In this way, analytical philosophy has seemed to achieve the point of view of eternity. As I mentioned in chapter 2, Spinoza says that it is the nature of reason to perceive things under a certain aspect of eternity. But the eternal aspect under which analytical philosophy regards its founding figures is anything but rational, for it turns on arbitrarily cutting philosophy off from—and marginalizing or sometimes even forgetting—its history.

One of the clearest expressions of this analytical break with the past emerges in a remarkable essay by Michael Dummett entitled, "Can Analytical Philosophy Be Systematic and Ought It to Be?" Dummett contends that, with the work of Frege, philosophy has reached a turning point and has finally "come of age" (p. 457). In a famous passage, Dummett claims:

> Only with Frege was the proper object of philosophy finally established: namely, first that the goal of philosophy is the analysis of the structure of *thought*; secondly, that the study of *thought* is to be sharply distinguished from the study of the psychological processes of *thinking*; and, finally, that the only proper method for analyzing thought consists in the analysis of *language*. (p. 458)

Dummett goes on to stress that "the acceptance of these three tenets is common to the entire analytical school" (p. 458).[11] He indicates that, by means of this turning point, philosophy can at last put behind it its wayward past in which practitioners of philosophy had "not yet attained a clear view of its subject-matter and goals" (p. 457). Dummett's work, in general, is filled with appreciation of the historical origins of analytical philosophy, and he has done an enormous amount to teach us about these beginnings.[12] Nonetheless, in this passage we can see the labeling of the philosophical past as a past of confusion coupled with the fresh air of a new beginning filled with wide vistas of promise and hope. In this separation of philosophy's past from philosophy's present, we have in paradigmatic form the discreteness to which the analytical philosopher is often drawn.

We see Russell as also expressing the view that analytical philosophy is a transformative moment in philosophy. Russell closes his book *Our Knowledge of the External World* with the pronouncement:

> The one and only condition, I believe, which is necessary in order to secure for philosophy in the near future an achievement surpassing all that has hitherto been accomplished by philosophers, is the creation of a school of men with scientific training and philosophical interests, unhampered by

---

[11] Notice that the features that Dummett lights on are different from my list of guiding themes, although, arguably, his focus on non-psychologistic thought can be seen as an expression of realism in my sense. In other aspects of his work, Dummett can be seen as challenging in welcome fashion each of what I have called three struts of analytical philosophy. It is for this reason that I said earlier that Dummett is an outlier among analytical philosophers.

[12] See especially Dummett, *Origins of Analytical Philosophy*. For an extremely helpful discussion of Dummett, I am indebted to Anat Matar.

the traditions of the past, and not misled by the literary methods of those who copy the ancients in all except their merits. (p. 242)

And it is clear from the beginning of that book that Russell, like Dummett after him, sees Frege as instituting the method that sharply separates philosophy's present from its past. Russell speaks of "the logical-analytic method in philosophy" and says that "the first complete example [of this method] is to be found in the writings of Frege" (p. v).

These passages from Dummett and Russell have helped to engender a perspective on philosophy to which many far less subtle and nuanced analytical philosophers seem to subscribe. According to this perspective, the contemporary philosopher cuts a figure much like that of the title character in *The Great Gatsby* by the great American novelist F. Scott Fitzgerald. Just as Gatsby seeks to shed the past and venture out into the new world, so too analytical philosophy, on this common view, seeks to inhabit a new world of philosophy with fresh opportunities and an unfettered new method for realizing its dreams, for exploiting the philosophical terrain. Unfortunately, Gatsby's outcome was not a happy one, and, as Fitzgerald reminds us, Gatsby, was—as we are—"borne back ceaselessly into the past." Perhaps, then, this example suggests that we would do well in philosophy to avoid this kind of attempt to break away from or forget the past. But how exactly can we do that?

An Isolationist Response on Behalf of the Study of the History of Philosophy

There is a possible way to deal with the forgetfulness on the part of analytical philosophy, a manner of opposition for which I have deep respect, even though, in the end, I take a different path. This response concedes the main point of the proponents of analytical forgetfulness: the study of the history of philosophy is a distinct enterprise from the activity of philosophy itself and should be pursued for its own sake, a sake independent of what is going on in contemporary philosophy. This defense of the study of the history of philosophy as separate but equal shares a kind of isolationism with analytical forgetfulness and, in so sharing, it manifests an inclination in favor of what I have called discreteness: the concerns in the history of philosophy are best seen as discrete and as independent of the concerns (whatever they might be) that actuate contemporary philosophy.

Again, I have admiration for those who adopt this approach to and defense of the study of the history of philosophy. But I want to note that, like the appeal to the apparent singularity that is Frege's work, this isolationist defense of the study of the history of philosophy brings with it arbitrary and non-rational divisions: why should the study of the history of philosophy and contemporary philosophy be regarded so differently? Further, with this isolationist tendency, historians of philosophy may seem to become complicit in their own marginalization within philosophy: for these historians agree with the key claim that makes the marginalization possible, viz. that the study of the history of philosophy is and should be separate from the pursuit of contemporary philosophy. (This complicity is, I would say, in the end is as ill-advised in the philosophical domain as it is in the political domain. We all know how well "separate but equal" worked out in political contexts.)[13]

How then can one respond to this disdain for the study of the history of philosophy without being complicit in this marginalization? Given that the disdain is, as we have seen, intricately bound up with more or less defining features of analytical philosophy—realism, the method of intuition, and discreteness—one cannot effectively counteract this neglect or disdainful forgetfulness without challenging central features of analytical philosophy. Let me put it for you starkly: if one does not challenge the combination of realism, the method of intuition, and the appeal to discreteness, one is destined to accept isolationism with regard to the study of the history of philosophy.

Ascent

Having raised the stakes in this way, I want to argue that the Parmenidean Ascent shows how this challenge can be met. More specifically, the Parmenidean Ascent— in particular, the Parmenidean Ascent with regard to meaning—enables us to undermine each of the struts that characterize analytical philosophy. With this attack on these struts, we can thereby also help to secure anew for the study of the history of philosophy its important status within—or as—and not merely alongside philosophy.

---

[13] I have discussed other methodological issues surrounding an isolationist approach in "Interpreting Spinoza: The Real is the Rational." For a recent, very insightful, and optimistic treatment of these matters, see Mercer, "The Contextualist Revolution in Early Modern Philosophy."

First, I challenge realism by invoking the Parmenidean Ascent with regard to truth (a Parmenidean Ascent that, as we saw in the previous chapter, flows from the Parmenidean Ascent with regard to meaning). Realism involves a commitment to the independence of the world and our ways of thinking about the world. Such independence embodies a *distinction* between our beliefs—even our true beliefs—and what those beliefs are about. Given the commitment to undifferentiated truth, there can be no such distinction between true belief and the world as envisaged by the realist. So the first strut is brought down by the Parmenidean Ascent with regard to truth.

Turn now to the second strut: the method of intuition. Because the method of intuition presupposes, as I indicated, some form of realism, and because realism is undermined by the Parmenidean Ascent with regard to truth, in making this Parmenidean Ascent we are also challenging the method of intuition.

Finally, consider the remaining strut: discreteness. This is the commitment to the independence of things or facts in general from one another. Such discreteness—embodying as it does the pervasiveness of external relations—is ruled out by the Parmenidean Ascent in general which is supported by my frequent, Bradleyan arguments for the unintelligibility of relations, including relations of distinctness.

Beyond the challenge to the method of intuition that I just sketched, I will explore further challenges to this method in chapter 11, where I more generally consider strategies for responding to opposition to the Parmenidean Ascent. Here—in the rest of this chapter—I want to focus on what the Parmenidean Ascent, especially with regard to meaning, can teach us in particular about the relation between philosophy and the study of its history.

If we make the Parmenidean Ascent with regard to meaning, then, as I argued, we reject discrete nuggets of meaning and instead come to regard meaning as located in the world as a whole with no differentiation between things that have meaning and things that do not, and with no distinction between meanings. The world is, as I put it, imbued with meaning. If we regard meaning in the Parmenidean way, then there is no good way to limit what is relevant to the meaning of a term, sentence, thought, or text, and what is not relevant. In seeking to understand, e.g., a particular philosophical text, anything—i.e. *anything*—we invoke or engage with can in principle be made relevant to its meaning. This is, in a way, Quinean holism with regard to meaning taken to its natural, Parmenidean extreme.

This holism run amok has momentous implications in two different directions for the study of the history of philosophy and for philosophy itself. First, given the Parmenidean Ascent with regard to meaning, the meaning of contemporary texts and positions is fixed by, inter alia, the meaning of older texts and positions in philosophy. Thus, in light of this Parmenidean Ascent, it is *of course* the case that the history of philosophy is relevant to contemporary philosophy and to the meaning of contemporary texts.

And in the other direction—perhaps more surprisingly—the meanings of older, historical positions and texts is fixed by, *inter alia*, the meaning of later texts and positions in philosophy, e.g., by the texts and positions in contemporary philosophy.

Since all is relevant to the meaning of all, there is no principled way to distinguish between philosophy and the study of its history. Philosophy expands to include what would normally be regarded as the study of its history. And the study of the history of philosophy expands to include what would normally be regarded as contemporary philosophy. Thus, in the study of the history of philosophy, we ignore contemporary philosophy at our peril, and the peril here is that in ignoring contemporary philosophy we may miss out on a source of meaning that the historical texts genuinely have. I am inclined to say that insofar as the study of the history of philosophy is authentically a study of the history of philosophy, it does not, cannot, and should not ignore contemporary philosophy. At the very least, given the Parmenidean Ascent, a dogmatic or doctrinaire isolationist or "separate but equal" approach to the study of the history of philosophy is dubious.

Similarly, contemporary philosophy cannot afford to ignore the history of philosophy. Indeed, I am inclined to say that insofar as the pursuit of contemporary philosophy is authentically a pursuit of philosophy, it does not, cannot, and should not ignore the history of philosophy.[14] Again, an isolationist approach is dubious.

Thus, the Parmenidean Ascent with regard to meaning leads to a Parmenidean Ascent—an eliding of distinctions in response to an explanatory demand—with regard to the alleged contrast between philosophy and the study of its history. Here the operative explanatory demand is the explanatory demand with regard to meaning: what is it in virtue of which texts (etc.) mean what they do?

---

[14] In chapter 11, I use a different argument to reach the same conclusion.

In this way, the Parmenidean Ascent provides a nice contrast to and antidote for the frozen-ness in a specious present that characterizes much of analytical philosophy. With the Parmenidean Ascent, *all* texts become permanently relevant to philosophy, permanently alive. To view philosophy thus is to see the past of philosophy as endlessly alive in its present. And, to take up this attitude is—in a way that is better grounded and less artificial than is the odd forgetfulness of much of analytical philosophy—to view things under an aspect of eternity. In this respect—to echo a theme from another great American novelist, William Faulkner—the past is never dead, it's not even past.[15]

Of course, given the radical nature of the Parmenidean Ascent, we may be able to go further than merely rejecting a distinction between philosophy and the study of its history. My argument here also points to the eradication of a distinction between philosophy and any "other" field of inquiry, and indeed between any "two" fields of inquiry. Although such a result should not be surprising in light of my general Parmenideanism, this outcome may seem to be a paradoxical self-undermining of my position. For my whole approach so far seems predicated upon there being a distinctive form of inquiry that is philosophy, upon the possibility of a philosophical investigation of substance, action, knowledge, etc. But now the very arguments I have given lead me to flirt with the idea that this presupposition is false. I will address this and other apparently self-undermining aspects of my position in chapter 9 and, in different and perhaps more powerful forms, in chapters 12 and 13.

---

[15] This quote is to be found in Faulkner's 1951 novel, *Requiem for a Nun*.

8
Metaphysical Explanation

I have undertaken Parmenidean Ascents in a number of central philosophical domains, including being, action, knowledge, meaning, and truth. In the previous chapter, I also embraced a Parmenidean Ascent with regard to the distinction between philosophy and the study of its history. In connection with this most recent Parmenidean Ascent in particular, I gestured at an apparently paradoxical, apparently self-undermining aspect of my Parmenidean endeavor. Each of these Parmenidean Ascents turns directly or indirectly on a certain explanatory demand, on a demand for a metaphysical explanation of a key philosophical notion. Given the pervasive connections between Parmenidean Ascents and metaphysical explanations, it is, perhaps, fitting that the final Parmenidean Ascent we will undertake regards the notion of metaphysical explanation itself. This last, and in some ways most dramatic, Parmenidean Ascent will lead us up to and into the very maw of paradox (in chapter 9), and it is here that the threat of self-undermining is most grave. And it is also here, as we shall see, that the reality of such self-undermining is most freeing. Apart from its direct path to self-undermining, the Parmenidean Ascent with regard to metaphysical explanation will be, in a certain respect, importantly different from the other Parmenidean paths on which I have embarked because it will invoke a notion of practical rationality that has not been explicitly employed in the previous cases.

Welcome Back

Let's begin this final Parmenidean Ascent with a round of applause for—an appreciation of—the work philosophers have done of late in order to rehabilitate the ancient notion of metaphysical explanation. Philosophers have recently gone to great lengths to acquaint or reacquaint their colleagues, students, and readers with this venerable notion. Roughly—and this characterization will suffice for our purposes—metaphysical explanation is the phenomenon whereby a thing, fact, object, or whatever, A, is the ground of another thing, fact, object, or whatever, B. Perhaps equivalently, B exists or obtains in virtue of A. This relation between A and B can be cashed out (but need not be) in terms of greater fundamentality: A is more fundamental than B. Or: A is the—or a—basis for B. B is at least partially metaphysically grounded in A.

And, of course, the grounding need not be spelled out as a relation between two items of whatever kind. Ground can be captured by means of a sentential operator (as we noted in chapter 3). Instead of "A stands in a grounding relation to B" (or something like that), we can say more austerely, as I just did, "B exists or obtains in virtue of A." No commitment here to a grounding relation.

Several restrictions are typically placed on grounding: it is asymmetric, irreflexive, and transitive. There are alleged counterexamples to each of these restrictions, and so there is controversy here. But these controversies need not detain us. The point for now is that grounding and the notion of metaphysical explanation have come back into vogue.

Such a notion had more or less fallen into disrepute or at least neglect, especially in so-called analytical philosophy, for much of the twentieth century. But in recent analytical philosophy, the notion has been revived, perhaps especially by the important work of Kit Fine.[1] The speed of the rehabilitation since the 1990s is all the more astounding in comparison to the slowness of the revival of the related notion of the modal over the course of the twentieth century when we philosophers took a great deal of time to get over some anti-metaphysical scruples that had achieved considerable influence. These, often Quinean, worries about the modal held great sway before they were, it seems, finally overcome. But have these qualms genuinely been overcome? Gideon Rosen thinks that the project of rehabilitating modal notions "is now more or less complete" and the value of this project is "beyond dispute."[2] Although I'm not so sanguine (quite the opposite, in fact, as we will see), I won't challenge this picture right now.[3] And while there are important doubts about grounding from dedicated critics[4] and also from conscientious

---

[1] Seminal papers in this regard are Fine's "Essence and Modality" and "The Question of Realism." Also extremely influential is Schaffer's, "On What Grounds What." Schaffer's approach to grounding differs in significant ways from Fine's, but these differences are neither here nor there—actually they're there and not here.

[2] Rosen, "Metaphysical Dependence," p. 134.

[3] I've told part of this less happy story about modality in "Essentialists versus Essentialism."

[4] E.g., Hofweber, "Ambitious, Yet Modest, Metaphysics"; Daly, "Scepticism about Grounding"; Wilson, "No Work."

proponents of grounding,⁵ the main impression one gets from checking in on the philosophical literature on grounding is that—as is now the case with modality—it's "all systems go." As Rosen says, "we have no reason to doubt that an adequate theory of this sort [concerning grounding] might be attainable."⁶

This confidence in grounding seems especially well-, well, well-grounded when one considers the substantial basis in intuition from which any theory of grounding may draw. Thus, the theorist of grounding claims or may claim support from intuitions or apparent intuitions to the effect that in certain cases one thing or fact grounds another. Consider, for example, Greta Garbo and her lonely singleton. It seems obvious that there is an asymmetrical dependence here: the singleton depends on Garbo and not vice versa.⁷ Equally—to use an example from Paul Audi—it seems that in virtue of its shape, the ball is disposed to roll. Also, dispositions seem to depend on categorical properties (solubility on a certain structure, etc.). Semantic facts seem to hold in virtue of non-semantic facts. Normative facts seem to depend on non-normative facts. And the list of intuitions favorable to grounding goes on. If the claim that there are cases of grounding is to be rejected, then one will have to contend with these intuitions, and doing so may not be pretty. Such an abundance and variety of intuitions don't go quietly into the night.⁸

Again, I applaud all these developments for their rigor, boldness, etc. These developments are all wrong, of course, but still I applaud. My praise is tempered in this way because I think that there are reasons to doubt that there are any instances of grounding, and indeed reasons to doubt the coherence of the notion of grounding. I believe that these reasons are broadly in keeping with the spirit of Quine's best argument against modality: what I call the argument from arbitrariness. In order to appreciate my strategy, note that one commonly accepted feature of grounding or of metaphysical explanation—along with transitivity, irreflexivity, and asymmetry—is its primitivity. As Ricki Bliss puts it, "The more or less received view among proponents of grounding ... is that the concept isn't analyzable—the concept of grounding is ultimately primitive

---

⁵ Audi, "Toward a Theory of the in-Virtue-of Relation"; Schaffer, "On What Grounds What"; Bennett, "Construction Area (No Hard Hat Required)," "By Our Bootstraps," and *Making Things Up*.
⁶ Rosen, "Metaphysical Dependence," p. 134.
⁷ For this kind of example, see Fine, "Essence and Modality" and just about any other paper in the literature on grounding.
⁸ Daly, "Scepticism about Grounding," discusses some strategies for challenging the significance of these intuitions.

in nature."[9] It is because of this widely attributed primitivity of metaphysical explanation that the lead-up to this Parmenidean Ascent will be different from other Parmenidean paths in this book. Typically, I have invoked an explanatory demand with regard to the target notion. Thus, I've pointed out how widespread the explanatory demand is in a given domain. I then—riding my Bradleyan steed—deploy this acceptance of the explanatory demand against the standard understanding of the phenomenon as differentiated. The strategy was different in the case of truth and in the case of the distinction between philosophy and the study of its history where the reliance on an explanatory demand was not directly in connection with the target notions—truth or the contrast between philosophy and the study of its history. Instead, the explanatory demand arose in connection with the notion of meaning which was presupposed in different ways by the target notions. In the current case, because of the broad appeal of the alleged primitivity of metaphysical explanation, there is less or even no commitment in the grounding literature to an explanatory demand with regard to metaphysical explanation. Thus, in order to facilitate the Parmenidean Ascent with regard to metaphysical explanation, I want—instead of invoking an explanatory demand with regard to metaphysical explanation or piggy-backing on another Parmenidean Ascent—to invoke practical rationality in a way that I haven't explicitly done before in this book. The force of my argument will thus *not* be that the proponents of metaphysical explanation violate an explanatory demand that they themselves insist on. Rather, I will argue that the proponents of metaphysical explanation—in offering metaphysical explanations—are committed to *acting* arbitrarily, without sufficient reason, in *positing* certain facts. Again, my argument here will be self-consciously analogous to—and in the spirit of—Quine's best argument against modality, viz. his argument from the arbitrariness that this notion involves. This Quinean argument—like my own argument against grounding and metaphysical explanation—is driven by a concern to avoid a certain form of practical irrationality.[10]

---

[9] Bliss, "Metaphysical Grounding," section 2. See also Rosen, "Metaphysical Dependence," p. 113; Schaffer, "On What Grounds What," pp. 364–65; Bennett, "Construction Area," p. 90; Rodriguez-Peyrera, "Why Truthmakers," p. 18.

[10] In rejecting ontological structure, I am in agreement with one of Fiocco's conclusions in his important paper, "Each Thing Is Fundamental: Against Hylomorphism and Hierarchical Structure." Like my argument, Fiocco's argument turns upon explanatory considerations. However, my argument is based on an attack on relations in general and thus is incompatible with any multiplicity of things. Fiocco doesn't invoke these more sweeping explanatory considerations, and so he embraces multiplicity and has no problem with relations as such.

A Challenge from Ockham

A focus of Quine's attack concerns the modal as extra-conceptual or extra-linguistic, i.e., the modal as a feature of objects in themselves and not as an offshoot of ways of conceiving or describing those objects. Of course, Quine has criticisms of the conceptual or linguistic notion of modality too—this is one thrust of his rejection of the analytic-synthetic distinction which I discussed in chapter 6. We'll return to his critique of conceptual or linguistic necessity later, but most relevant for our purposes now is Quine's attack on modality as worldly, as "out there." His attack invokes the specter of arbitrary action: without appealing to a basis in the conceptual or the linguistic, we have no principled way to sort the properties of objects into necessary and contingent. Drawing any such distinction is "invidious,"[11] exhibits "favoritism among the traits of an object,"[12] and "means adopting a frankly inequalitarian attitude toward the various ways of specifying the object."[13] And this lack of a principled path through the modal is the main reason, I believe, Quine warns against venturing into "the metaphysical jungle of Aristotelian essentialism."[14] I interpret this concern with invidiousness and favoritism as a worry about arbitrary action, about the lack of a principled basis for drawing modal distinctions.[15] Quine's worry is an inherently rationalist one: it is a claim that to draw modal distinctions is to act without reason, and it is a claim that modal distinctions are to be rejected on that basis. To call this move rationalist is not, of course, to deny that Quine is motivated by empiricist reasons as well. Such is the beauty of rationalism—seen as the concern to avoid brute facts—that it is, in fact, surprisingly compatible with empiricist views. It may seem odd to put Quine in the rationalist camp to even this limited extent, but I believe, as I indicated in chapter 6, that Quine had a clandestine love affair with rationalism and with that hallmark of rationalism, the Principle of Sufficient Reason, or the PSR.

Most now think that Quine's attack on modality did not succeed. I have argued elsewhere that a souped-up version of his attack does succeed, but

---

[11] Quine, "Reply to Professor Marcus," p. 184; Quine, "Reference and Modality," p. 155. Cf. Lewis in *Counterfactuals*, p. 39, where he rails against what he sees as the essentialist's making "a mystery of those facts [of *de re* modality] by denying us any way to explain why there are some sorts of transworld identities but not others." See also Lewis, *On the Plurality of Worlds*, section 4.5.

[12] "Reference and Modality," p. 155. See also Cartwright, "Some Remarks on Essentialism," p. 619.

[13] "Reply to Professor Marcus," p. 184.

[14] Quine, "Three Grades of Modal Involvement," p. 176.

[15] For further discussion of this reading of Quine's objection, see Della Rocca, "Essentialism vs. Essentialism."

this is another story—actually, it's the same story, but that it's the same story is another story. Exploring how this revamping of Quine's argument would go requires exploring more nuances about our modal locutions than we can go into here. I note, however, that the scope of my criticism in chapter 11 of what I call the method of intuition can be seen as indirectly supporting Quine's case against modality.

Quine would, doubtless, reject the notion of grounding, if only because of the modal implications that this notion is often thought to have. Further, being fundamental or non-fundamental is a feature that is usually thought of as worldly or "out there": fundamentality is a feature that objects have in a way that is not mind dependent or language dependent.[16] Later, I will discuss briefly a non-standard view according to which grounding is a non-worldly, conceptual affair. But now I want to investigate whether a Quinean charge of arbitrariness against these mind- and language-independent features can be developed. I think such a worry may be behind some of the critiques of grounding as dark and obscure that we find among some of the skeptics about fundamentality. But this charge has not been articulated in the case of grounding, as far as I know. Perhaps one who comes closest—ironically, but not surprisingly given his insight into and command of the issues—is Schaffer, and it is to this criticism that I now turn.

The criticism is this: grounding and a structured ontology violate the universally beloved methodological principle, Ockham's Razor. The principle is often formulated as "A plurality is not to be posited without necessity" or as "Entities are not to be multiplied beyond necessity."[17] Exactly why we should abide by Ockham's Razor is not immediately apparent. A side benefit of the ensuing discussion in this chapter is that it will, I hope, throw some light on the Razor's appeal. The important points for now are that this precept is widely and wildly popular, and thus that if a structured ontology does indeed

---

[16] Audi stresses this point in "Toward a Theory of the in-Virtue-of Relation."

[17] In Latin: "*Pluralitas numquam ponenda est sine necessitate*" and "*Entia non esse multiplicanda praeter necessitate.*" For discussion of the origins in medieval philosophy of these formulations of the Razor, see Brampton, "Nominalism and the Law of Parsimony"; Maurer, "Method in Ockham's Nominalism" and "Ockham's Razor and Chatton's Anti-Razor." Apparently, the former of these two formulations is more genuinely Ockham's; the latter version was made popular by later thinkers, including Leibniz. Thus, Leibniz says, "The general rule which the nominalists frequently use is that entities must not be multiplied beyond necessity" ("Preface to an Edition of Nizolius," in Leibniz, *Philosophical Papers and Letters*, p. 128, Gerhardt IV 158). For a detailed discussion of different versions of Ockham's Razor and for critical analysis of different uses of those different versions, see Sober, *Ockham's Razors: A User's Manual*.

violate Ockham's Razor, then this is a very serious challenge to the notion of grounding.

How does this criticism arise? First, some background. As I noted, grounding is usually seen as a primitive notion. Still, we can say enough about what this relation is supposed to be and about what other notions may be defined in terms of it to be able to say that the grounded derives from—has its source in—its ground or grounds. As Schaffer puts it, "The posterior is grounded in, dependent on, and derivative from [the primary]."[18] Similarly, Leibniz, in a passage quoted by Schaffer,[19] says that the reality of non-fundamental entities is "borrowed" (*mutuata*) from more fundamental entities.[20] For proponents of grounding, the grounds are rich enough to give rise to all other beings. The grounded are somehow, as Schaffer puts it, "latent" in the grounds.[21] Or, shifting the vocabulary, Louis deRosset says that, for the proponent of grounding, the less fundamental are "fully explicable solely by reference to" the fundamental.[22] Given that the grounded is latent in the grounds, why bother positing the grounded? It seems gratuitous to do so, for whatever we think we might need the grounded for—whatever work the grounded might do—can always be done simply by staying at the fundamental level because the non-fundamental is already contained within the fundamental.

Of course, we might think we need a certain non-fundamental item, B, in order to explain an even less fundamental item, C. Explaining C is something the fundamental item A cannot do on its own. However, since A is so very rich, it already contains both B and C. If C is explained by and thus latent in B, and if B is latent in A, then C is latent in the fundamental thing A as well. We can't say we *need* the non-fundamental to explain what the non-fundamental explains because if one grants that all the non-fundamental items are latent within the fundamental, then it becomes redundant to posit the non-fundamental as distinct from the fundamental. Thus, Schaffer acknowledges, "There is redundancy in what exists."[23] In positing the non-fundamental we

---

[18] Schaffer, "On What Grounds What," p. 351.
[19] Schaffer, "Monism: The Priority of the Whole," p. 37n12.
[20] Leibniz to de Volder, June 30, 1704, Gerhardt II 267. Cf. Fine, "Any element of the ontology can be constructed from the basic elements of the ontology by means of constructors in the ontology" ("The Study of Ontology," p. 267).
[21] Schaffer, "On What Grounds What," p. 378.
[22] deRosset, "Getting Priority Straight," p. 74n7. Cf. Audi, "Grounding: Toward a Theory of the in-Virtue-of Relation."
[23] Schaffer, "From Nihilism to Monism," p. 189. See also Schaffer, "Monism," section 2.2.1: "if the proper parts explain anything at all, they are redundant."

are, it seems, multiplying entities without needing to do so. In other words, the proponent of grounding, in positing non-fundamental entities, violates Ockham's Razor.

In response to this worry, Schaffer follows that old metaphysical dictum, "When in trouble, modify." He makes what seems to be the reasonable move of modifying Ockham's Razor: "I think that Occam's Razor needs revision to distinguish *fundamental* entities from *derivative* entities."[24] Similarly: "Occam's Razor should be modified to take into account the notion of basicness."[25] Thus, Schaffer contends, only fundamental entities should not be posited without necessity. For Schaffer, we should not play fast and loose with the fundamental: we should posit such entities only if we have to. But, given that non-fundamental entities are—as Schaffer acknowledges—explanatorily redundant, we are free to posit them even when it is not necessary to do so. Thus, Schaffer embraces explanatory redundancy in certain cases: "Redundancy is tolerable provided the redundant entities are properly grounded in what is basic."[26]

In taking this line, Schaffer affirms the principle that

(N) Nothing non-fundamental is posited with necessity.

This emerges when Schaffer says, "Occam's Razor cuts against both explanatorily redundant and epiphenomenal entities, as there can be no need for positing either."[27] Since Schaffer holds (as we have seen) that non-fundamental entities are explanatorily redundant, he is committed to the claim that non-fundamental entities need not be posited, i.e., Schaffer is committed to (N).

(N) and modified Ockham's Razor can be seen as required by what Schaffer calls the "bang for the buck" principle: "What one ought to have is the strongest theory (generating the most derivative entities) on the simplest basis (from the fewest substances [fundamental entities])."[28] Or, as Schaffer says:

---

[24] Schaffer, "Why the World has Parts," p. 87.
[25] Schaffer, "Monism," section 2.2.2.
[26] Schaffer, "From Nihilism to Monism," p. 189. For a similar proposal, see Cameron, "Truthmakers and Ontological Commitment," p. 14. In the same vein, deRosset ("Getting Priority Straight," p. 77) considers a "judicious use of Ockham's Razor" which amounts, I believe to the modified Ockham's Razor.
[27] Schaffer, "Monism," section 2.2.1.
[28] Schaffer, "On What Grounds What," p. 361; see also "On What Grounds What," pp. 377–78.

> An ontological system should optimally balance simplicity and strength, positing as few fundamental entities as possible (simplicity), grounding as many derivative entities as possible (strength). ("Why the World Has Parts," p. 88)

In other words: go for more entities (bang) if you can, as long as you keep the number of fundamental entities (buck) to a minimum.[29] If this principle is our guide, then we cannot afford to abide by the full-blown Ockham's Razor which can be read as trying to minimize bang. Because, for Schaffer, something like the bang for the buck principle is obviously a good idea to abide by, we need to modify Ockham's Razor. Schaffer's modification seems to be the best way to meet this need. So, for Schaffer, within certain limits, we are encouraged to posit non-fundamental entities even if we don't need to do so. This is a violation of the full-blown Ockham's Razor but not of the modified Ockham's Razor, which, for Schaffer, is all we want or need.

I believe that not only Schaffer but *any* proponent of grounding and of a structured ontology must endorse (N) and modify Ockham's Razor. A proponent of grounding might challenge this general claim by arguing that the non-fundamental *is* posited with necessity: simply by positing the fundamental we automatically posit the non-fundamental because, as we've stipulated, the non-fundamental has its source in, is somehow necessitated by, the fundamental. Thus, according to this challenge, the non-fundamental (like the fundamental) is posited with necessity. So, the challenger claims, the proponent of grounding does not come into conflict with Ockham's Razor even in its unmodified form.

This challenge, however, does not appreciate the force of Schaffer's insight that the proponent of grounding is committed to (N). We can easily grant—as the challenger insists—that *if* fundamental things necessitate non-fundamental things, then the non-fundamental is posited with necessity. The question, however, is, should the proponent of grounding and should a fan of unmodified Ockham's Razor grant that the fundamental genuinely necessitates something distinct from the fundamental?

If a fundamental thing, A, necessitates the distinct non-fundamental thing, B, then, as we have seen, whatever can be explained by B is already contained within A. If something could be explained by B that was not already latent within A, if it could not already be explained by A, then where

---

[29] For other constraints Schaffer places on positing entities, see "On What Grounds What," p. 359.

did this extra explanatory power in B come from? If it came from A itself, then A could already explain what B explains, and so there is no extra explanatory power in B after all. If the extra explanatory power in B did not come from A, then in what sense is B fully grounded in A? So A can explain whatever B explains. Given that B has no explanatory power over and above A, what need is there to posit this distinct item, B?

Support for the contrary view that the grounded has its own explanatory value might be thought to derive from the idea that grounding is a species of the relation of determination, another species of which is causation. Since, it might be claimed, an effect has its own explanatory value distinct from its cause, likewise the grounded has its own explanatory value distinct from its ground.[30] However, it is far from clear in what respects we should see grounding as similar to causation even if both relations are kinds of determination. In addition to this worry, one should note that the claim that effects have their own explanatory value distinct from their causes is also far from clear and can be challenged.[31] Thus, this argument for seeing the grounded as having its own explanatory value is problematic on more than one front. Of course, this matter requires further discussion, but we can see at least some of the reasons that I am happy to go along with many proponents of grounding in seeing the grounded as having no separate explanatory value.

Given this feature of any grounding situation, we can ask: if anything that B explains can already be explained by A, then what reason is there to accept the scenario—call it "S1"—in which A grounds or necessitates the distinct B, instead of the scenario—call it "S2"—in which A does not necessitate or ground the distinct B and there is, indeed, no distinct B? Each scenario possesses the same explanatory value. However, the proponent of grounding chooses S1 over S2, and in so doing the proponent of grounding posits more objects than would otherwise be posited. That is, the proponent of grounding posits more objects than would be posited in S2. Thus, given the availability—and equal explanatory value—of S2, a scenario with only A, B does not need to be posited after all: we could stick just with A. If we were to do so, we would not suffer a loss as far as explanatory value is concerned. On the contrary, as I will argue later, a view that posits only A has the advantage of avoiding

---

[30] Audi, "Grounding: Toward a Theory of the in-Virtue-of Relation," seems to support the view that the grounded has its own explanatory value in this way.
[31] I take some steps toward an argument for this claim in Della Rocca, "Violations of the Principle of Sufficient Reason" and in "Playing with Fire: Hume, Rationalism, and a little bit of Spinoza."

some of the unintelligibility of a view that posits B as well as A. From this perspective, i.e., given the availability of S2, it seems that if B is posited, then it is posited without necessity. Thus, in adopting S1, the proponent of grounding would be violating unmodified Ockham's Razor. And so the proponent of grounding needs to modify Ockham's Razor and accept (N) after all.[32]

Despite the fact that Schaffer (rightly, as I have just argued) endorses (N), he does sometimes say that non-fundamental entities may be needed for semantics.[33] Schaffer makes this claim in response to Horgan and Potrč who devise a semantics without any ordinary objects in the associated ontology.[34] Schaffer counters that ordinary objects are needed to get the semantics going if we adopt a version of iterated supervaluationism. As he says, the proper parts of the cosmos "provide the needed extensions" for our terms.[35] (The details are irrelevant here.) For Schaffer, then, non-fundamental things are needed after all. Strictly, however, this goes against (N), and if the non-fundamental is needed for semantics, then there may be no need, after all, to modify Ockham's Razor.

But are the non-fundamental entities really needed or posited with necessity for this reason? This is far from clear. First of all, as Schaffer acknowledges, we may be able to devise a semantics without the non-fundamental as extensions. This is Horgan and Potrč's view. While Schaffer presses them because their view needs to be worked out further, their project is worth pursuing.[36] Moreover, and more importantly, do we really need to do semantics anyway? Perhaps the fundamental level is so rich on its own that not only are non-fundamental objects not needed, but also semantical relations, often between non-fundamental objects, are not needed either. Without positing the non-fundamental, it might be thought, one no longer really needs semantical relations (at least not for terms that apparently refer to the non-fundamental). It may be that, with only the fundamental in the picture, semantical relations just go out the window. In short, with just the fundamental, there may be no need for semantics in part because often one or both of the relata in a semantical relation are non-fundamental. This dismissal of semantical relations may seem to be a high price to pay, but two things here: First, I have already argued—by my Parmenidean Ascent with regard to meaning—that semantical relations are to be dismissed. Second, I think that anyone who

---

[32] For a similar line of argument, see Kim, "The Nonreductivist's Troubles with Mental Causation."
[33] "Why the World Has Parts," pp. 82, 83.
[34] Horgan and Potrč, *Austere Realism* and "Existence Monism Trumps Priority Monism."
[35] Schaffer, "Why the World Has Parts," p. 82.
[36] D'Ambrosio, "Monogamy: Or How to Make a Commitment to Only One Thing and Stick with it.," offers a powerful response to Schaffer on precisely this matter.

takes seriously the stratification of reality, as Schaffer and his followers do, should likewise take seriously the claim that semantical relations may not be at the fundamental level. If this is so, then there may be no need to posit semantical relations and thus no need to posit non-fundamental objects for the sake of semantical relations.

So for two reasons, it's not at all clear that semantics indicates that non-fundamental entities need to be posited: First, there may be some other semantics besides one that requires non-fundamental objects to serve as extensions. (Here I acknowledge Horgan and Potrč). Second, with just the fundamental, there may be no need for a semantics as ordinarily understood. (Here I depart from Horgan and Potrč).

Bracketing this concern about Schaffer's view that the non-fundamental is needed to provide extensions for our terms, I want to address head-on his modification of Ockham's Razor, a modification to which, as I have argued, any proponent of grounding is committed. I want to argue that this reconstrual of Ockham's Razor is untenable and that there is something deeply problematic about positing the non-fundamental without necessity, as Schaffer does and as any proponent of grounding should do. The worry at bottom is that such positing is an act performed for no good reason and that it brings with it an unacceptable arbitrariness or worse.

Sine Necessitate. Sine Ratione

To see why, let's draw a potential distinction between positing something with necessity and positing it for a reason. It may seem that the latter notion is weaker than the former: if something is posited with necessity, then it is posited for a reason (e.g., whatever necessitates the positing of a thing can provide a reason for positing it), but, it seems, the converse does not hold, i.e., even if something is posited for a reason, it does not seem to follow that that reason necessitates positing that thing or, in general, that the thing is posited with necessity. I want to show first that, for Schaffer and other proponents of grounding, non-fundamental things are posited for a reason. I will then show that if non-fundamental things are posited for a reason, they are—contra modified Ockham's Razor and (N)—posited with necessity. And since, as we have seen, the proponent of grounding needs modified Ockham's Razor in order to save the commitment to non-fundamental things, a structured ontology seems to be itself razed.

Let's do the first point first: for the proponent of grounding, a non-fundamental thing is posited for a reason. If the non-fundamental is not only not posited with necessity, but is posited for no reason, then we are under no rational constraint with regard to the non-fundamental. We can posit non-fundamental things at will, arbitrarily. If that's the case, then why not give up rational constraints as well with regard to positing the fundamental? That is, why not posit the fundamental without reason and thus without necessity? If we are going to make arbitrary moves at the non-fundamental level, why not at the fundamental level as well? But doing so would violate modified Ockham's Razor (as well as full-blown Ockham's Razor). So it seems unacceptable—and, I believe, it would seem unacceptable to Schaffer and to other proponents of grounding—to say that a non-fundamental thing is posited for no reason. The general point is that moves within one's metaphysics should not be made without reason. This seems to me to be a non-negotiable feature of any metaphysical (or even perhaps of any philosophical) system.[37] "Who wants an arbitrary or irrational metaphysics?" I ask rhetorically.

Again, however, even though the proponents of grounding must hold that the non-fundamental thing is posited for a reason, they must deny that it is posited with necessity, or else they would have to give up modified Ockham's Razor which is essential to the defense of a structured ontology. The key question is, is it possible for non-fundamental things to be posited with reason but without necessity? I don't think so, and here's why.

Let's say we posit a non-fundamental thing, NF, and do so—as we have just seen—for a reason. This reason—whatever it is—will be among the totality of reasons one has for positing objects or for not positing objects in this situation. Call this totality "R." These reasons may even include Schaffer's bang for the buck principle which I am willing to grant for the moment for the sake of argument. Perhaps a reason to posit NF is that doing so enables us to abide by the bang for the buck principle.

R, we are assuming, does not dictate, does not require, does not necessitate positing NF. This is merely a manifestation of Schaffer's claim that NF is not posited with necessity. If R does not necessitate positing NF, but, as the proponents of grounding must hold, R does include and provide a reason for positing NF, then this could only be because one of the following three scenarios obtains.

---

[37] I might also go so far as to say that it is the sole non-negotiable feature of a metaphysical system.

Either the reasons in R for positing NF or the reasons in R for not positing NF are equally balanced so that one has overall no more reason to posit NF than not to posit it. In this situation, given the totality of reasons, whatever one does, one would be acting arbitrarily, and so positing NF would be arbitrary and indeed without reason. There would be no reason to posit NF instead of not positing NF. This is unacceptable: again, our metaphysical moves should be more principled. In particular, our metaphysical moves should not be choices in the manner of Buridan's ass.

Next scenario: although positing NF is not necessitated, the reasons for positing NF are stronger, better, than the reasons for not positing NF. In other words, taking into account all reasons for positing in this situation, including, perhaps, the bang for the buck principle which, again, I am granting for the sake of argument, one has more reason to posit NF than not to posit it. In this light, if one does not posit NF, then, given that the totality of reasons points to NF, one would not only be acting arbitrarily but one would also be acting positively irrationally. This would be a form of ontological akrasia, and this too is unacceptable: once again, our metaphysical moves should be more principled. And, as before, I ask a rhetorical question, "Who wants an akratic metaphysics?" So one *must*, on pain of an unacceptable irrationality, posit NF: not only is NF posited for a reason or reasons, but those reasons also necessitate positing NF. This result is contrary to (N) and to modified Ockham's Razor.

Final scenario: positing NF is not necessitated and the totality of reasons, R, contains more reason not to posit NF than to posit it. In this situation, it would be irrational to posit NF, and thus, on pain of irrationality again, it is necessary *not* to posit NF. In this situation, positing NF is unacceptable: again, we expect more from our metaphysical moves than that they take place without or against reason.

So, of the three situations, the only one in which NF is posited for a reason that is overall good, i.e., the only one in which we have overall more reason to posit NF instead of not positing NF is also a situation in which positing NF is necessitated. As we saw, if NF is posited for a reason that is not overall good or better than the alternative, then one is acting arbitrarily or even irrationally, and that is unacceptable in the construction of a metaphysical system. But if NF is posited for a reason that is overall good and if one is thus positing non-arbitrarily and rationally, then one is positing with necessity: one is positing because one *needs* to do so in order to avoid an unacceptable irrationality or arbitrariness. In short, reasons for a certain course of action, if they are good and better than reasons for any alternative course of action, necessitate.

In reaching this conclusion, I am denying that one's reasons for making a metaphysical move can leave it open whether one should act in a certain way: if the reasons are reasons but don't dictate because there are equally good reasons on the other side, then whatever one does is at best arbitrary and thus unacceptable. And, of course, if the reasons are *not* equally good, then one has to go where the preponderance of reasons points. Thus, I am, in effect, insisting that, when it comes to the construction of a metaphysical system, there is no place for reasons that are reasons but nonetheless give one leeway. Not only am I rejecting ontological akrasia and ontological Buridan-style choices, but I am thus also rejecting ontological analogues of satisficing and supererogation and any kind of situation in there is room for rational prerogatives in one's metaphysical theorizing.

So, there cannot be the middle ground the proponent of grounding needs; they cannot occupy the position that NF is posited for a reason but without necessity. Thus, if NF is to be posited at all, it is posited with a reason and with necessity. This goes against modified Ockham's Razor which the proponents of grounding need in order to save a structured ontology.

In response to an earlier version of my argument against the coherence of modifying Ockham's Razor in the way that Schaffer proposes, Schaffer has proceeded—not by addressing the three-scenario dilemma that I have just raised—but by drawing an analogy between his way of modifying Ockham's Razor and other clearly rational and coherent procedures for putting restrictions on general principles of action. First, Schaffer considers the difference between two practical principles:

(a) Never use anyone's property without necessity.

and

(b) Never use anyone else's property without necessity.

(b) seems to be a perfectly reasonable dictum and, for the same reason, (a) seems perfectly unreasonable, for (a) overlooks the leeway, the freedom, one typically has in deciding to use one's own property. (a) fails to take account of the fact that using one's own property "does not violate any norms of property use."[38]

In the same way, Schaffer suggests, we should treat the following two, now-familiar dicta:

(c) Don't multiply entities without necessity.

and

(d) Don't multiply fundamental entities without necessity.

Schaffer claims that (d) (just like (b)) is a perfectly reasonable norm and that (c), like (a), is perfectly unreasonable, for (c) overlooks the fact that positing derivative entities "does not violate any norms of conceptual economy."[39]

I would like to point out in response that there is a crucial difference between the property case and the case of positing entities. In the property case, (b) is OK and (a) is not *because* one has leeway or freedom or discretion to use one's own property. Typically, one may use one's own property however one sees fit. One may use one's own property at one's whim or arbitrarily. The use of one's own property is thus properly exempt from the bounds of any constraint such as the one (a) imposes. By contrast, in the positing entities case, there is no analogous leeway or freedom or discretion, no analogous possibility of acting on a whim or arbitrarily. And that's because we're doing metaphysics, after all! In our metaphysical theorizing, as I have already said, our actions or our metaphysical moves should not be arbitrary. Nor do I believe that, on the conception of metaphysics that metaphysicians such as Schaffer operate under, our metaphysical moves may be mere matters of choice or discretion. Rather, our metaphysical moves, as I have said, should be dictated by one's overall reasons for making a metaphysical move or, in this case, positing entities. There is no room for discretion here.

So, because of the relevant disanalogy between the property case and the positing case, I argue that the fact that (b) may be legitimate as a norm of property use (while (a) is not) does not give us a reason to think that (d) is likewise legitimate as a norm of positing entities (while (c) is not).

---

[38] Schaffer, "What Not to Multiply Without Necessity," p. 659.
[39] Ibid., p. 660.

Of course, a defender of Schaffer may assume that (d), like (b), "does not violate any norm of conceptual economy," but, in the absence of any good reason to think that these cases are relevantly analogous, such an assumption would simply beg the question. Thus, I stand by the above argument against the coherence of modifying Ockham's Razor.

Having cut away the middle ground that a proponent of a structured ontology requires, we can restate Ockham's Razor in equivalent terms: "Not only should entities not be posited without necessity (*sine necessitate*), entities should also not be posited without reason (*sine ratione*)."

Thus, given that, as proponents of grounding would agree, the non-fundamental, if posited at all, is to be posited for a reason, there is no way to avoid commitment to the full-blown form of Ockham's Razor. But because, given the nature of grounding, a structured ontology must violate the full-blown form of Ockham's Razor, it follows that a structured ontology is unacceptable: it must violate the form of Ockham's Razor—the full-blown form—to which it is inevitably committed. In this light, we can see that it is not the case that a view that does not posit the non-fundamental suffers a loss of reality or explanatory value by eschewing the non-fundamental. On the contrary, by positing only the fundamental, such a view is better off for it avoids the arbitrariness and irrationality to which a structured ontology is inherently vulnerable.

To sum up the argument so far: To save a structured ontology, the proponents of grounding need to draw a distinction between positing with reason and positing with necessity. But the problem for supporters of grounding is that (overall) reasons for positing necessitate positing on pain of an irrationality of a kind that we should avoid in our metaphysical theorizing. Thus, the distinction between positing with reason and positing with necessity is ruled out. And if you want to respond to this argument by defending the value of pursuing metaphysics in an irrational manner, please be my guest.

This line of thought is, perhaps, a sophisticated—souped-up—version of a Quinean charge of invidiousness. There is, metaphysically speaking, no principled distinction between the fundamental and the non-fundamental, the prior and the posterior. Drawing any such distinction requires one to act arbitrarily or irrationally—just as, in Quine's critique of modality, drawing any distinction between the necessary and the contingent understood as mind- or language-independent features would have to be arbitrary. I have taken the Quinean criticism of modality—a criticism over which victory has been all but declared—and reshaped it to address issues of fundamentality. And in this troubling form, Quinean troubles have come back to haunt proponents of grounding.

In this light, we can see that at least part of the appeal of Ockham's Razor—full-blown Ockham's Razor—is that it rejects irrational or arbitrary actions in the service of metaphysics. And correlatively, the problem with modified Ockham's Razor is that—in its tolerance of redundancy and thus of violations of full-blown Ockham's Razor—it tolerates the positing of objects for no good reason. One reason to embrace full-blown Ockham's Razor is that it, unlike modified Ockham's Razor, does not countenance such irrational and arbitrary actions.

You might say, though, "Even if we abide by full-blown Ockham's Razor in this situation, positing is arbitrary: when faced with the choice of positing or not positing non-fundamental objects, either choice is arbitrary. So why should there be this bias against positing more objects if not positing is equally arbitrary?" But to raise this objection is to misunderstand the way that Ockham's Razor works in this context: given that we have certain objects—the so-called fundamental objects—the Ockhamian (Ockhamite? Ockham-esque? Ockhamamie?) question is, "Should we posit more?" Well, in this situation, there is no reason to posit more. But there is a reason already, presumably, to posit what you already have, i.e., there is reason already to posit the so-called fundamental objects with which you start. So keeping the status quo has a reason, but positing more things does not.

An Argument from Conceptual Priority

This attack on modified Ockham's Razor is, at the same time, an attack on the bang for the buck methodological principle which, as we saw, more or less dictates modified Ockham's Razor. Because of this connection, it behooves us to look at a direct argument Schaffer gives for the bang for the buck principle. This principle must be wrong, given the previous argument against modified Ockham's Razor, but exactly how is it wrong? Schaffer says that the "best recourse" for defending the ontologically oriented bang for the buck principle is to appeal to what might be seen as a conceptual bang for the buck principle.[40] According to this principle, a conceptual system which defines

---

[40] Schaffer, "Why the World Has Parts," p. 87.

more concepts (i.e., gets more conceptual bang) on the basis of the same or a smaller number of primitive concepts (i.e., for the same or less conceptual buck) is preferable to a conceptual system that falls short in these ways. Schaffer argues (plausibly) that just as a conceptual system that respects a bang for the buck principle is to be preferred, so too an ontological system that respects a bang for the buck principle is to be preferred. Since the conceptual bang for the buck principle is, for Schaffer, clearly to be adopted, he accords the same status to the ontological bang for the buck principle (and to modified Ockham's Razor which it dictates).

There are at least two ways to challenge this argument. (I'll leave aside here questions about the way in which the overall simplicity of a system is to be measured.) First, one might reject Schaffer's analogy and say that even if conceptual simplicity, priority, and structure are OK, ontological simplicity, priority, and structure are not. This may be a viable way of challenging Schaffer's argument, but it's not the path for me because it seems pretty unprincipled. Why should the two kinds of (apparent) priority, etc. be treated so differently?

Instead, continuing in my Quinean vein, I want to challenge, as Quine does, the notion of conceptual simplicity, priority, and structure (as well as ontological simplicity, priority, and structure). Accepting any conceptual structure requires one to act arbitrarily, just as does accepting any ontological structure (and just as, for Quine, does accepting any distinction between necessity and contingency). The challenge to conceptual structure as arbitrary is, I take it, one upshot of Quine's critique of the analytic/synthetic distinction, as we discussed in chapter 6: any such joint in the conceptual, any such distinction, is arbitrary. More generally, given the holism of concepts, there is no principled way to structure concepts. The aversion to arbitrariness at work in Quine's rejection of the analytic-synthetic distinction and in his holism is evidence of his affinity to rationalism. Given the rationalist force behind Quine's critique of analyticity, I am happy to adopt this critique and to use it as a way of showing how one might block Schaffer's argument from conceptual priority to ontological priority. Of course, much more needs to be said in order to defend properly the rejection of conceptual structure, but the main outlines of my response to Schaffer's direct argument for the bang for the buck principle should be clear: even if conceptual priority and structure and ontological priority and structure should be treated as analogous, one cannot use the ultimately arbitrary notion of conceptual priority and structure to make a case for the equally arbitrary notion of ontological priority and structure. So I reject, for broadly Quinean reasons, not only ontological structure but also conceptual structure. We have, then, not only a flat ontology, but also a flat conceptual landscape.

Once we take this line, we can see how to thwart a different attempt to save the notion of grounding. As I mentioned, grounding is typically seen as a worldly relation, independent of ways of conceiving of—or referring—to things. Perhaps, then, in light of the argument against ontological grounding that I have offered, one might be willing to see grounding as merely conceptual in nature and not as a feature of objects that is "out there." This move would be analogous to the anti-essentialist move of making modal features concept dependent or language dependent.[41] On this conceptualist view of grounding, conceived in one way, x depends on y, but conceived in another way it may not be the case that x depends on y.[42] This move would salvage some kind of grounding, even if it is not the worldly form of grounding that friends of grounding typically have in mind.

However, even this attempt must be abandoned in light of the Quinean considerations I have invoked against conceptual structure. To tie dependence to ways of conceiving things is to appeal to some kind of conceptual structure or connection which would fall under the Quinean axe.

Ascent

If, for all the reasons I have offered, we are to reject a structured ontology, then what are we to do with the powerful intuitions invoked near the beginning of this chapter, intuitions that affirm that there are grounding relations—e.g., intuitions of priority relations which it comes to poor Greta Garbo and her lonely singleton, when it comes to categorical properties and dispositions, etc.? Having tried and failed to make sense of ontological priority because it leads to irrational action and unacceptable arbitrariness, it's no longer clear why we should accord any weight to these intuitions at all. That is, it is no longer clear that we should follow intuition or apparent intuition and say that there are cases in which one thing or fact grounds another. Indeed, as I will argue in chapter 11, I believe that in most, if not all, cases relying on so-called intuitions in philosophy is arbitrary in something like the way that drawing

---

[41] See Della Rocca, "Essentialism vs. Essentialism"; Lewis, "Counterparts of Persons and their Bodies" and *On the Plurality of Worlds*, chapter 4, section 5.

[42] Fatema Amijee in "Relativism about Fundamentality" defends the similar view that the fundamentality of an entity is relative to particular ways of explaining that entity.

distinctions of ontological priority and posteriority requires us to act arbitrarily, and in something like the way that drawing distinctions of conceptual priority and posteriority requires us to act arbitrarily.

Where, then, are we? Relying on the notion of the metaphysical explanation of one thing in terms of another, and thus relying on a structured ontology, commits us to irrational action in a way that is and should be unacceptable in our metaphysical theorizing. The source of the difficulty here is that the kind of metaphysical explanation we were longing to legitimate is what may be seen as *relational* metaphysical explanation: explanation of one thing in terms of—in relation to—another. It is because of this relationality that we were, in offering such metaphysical explanations, positing the less fundamental without needing to, and thus we were acting irrationally in our metaphysical theorizing.

So, the argument so far is an argument against differentiated or relational metaphysical explanation, just as—as we saw—the analogous arguments in previous chapters were against differentiated or relational substance, action, knowledge, meaning, and truth. And, as before, the worry is not merely that there is no differentiated metaphysical explanation, but that such explanation is unintelligible, that the notion of such explanation is somehow incoherent. This denial of coherence is a deep skepticism about ontological structure, as deep as the skepticism in previous chapters about the very notions of being, action, knowledge, and meaning. The difference, though, between this case and previous ones is that in this case we have reached the skeptical, anti-relational conclusion, not directly through a Bradleyan argument that engaged with an explanatory demand in the relevant domain; we have, instead, reached this conclusion through a style of argumentation inspired by Ockham's Razor and a concern to avoid a certain kind of practical irrationality.

As in the previous chapters, we can, it seems, save the relevant notion—in this case, that of metaphysical explanation—by advancing to a non-relational version of the phenomenon, i.e., by stripping metaphysical explanation of relationality or avoiding the associated problematic use of sentential operators such as "because." As in the previous cases, metaphysical explanation must be non-relational, if we are to have metaphysical explanation at all. And thus, in giving up relational metaphysical explanation, we must also give up a structured ontology.

Without structured ontology, without grounding relations, we give up relations in general because relations in general presuppose, as we have seen, grounding relations. (Recall that relations, by their nature, are partially grounded in their relata.) So, there are no relations, and in particular there are no relations of distinction, and thus, we reach monism again—a radical form of monism without distinctions.

In keeping with this monism and this non-relational metaphysical explanation, it must be the case that there are no explanations *of* some things *in terms of* things.

There cannot be an explanation *of* something. This "of" would import a relation between the explanation and what it is allegedly an explanation of. This rejection of of-ness is in the spirit of the rejection of aboutness in chapter 6.

Equally, I am rejecting explanation of one thing *in terms of* something. The "in terms of" is relational too and must be gotten rid of.

Further—and even more radically—this also means that, since grounding is now ruled out, relations which, as we have seen, presuppose grounding are also ruled out. Thus, there cannot be any relations, in particular, between metaphysical explanation and what is not metaphysical explanation. And thus there cannot be any distinctions (i.e., any relations of distinction) between one metaphysical explanation and another.

So, metaphysical explanation must be thoroughly non-relational: not *of* anything, not *in terms of* anything, and not differentiated from anything else. We can have only non-relational explanation, non-differentiated explanation, non-individuated explanation. Thus, all is explanation, in the same way that, as we saw, all is substance, all is action, etc. And as with the terms, "substance," "action," etc., "explanation" is now something like a mass term. There are no metaphysical explanations, not even one metaphysical explanation. There is just metaphysical explanation. And it may be that, at the divine level at least, Aquinas approaches this view when he says, as we noted in chapter 5, that God is God's intellect or understanding (*Summa Contra Gentiles* I 45). With the claim that all is explanation, we have another—and indeed our final—Parmenidean Ascent, a Parmenidean Ascent with regard to metaphysical explanation itself. Actually, of course, this is the same Parmenidean Ascent all over again.

9
Paradox and the Joy of Self-Undermining

It's time to confront a specter that's been haunting this project from the beginning and has now—with chapter 8's Parmenidean Ascent with regard to metaphysical explanation and with the concomitant attack on differentiated metaphysical explanation—become especially acute and something we can no longer ignore. If, as I've just argued, differential metaphysical explanation is unintelligible and thus ruled out, then we are not entitled to the explanation *of* one thing *in terms of* something. But look—so the objection goes—we've used or attempted to use such metaphysical explanations throughout this book, particularly when we issued various explanatory demands concerning being, action, knowledge, meaning, etc. And we employed such metaphysical explanation when we issued—starting in chapter 3 and throughout subsequent chapters—a demand for an explanation *of* relations, when we said that relations must not be free-floating and must be explained *in terms of*, grounded in, (at least) their relata. But it now turns out that we weren't entitled to make any of those demands, because there isn't a coherent notion of differential metaphysical explanation at all. In this way, my overall arguments—in relying on notions that I come to see, by virtue of those very arguments, as illusory—are self-undermining.

The above line of thought is not the only way the threat of self-undermining can be seen as arising for me. Consider the difficulty I have in even stating my position. If, as I've been arguing at various points in this book, relations are to be rejected as unintelligible, then how can my position with regard to being or action or knowledge or meaning, etc., even be articulated? Such articulation requires making statements and, in particular, making statements with structure—perhaps subject-predicate structure—statements that thus exhibit relations. But, again, relations are ruled out or unintelligible, so the views I have expressed early and late in this book cannot, it turns out, be coherently articulated. Again, my position seems to be in some way self-undermining. My own arguments lead to the conclusion that I can't even state my own position (and, of course, that I can't even state that I can't state my own position, etc.).

The Parmenidean Ascent. Michael Della Rocca, Oxford University Press (2020).
© Oxford University Press.
DOI: 10.1093/oso/9780197510940.001.0001

But wait, there's more: yet another way to see the threat of self-undermining as arising is to return to a point I made at the end of chapter 7, after making the Parmenidean Ascent with regard to meaning and exploring the implications of that Parmenidean Ascent. One conclusion I drew is that there is no distinction between philosophy and any, apparently, other field of inquiry. Thus, there is, it seems, no distinctively philosophical inquiry into relations, substance, action, etc. of the kind that I apparently have been trying to conduct. So, what then am I or we doing in trying to conduct the investigation that I've been trying to conduct? Again, the coherence of the entire project seems to be called into doubt by means of my very way of conducting this project.

Finally, the threat of self-undermining was apparent at the beginning of this work when I noted (approvingly) that Parmenides' rejection of non-being, negation, and distinctions threatens to undermine itself because Parmenides mentions and makes use of non-being, negation, and distinctions in the course of establishing and articulating his position.

All this self-undermining puts us in a difficult position. (I can hear you say: "what do you mean '*us*'?") The earlier arguments in this book, relying in one way or another, as they do, on the now-discredited notions of relations and of relational metaphysical explanation, seem to be unintelligible. How, then, can we (or I) rely on them as I (or we) do in order to reach metaphysical conclusions?

In a word (actually, two words): we can't. And this is because I am challenging the very notion of reliance in a metaphysical context or the notion of metaphysical structure that such reliance presupposes.

I grant that the arguments involved in various forms of the Parmenidean Ascent are, by my own lights, incoherent or—to use a Wittgensteinian term—nonsense. Nonetheless, these arguments can be regarded as a ladder that we climb up and then throw away when we realize that they are nonsense. And in climbing, in—as I might say—ascending, we—as Wittgenstein might say—see the world aright in the sense that we are, finally, free of the illusion of distinctions, especially the distinctions that we appeal to in carrying out certain forms of metaphysical thinking. In other words, I've used relational metaphysical argumentation in order to undermine and thus transcend or overcome relational metaphysical thinking itself. Paradoxically, what I have offered is a relational metaphysical challenge to relational metaphysics itself. Indeed, I believe that I have earned—through my various Parmenidean Ascents—the right to challenge and reject and transcend or overcome relational metaphysics. And I have earned this right precisely because I argued against such metaphysics by using relational metaphysics itself. The lesson is that, because of this self-undermining argument, we cannot coherently endow any claim with relational metaphysical significance. Relational metaphysical thinking undermines itself, and through its doing so, we come to see that relational metaphysical thinking is to be rejected and overcome.

In alluding to Wittgenstein here and by invoking him as a fellow self-underminer, I do not claim that, in the *Tractatus Logico-Philosophicus* or elsewhere, Wittgenstein makes a Parmenidean Ascent, and I advance no particular interpretation of Wittgenstein.[1] I do think, however, that, despite a general affinity between Wittgenstein's position and my own, he would not be likely to look favorably upon my Parmenidean and Bradleyan rejections of distinctions and multiplicity. In the *Tractatus*, Wittgenstein can be seen as seeking to secure the possibility of logic and as seeking to preserve distinctions presupposed by logic such as the distinction between different contexts in which the same term can appear. I would argue that this kind of distinction, like all others, has got to go. Nor do I think that appealing to a distinction between so-called categorematic and syncategorematic differences—as Irad Kimhi insightfully does in order to present his own system in a Tractarian spirit and to preserve the possibility of logic—enables Wittgenstein or Kimhi to avoid the kinds of Bradleyan and Parmenidean worries about differences that I have raised and that Wittgenstein and Kimhi are sensitive to. It's noteworthy that Kimhi's book, although framed in response to a Parmenidean problematic concerning negation and distinctions, ends up in a distinctly non-Parmenidean place in which distinctions of some kind are invoked and the possibility of metaphysics—in my terms, relational metaphysics—is preserved.[2]

For me, the self-undermining of relational metaphysics is—as I said in chapter 1 in connection with Parmenides—a feature, not a bug. A view so radical as to deny, as Parmenides and I do, that there are any distinctions or any relations and indeed to deny the very coherence of the notion of relations must be a view that cannot coherently be stated—or said—and cannot coherently be argued for, i.e. cannot be argued for without undermining itself.

---

[1] For the record, I am broadly in sympathy with a so-called resolute reading of the *Tractatus*. See Diamond, *The Realistic Spirit*, chapter 6; see also Conant and Diamond, "On Reading the *Tractatus* Resolutely"; and, for further evaluation of a resolute reading, see Goldfarb, "Metaphysics and Nonsense," and "*Das überwinden*: Anti-Metaphysical Readings of the *Tractatus*." For an opposing position, see Hacker, "Was He Trying to Whistle It?"
[2] See Kimhi, *Thinking and Being*, p. 161. For a fuller discussion of the connections between my view and Kimhi's see my "Parmenides' Insight and the Possibility of Logic."

Bradley expresses a similar insight when he speaks of the "happy suicide" of relational metaphysical thinking.[3] The self-undermining in this case thus shows that we—Parmenides and Bradley and I and other fellow travelers—are on the right track, are doing things right. And so this self-undermining is a virtue, not a vice.[4]

Indeed, this self-undermining is just a manifestation of the skeptical vein that runs through this book. Not only am I advancing a skeptical challenge to the coherence of central philosophical concepts such as being, action, knowledge, meaning, etc., but I am also advancing a skeptical challenge to any arguments that invoke the notion of differentiated, relational metaphysical explanation or dependence. Thus, this challenge applies to the coherence of the very arguments I invoke to show that those concepts are incoherent. The claim is not just that there may be no differentiated, relational metaphysical explanations, but also that we have no coherent notion of such explanation and thus that we can't advance metaphysical arguments, not even our own metaphysical arguments designed to show that certain concepts are incoherent. This undermining of even our own relational metaphysical arguments is skeptical in a particularly radical way. And, here again, it's particularly noteworthy that, as I mentioned in chapter 3, Bradley sees matters in these skeptical terms.[5]

One of my dear colleagues once said when alluding to and criticizing my view: "There's gotta be a *reductio* in there somewhere." And all I can say is, I certainly hope so! My view requires and thrives upon such a self-undermining, and I believe that in arguing—relationally—against the intelligibility of relations, in making all my Parmenidean Ascents, things are proceeding in a self-undermining fashion, just as I had planned. Remember what I said in the proem: my arguments are probably more rationalist and more skeptical and more Parmenidean than you may suspect. Those rationalist, skeptical, and Parmenidean extremes are all on display in this brief chapter.

But what exactly is it to throw away the ladder and to transcend relational metaphysical thinking? One important answer to this important question is that to throw away the ladder is simply to divest the arguments and the claims that we have made of any relational metaphysical significance, the

---

[3] *Appearance and Reality*, pp. 150, 152. For further discussion, see Candlish, *The Russell/Bradley Dispute*, p. 96; Hylton, *Russell, Idealism, and the Emergence of Analytic Philosophy*, pp 68–71.
[4] A virtuous feature, not a vicious bug.
[5] Bradley, *Appearance and Reality*, p. xii.

kind of significance that trades in explanations-of and explanations-in-terms-of.[6] It is this of-ness, this relationality, that is problematic about relational metaphysical thinking. Thus, there is a sense in which, in making the Parmenidean Ascent and throwing away the ladder, we are no longer able to articulate anything, if by "articulate" we mean offering a treatment (in Latin *tractatus*) *of* things, or an explanation *of* things, *in terms of* things. We can, in this light, no longer say or think anything, as long as such saying or thinking presupposes relations and distinctions. As Parmenides says, non-being cannot be thought.

With the undermining of explanations-of and with the breaking down of the particular attempted explanations that we have relied on to get to this point, we can revert for the second time in three paragraphs to the proem. But this time I would like to reverse my thought or apparent thought in the proem. I said in the very first sentence of this book that I have often thought it ironic that the writings of the great monist, Parmenides, are available to use only in the form of fragments. But now we can see that it need no longer appear ironic that Parmenides' writings come to us in this state, for these fragments have the form of broken-down attempts at thought, attempted explanations-of. Such fractured non-statements are perhaps, we can now see, the most that we can hope for when we attempt to do metaphysics, and so the fragmentary character of Parmenides' writings now seems altogether appropriate.

At the same time, by throwing away the ladder and making the Parmenidean Ascent (in its various ["various"] forms), we also see the world aright in that we strip our arguments or statements of unintelligible, relational metaphysical import, and, in particular, we strip them of any kind of attempt to match an independent world. Freed of the burden of attempted matching, we and our words are no longer obligated to stand in a certain relation to the world. Instead, we and our words are (happily) now free, free to play, perchance to joke.[7] Enjoying this freedom from relations and the concomitant freedom to play is a way of seeing the world aright, without illusions; it is, perhaps, a kind of non-relational seeing, non-relational explanation of the kind that the previous chapter led us to seek out. I will exhibit

---

[6] Of course, this may be easier done than said.
[7] Here, among others, the spirits of Richard Rorty (in *Philosophy and the Mirror of Nature*) and of Sextus Empiricus loom large for me.

this kind of freedom from the illusion of relational metaphysical explanation in chapter 12.

In a way, once we make the Parmenidean Ascent—in making the Parmenidean Ascent—nothing looks the same because our words are stripped of the illusion of relational metaphysical significance, a metaphysical significance to which we previously tried to anchor our ideas. But, at the same time, everything looks the same, for we may use (or at least appear to use) the same words as before, though without the incoherent metaphysical accretions that we are now trying to identify and eliminate. In chapter 13, I will exhibit this kind of use of the same words but without the metaphysical significance that we may have previously incoherently attributed to them.

Equally, however, because we and our words are, we now realize, free of the duty to match an independent reality, we are also free to speak and to think and to be in new ways. The Parmenidean Ascent in this respect is fundamentally non-conservative and allows for radical change. This is a theme I will discuss in chapter 11.

All this ascent and overcoming and self-undermining is, perhaps, well and good, but a different kind of question now takes shape: What is the *significance for us* of these metaphysical/non-metaphysical musings? Why should they *matter to us*? What is at stake for us in all of this high-flying self-undermining?[8] A full answer to these questions would require an exploration of the Parmenidean Ascent with regard to moral notions, such as goodness and virtue. As I mentioned earlier (in the proem and chapter 4), I'm largely bracketing in this book the Parmenidean Ascent with regard to moral notions. But I can make some initial observations and suggestions in response to the question about mattering, observations to be developed in future work.

First, I would say that freeing ourselves from metaphysical confusions of relationality should and does matter to us.

Second, and perhaps more positively, I would also say that this freedom from metaphysical relations is at the same time a freedom to speak, to think, to play, and simply to be in the same way and also in new ways.

Finally, recall that the seeing that we achieve with the Parmenidean Ascent and with freeing ourselves from relational illusions is itself non-relational. As non-relational, this seeing is not distinct from what is seen. This is because there can be no intelligible relation that this non-relational seeing

---

[8] I am indebted here to a memorable question from Hagi Kenaan.

stands in, not even (as we have seen) a relation of distinction. And so, this non-relational seeing is not distinct from, *inter alia* ("*inter*" "*alia*"), what is seen, and so it is not distinct from the world that is seen aright. In this way, in making the Parmenidean Ascent—and in seeing in this way—we literally are or become or are no longer distinct from the world, or at least our seeing is or becomes or is no longer distinct from the world. Thus, with the Parmenidean Ascent, we, in a way, gain the world.

In so gaining the world, we do not, contrary to a familiar worry, lose our souls. And, more generally, we do not lose anything real. The distinctions, the differentiation, the relations that we leave behind are not real. What is real about us is best captured by appealing simply to the world and to ourselves without distinctions. All we lose in making the Parmenidean Ascent are the apparent distinctions, the apparent relations which we can now see were illusory anyway, were not real anyway.[9]

But, certainly, given our susceptibility to illusion and given our apparent limitedness, we may be unable to fully divest ourselves of metaphysical incoherence and unintelligibility. What, then, are we to do? We can embrace the fact that the more we free ourselves from metaphysical illusions and from the unintelligible load of relations, the more we will see the world aright and the more our seeing will simply be the world itself. This is the standard to which we may aspire, the standard of freeing ourselves more and more from the illusion of relational metaphysics. The more we do so, the more free we and our words become to play, to joke, instead of being held down by an incoherent standard. This, then, is what is at stake for us in the Parmenidean Ascent: our very freedom and the freedom of our words to be—without relational metaphysics—and to play.

---

[9] I pursue a similar theme in my interpretation of Spinoza in "Perseverance, Power, and Eternity: Purely Positive Essence in Spinoza."

10
Tamers, Deniers, and Me

"OK, here it comes," I say to the reader as I see that, with chapter 9, a limit to their patience has been reached.

And the reader—perhaps you—says, "You bet, it's coming. How can we take your view seriously? The abandonment of relational metaphysics, the abandonment of all distinctions, the embrace of self-undermining? You have to be joking."

And I say: "Yes, indeed, I do have to be joking, for, as I argued in chapter 9, engaging in joking and, more generally, play is (happily) all we can do once we abandon the incoherent aims of a certain kind of pervasive attempt at metaphysical thinking."

And I must also reiterate at this point: "Don't mistake the fact that you don't like my conclusions for an argument against them."

But, I'm no dummy, I can see how things are: pointing out the positive arguments that—paradoxically, no doubt—lead to my extreme position will, given the state of things in philosophy, never be enough, by itself, to ward off what I call the Great Resistance, the dismissal of or the refusal to engage with the Parmenidean Ascent.

Part of the reason for such resistance, at least in some quarters in analytical philosophy, is that the Parmenidean Ascent and the powerful rationalist considerations I have advanced on its behalf run counter to what I called in chapter 7 three struts of analytical philosophy: realism, discreteness, and the method of intuition.

First of all, as we saw especially in chapter 6, the Parmenidean Ascent, particularly in the guise it takes with regard to truth, conflicts with realism which sees the world and the facts in it as, in general, distinct from and independent of thoughts or beliefs about the world.

Second, the Parmenidean Ascent in general, with its rejection of relations and distinctions is also opposed to the discreteness—to the looseness and separateness—of things which, as I have mentioned, is so prized in various stretches of analytical metaphysics.

The Parmenidean Ascent. Michael Della Rocca, Oxford University Press (2020).
© Oxford University Press.
DOI: 10.1093/oso/9780197510940.001.0001

Finally, as has been apparent throughout this book, the Parmenidean Ascent, time and again, violates the method of intuition by advancing counterintuitive claims or claims that go against so-called common sense. By undermining—and, indeed, deeming incoherent—our ordinary understanding or intuitive understanding of being, action, knowledge, meaning, etc. as differentiated, the Parmenidean Ascent goes against the method of intuition which seeks to preserve and accommodate the ordinary grasp of such notions.

Given the deeply heterodox character of the Parmenidean Ascent, it will be difficult for it to be taken seriously. For this reason, in this chapter and the next—the last two more or less conventional chapters in this increasingly less conventional book—I want to take up means of pushing against this resistance that are perhaps less direct and perhaps more dialectically effective than merely presenting positive arguments, as I have been doing, for my position.

Thus, in chapter 11, I take aim at the methodology—the Method of Intuition—that undergirds the Great Resistance and supports, for better or worse, so much metaphysical theorizing nowadays and supports so much else that is going on in contemporary and recent philosophy, particularly in analytical philosophy.

In the current chapter, I want to challenge a perennial, hopeful, sober, and to some extent conciliatory strategy designed to avoid extreme results of the kind that I have reached. This strategy focuses on the rationalist character of my arguments throughout this book, my pervasive reliance on various kinds of explanatory demands. Perhaps—so the perennial strategy goes—things go wrong, as they have gone wrong in this book, only because we have tried to extend such extend such explanatory demands too far, only because we have tried to use some versions of the Principle of Sufficient Reason (PSR)—the principle according to which each thing or fact has an explanation—in too unrestricted a fashion. We saw this principle—in some form—as driving Parmenides' arguments in what came to be his fragments. This principle has—again, in some form—been expressed in the explanatory demands I have cited and invoked throughout the book and in chapter 8's insistence on avoiding arbitrary, Buridan-like actions. But again, perhaps this rationalist thrust on my part goes too far. Perhaps we should simply limit the PSR or, as it were, tame it, so that, once properly constrained and put in its proper place, it no longer leads to the wild, metaphysics-destroying results that I have in my rationalist, happily self-undermining fashion advanced throughout the book.

I will put forth, in this chapter, an argument designed to put pressure on this conciliatory and apparently judicious taming strategy, an argument designed to suggest that the taming strategy is, in the end, incoherent. I will argue, in particular, that the means the PSR-tamer follows and must follow in order to limit the PSR inevitably leads to an untamed PSR, and thus the taming strategy is inherently unstable in a way that would be unacceptable to it proponents. In my discussion of tamers in this chapter, the focus will be on Kant and on contemporary philosophers of grounding or metaphysical explanation such as Shamik Dasgupta, but my argument will apply to PSR-tamers in general.

My procedure here thus amounts to an indirect argument for the PSR: a little use of the notion of explanation goes a long way, indeed it goes all the way, and in going all the way to the full-blown PSR, this tamed PSR undermines itself.

I will begin with a general characterization of the motivations for and the historical origins of the taming strategy before moving on to my way of showing that this strategy won't work.

Breaking Up Is Hard to Do

I begin with a quasi-historical quasi-overview of the vicissitudes of the PSR. When it comes to the PSR many philosophers just can't seem to let go. It could be argued—and I would argue—that this principle was there at the beginning for us philosophers, guiding, for example, as we saw in chapter 1 the thought of Parmenides and of those many who responded to the challenges posed by his thought. And the PSR has subsequently *explicitly* sustained philosophy at other points in its history (especially, I would say, in the heyday of philosophy that was the seventeenth century). I would also argue that the principle has *implicitly* helped propel philosophy throughout its entire history down to the present day.

Despite the good times, philosophers have come to see—or have come to think they see—that the PSR just can't be right. After all, the PSR seems to have so many untoward consequences. Thus, bracketing my extreme, PSR-inspired arguments in this book, we can point to some prominent and allegedly unsavory apparent consequences of the PSR such as necessitarianism—the thesis that all truths are necessary—and the identity of indiscernibles—the view that no two things are exactly alike, and the denial of free action.[1] Because of these apparent consequences that many would regard as implausible or even outrageous, perhaps it's just better all around for there to be a parting of the ways of philosophy and the PSR. It's no one's fault. It's just that, perhaps, philosophy and the PSR weren't made for each other.

Still, we can't help but think of the great fun that we philosophers have had with the PSR in the glory days before things all turned bad. The PSR and we were good together, weren't we? And when things were good, they were really good: the breathtaking confidence in our ability to find the world and things within it intelligible was a heady and invigorating feeling.

And, as with many a first love, the memory of this feeling has proven to be resilient, and it keeps drawing us back in. Many of us find that we keep returning to the PSR, perhaps with the hope that *this time* things will be different. Perhaps this time, we can have our PSR without its excesses; perhaps this time we or the PSR can be made to settle down. Thus, it is that hope springs eternal. And so we philosophers, wisely or not, keep returning.

The strategy or the wish here is that we can have a reformed version of the PSR, suitably restricted or limited or, as I put it, tamed. The PSR with its wings clipped will be a version that we can live with, that won't crash and that won't crush us as has happened so many times in the past. Don't we—so the thought goes in our weaker moments—owe it to ourselves or to the memory of our past relationship with the PSR to give the taming strategy a chance? And so are born the PSR-tamers, a hopeful and yet serious bunch.

The PSR-tamers must be distinguished from the more hard-hearted PSR-deniers who say outright that the PSR is false: they give up the PSR and give us nothing in its stead. The deniers do not, it seems, seek to revive the PSR in a limited form, a form that we can console ourselves with and show off to our friends.

The PSR-tamers, of course, deny the unrestricted form of the PSR, and so in a way the PSR-tamers are PSR-deniers. But when I use the term "PSR-denier," I have in mind those who reject the unrestricted PSR *and*, unlike the PSR-tamers, do not replace it with a limited version of the PSR.

---

[1] For the connection between the PSR and necessitarianism, see van Inwagen, *An Essay on Free Will*, pp. 202–4, and Bennett, *A Study of Spinoza's Ethics*, p. 115; for challenges to this alleged implication, see Levey, "The Paradox of Sufficient Reason," and Amijee, "Explaining Contingent Facts." For the identity of indiscernibles, see chapter 7, note 9.

230 THE PARMENIDEAN ASCENT

Both the PSR-tamers and the PSR-deniers must, of course, be contrasted with those, perhaps benighted, souls who seem to live in the past and who seem to embrace an unrestricted, unclipped, untamed version of the PSR. Such philosophers are, perhaps, to be admired and, perhaps, pitied as extremists often are. Whatever one's attitude toward these extremists, such philosophers nowadays seem non-existent or almost so, with the possible exception of the likes of me (and, as we'll see at the end, perhaps even the likes of me should be deemed non-existent too). We might call those in this last category "PSR-affirmers," and I will do that sometimes, though we'll see eventually that there may be reason to avoid this label.

Who are examples of these kinds of folks? The first thing to note is that in many cases, the classification is difficult, and it may be a vague matter whether some philosopher falls into one or another of the three categories. We'll return to this point. Nonetheless, there are some pretty clear examples. Take the category of the likes of me (or of PSR-affirmers): among contemporary philosophers, we have, perhaps, a clear enough example of the likes of me in me, for I seem at some points to be sympathetic to a pretty unrestricted version of the PSR.[2] Looking back to philosophy's glory days (or dark days, if you like), we can spy others who fall into the pro-PSR camp, including (again, perhaps) Parmenides, Spinoza, Leibniz, Wolff, du Châtelet, Baumgarten, Bradley, and many others.

In the category of PSR-deniers, I would place Hume, who, as I've argued elsewhere, has a powerful argument against the PSR and who seems not to want to give us a limited version of it. Russell may fall into this category too (as we'll see). Perhaps David Lewis does too.[3]

And who are the PSR-tamers? One is perhaps Kant who feels the pull of the PSR but also urgently seeks to limit it. For Kant, the PSR legitimately applies within experience, within the realm of objects of possible experience. In Kant's terminology, in its legitimate use, the PSR is an "immanent" (*immanente*) principle (*Critique of Pure Reason* A295–96/B352),[4] a principle "whose application stays wholly and completely within the limits of possible experience." What Kant rejects are transcendent principles which "would fly beyond these

---

[2] See my "PSR."
[3] See Hume, *Treatise* 1.3.3. On Hume, see Della Rocca, "Playing with Fire." See also Russell, "Some Explanations in Reply to Mr. Bradley," and Lewis, *On the Plurality of Worlds*, pp. 128–31. This is Lewis' response to Unger's, "Minimizing Arbitrariness."
[4] Unless otherwise noted, all references to Kant will be to his *Critique of Pure Reason*. I follow the standard practice for referring to passages from the A and the B editions of the *Critique*.

boundaries," and thus he rejects the transcendent use of the PSR. For Kant, every event that can be experienced has a cause[5] and is thus conditioned, has a ground. But we cannot legitimately posit the existence of an unconditioned being that serves as the ultimate ground of all the events that are caused, all the things that have a condition (A307/B364). We cannot, as Kant puts it elsewhere, employ the concept of causation to achieve "theoretical cognition of things" that "extend beyond the limits of possible experience."[6] In so moving from the conditioned to the unconditioned, which would be the explanation of all particular conditioned things, we would be seeking to apply the PSR not just to a particular object or event that can be experienced, rather we would be seeking to apply the PSR also to the totality of particular objects or events we can experience. For Kant, this would be to attempt to transcend experience and would be to adopt—as Kant puts it—a *dogmatic* position, to make a claim to know the way the world is independent of our experience of it.

Why, for Kant, are we not permitted to transcend experience in this way? I realize, of course, that I cannot hope in this finite space and time to do justice to Kant's views on this matter, but here are, I think, some central strands in Kant's thinking. Return to the issue of our positing an unconditioned ground of all particular conditioned things. That such an unconditioned being exists is not an analytic truth. This denial by Kant is a reflection of his rejection of the ontological argument—an argument which claims that the existence of God or of a being that is the explanation of the whole series of conditioned beings follows from the very concept of God, the concept of such an unconditioned being. Thus, since the existence of such a being is not an analytic truth, if its existence is to be known, it must be known by means of a synthetic judgment. For Kant, there are two kinds of synthetic judgment by which we can achieve knowledge: synthetic *a posteriori* judgments and synthetic *a priori* judgments. That is, such a being—if its existence is to be knowable at all—must be something whose existence must be shown to us through experience (as would be the case if we are dealing with a synthetic i judgment) or whose existence is somehow a condition of the possibility of experience (as would be the case if we were dealing with a synthetic *a priori* judgment).[7] But, for Kant, the unconditioned is not an object of experience

---

[5] See Kant, *Critique*, A189/B232

[6] "On a Discovery Whereby Any New Critique of Pure Reason Is to Be Made Superfluous by an Older One," p. 293.

[7] On the two kinds of synthetic knowledge for Kant, see Hogan: "all theoretical synthetic cognition requires reference to the general form or particular content of sensibility," "Metaphysical Motives of Kant's Analytic-Synthetic Distinction," p. 270. Hogan goes on to quote from Kant's "On a Discovery,"

(A308–9/B365): anything we experience is conditioned by other things. Nor is the existence of an unconditioned being a condition of the possibility of experience. Famously, Kant thinks that in some way, certain forms of sensibility—space and time—are conditions of the possibility of experience and certain fundamental concepts—what he calls "categories"—are also (but in a different way) conditions of the possibility of experience, concepts such as those of cause and of substance. That is why, for example, we can know *a priori* for Kant that every event that can come within our experience has a cause. But while there being causally related events in space and time is a condition of the possibility of experience, there being an unconditioned being that is the ultimate explanation of all events is *not*, for Kant, a condition of the possibility of experience. So, because the existence of an unconditioned being is not an analytic truth and because such a being is not apprehended through experience, nor is such a being's existence a condition of the possibility of experience, it follows, for Kant, that we cannot know that there is such an unconditioned being.

We can now see that in positing an unconditioned explainer (i.e. an unconditioned conditioner, or if you will, an unmoved mover), we were seeking to apply the PSR—the claim that everything has an explanation—to something that we cannot experience and that is not a condition of the possibility of experience—viz. the entire series of conditioned things. Kant says that we cannot legitimately use the PSR in this way, that we must, in other words, clip the PSR's wings, limit it to objects that we can experience.

Kant also argues that if we do not so limit the PSR—if we attempt to apply the PSR dogmatically to reach substantive conclusions about the world that outstrip the bounds of experience—we philosophers will be embroiled, as we have been for centuries, in interminable disputes, in contradictions (the antinomies), and in empty metaphysics, such as the positing of a substantial self (the paralogisms).[8] Moreover, if we give the PSR unrestricted scope, then we will unleash a determinism that undermines freedom. Kant holds that if the PSR is true, then all freedom must be denied (Bxxviii–xxix).[9] These

---

p. 328: "The principle of synthetic judgments in general [is] that they are only possible under the condition that an *intuition* underlies the concept of their subject, which, if the judgments are empirical, is empirical, and if they are synthetic judgments *a priori*, is a pure intuition *a priori*."

[8] Thus Melamed and Lin ("Principle of Sufficient Reason"): "Kant restricts the validity of the PSR to human experience, i.e. to things which appear in space and time. Any use of the PSR that transgresses the boundaries of human experience is bound to generate antinomies."

[9] For a very illuminating treatment of the role that freedom plays in Kant's understanding of the PSR, see Hogan, "Metaphysical Motives of Kant's Analytic-Synthetic Distinction," especially pp. 291–93.

reasons—the antinomies, the paralogisms, the denial of freedom—give Kant a *motivation* to avoid these undesirable consequences. But Kant earns the *right* to limit the PSR by virtue of his claim—which I have just outlined following Omri Boehm's important work on the subject[10]—that there is no way to be justified in applying the PSR beyond experience.

For Kant, this is precisely where some great rationalists were tripped up. They employed an unrestricted PSR illegitimately, in Kant's eyes, and with disastrous consequences. (And you can just imagine what he would say about the rationalist, skeptical, Parmenidean path I am pursuing.) Kant thinks that we must limit the PSR to avoid these consequences, we must take a less dogmatic, more critical, cautious approach. In so doing, we will make the world safe for metaphysics; we will, in Hume's words, be able finally to "cultivate the true metaphysics with some care in order to destroy the false and adulterate."[11] I will investigate and critique Kant's case for taming the PSR in this way shortly.

Jumping ahead more than 200 years, we find another instance of a PSR-tamer in Shamik Dasgupta.[12] Like Kant, Dasgupta thinks that there is strong reason to limit the PSR, but—also like Kant—he doesn't want to give it up entirely. Dasgupta takes seriously and is clearly drawn to, but doesn't quite endorse, a fairly robust but still restricted version of the PSR. Dasgupta takes up the PSR insofar as it concerns the explanation of *facts* (as opposed to objects), and, according to the version he is drawn to, all non-autonomous facts have explanations. A non-autonomous fact is a fact that is, as Dasgupta puts it, apt for explanation, a fact that is suitable for explanation. Thus, according to the idea he proposes, all non-autonomous facts—all facts that are apt for explanation—do have explanations. The other facts—the autonomous facts—are not apt for explanation, and so the fact that these autonomous facts do not have explanations is not a threat to the PSR: everything that is suitable for explanation has an explanation.

For Dasgupta, the autonomous facts are essentialist facts, facts such as that it is essential to triangles to have three sides, that water is essentially H_2O, that it is essential to Greta Garbo's singleton set that it contains Greta Garbo as its only member, etc.[13] Such facts are autonomous because, in answer to

---

[10] Boehm, *Kant's Critique of Spinoza*, and "The Principle of Sufficient Reason, the Ontological Argument, and the Is/Ought Distinction."
[11] *An Enquiry Concerning Human Understanding*, section 1.
[12] Dasgupta, "Metaphysical Rationalism."
[13] Dasgupta, following Fine, uses the example of singleton Socrates. Here, as elsewhere in this book, I shamelessly change the example to one involving Greta Garbo.

the question—e.g., why is it essential to being a triangle that triangles have three sides?—there is nothing more to say beyond saying that that's just what triangles are. Similarly, Dasgupta says:

> suppose that it is essential to water that it is a substance composed of H_2O and suppose someone asks what explains this? ... It is ... hard to know what to say other than that is *just what water is*! And in saying this one is ... most naturally heard as sidestepping the question rather than giving it a serious answer. (Dasgupta, "Metaphysical Rationalism," p. 386)

In effect, for Dasgupta, the PSR doesn't apply when it comes to essentialist facts, perhaps in something like the way that, for Kant, the PSR doesn't apply when it comes to matters that transcend experience. In limiting the PSR—in taming the PSR—in the way he does, Dasgupta is eager to incorporate some version of the PSR into a metaphysical system that exhibits a sophisticated structure replete with fundamental facts: facts that are without explanation, that are not apt for explanation, and that serve as the basis for all other facts.

Besides Kant and Dasgupta, other PSR-tamers may include various stripes of monists, such as Jonathan Schaffer who holds, as we saw in earlier chapters, that all concrete things that are contained within the cosmos are explained by and thus metaphysically posterior to the cosmos itself. This view—which Schaffer calls "Priority Monism"—embodies a restricted version of the PSR where each non-fundamental concrete thing is explained.[14]

There are, perhaps, many other PSR-tamers. However, as I noted, it is sometimes hard to know whether to categorize individual philosophers as PSR-tamers or not. Still, the important point for our purposes is that there are at least three possible positions with regard to the PSR—the tamers, the deniers, and the likes of me or the PSR-affirmers—and that the taming strategy has been and is an attractive option for a sober-minded philosopher who is nonetheless willing to be daring to some degree.

The history of PSR-tamers is, in a way, charted in Arthur Lovejoy's wonderful book *The Great Chain of Being*. Lovejoy outlines what he sees as the increasing movement in the history of philosophy away from the PSR as philosophers came to realize some of its apparently unwelcome implications.

---

[14] Schaffer, "Monism: The Priority of the Whole."

These philosophers may have retained some local applications of the PSR, Lovejoy notes, while they rejected a full-blown PSR.[15] In general, Lovejoy sees the movement away from the PSR as a salutary development. However, while I deeply appreciate Lovejoy's insight into the implications of the PSR and into the reasons for seeking to tame it, I want to argue in this paper that it is actually the tamers of the PSR who face a particularly pernicious threat of incoherence that the PSR-deniers and PSR-affirmers alike may be able to avoid. This is not to deny, of course, that PSR-affirmers (including me) may face their own threat of incoherence. However, the PSR-affirmers do or can embrace this incoherence in a way that the PSR-tamers cannot embrace the threat of incoherence that they face. I will return to this point at the end of the chapter.

Before I begin trying to make trouble for the PSR-tamers, let me call attention to the fact that in other cases too we may see similar taming strategies at work. Thus, turn once again to the thesis of monism and focus, in particular, on monism in its most radical form. This radical monism would be the thesis that there is no multiplicity whatsoever and no distinctions of any kind. There is only—or, at most—one object of any kind. Such a radical monism may be embraced by Parmenides and by Bradley (and by me). Other philosophers are drawn to monism but seek to avoid the counterintuitive consequences of the radical monism that allows for no distinctions at all. One limited version of monism—one, as it were, tamed version of monism—is Schaffer's already mentioned priority monism, according to which there is only one fundamental object, the cosmos itself. For Schaffer, this object contains very many smaller individuals—perhaps as parts—which are genuinely distinct from each other and from the cosmos itself. This is a version of monism because it allows only *one* fundamental (concrete) object, but at the same time makes the world safe for multiplicity. According to priority monism, the thesis of monism—when properly tamed—doesn't require that there be no multiplicity at all, just as, according to Kant and Dasgupta, the PSR doesn't require that every fact whatsoever has an explanation. With priority monism, we can have a recognizable and robust form of monism which nonetheless restricts oneness to fundamental things, just as with Kant and Dasgupta we have a recognizable and robust form of the PSR which

---

[15] See Lovejoy's discussion of Cusanus: "He well illustrates . . . the tendency of medieval writers who reject the principles of plenitude and sufficient reason in general terms, to argue unhesitatingly from these premises in other cases," p. 114.

nonetheless restricts the application of the PSR. With monism, as with the PSR, it's difficult for at least some philosophers to let go completely. Again, breaking up is hard to do. And, course, one shouldn't be surprised that when it comes to monism in particular, breaking up—i.e. breaking up into a multiplicity of distinct elements—is far from easy!

Insights from a Widely Mocked Argument

To begin to put pressure on PSR-tamers and to cast doubt on their taming strategy, I want to turn to an argument for the PSR that practically no one loves, perhaps eventually not even its author, Leibniz, who seems to have largely abandoned it after having advanced it early in his career.

I should say right off that, although I find this argument oddly attractive, I do not aim to rehabilitate this argument for the PSR, to show that it can somehow be made to work.[16] My aim here is different: I believe that exploring the workings (or the non-workings) of this argument will lead to important insights about the connections between the PSR and the radical form of monism mentioned earlier, according to which there are no distinctions whatsoever and there is at most only one thing. I will from now on refer to this radical monism as RM. It is this connection to RM that will, in the end, threaten to undermine the strategy of PSR-taming.

So let's look at this little Leibnizian argument. Here it is in Leibniz's own words in a piece written in 1671–72, but which he never published. I use a modified version of Adams' translation:

Proposition: Nothing is without a reason, or whatever is has a sufficient reason.
Definition 1. A *sufficient reason* is that which is such that if it is posited, then the thing is.
Definition 2. A *requisite* is that which is such that if it is not posited, then the thing is not.
Demonstration:
[1] What is, has all [its] requisites.
For if one [of them] is not posited, then the thing is not (*by def. 2*).

---

[16] In other work (in progress), I offer a kind of defense of Leibniz's argument, but my purposes here don't require doing so now.

[2] If the requisites of a thing have all been posited, then the thing is.
For if it is not, it will be kept from being by the lack of something, that is, a requisite.
[3] Therefore, all the requisites are a sufficient reason *by def. 1*.
[4] Therefore, whatever is has a sufficient reason.
(A VI, ii, 483)[17]

Claim [4] is obviously a version of the PSR.

As most who have discussed this argument seem to agree, the argument seems to be question-begging. The problem seems to be claim [2]. Leibniz does give a brief argument for this claim: "For if it is not, it will be kept from being by the lack of something, that is, a requisite." However, it seems, no competent opponent of the PSR should be willing to grant that [2] is true or that Leibniz's little argument for [2] carries any weight. After all, an opponent of the PSR can see the denial of the PSR as amounting to the claim that even when all the conditions required for x's existence are given, x could still—brutely, for no reason—fail to exist. By excluding such a possibility in [2],

---

[17] Here it is in Latin:

Propositio: Nihil est sine ratione seu quicquid est habet rationem sufficientem.
Definitio 1: Ratio sufficiens est qua posita res est.
Definitio 2: Requisitum est quo non posito res non est.
Demonstratio:
Quicquid est, habet omnia requisita.
Uno enim non posito non est per def. 2
Positis omnibus requisitis res est.
Nam si non est, deerit aliquid quo minus sit, id est requisitum.
Ergo Omnia Requisita sunt ratio sufficiens per def. 1
Igitur quicquid est habet rationem sufficientem.
Q.E.D.

A version of this argument also appeared in Leibniz's *Confessio Philosophi*: "Whatever exists, at any rate, will have all the requisites for existing; however, all the requisites for existing taken together at the same time are a *sufficient reason for existing*. Therefore whatever exists has a sufficient reason for existing," *Confessio Philosophi*, p. 33; "*Quicquid existit, utique habebit omnia ad existendum requisita, omnia autem ad existendum requisita simul sumpta, sunt* **ratio existendi sufficiens**; *Ergo quicquid existit, habet rationem existendi sufficientem*," *Confessio Philosophi*, p. 32)

The argument also appeared in a paper entitled "De Existentia" (from 1676; *De Summa Rerum* 110–13): "For existence, it is necessary that the aggregate of all requisites is present. A requisite is that without which a thing cannot exist. The aggregate of all requisites is the full cause of a thing. There is nothing without a reason; for there is nothing without an aggregate of all requisites (*Ad existentiam necesse est aggregatum omnium adesse Requisitorum. Requisitum est id sine quo res esse non potest. Aggregatum omnium requisitorum est causa plena rei. Nihil est sine ratione. Quia nihil est sine aggregato omnium requisitorum*)."

Finally, an echo of this argument emerges in Leibniz's correspondence with Clarke, letter 5, section 18: "the nature of things requires that every event should have beforehand its proper conditions, requisites, and dispositions, the existence whereof makes the sufficient reason of such an event" ("*la nature des choses porte, que tout evenement ait prealablement ses conditions, requisits, dispositions convenables, dont l'existence en fait la raison suffisante*"), Gerhardt VII 393/Loemker 698.

Leibniz is thus, it seems, tacitly assuming the PSR in the course of an argument purporting to show that the PSR is true. Robert Adams puts this point as follows: "anyone who denies the Principle of Sufficient Reason will suppose that when all the necessary conditions of a thing's existence are given, there must still remain both a possibility of its existing and a possibility of its not existing" (Adams, *Leibniz*, p. 68).[18] So without further defense of claim [2], the argument for the PSR seems to go nowhere.

Now I don't want to kick an apparently bad argument when it's down, but I would like to point out a problem in the way the argument is expressed, a minor weakness that is potentially very illuminating. By Leibniz's own lights, [2] and other claims in the argument require a certain modification. As it stands, [2] may appear to be trivially true in a way that Leibniz certainly does not intend. Thus, x's existence itself may seem to be a requisite of x. After all, x's existence is such that if it is not given, then x does not exist. If x's existence does count as a requisite for x, then claim [2] is trivially true: if the requisites for x—including x itself—have all been given, then, of course, x exists. Leibniz would not want his key premise to be trivial in this way; Leibniz would want [2] to be more than the tautology that if x exists, then x exists.

Similarly, in criticizing Leibniz's argument and in criticizing claim [2], Leibniz's opponent will also want to see [2] as more than just a tautology. Leibniz's opponent, as we have seen, wants [2] to be false and the assertion of [2] to be question-begging. The opponent does not want [2] to be true and trivially so.

Both Leibniz and his opponent, then, in order to avoid trivializing [2], would want to specify somehow that the relevant requisites of x do not include the existence of x itself.[19] Thus, both Leibniz and his opponent would agree that [2] may be better expressed as:

[2'] If x has requisites other than itself and these requisites are all posited, then x exists.

It's the other-ness invoked in [2'] that will prove to be of most interest to us.

---

[18] See Look, "Grounding the Principle of Sufficient Reason," p. 204.

[19] Adams recognizes this point when he says that that opponent of Leibniz would regard [2] as question-begging "unless trivially necessary conditions (such as the thing's existence itself) are included among its requirements, in which case the sum of the requirements will constitute a sufficient reason only in a very uninteresting sense of 'reason,'" p. 68.

Instead of modifying [2] in this way to include other-ness, we might instead want to build the notion of other-ness into the very notion of a requisite. One way to do this would be to modify Definition 2 along these lines:

Definition 2': A requisite of x is something other than the existence of x which is such that if it is not posited, then x does not exist.

Whether we make the modification explicit in [2] or earlier in Definition 2, there will be important implications for our understanding of claims later in Leibniz's argument. The key point is that the notion of other-ness ("other than x") must be introduced into the argument at some point. It doesn't matter for our purposes whether this introduction occurs in Definition 2 or in claim [2].[20]

Sticking with the modification of [2] as [2'], we can see the argument in this way:

Definition 1. A *sufficient reason* is that which is such that if it is posited, then the thing is.
Definition 2. A *requisite* is that which is such that if it is not posited, then the thing is not.
Demonstration:
[1] What is, has all [its] requisites.
For if one [of them] is not posited, then the thing is not (*by def. 2*).
[2'] If x has requisites other than itself and these requisites are all posited, then x exists.
[3'] Therefore, all the requisites of x other than x itself are a sufficient reason *by def. 1*.
[4'] Therefore, if x exists and has requisites other than itself, then x has a sufficient reason.

---

[20] For more on Leibniz's notion of requisites, see Di Bella, "Leibniz's Theory of Conditions." Di Bella points out (p. 69) that while in some early works (such as the passage I am focusing on in the main text as well as in "De Exisentia") Leibniz's wording suggests that requisites are mere necessary conditions, in other passages it is clear that Leibniz sees requisites as by definition *prior* in nature to what they are requisites for. In this sense of "requisite" which invokes priority, the notion of other-ness will be built into the definition of "requisite." Thus Leibniz says, in the piece "*Definitiones notionum metaphysicarum atque logicarum*" (1685?), "*requisita est conditio simplicior, seu ut vulgo vocant natura prior*"(A VI.4.627).

With the argument so revised, its key proposition—[2']—is no longer clearly trivial and, more importantly for our purposes, we are now in a position to bring out a connection between a variety of monism and Leibniz's argument for the PSR. The version of monism I have in mind is the very radical version of monism—RM—that I've mentioned already, one according to which there are no distinctions whatsoever, and there is (at most) only one thing.

Of course, it may be that this extreme version of monism is not really a form of monism—one-ism—at all, for it may be that to say, as I have said in chapter 3 and elsewhere, that there is *one* thing already presupposes that there are distinctions—at least possible distinctions—between the one thing and other things, and distinctions among numbers. In that case, the view I have in mind according to which there are absolutely no distinctions would not be a version of one-ism (monism) after all. Perhaps then you should not call the view I'm assuming a kind of monism. So be it. Or rather, since the term "it" may problematically presuppose individuation and number and at least possible differentiation: so be. Or even better, since the "so" may indicate a manner of being distinct from being itself: be. That would suit me just fine, as we'll see later. On the view I have in mind, then, there would thus be being, but no plurality of beings and not even one being. ("Being" would then be something like a mass term, as I suggested in chapter 3.) Perhaps, then, the view I have in mind is not best called "monism." Perhaps it should be called "being-ism." But because the term "monism" is more familiar and is clear enough, I will continue to speak in terms of a monism of a particularly radical variety. And I ask that when I mention monism or RM you keep in mind that I have in mind the view that there are no distinctions whatsoever.

I want to explore now the implications for our modified Leibnizian argument if we assume that monism of this radical form is true. Never mind that this extreme view is highly implausible and even outrageous. I know it is, and—I say this with all due consideration—*I don't care*. This is, in part, because, as I have mentioned already and as I will elaborate in chapter 11, to my way of thinking, the implausibility of a view is no knock against it and is certainly not a disqualifying feature of a view. More relevantly on this occasion, I don't care about the implausibility of this form of monism because my main aim is not (yet) to endorse or defend this radical monism; rather I'm just assuming RM, for the sake of argument, to see what effect such an assumption has on the Leibnizian argument for the PSR. So let's see what happens.

Look, in particular, at [2'] and [4'].

[2'] If x has requisites other than itself and these requisites have all been posited, then x exists.
[4'] If x exists and has requisites other than itself, then x has a sufficient reason.

And recall that [4'] is a form of the PSR.

Notice that the antecedent of [2'] and the antecedent of [4'] are conjunctions, one conjunct of each of which is the claim that x has requisites other than itself. On the assumption of RM—the claim that there are no distinctions and thus no other-ness—this conjunct is false: there is nothing that has requisites other than itself. But now since, on our assumption of RM, this conjunct as well as the antecedent of the conditional [2'] is false, it turns out that [2'] itself is true. Similarly, [4'] has a false antecedent and thus [4'] itself is also true (and [4'], as we have seen, follows in part from [2']). In other words, on our (big) assumption of RM, the key claim—[2']—in the modified Leibnizian argument for the PSR is true, and thus the PSR is true. The PSR is true in the sense that there is no thing that exists, has requisites other than itself, and lacks a sufficient reason.

It may be relevant here how one phrases [2'] and [4']. I have phrased them so that the claim that there is a multiplicity of things (other than x) is an explicit conjunct of the antecedents of these conditionals. It is the falsity of this conjunct that makes the conditionals true. However, we could instead phrase the antecedents so that the claim of other-ness is a *presupposition* of the antecedents and not a conjunct. For example, we might say in the case of [2']: "If all the requisites of x other than x itself are posited, then x exists." (And similarly for [4'].) Here the other-ness is not an explicit claim in the antecedent, but a presupposition of the antecedent. In this case, the antecedent may—depending on how one understands presupposition—be regarded not as false, but as truth-valueless. And so [2'] would not be true but truth-valueless. (Similarly for [4'].)[21]

Even if we phrase [2'] and [4'] in this way and even if they thus lack truth-values, the key point stands: if RM is true, then some version of the PSR is true, or at the very least there are no counterexamples to the PSR. The PSR can be seen as a claim to the effect that no thing x meets the following three conditions: x exists, x has requisites other than itself, and x lacks a sufficient reason. RM dictates that no thing meets all three conditions. And so, if RM

---

[21] I am indebted to Sam Berstler here.

is true, then the PSR (at least in this form) is true, or at least, there are no counterexamples to the PSR. There are no things that exist without a sufficient reason.[22]

I freely acknowledge that [4'] and the PSR arrived at through the assumption of RM is in a certain way vacuous. RM—the claim that there are no distinctions whatsoever—is so radical that it renders [4'] true (or without counterexamples) through what might seem to be a logical "trick" that turns on the truth-value (or lack thereof) of certain conditionals with false antecedents. By the same token—i.e. by virtue of the same logical "trick"—not only is [4'] true (or without counterexamples) but also other lovely claims are equally true (or without counterexamples). Thus, consider an antirationalist counterpart of [4'], [4'AR]:

[4'AR] If x exists and has requisites other than itself, then x *lacks* a sufficient reason.

RM is so radical that both [4'] and [4'AR] are true (or are at least without counterexamples), that is, if x exists and has requisites other than itself, then a certain claim is true and the contradictory of that claim is true.

So, yes, the version of the PSR argued for on the basis of RM is in this way vacuous, but—and again I say this with all due consideration—*I don't care.* The emptiness of the PSR arrived at in this way doesn't threaten my aim in this chapter which, in the end, is to suggest that the taming strategy is incoherent. In fact, as we will see near the end, this emptiness only enhances the strength of the negative conclusion I will ultimately reach about the taming strategy.

Of course, Leibniz would reject the modified Leibnizian argument as a way to establish the PSR. Leibniz—as is well known—seeks a more robust PSR—he seeks not only the truth of [4'], but also the falsity of [4'AR]. And the fact that he would reject this way of arguing for the PSR is ultimately due to Leibniz's rejection of RM which drives this argument for [4']. Leibniz would not want to accept any form of monism, let alone a form of monism as strong as RM, in order to support the PSR. Despite some early, occasional flirtation with monism, Leibniz is decidedly not a monist, and so he would not want to deploy this argument.

---

[22] It is worth noting that if, instead of modifying [2] as [2'], we modify Definition 2 as Definition 2', the antecedents of [2] and [4] are still false (or without truth-value) because now the very notion of requisite includes the notion of priority or other-ness.

But what Leibniz might or might not want is not my focus here. I am interested instead in how a PSR-tamer would react to my modified Leibnizian argument. First, note that PSR-tamers must, like Leibniz, reject this way of arguing for [4'], i.e. must reject arguing for [4'] on the basis of RM. This is so because this version of the PSR is true because RM (which we are assuming) is true. This version of the PSR may be true for other reasons as well, but it's true at least in part because RM is true. And the point that I want to highlight here is that RM is unacceptable both to Kant and to Dasgupta (and, I would suspect, to any PSR-tamer). Thus, Kant must reject RM because his system is (as I like to put it) rife with distinctions of various kinds: between noumena and phenomena, between intuitions and concepts, between sensibility and understanding, between *a posteriori* judgments and *a priori* judgments, between different regions of space, and between different moments in time, etc. Similarly, Dasgupta's system is, as we saw, in the service of a structured ontology which is (as I still like to put it) rife with distinctions—distinctions between more and less fundamental things.

Further, not only must PSR-tamers reject, as Leibniz would, this way of arguing for [4'], but also—and perhaps more importantly—they must, unlike Leibniz, reject [4'] itself. The version of the PSR arrived at—[4']—would be too sweeping, too untamed, a version of the PSR for both Kant and Dasgupta, and I suspect for PSR-tamers in general.

First, consider Kant's position. As we saw, for Kant, we cannot legitimately seek to explain the existence of the entire series of conditioned beings. Such a limitation is essential to Kant's taming project. Notice, however, that this total series has requisites other than itself, e.g., among the requisites of the series are the individual members of the series, as well as the properties of being a series, of containing individual events as members, etc. Thus, in order for there to be such a series of conditioned beings, there must be, e.g., the individual events in the series and there must be the properties of being a series of events, etc., a series that contains individual events as members. The fact that there are these requisites is enough to trigger the application of [4'], the version of the PSR we are currently considering.

[4'] If x exists and has requisites other than itself, then x has a sufficient reason.

Since this total series has requisites other than itself and since, by [4'], anything which has requisites other than itself has a sufficient reason, it follows that the total series has a sufficient reason. But this result—this kind of application of the PSR—would, of course, be unacceptable to Kant. Thus, Kant must reject the version of the PSR, [4'], that we have arrived at with the help of the Leibnizian argument and with the help of RM.

Consider next the attitude Dasgupta must take to [4'] and the version of the PSR we are now considering. Recall that, according to the position Dasgupta articulates, all and only facts that are apt for explanation have explanations. Essentialist facts, e.g., that water is essentially H_2O or that Greta Garbo's singleton set essentially contains Greta Garbo as its only member, are not apt for explanation, and so the PSR does not apply to them. Such facts do not have or need a sufficient reason. However, notice that, e.g., the fact that Greta Garbo's singleton set essentially has Greta Garbo as its only member has requisites: for example, it is a requisite of this fact that the nature of set-membership be such that the sole member of a singleton set is essential to that set.[23] Also, and even less controversially, other requisites of the fact that Greta Garbo's singleton set essentially has Greta Garbo as its only member include the fact that that set has Greta Garbo as its only member and the fact that Greta Garbo exists.[24] Since the fact that it is essential to {Greta Garbo} that it contains Greta Garbo has requisites, and since, according to [4'], i.e. the version of the PSR under consideration, anything that exists and has requisites other than itself has a sufficient reason, it follows that the essentialist fact that singleton Greta Garbo essentially contains Greta Garbo as its only member *does* have a sufficient reason, an explanation, after all—contrary to Dasgupta's guiding claim that such a fact does not have an explanation. Thus, Dasgupta, no less than Kant, must reject [4'] and the version of the PSR it expresses. This version of the PSR is too untamed, not restricted enough, for the likes of Kant and Dasgupta.

I suspect that other PSR-tamers would likely also find [4'] and this version of the PSR too untamed. Consider, e.g., Schaffer who, as we have seen, also holds a tamed version of the PSR: all concrete things other than the cosmos

---

[23] Here I disagree with Dasgupta when he denies that the essentialist fact about this set is grounded (at least in part) in the fact that it is essential to the set-membership relation that it is essential to any set that it has the members that it has. Dasgupta explicitly denies the claim that the fact that it is essential to {Socrates} to contain Socrates as its only member is "grounded (at least in part) in the fact that it is essential to the set-membership relation that it is essential to any set that it has the members it has," p. 389. Dasgupta gives no reason, as far as I can see, for denying that the nature of the set-membership relation is a partial ground of the essentialist fact in question. I suspect that Dasgupta's position here is a reflection of the unargued assumption in much of the grounding literature that general facts are grounded in their particular instances.

[24] Here I am indebted to Fatema Amijee.

itself have explanations. Since the cosmos itself has requisites, e.g., being a concrete object, having the property of being a ground, etc., the cosmos would, according to [4'], have a sufficient reason. Thus, Schaffer who denies that the cosmos has an explanation cannot accept [4']; he must tame the PSR.

Fortunately for the PSR-tamer—at least fortunately so far—a PSR-tamer can reject this argument for [4'] simply by rejecting RM which, at this point, there is no pressure on the PSR-tamer to accept. Thus, although the PSR-tamer must reject [4'] as too sweeping or untamed, there is, as yet, no pressure on her through RM to accept the unacceptable [4'].

A Difficult Position for PSR-Tamers

My aim so far has not been to argue that the PSR-tamers face any inconsistency or other difficulty. My aim has been simply to begin to show how a certain radical form of monism and a rather untamed version of the PSR may be connected. However, this connection, while not in itself problematic, may—when combined with certain arguments that I shall now sketch—prove to be very damaging indeed for the projects of Kant, Dasgupta, and PSR-tamers more generally.

To put the PSR-tamers in this difficult and, in the end, untenable position, I would like to argue for the view that not only does RM entail some untamed version of the PSR, but also that some rather modest form of the PSR—one that would prima facie be acceptable to PSR-tamers—entails RM. In other words, I seek to show, first, that PSR-tamers are committed to RM—a result that they would find most uncongenial.

One way to uncover such a commitment is through the kind of Bradleyan argument that I invoked in chapter 3 and that, in order to highlight the role of the PSR in these proceedings, I will deploy here using an order that is the reverse of the order that I followed in chapter 3. This kind of link between the PSR and RM can also be elicited through the Parmenidean argument I discussed in Chapter 1 and also through a Humean argument that I will outline briefly later in this chapter. But I will focus mostly on the Bradleyan argument here.

So—in my backward-looking fashion—let's see what we need to do in order to reach RM. First, note that if there are no relations at all, then there are no relations of distinction and thus, as I showed earlier, RM of the kind that I am interested in is true.

246   THE PARMENIDEAN ASCENT

But why should it be the case that there are no relations at all? One might argue that there are no relations because relations are unintelligible. This step turns on the claim that if something—some purported fact, say—is unintelligible, then it does not exist or obtain. I'll return to this step shortly—it obviously depends on something like the PSR.

Continuing to work backward, let's now ask: why should it be that relations are unintelligible? In answering this question, the PSR is again at work: relations are unintelligible because there is no way to ground them, to provide a metaphysical explanation of them. For any given relation, there is nothing in virtue of which that relation obtains.

But why should this be the case? My reasons should by now be familiar: relations are—by their nature—not free-floating, that is, relations are—by their nature—grounded in (at least) one or more of their relata. By its nature, a relation depends on (at least) its relata. Such a dependence—the relation's not being free-floating—seems to be part of what a relation is, just as it is part of the nature of a singleton set to depend on its only member. One can see this rejection of free-floating relations as a manifestation of the PSR: a free-floating relation would be without a sufficient reason and, as such must be rejected.

One can also see the further claim that not being free-floating is built into the nature of a relation as a manifestation of the PSR. If relations cannot be free-floating, but this inability to float free is not due to the nature of the relations, then what would the explanation be for the inability to float free? This inability would seem to be arbitrary and would thus, perhaps, be a brute fact unless this inability has its source in the nature of the relation.

Further, as I stressed in chapter 3, it seems to be generally true that if one thing is built into the nature of another thing, then the second thing depends on the first.[25] In the case at hand, because standing in a relation of grounding to one or more of its relata is built into the nature of any relation, it follows that our relation R depends not just on its relata, but also depends on the relation of grounding that it stands in to one or more of its relata. Call this relation of grounding, R'. Thus, R depends not only on its relata, but also on R' (the relation of grounding between R and one of its relata). I will call the relatum in question "A." So R' is the relation of grounding between R and A.

Now, as Hume might say, in our sifting humour, we must ask: what does R' depend on? R', by its nature, stands in a grounding relation to *its* relata, R

---

[25] See, again, Fine, "Senses of Essence," p. 61; "Ontological Dependence," pp. 275, 283–84.

and A. Thus, it is built into the nature of R' that it stands in this further relation of grounding which I'll call R". But what does R" depend on? Answer: *its relata plus* a further relation of grounding, R''' between R" and its relata, etc. We are clearly off, as we first saw in chapter 3, on an infinite regress, a regress that seems to be vicious. Grounding R depends on *first* grounding R' which depends on *first* grounding R", etc. This chain of grounds not only can never be completed, but it can never even get started: the chain of grounds can never, as it were, get off the ground.

One can also see the emptiness of the grounding of R by pointing out that not only is there an infinite regress, but there is also a circle of grounds. Thus: R' depends on its relata, R and A. But, as we have seen, R, in turn, depends in part on the relation R' of grounding which it stands in to A. So R' ultimately depends in part on R' itself. This is a circle. This is a problem.

Notice that this argument seems to depend at three points at least on the PSR: first, in the claim that if relations cannot be grounded or metaphysically explained, they don't exist or are not real; second, in the claim that relations cannot be free-floating, they must be grounded at least in their relata; and third in the claim that being grounded in its relata is built into the nature of a relation. Russell, for one, explicitly notes that the kind of regress I have called attention to turns on some form of the PSR ("Some Explanations in Reply to Mr. Bradley," p. 374).[26] In this light, we can represent the argument as an argument from the PSR to the denial of the existence of relations and thus to the radical form of monism in which there are no distinctions whatsoever.

There is at least one other way to show that the PSR leads to RM. This argument is a chain of thought made possible by—of all people—Hume. I have developed this argument in my paper, "Playing with Fire." I won't repeat the details of this argument here, but let me offer some highlights of this other line of thought; a line of thought that does not turn on—at least not explicitly—the kind of regress argument I just invoked.

Let's consider the contrapositive of the conditional we are focusing on. That is, instead of examining the conditional if PSR, then RM, let's turn to the contrapositive (which, of course, is equivalent to the original conditional): if not-RM, then not-PSR. It is in this form that Hume's anti-rationalism most clearly takes shape.

Thus, let's begin with the denial of RM and thus let's assume that there are some distinct things. Let's assume that these distinct things include A and

---

[26] There will be more on the Russell-Bradley-PSR connection in chapter 11.

B. If there are these distinct things, then can there be any necessary connection between them? Hume's answer is "no." If there are necessarily connected things, then—for Hume—they cannot be genuinely distinct. This is Hume's famous and popular principle that there can be no necessary connections between distinct existences.[27] Given this principle, it follows that no distinct things can be necessarily connected and thus, if (as Hume thinks)[28] causation requires necessary connection, no distinct things can be causally connected. For Hume, then, the denial of RM, the acceptance of distinctions, together with the principle that there are no necessary connections between distinct existences, leads to the view that one thing, B, cannot be necessarily or causally connected to A or to any other distinct thing. Given the Leibnizian understanding of sufficient reason which we articulated earlier—a sufficient reason is some thing or things distinct from B which guarantee or necessitate the existence of B—it turns out that there is no sufficient reason for B. Thus, the PSR is false. (This is, in effect, Hume's argument in *Treatise* 1.3.3.)

Of course, this path from not-RM to not-PSR is only as strong as the support for Hume's claim that there are no necessary connections between distinct existences. In the interest of time and space, I won't explore this support here except to note that I have argued elsewhere that perhaps the best way to support the no-necessary-connection principle is by invoking the PSR.[29] But then what justification for the no-necessary-connection principle is available to Hume who (as I've mentioned) denies the PSR? This is a major threat facing Hume's system, but one that need not concern us here.

The main point to be gleaned from the sketch of the Humean argument is that we can see our way clear to another argument—apparently separate from the regress argument—for there being a path from the PSR to RM (or from the denial of RM to the denial of the PSR). I will, in what follows, continue to focus, however, on the regress argument as a way of showing the connection between the PSR and RM, but the points I make below can be adapted to the Humean argument as well.

---

[27] Thus, *Treatise* 1.3.6: "There is no object, which implies the existence of any other if we consider these objects in themselves." *Treatise* 1.3.15: "Any thing may produce any thing. Creation, annihilation, motion, reason, volition; all these may arise from one another, or from any other object we can imagine . . . no objects are contrary to each other, but existence and non-existence." See also Armstrong, *A Combinatorial Theory of Possibility*, pp. 115–17.

[28] See, e.g., Hume, *Treatise* 1.3.2.11

[29] Della Rocca, "Playing with Fire." See also Han, "Identity, Dependence, and the Problem of Alienation," and Amijee, "The Rationalist Foundations of Hume's Dictum."

If one is so minded, the natural way to reject the pressure the regress argument generates to accept RM is simply to deny the PSR on which the argument turns and, in particular, to deny that relations cannot be free-floating, to deny that they are by their nature grounded in at least their relata. This is, in effect, the move Russell makes in response to the Bradleyan argument: he simply denies the PSR—at least insofar as it applies to relations. Russell says that this argument "seems to rest upon some law of sufficient reason," and he goes on to say that "the search for a 'sufficient reason' is mistaken" (p. 374). And, of course, denying the PSR is the natural move for Hume to make as well, for he is only too eager, as we have seen, to reject the PSR.

So it seems pretty straightforward for a PSR-denier—such as Russell and Hume—simply to deny the PSR and thus to cleanly avoid RM to which the PSR leads.

Other responses to the regress argument rely on—perhaps less explicit—denials of the PSR. As we saw in chapter 3, one common strategy is to allow that there are infinitely many relations of grounding—R', R'', R''', etc.—but to deny that this regress is vicious. For the regress not to be vicious, one would have to say the following: although there are these infinitely many relations—i.e. although R stands in grounding relation R', and R' stands in grounding relation R'', etc.—the grounding relation in which R stands is not built into the nature of R, and the grounding relation in which R' stands is not built into the nature of R', etc. The regress would be vicious only if there is a regress of dependence relations whereby one relation is prior to another which in turn is prior to another, etc. But, if the relevant grounding relations are not built into the nature of the relations in question, then, one might say, there is no way for the regress of dependence relations—where each depends on other relations that are prior to it—to get going.

One way to develop this view is to state that, although R depends on its relata, A and B, and although R stands in a grounding relation R' to A (say), R does not depend on R'. This way of pursuing the non-vicious regress strategy requires drawing a distinction between the relata, A and B, on the one hand, and the grounding relation R', on the other. The relata are built into the nature of the relation R, but the grounding relation R' is not. But why should there be such a differential treatment of R' and the relata? It seems fundamental to R that there be these relata. But it seems equally fundamental to R that there be this grounding relation R' that R bears to A. Again, because relations are by nature not free-floating, they seem by their nature to stand in such grounding relations. On what basis could the distinction between R' and the relata be drawn when it comes to being part of the nature of R? The distinction appealed to here by the non-vicious regress strategy thus seems arbitrary. There seems to be nothing in virtue of which this distinction between R' and the relata obtains. And so, to appeal to such a distinction is, in effect, to appeal to a violation of the PSR. Here again, the response to my regress argument is or requires the denial of the PSR.

A different, but related response to my regress argument also comes from a challenge to the crucial step in that argument, i.e. to the claim that a relation by its nature depends on the grounding relation between it and its relata or, in my terminology, the claim that R depends on R'. The challenge here is that this position fails to take account of the distinction between the constitutive essence of a thing and its consequential essence. However, as I argued in chapter 3, this distinction cannot be drawn in a non-arbitrary way, and so the appeal to this distinction in challenging the regress argument also depends on the denial of the PSR.

I believe that any response to the regress argument will appeal to brute facts in one way or another, i.e. will turn on denying the PSR. Such a strategy of response is, it might seem, perfectly legitimate, but the key question for us is: is the strategy of denying the PSR in order to avoid RM open to the PSR-tamers, to those who are fond of the PSR but who seek to limit its application?

To answer this question, notice first of all that PSR-tamers have to reject the conclusion of the argument from some form of the PSR to RM. We've seen already that Kant, Dasgupta, and perhaps PSR-tamers in general are (like most philosophers) committed to the denial of RM. But, if the use of the PSR in the argument from the PSR to RM is within the scope of the PSR that is approved by PSR-tamers, then the PSR-tamers are in trouble.

Let's see first if Kant gets into this kind of trouble. As we saw, Kant is a fan of the PSR, but, as a tamer, he is a fan only to a limited extent. He appreciates the PSR's application to items—things or facts—within possible experience. He doesn't welcome the use of the PSR to explain or posit something that transcends experience, such as the total series of finite objects or particular facts or events. Further, while he allows and requires explanation of conditioned things—things that depend on other things—he doesn't allow such explanation to lead us to the conclusion that something unconditioned exists, something that is not dependent on other things. Thus, for Kant, we must, in our use of the PSR, beware of attempts to transcend experience and beware of appeals to the unconditioned. However, uses of the PSR that obey these strictures are legitimate for Kant. That is part of the point of the taming strategy.

Consider now the regress argument for the non-reality of relations. This argument focuses on R—any old relation—and shows that the relation is unintelligible, not real, and does not obtain. Since R was chosen at random, the conclusion here applies to relations in general: there are, in general, no relations and thus no distinctions. Recall that RM—radical monism—as I am using the term is not committed to the claim that there is positively one (big) object. All RM amounts to is the claim that there are no distinctions. Notice that in reaching this conclusion, the regress argument does not appeal to an unconditioned being. Nor does the argument at any point appeal to something that transcends possible experience. The argument focuses on a random relation, R, a relation that can be an object of possible experience, for example, a spatial relation between two objects A and B. This relation must, by its nature, be grounded in at least one of its relata, A, and also in R' the relation of grounding between A and R. We have not transcended experience at this point, nor have we appealed to an unconditioned thing, and we certainly have not claimed knowledge of an unconditioned being. When we see that R' must be, by its nature, grounded in R", etc., we still do not appeal to the unconditioned, and we still do not transcend possible experience.

One might think, however, that in appealing to an infinite regress of grounding relations, the Bradleyan argument that I have offered does transcend the bounds of experience. Perhaps this is so, but this infinite regress is really beside the point here, for, as I have stressed, even if we bracket the issue of infinite regress, there is still an obvious problem: the problem of circularity. R depends on R' which in turn depends on R. It's not at all clear how a Kantian concern about transcending experience can short-circuit the concerns raised by the circularity of this very tight circle.

Even within the constraints dictated by Kant's way of taming the PSR, there does not seem to be a way to stop the regress argument from going forward. If Kant had denied the PSR outright or if Kant had denied that the PSR applies to relations, then he would, as we have seen, be in a position to reject RM. But he doesn't reject the PSR outright, and he doesn't (and I would say can't) deny that the PSR applies to relations: he's a tamer, not a denier, after all. The limited version of the PSR that he accepts does allow the regress argument to go forward. And so Kant has, I argue, no way to resist the PSR's push to RM, to radical monism of a kind that he obviously wants to reject in light of his general commitment, as we have seen, to various kinds of distinctions (at least to distinctions within experience).

Of course, the matter of whether Kant can resist the force of the argument from PSR to RM is not settled by what I have said so far, and I cannot hope to settle it in this chapter. But while we are focused on this topic, let us consider some possible strategies a Kantian might whip out in order to resist the force of this argument. I regard these strategies as unsuccessful.

One possible response on behalf of Kant stresses that he does not seek to make claims of knowledge about the world independent of experience. Thus, Kant seeks, as I mentioned, to avoid dogmatism. So perhaps, then, Kant could agree that within experience, the PSR holds and that, in particular, the regress argument shows that *within experience* there are no relations and that *within experience* some form of monism is true. But—so the response continues—the regress argument is compatible with there being relations in the world insofar as the world is independent of experience and compatible with monism thus being false of the world insofar as the world is independent of experience.

However, for a number of reasons, this response would be unacceptable from a Kantian point of view. One reason is this: Kant cannot hold that within experience there are no relations. For Kant, treating space and time as forms of sensibility—a crucial move in his argument leading up to the limitation of the PSR—requires that within experience there is, as it were, a framework of multiplicity in which objects of experience can and do stand in relations. This commitment to relations within experience is pervasive in the *Critique of Pure Reason* and elsewhere in Kant, and especially so, e.g., in the Amphiboly where Kant advocates the possibility of objects within experience that are differentiated only by the fact that they occupy different regions of space and time. Kant's treatment of space and time thus presupposes, in particular, relations of distinction within the realm of experience. And so this potential strategy for resisting the movement from the PSR to monism is not available to Kant.

A second response on behalf of Kant is more sophisticated, but in the end no more successful. According to this line of thought, when Kant clips the wings of the PSR in his Critical period and offers a new and unprecedented defense of the PSR, the version of the PSR that he has in mind is one according to which there must be a rule-governed succession of events in the realm of experience. Béatrice Longuenesse brings out this point well. She notes first that, for Kant, "the only objects for which one *can* affirm the universal validity of some version of the principle of sufficient reason" are "the objects of perceptual experience" ("Kant's Deconstruction of the Principle of Sufficient Reason," p. 68). She goes on to note that, for Kant, the version of the PSR which he is able to prove concerns the succession of states in the objects that are experienced. Any such succession, for Kant, "presupposes something else upon which it follows according to a rule" (p. 78). And the reason for this presupposition is, of course, as Kant famously argues, that without a sequence of events in experience that proceeds in a rule-governed fashion, the experience that allegedly contains these events would lack the unity required for it to be an experience at all. As Longuenesse points out, Kant sees this focus on the explanation of a succession of events concerning objects of experience as the only adequate way to prove—offer a solid ground for—the PSR. Thus, Kant says that "all attempts to prove the principle of sufficient reason have ... been in vain" (A783/B811). He also says that his own arguments in the Analogies have succeeded where the arguments of others have failed (A217/B265). Kant thus, as Longuenesse puts it, restricts "the principle of reason of things and their determinations to a principle of the determination of an *objective temporal order*" (p. 80).[30]

The upshot of this reading of Kant, for our purposes, is that Kant's limited version of the PSR is, at most, a principle concerning the explanation of events in an objective temporal order. But, recall that the argument from the PSR to RM turns not on the explanation of events, but rather on the explanation of relations, such as R. It was a claim about the need for an explanation of relations in general that got the regress going. However, if Longuenesse is right, Kant, in embracing the PSR, is not committed to the explanation of relations in general, but only to the explanation of events.

In response, I say that, while Kant does focus on the explanation of events, it is not clear that he is not also committed to the explanation of relations in general. Notice that what Kant affirms, as Longuenesse stresses, is the explanation of events in *an objective temporal sequence*. Thus, what is being explained is events in their objective *succession*. But the succession in question is itself a kind of relation, a relation between the events in question. So, Kant's version of the PSR is committed to the explanation of a certain relation (the relation of objective succession between particular events). But then why isn't Kant equally committed to the explanation of other relations

---

[30] See also Hogan, "Metaphysical Motives," p. 281; Watkins, *Kant and the Metaphysics of Causality*, p. 199.

concerning objects? That is, why isn't Kant equally committed to the explanation of what might be called other objective relations, such as, e.g., the relation R between objects A and B, or the relation of objects A and B being 5 feet apart, or the relation between A and one of its properties, etc.?[31]

Here's another way to make the same point. Notice a certain similarity between the argument of the Second Analogy and the regress argument that leads from the PSR to RM. The worry in the Second Analogy is that there be no—what might be called—free-floating events, no event that is not tethered to, not grounded in, not explained by other things. Similarly, we might say, as I have indeed said, the concern in the regress argument is that there be no free-floating relations. And my point here is that it is not clear why Kant would be concerned about free-floating events (in the Second Analogy), but not concerned about free-floating relations. After all, in the case of relations, one can say that if a given relation, R, is not tethered to or explained by (at least) its relata, then we could have the very same relations with different relata at different times and in different situations.[32] This unmooring of relations from the objects that stand in and allegedly ground these relations would, I believe, be as big a threat to the unity of experience as the unmooring of events from one another would be if we lacked an objective temporal order, according to Kant.

But if there cannot be free-floating relations, then we—and Kant—are in a position to say that standing in these tethering relations, these grounding relations, is essential to or part of the nature of a given relation. In the same way, it may be essential to a particular event that it stand in a relation of succession to other events whereby the first event is explained by the other events. And if this is the case—if it is part of the nature of a relation to stand in such grounding relations—then our regress in all its glorious viciousness is off and running.

So I do not regard this strategy—the strategy of arguing that Kant can coherently limit his version of the PSR to objective temporal successions among events and not apply the PSR to the explanation of relations—as successful. Kant has, I argue, no good basis on which to limit his PSR in this way to avoid the regress argument and to avoid RM.

---

[31] We might also put this question by asking: why isn't Kant equally committed to the explanation of A and B in their objective relatedness?

[32] This analogy between free-floating events and free-floating relations is made even stronger if facts, including relational facts, are seen as certain kinds of events.

Dasgupta gets into similar difficulties. He is willing to apply the PSR to all facts with the exception of essentialist facts such as the fact that water is essentially H_2O, the fact that singleton sets essentially depend on their sole members, etc. Essentialist facts are the exception, Dasgupta says. They are not apt for explanation. However, at no point does the regress argument I have offered seek to apply the PSR to essentialist facts. The facts for which explanations are demanded in the argument are facts such as that relation R exists or obtains, the fact that relation R' (the relation of partial grounding) exists or obtains, etc. At various points, the argument does invoke the claim that, e.g., standing in certain grounding relations is essential to R or R', but the essence of a given relation was not itself something for which an explanation was sought. Rather, the essence of a given relation was invoked to reveal a given fact that is not an essentialist fact, e.g., the fact that R stands in a grounding relation, R' to A, or the fact that R' stands in a grounding relation to R'', etc. At no point does the argument invoke or seek an explanation of an essentialist fact.

Thus, given that Dasgupta is friendly toward the PSR in general, he has to allow—or has no way of preventing—the argument for RM from going forward. But, of course, as we have seen, Dasgupta cannot accept that conclusion in light of his general commitment to a structured ontology replete (and, indeed, rife) as it is with many relations and many distinctions.

The problem the argument for RM poses for Kant and Dasgupta is, I believe, also a problem for PSR-tamers in general. As long as the PSR-tamer cannot invalidate the rather limited use of the PSR in my argument for RM, then PSR-tamers in general are committed to RM, a thesis that some, if not all, PSR-tamers find repellent. I can't think of a way for a PSR-tamer—while still remaining friendly to the PSR in general—to invalidate the limited use of the PSR made in the argument for RM. But if a PSR-tamer has any proposals for a legitimate limitation, then, of course, I am all ears.

An Untenable Position for PSR-Tamers

But the problem for PSR-tamers is even more dire than I have indicated so far. This is because not only does a very limited use of the PSR entail RM, but, as we have seen with the modified version of the Leibnizian argument for the PSR, RM entails a very robust form of the PSR, viz. a form of the PSR that is not restricted to the conditioned or to possible objects of experience or to non-essentialist (non-autonomous) facts. So not only are PSR-tamers committed to RM surprisingly and in a fashion most likely unwelcome to them, but PSR-tamers are also committed to an unrestricted form of the PSR. This commitment indicates that the PSR-taming strategy is simply incoherent: PSR-tamers, as such, seek to limit the PSR, but their limited versions of the PSR commit them to an unlimited version of the PSR, in contradiction to their stated goal of limiting the PSR.

To put the point simply: a restricted PSR leads to RM which leads to an unrestricted PSR. That is, a commitment to a restricted PSR—the hallmark of the taming strategy—leads to an unrestricted PSR—the hallmark of the rationalist opponent of the taming strategy. This result is enough to indicate that the taming strategy is incoherent.

But another at least equally unacceptable result is now apparent. Not only does the limited form of the PSR that tamers embrace commit them to an unrestricted PSR in the form of [4'], but it also commits them to a position so radical that this unrestricted PSR to which they are committed is—as I outlined earlier—empty. This is because, as we have seen, when one is committed to an unrestricted PSR through RM, one is committed to the view that if something exists and has requisites other than itself, then it has a sufficient reason and one is also committed to the view that if something exists and has requisites other than itself, then it does *not* have a sufficient reason. This dual commitment—when combined with the view embraced by PSR-tamers that there are things with requisites other than themselves—leads, for a PSR-tamer, to a commitment to a contradictory pair of claims. This commitment to contradictory claims by the taming strategy reveals in a rather stark manner that this strategy is incoherent.

This incoherence in the taming strategy shows that it may be time for philosophy either to embrace the PSR fully or to deny it outright. At the very least, we can see that the taming strategy in which breaking up with the PSR is followed by a limited return to the PSR is not so easy to bring off successfully.

I would argue that, for the kinds of reason that the PSR-taming strategy is incoherent, so too are at least some forms of the monism-taming strategy. Consider a monism-taming strategy in the form of Schaffer's priority monism. This view is, as we have seen, committed to a limited version of the PSR: all non-fundamental objects are explained by the cosmos itself, but the cosmos itself is left unexplained, ungrounded (or perhaps the cosmos itself is not apt for explanation). Thus, as we saw, this form of tamed monism is committed to a restricted form of the PSR.

But now consider the argument for RM from the need to explain relation, R: the existence or obtaining of R is not the cosmos itself, and so it must be explained, and it must be explained in part in terms of the grounding relation, R', which must, in turn be explained in terms of a further grounding relation, etc. The regress here leads to the denial of distinctions and to a form of RM which is incompatible with tamed monism, at least incompatible with tamed monism in the form of Schaffer's priority monism. (And, of course, there is the associated circle to which I have already called attention.) Further, as is the case with the tamed PSR, this tamed monism leads to an empty version of the PSR which—in combination with Schaffer's commitment to objects that have requisites distinct from themselves—leads to contradictory claims. Other forms of tamed monism are likely to go down in similar fashion.

In cutting away the ground that Kant, Dasgupta, and others want to stand on—in eliminating their restricted versions of the PSR—my argument is really an argument against a tamed, middle-ground position in which one limits the PSR. If one is to use the PSR at all, then one must, as it were, go all the way. Thus, my argument against PSR-tamers in this chapter is of the same general form as my defense of the PSR in my 2010 paper, "PSR." There, as well as here, I argue that one cannot coherently be half-hearted in one's defense of the PSR. There my focus was not so much on some sophisticated attempts to limit the PSR (as in Kant and Dasgupta), but on some apparently innocuous, everyday appeals to explicability that can, as I argued, quickly lead to a full-blown PSR. But the outcome in that paper as in this chapter is the same: the middle ground is untenable. So much for the taming strategy.

Breaking Up

And what about the non-tamers mentioned at the beginning of this chapter? The PSR-deniers seem to be in a better position than the PSR-tamers: PSR-deniers don't obviously undermine the guiding theme of their position, as PSR-tamers seem to. This self-undermining of the PSR-tamers comes about through their commitment to a restricted form of the PSR, a commitment that is—officially—nowhere to be found in the position of a PSR-denier.

However, the PSR-deniers are better off than PSR-tamers only as long as they are true PSR-deniers and do not, in fact, smuggle in a limited form of the PSR. Doing so would lead to incoherence, for, as we've just seen, the limited form of the PSR leads to the unrestricted form of the PSR which the

PSR-deniers certainly want to avoid. Here the difficulty—alluded to earlier—in categorizing philosophers as PSR-tamers becomes salient. Some PSR-deniers may be drawn to a limited form of the PSR. And I would say that this is one place where Hume gets into trouble. Despite his stand against the PSR, Hume flirts too much with the PSR, and doing so threatens his entire system, as I've argued in "Playing with Fire."

And what about the other category that I introduced at the outset: the likes of me? This is the category I tentatively called the PSR-affirmers, those who endorse an unrestricted form of the PSR which entails, as we have seen, a radical monism according to which there are absolutely no relations and no distinctions, and, indeed, relations are unintelligible. Such a philosopher—who does not try to limit the PSR—may avoid the particular kind of internal incoherence and the commitment to contradictory claims that, as we have seen, such limitation brings and that threatens PSR-tamers.

Nevertheless, such a philosopher encounters their own threat of incoherence, as I stressed in chapter 9. For example, such a strong PSR leads to the denial of the relations presupposed by the PSR and also leads to a view that cannot coherently be articulated. To the extent that, in appealing to the notion of sufficient reason, one is appealing to differentiated metaphysical explanation, the proponent of an unrestricted PSR must regard the notion of sufficient reason itself as unintelligible. Thus, the proponent of an unrestricted PSR may, in Wittgensteinian fashion, face the prospect of self-undermining. So it might seem as if the proponent of an unrestricted PSR is, in the end, no better off than a PSR-tamer.

However, as we also saw in chapter 9, the proponent of this extreme PSR can and should welcome the incoherence and the destruction of relational metaphysics to which the rationalist rejection of relations leads. By contrast, the PSR-tamer—perhaps, by definition—seeks to occupy a relatively moderate and non-extreme position. Such a tamer thus cannot readily embrace self-undermining in the way that I have argued a proponent of an unrestricted PSR, a proponent of unrestricted use of explanatory demands, can and should.

In this light, perhaps, the label "PSR-affirmer" is not appropriate because, as I've indicated, the ability to articulate a metaphysical position is something that is, in the end, abandoned by the extreme rationalist. At the same time, there is a sense in which this extreme rationalist welcomes self-undermining in a way that the more moderate rationalist, such as Kant and Dasgupta and PSR-tamers more generally cannot. And in this respect, the position

I previously called that of the PSR-affirmer is at an advantage over that of the PSR-tamer.

In ultimately abandoning the PSR itself during its exit from—its ascent out of—relational metaphysics, is the philosopher formerly known as the PSR-affirmer a PSR-denier after all? No, and this is because the PSR-denier seems to invoke the notion of relational metaphysical explanations: the PSR-denier denies that for each fact there is something that stands in an explanatory relation to it. This denial is thus itself a relational metaphysical position. The philosopher formerly known as a PSR-affirmer, in embracing self-undermining, challenges the coherence of relational metaphysical claims as such, even the claims of the PSR-denier. The position of the philosopher formerly known as the PSR-affirmer is or seems to be that the very notion of differentiated truth (as explained at the end of chapter 6) is incoherent. The PSR-denier, in denying the PSR, is not—unlike the philosopher formerly known as the PSR-affirmer—challenging the very notion of such truth or of the failure to attain such truth. Again, the PSR-affirmer's position, in undermining itself, is without metaphysical significance. By contrast—and to their disadvantage—the PSR-denier's position (as well as, of course, the PSR-tamer's position) is fraught with such significance.

I want to close on yet another paradoxical and yet another ironic note. At the outset of this chapter, I mentioned that the position of the PSR-affirmers is so extreme that there may not actually be any PSR-affirmers; PSR-affirmers may not actually exist. We can now see in an unexpected way how this might be so. As I have argued (or "argued"), if the PSR in restricted form is true, then RM is true. And if RM is true, then there are no distinct individuals; in particular, there are no PSR-affirmers as distinct individuals, and there are no philosophers like me as distinct individuals. If that is the case, then those who, perhaps like me, seem to affirm the PSR in unrestricted form are, despite being, in a way, right, are also, in a way, non-existent after all.

11
The Taming of Philosophy

In chapter 10, I sought to dispense with one important strategy of resisting my Parmenidean conclusions, viz. the strategy of taming or limiting the PSR. But despite the significance of the attempts to tame the PSR by Kant, certain contemporary metaphysicians, and others, these sophisticated approaches are, perhaps, not the biggest challenge to the Parmenidean Ascent. An even bigger road-block may simply be the fact that the results and implications of the Parmenidean Ascent are so very implausible, so extreme, so contrary to intuitions and to common sense. As philosophers we have, especially in recent years spanning the lifetimes of all existing philosophers, become conditioned to avoid the implausible or the extreme. The source of this resistance is what I called in chapter 7 the "method of intuition" (MI) which I identified as one of the struts of analytical philosophy in particular. Of the three struts I singled out—realism and discreteness, in addition to the MI—the hardest, perhaps, to counteract and the one that I have done the least so far to challenge directly is the MI. In this chapter, I want to take some steps toward filling this gap. I will take on the formidable task of arguing that the fact that a view is implausible or counterintuitive or goes against common sense is *not* a mark against that view. Because the concern to avoid the implausible is part of the motivation for the (misguided) principle of charity that too often guides the interpretation of texts in philosophy, in challenging the bias against the implausible, I will also be challenging the principle of charity that was discussed in chapter 1. But how does one go about challenging such a pervasive methodological bias against the implausible or counterintuitive or non-commonsensical?

My attack will be two-fold. First, I'll explain why the MI is philosophically deeply problematic: it is unduly conservative, unduly (in some versions of the MI) psychologistic, and unduly arbitrary. In developing these criticisms, I build upon and generalize the brief objection to the MI that I raised in chapter 7. Then, I will narrate a historical drama and, by this

THE TAMING OF PHILOSOPHY 261

means, argue that the recent ascendancy of the MI has a source in a glaringly ineffective and perhaps even question-begging move made by Russell and Moore at the turn of the twentieth century against what is, in effect, a radical Parmenidean position. By unmasking the problematic and, ultimately, philosophically toothless arguments that were crucial in setting analytical philosophy on its merry path to the MI, I will challenge in a new fashion the MI and one of the underpinnings of analytical philosophy itself. Indeed, as we will see, my challenge is equally a challenge to any philosophy that relies on the reality of relations. Here my skepticism reaches a new pitch. This skepticism can now be seen as not merely a skepticism about the coherence of some of our fundamental philosophical concepts and not merely a skepticism about arguments that make use of the notion of metaphysical explanation (including the very arguments I have made challenging these concepts), but as also a skepticism about the possibility of philosophy itself as it is ordinarily practiced. The alternative to ordinary philosophy is, of course, the Parmenidean Ascent that I have been advancing throughout this book, an option that, I believe, will come to appear as more available through the skeptical challenge that I offer in this chapter.

As I said in chapter 7, the MI licenses the rejection of a philosophical view if it is contrary to commonsense belief or if it somehow goes against our intuitions. As I also mentioned, analytical philosophers, in particular, tend to see appeals to common sense or to intuition as a way of trying to advance or settle philosophical disputes. According to this method, the—or a—job of philosophy is to "accommodate" as many intuitions or commonsense beliefs as possible. I will explore the nature of—and the perils of—this accommodation shortly.

But, before doing so, I would like to make a historical observation: while reliance on intuition and the desire to avoid implausible claims is a perennial feature of philosophy, the dependence on this method has not always been as prominent as it has been of late (and, by "of late," I mean the last hundred years or so).[1] Although there were, of course, prior to the twentieth century, philosophers who were more or less subservient in their philosophy to intuition and, in some cases to common sense, and although, as I acknowledge, one can find elements of the MI in just about

---

[1] It is, perhaps, a manifestation of the significance of the history of philosophy to philosophy itself [*failure of philosophy to make any progress*] that "of late" can, when discussing philosophy, cover a period of more than a century.

any historical philosopher, nonetheless, with the rise of analytical philosophy in the twentieth century—and for reasons that we will begin to explore later—intuition or common sense came to dominate philosophy to, perhaps, a greater extent than previously. Before the twentieth century, it is much easier to find philosophers—such as, in reverse chronological order, Bradley, Nietzsche, Hume, Leibniz, Spinoza, Sextus Empiricus, Parmenides, and many others—who seem to be able to do philosophy without continually checking that their intuitions or commonsense beliefs continue to thrive in the hothouse of philosophical reflection. These philosophers and many other historical figures in philosophy do not assume that their own philosophical views have to accommodate either commonsense beliefs or fallible intuitions or fallible intellectual seemings. Rather, many historical figures in philosophy tend to focus more directly than do more dedicated practitioners of the MI on the generally non-psychological subjects with which they are engaged and do not build their systems around fallible intuitions. These philosophers, perhaps, do not turn their backs entirely on the MI, and in recent philosophy one can find philosophers less concerned than some others with intuitions, but the general differences between recent and not-so-recent philosophy are striking.

These sweeping claims lead to the two questions that will guide me throughout this chapter: "Is it good?" and "Why now?" More subtly: In what respects is the MI to be applauded and in what respects is it to be criticized? And: Why has the MI become so popular recently? My answers to the two guiding questions are, perhaps surprisingly, closely intertwined. The historical story I tell near the end of this chapter will help us to understand what is wrong with the MI and will clear the way for our appreciation of an alternative to the MI. Here the assiduously neglected F. H. Bradley will be pivotal to our discussion for not only does he straddle the nineteenth and twentieth centuries and not only is he a particularly clear example of one who rejects the MI, but it is also this example that—in a negative fashion—provided much of the impetus for the ascendancy of the MI.

The story that I will tell and the assessment that I will offer are, I know, by necessity incomplete, but this perspective also provides, I believe, a provocative and needed challenge not only to certain ways of doing philosophy, but also perhaps to philosophy itself. And this perspective is one from which we can better appreciate the power of the Parmenidean Ascent.

Intuition and Accommodation

Let us look more closely at some forms the MI can take. As I mentioned in chapter 7, philosophers sometimes seem to use the terms "intuition" and "common sense" more or less interchangeably. But others seem to reserve the term "intuition" for a kind of intellectual seeming or rational insight. Those who regard such attitudes as ordinary beliefs or as expressions of common sense (whatever that is) or as evident in the workings of ordinary language (whatever that is) include G. E. Moore, Lewis, Sider, etc. who, as we will see, make it at least part of their mission to account for ordinary beliefs. The latter philosophers who regard intuitions as intellectual seemings include George Bealer and John Bengson. These philosophers do not regard intuitions as beliefs but rather as an epistemically privileged, but nonetheless fallible, kind of intellectual seeming or rational insight.[2] Whenever I speak about the MI, I will, unless I explicitly note otherwise, have in mind both the commonsense version and what might be called the more refined version of the MI. And, as we'll see, the criticisms I make of the MI apply either to one or to both forms of the MI.

Many proponents of the MI concentrate on certain attitudes—intuitions or commonsense beliefs—toward particular cases of a general phenomenon. These attitudes concern whether such-and-such is a case of knowledge, causation, intentional action, free action, good or bad or right or wrong action, etc. Think: Gettier cases, Frankfurt-style cases, trolley problems, etc. Discussions of such cases or of intuitions or commonsense beliefs about them have been for many years, and continue to be, a staple—or the staple—of the diet of many philosophers.

For practitioners of what I am calling the MI, such intuitions often play a crucial role in constructing an overarching theory that accommodates such intuitions. As we'll see, the goal of such practitioners of the MI is often to put intuitive responses to cases in touch with often extra-intuitive principles by means of which we can codify, generalize upon, and perhaps explain these intuitive responses.

Some philosophers, of course, eschew—on philosophical grounds—any such use of general principles. Although these philosophers reject philosophical theorizing of the generalizing sort, they nonetheless accord our intuitions a central role in whatever philosophical accounts they offer in a

---

[2] See the references in chapter 7, note 4.

given domain. A prime example of such theorists are the so-called moral particularists.[3] We can also at least conceive of similarly particularist approaches in other areas such as metaphysics or epistemology.[4] Because particularist and non-particularist purveyors of the MI each give intuitions (though in different ways) a central role in their theorizing, they will each be subject to the kinds of critiques I make against the MI.

Finally, the MI need not be focused just on intuitions about cases. One may also appeal directly to intuitions about general principles, i.e. principles that would apply to or explain a range of cases. But intuitions about cases are usually thought to be stronger than, and thus to enjoy primacy over, intuitions about general principles.[5] Whether or not this is the case, I will continue to focus for the most part on intuitions about cases because such intuitions are more often discussed, but I note that the criticisms I make concerning the version of the MI that focuses on intuitions about cases will apply to the more general version of the MI that concerns intuitions about principles as well as about cases.

Perhaps the most prominent version of the MI and, indeed, the predominant method at work in philosophy today is the method of reflective equilibrium (hereafter: MRE).[6] On this view, although our intuitions about cases are in *a* driver's seat and are owed *some* deference, they are not in the only driver's seat. Thus, they are subject to revision and reconstrual when they conflict with well-supported principles. There is thus, for the MRE, a reasonable and, one might say, fair distribution of weight between intuitions and principles: each has some, but not total, power over the other. Intuitions about cases can lead us to reject certain principles or certain proposed principles which conflict with those intuitions AND principles can, in certain cases, lead us to reject intuitions which cannot be accommodated by the principles. The intuitions are especially likely to be given up or at least modified in a case in which there is a plausible explanation of the fact that we were initially inclined to endorse the intuition.

---

[3] See Dancy, "Moral Particularism," and the essays in Hooker and Little, *Moral Particularism*.

[4] Anscombe espouses a view that might be called "causal particularism." See Anscombe, "Causation and Determination."

[5] See McMahan, "Moral Intuition"; Bealer "The Incoherence of Empiricism," p. 104; Bealer, "Intuition and the Autonomy of Philosophy," p. 205; Kagan, "Thinking about Cases," pp. 46, 60.

[6] On the popularity of the MRE, see DePaul, "Why Bother with Reflective Equilibrium?," p. 294, and Kelly, "Common Sense as Evidence: Against Revisionary Ontology and Skepticism," p. 57.

The MRE was, perhaps, first made explicit—though not given its name—by Nelson Goodman in his discussion of the justification of deductive and inductive reasoning:

> [R]ules and particular inferences alike are justified by being brought into agreement with each other. *A rule is amended if it yields an inference we are unwilling to accept; an inference is rejected if it violates a rule we are unwilling to amend.* The process of justification is the delicate one of making mutual adjustments between rules and accepted inferences. (Goodman, *Fact, Fiction, and Forecast*, p. 64; emphasis in original)

Around the same time, John Rawls described the method in his 1951 paper "Outline of a Decision Procedure for Ethics," and he later gave the method its name and elaborated it in *A Theory of Justice*.[7] Rawls speaks mostly not of intuitions but of our "considered judgments" "against which conjectured principles can be checked" (p. 51) in a "process of mutual adjustment" (p. 20n7).[8]

To see the reach of the MRE, I'll point out just two examples of philosophers far removed from moral and political philosophy who nonetheless espouse this method. Thus, take David Lewis whose work is pre-eminent in metaphysics and other areas. Lewis says, "a reasonable goal for a philosopher is to bring them [our intuitions] into equilibrium. . . . If we lose our moorings in common sense . . . the trouble is that we settle for a very inadequate equilibrium."[9]

Notice that Lewis, a philosopher who espouses such radical views as modal realism, counterpart theory, and perdurantism, nonetheless sees his positions as based securely in intuitions and ordinary beliefs, and he sees as his goal the establishment of a stable equilibrium. Lewis doesn't mention Rawls in these passages, but it's clear, especially in the first of the two passages I just quoted, that he means to call the Rawlsian approach to mind.

---

[7] In light of the equitable distribution of weight between intuitions and principles, it is, perhaps, not a mere coincidence that this inherently fair method should be most prominently developed by the thinker who introduced the notion of justice as fairness.

[8] For a sophisticated articulation and defense of the MRE, see Elgin, *Considered Judgments*, chapter 4.

[9] Lewis, "Introduction," p. x. See also the passage from Lewis, *Counterfactuals*, p. 88, (quoted in chapter 7); see Lewis, "Elusive Knowledge" (p. 419), where he favors a certain account of knowledge because "[i]t demands less frequent corrections of what we want to say." See also Lewis' "Rule of Conservatism" later in the same paper (p. 433).

Ted Sider—another metaphysician—articulates a methodology very much in the same vein and emphasizes the accommodation of ordinary beliefs: "One . . . develops a theory preserving as many of these ordinary beliefs as possible, while remaining consistent with science."[10] I'll return to these passages from Lewis and Sider.[11]

Some versions of experimental philosophy fall within the general MRE camp. These approaches typically investigate and critique our intuitions understood as ordinary beliefs, in order to see which of them are worth keeping. These views thus seek, upon that basis, to come up with principles.[12] Such accommodation of intuitions—at least of some kind—is also the goal of the MI.

George Bealer's view is not a version of the MRE, for Bealer, unlike Lewis, Sider, Rawls, and others, does not begin with ordinary beliefs, but rather with a quasi-perceptual state of seeing. Nonetheless, because Bealer recognizes that even intuitions in his sense are fallible, intuitions may need to be rejected in order to accommodate principles or other intuitions.[13] Because of the mutual accommodation between intuitions and principles in his system, even Bealer's methodology resembles, in this crucial respect, a version of the MRE.

Thus, there is a common commitment to some form of the MI—a commitment to reliance either on commonsense beliefs or fallible intuitions—running through much of contemporary and recent philosophy.

Indeed, reliance on some form of the MI may come to seem inevitable. Without the ballast apparently provided by intuitions understood as commonsense beliefs or as fallible intellectual seemings, what legitimate basis could one have for starting with whatever starting points one starts with? Philosophy which gives sole weight to extra-intuitive principles or other factors as opposed to intuitions seems to be philosophy without moorings, philosophy in danger of listing dangerously from side to side, a philosophy plagued by what Lewis calls "a very inadequate equilibrium."[14] For this reason, very many contemporary and recent philosophers seem to regard the MI as well-nigh unavoidable: abjuring commonsense beliefs or ceasing to rely on fallible rational insights would leave us, it may seem, in a very undesirable skeptical position with no way to pursue philosophical inquiry in a principled way. And the examples of apparently failed metaphysical systems

---

[10] Sider, *Four-Dimensionalism*, pp. xv–xvi.
[11] See also Schaffer, "From Nihilism to Monism," p. 175. There he is guided by what "commonsense methodology demands."
[12] See Alexander, Mallon, and Weinberg, "Accentuate the Negative."
[13] For references concerning the fallibility of intuitions, see chapter 7, note 6.
[14] Lewis, "Introduction," p. x.

from the past when the MI may not have been as prominent as it is today only serve to underscore the air of inevitability of the MI.

This apparent inevitability of the MI only serves to make it all the more troubling that there are, as I will now explain, deep objections to the MI. I will elicit three related difficulties with the MI, each of which is an instance of what I call the taming of philosophy, i.e. of philosophy's arbitrary limitation of its inquiries, philosophy's arbitrary limitation of itself. In the previous chapter, we considered views which seek to tame the PSR in particular by arbitrarily limiting its scope. In the current chapter, I will focus on the phenomenon of taming philosophical inquiry more generally. These difficulties that I raise here for the taming strategy in general will enable me to answer the first guiding question—Is the MI good?—in the negative, and they will also lay the groundwork for the historical considerations I will invoke to answer the second guiding question—Why did the MI become so popular? These challenges to the MI will help pave the way for a philosophy untamed and at the same time help pave the way for the Parmenidean Ascent.

Is It Good?—Taming and Conservatism

A standard objection to the MI in general and to the MRE in particular—though as we will see, an objection that is, in some respects, unfair—is that such a method is too conservative: it doesn't allow for the radical changes in beliefs that may sometimes be required by the phenomenon one is investigating. The charge is that proponents of this method privilege certain starting points which are not worthy of such privileging. And the worry is that with such unjustified starting points, the whole edifice that one erects is rendered arbitrary.

This criticism is more obviously appropriate when directed against a version of the MI that privileges ordinary, commonsense beliefs. Ordinary beliefs are just ordinary, after all. Why should they get any special treatment and constrain where we begin and where we wind up in our philosophical investigations? Reality—or our inquiry into it—may demand radical revision in our beliefs, and if we are beholden to common sense, then it may be unjustifiably difficult to make the required changes.

Such conservative—and ultimately, arbitrary—fealty to common sense is widespread in philosophy, particularly over the last one hundred years, though also among certain historical figures. Thus, let me just mention

Berkeley and Moore as explicit proponents of commonsense philosophy who are, I believe, vulnerable to this charge of arbitrary conservatism. But let me also highlight two widely admired contemporary philosophers who, surprisingly perhaps, are subject to the same criticism. Thus, consider one of Sider's methodological musings part of which was quoted earlier:

> One approaches metaphysical inquiry with a number of beliefs. Many of these will not trace back to empirical beliefs, at least not in any direct way. These beliefs may be particular, as for example the belief that I was once a young boy, or they may be more general and theoretical, for example the belief that identity is transitive. One then develops a theory preserving as many of these ordinary beliefs as possible, while remaining consistent with science. (*Four-Dimensionalism*, pp. xv–xvi)

This is an extremely conservative methodology: one may depart from ordinary beliefs, but one must not go too far; one must always return to common sense as much as possible.

Lewis gives expression to a very similar methodology. On Lewis' view (as well as Sider's apparently) one may "give up" an intuition or ordinary belief, but in order to do so one must first show how such giving up enables one to hold onto many other ordinary beliefs and to do so within a stable system of beliefs. Lewis' methodology, like Sider's, is deeply conservative. As Lewis explicitly announces, "theoretical conservatism is the only sensible policy for theorists of limited powers, who are duly modest about what they could accomplish after a fresh start."[15] Even the most apparently exotic views, according to this methodology shared by Lewis and Sider and many others, must in the end return home and be grounded in common sense.

An explicitly and similarly conservative view (focusing on the nature of perception) is embraced by James Pryor:

> [W]e start with what it seems intuitively natural to say about perception, and we retain that natural view until we find objections that require us to abandon it. This is just sensible philosophical conservatism.[16]

---

[15] Lewis, *On the Plurality of Worlds*, p. 134. See also Symons, "Intuition and Philosophical Methodology," p. 82.

[16] Pryor, "The Skeptic and the Dogmatist," p. 538. For further examples of such conservatism, see Harman, "Skepticism and Foundations" (esp. p. 8), and "Three Trends in Moral and Political Philosophy." Paul similarly stresses "the value of minimizing . . . radical reinterpretations of our

To point out this conservatism is not yet to criticize Lewis et al., but the criticism is not far behind, for the worry is that this privileging of ordinary beliefs is arbitrary and unjustified. Yes, it may feel good to return home to the comfort of familiar beliefs, but not all homes are worth returning to. Many of our ordinary beliefs are the products of less than reputable sources, e.g., in the case of moral opinions such as judgments that, as Peter Singer puts it, "derive from discarded religious systems, from warped views of sex and bodily functions, or from customs necessary for the survival of the group in social and economic conditions that now lie in the distant past."[17] Without a good reason for requiring a return to commonsense beliefs, a philosophy generated by this methodology seems unavoidably arbitrary.

The arbitrariness is not removed by claiming, as Lewis does as I noted, that a philosophy not anchored in common sense is inadequate. Even if a philosophy not grounded in common sense is inadequate—and I am by no means convinced that it is, but let's grant this point for the sake of argument—this doesn't mean that the comforts of stability and common sense should have any bearing on successful inquiry. If the starting points in common sense are arbitrary, then any system based on common sense—no matter how stable—is also arbitrary.

Thomas Kelly—a Moorean defender of common sense[18]—acknowledges the possibility that our prephilosophical beliefs are off the mark and, at the same time, he seems unperturbed by this possibility:

> A case in which our prephilosophical beliefs about what there is or what we know are in fact radically in error is a case in which we are maximally ill-positioned to find such truths [deep truths in metaphysics and epistemology]. It is one in which we sit down to play the exceedingly difficult games of metaphysics and epistemology having been dealt a particularly bad hand. If these are indeed our circumstances, it would be a mistake to assume that an adequate philosophical method ought to provide us with a rational path out of the darkness and into the light. ("Common Sense as Evidence," p. 58)

---

commonsense language and beliefs," "Metaphysics as Modeling," p. 23. See also Strawson's views as discussed in Dutilh Novaes and Geerdink, "The Dissonant Origins of Analytic Philosophy."

[17] Singer, "Sidgwick and Reflective Equilibrium," p. 516.
[18] See especially Kelly, "Moorean Facts and Belief Revision, or Can the Skeptic Win?"

Kelly seems to hold that we should, in general, stick with our prephilosophical beliefs even though they might be very inadequate guides to the world. In light of this possibility, there seems to be no non-arbitrary basis for preferring these prephilosophical beliefs as starting points. Here we have again the combination of conservatism (stick with our original beliefs, by and large, i.e. dance with who brung ya) and arbitrariness.

The charge of unjustified conservatism has often been leveled at Rawls' MRE. Indeed, the charge by Singer recently quoted is directed against Rawls. But here the criticism is not as clearly on target, and that is because Rawls is not as beholden to common sense as philosophers such as Sider and Lewis are. Rawls can go some distance toward rebutting the charge of conservatism (and thus of arbitrariness) by pointing out, first, that the opinions about cases to which he accords weight in the process of achieving reflective equilibrium are not just any judgments but our "considered judgments." Further, and especially after the original edition of *A Theory of Justice*, Rawls stresses that the kind of reflective equilibrium he has in mind is the "wide" variety according to which, in one's deliberations, one brings to bear not just considered judgments about cases but also background facts concerning persons and morality. Such further theoretical background may provide more room for criticism and revision of ordinary beliefs and of considered judgments.[19]

Bealer, also a proponent of the MI, like Rawls does not give pride of place to commonsense or ordinary beliefs.[20] Indeed, as we saw, Bealer's focus is not on beliefs at all, but on what he sees as the kind of just seeing that is constitutive of intuitions.[21] Because—in these different ways—they do not dwell on common sense, both Bealer and Rawls may be able to rebut (at least initially) the charge of undue conservatism or undue reliance on existing beliefs.

Nonetheless, even if they rely on intuitions of some kind which may—in different ways—be remote from common sense, both Bealer and Rawls may still face a charge of undue privileging of certain states or graspings over others. For we can ask: why should intuitions in Bealer's sense or considered

---

[19] See Rawls, "The Independence of Moral Theory," pp. 7–8. Scanlon, "Rawls on Justification," p. 150, stresses the flexibility of wide reflective equilibrium in his response to the charge of conservatism. See Mühlebach, "Reflective Equilibrium as an Ameliorative Framework in Feminist Epistemology" for interesting observations on the usefulness of wide reflective equilibrium in offering a feminist response to feminist criticisms of the MRE as conservative.

[20] Bealer, "The Incoherence of Empiricism," pp. 103–04; "Intuition and the Autonomy of Philosophy," p. 211.

[21] Bengson, "The Intellectual Given," p. 728, stresses how the method of intuition—in the sense of intellectual seemings—is potentially subversive of ordinary beliefs and can potentially reach radical new conclusions.

judgments in Rawls' sense be our starting or focal points?[22] It may be that a sharper, more radical departure from even our refined intuitions or from our considered judgments is required. After all, the intuitions and judgments are, as Bealer and, presumably, Rawls would admit, fallible. Antecedently, there is no reason that we should attune our theories to fallible intuitions rather than adopt some other, extra-intuitive starting point.[23] Thus, the method of refined intuition or of considered judgments in wide reflective equilibrium, like the MI generally, may be too conservative in blocking or hampering departure from our ordinary beliefs or from fallible intuitions. Thus, this method may—like the MI generally—arbitrarily treat certain starting points or focal points as good.[24]

Again, this closing-off of certain radical options, this arbitrary limitation of one's philosophical perspective that is characteristic of the MI, is what I call the taming of philosophy. The taming of philosophy may preclude the possibility of overturning our existing convictions, and may unjustifiably shut us off from exotic, unusual views. We will see shortly two other manifestations of this taming that the MI ushers on stage.

Of course, as I noted, without appealing to intuitions of some kind there may be no reason for starting at whatever point one starts at in philosophical inquiry. Thus, damned if you do (appeal to intuitions), damned if you don't. Or, more specifically, arbitrary if you do appeal to intuitions, arbitrary if you don't. This may be so, but even if it is, then this result would merely go to support the skeptical claim that whether or not one relies on intuitions, one has no principled or justified starting point, and that there is no way forward for philosophical inquiry. But, then, as I am fond of saying in my skeptical way: so much the worse for us. The fact (if it is a fact) that any other starting point besides intuition is also arbitrary doesn't undermine the fact that starting with one's intuitions (of one kind or another) is itself arbitrary. Yes, it would be nice for us to have non-arbitrary starting points, but if we don't we don't, and no amount of pinning one's hopes on intuitions or considered judgments will alter this picture.

This latest dimension of skepticism is in addition to the forms of skepticism to which we have been led in previous chapters. That is, the skepticism

---

[22] See Hare, "Rawls' Theory of Justice—I," p. 147.
[23] See Cummins, "Reflection on Reflective Equilibrium," p. 124.
[24] For a very compelling criticism of something like the MI as too conservative—a criticism different from, yet consistent with, the objections developed here—see Rinard, "Why Philosophy Can Overturn Common Sense."

here is in addition to skepticism about the coherence of the very notions of substance, action, knowledge, meaning, and explanation and in addition to skepticism about the coherence of the very arguments that lead to this claim that these notions may be incoherent. The new dimension of skepticism here concerns philosophy's ability to have non-arbitrary starting points and thus to proceed in a non-arbitrary fashion.

So the first criticism of the MI and the first part of my answer to the question, "Is it Good?," is to point out that the MI inevitably generates a system of claims that is arbitrary and conservative. This is the first respect in which the MI leads to the taming of philosophy.

Is It Good?—Taming and the Antiquarianism of the Present

The first charge of taming was that this focus on our intuitions—refined or not—engenders an arbitrary conservatism. The second charge of taming dwells not so much on the conservatism of the MI, but on the fact that the MI centers on our intuitions, what, on some views, may be seen as bits of our psychology. The worry here is that this focus makes the MI inherently unsuited for providing philosophical accounts. The criticism in this section applies only to those forms of the MI that call for philosophical systems centered on commonsense beliefs (as in Moore, Lewis, and Sider) or on considered judgments (as in Rawls and Goodman). The version of the MI found in Bealer and Bengson according to which intuitions are intellectual seemings is, for reasons I will explain shortly, not threatened by the particular criticism I advance in this section.

When one adopts the MI according to which intuitions are commonsense beliefs or Rawlsian considered judgments, one's focus is not directly on the world itself; rather one's focus is directly on our intuitive beliefs or judgments about the world, i.e. on bits of our psychology instead of on bits of extramental reality. Perhaps one so focuses with the ultimate goal of getting at reality through our intuitions. However, at least for these versions of the MI, the initial focus is on the intuitive beliefs themselves which are treated as evidence for the philosophical conclusions we reach. It is precisely because Bealer's version of the MI does not treat intuitions as evidence, but rather as intellectual seemings or direct perceptions of philosophically relevant facts that this version of the MI is not vulnerable to the criticism I offer in this section. But, with other versions of the MI, philosophy becomes in the first instance more of a recording of opinions or apparent insights into reality than an account of reality itself. Timothy Williamson describes this kind of approach well:

> [Many contemporary analytic philosophers] think that, in philosophy, ultimately our evidence consists only of intuitions.... [T]hey take that to mean not that our evidence consists of the mainly non-psychological putative facts which are the contents of those intuitions, but that it consists of the psychological facts to the effect that we have intuitions with those contents, true or false. (Williamson, *The Philosophy of Philosophy*, p. 235)

> Philosophers' uncritical talk of philosophy as relying, for better or worse, on "intuitions" often manifests the misconception that our evidence in philosophy consists of psychological facts about ourselves rather than facts about the philosophical topic itself. (Williamson, interview in Hendricks and Symons, *Formal Philosophy*, p. 222)

One problem with this approach is that the emphasis on our intuitions seems to be misplaced: with the MI understood as focused on commonsense beliefs or with the MRE, we are being asked to "check" our theories against our intuitions.[25] But instead of focusing on our intuitions about facts or the world, we should be focusing on those facts or the world themselves—after all, that is what we in our philosophical theories are primarily trying to understand. This errant emphasis renders philosophical accounts that purport to be of reality unnecessarily and illegitimately subjectivist. Williamson makes a similar point in inveighing against MRE:

> [P]hilosophy is often presented as systematizing and stabilizing our beliefs, bringing them into reflective equilibrium: the picture is that in doing philosophy what we have to go on is what our beliefs currently are, as though our epistemic access were only to those belief states and not to the states of the world that they are about. This picture is wrong; we frequently have better epistemic access to our immediate physical environment than to our own psychology. (Williamson, *The Philosophy of Philosophy*, p. 5)

---

[25] See Hare, "Rawls' Theory of Justice—I," p. 145.

It's as if Rawls and other proponents of the commonsense version of the MI or of the MRE are guilty of placing not so much a veil of ignorance but rather *a veil of intuitions* between us and reality. By dwelling more directly on our intuitions about the world than on the world, a philosophy guided by these forms of the MI becomes oddly detached from the philosophical subject matters with which it seeks to concern itself. Philosophy under the MI is philosophy without its moorings in reality. Earlier I said that it *may be* the case that philosophy that is not in the spirit of the MI is also philosophy without moorings, philosophy without an adequate basis for its starting points. Now we see, however, that whether or not such approaches other than the MI lack moorings, philosophy in the spirit of the MI is not well grounded.

The problem here is another instance of the taming of philosophy. By drawing back our focus onto us and psychology, these versions of the MI detach us from the philosophical matters we are taken up with, and so, once again, philosophy's engagement with reality is limited. And, crucially as before, this limitation seems to be arbitrary and unjustified: what basis is there for thinking that certain of our intuitions should be a guide to facts or the world?

And in this there is a bit of irony. In becoming in many cases more directly focused on our thoughts, than on the relevant philosophical subject matter, philosophy under these versions of the MI comes to resemble nothing so much as what is often derided as mere doxography, the recording of belief systems without being primarily concerned with the truth of the beliefs in those systems. Similarly, Hare likens the MRE to anthropological theories:

> the only "moral" theories that can be checked against people's actual moral judgments are anthropological theories about what, in general, people *think* one ought to do, not moral theories about what one ought to do. (Hare, "Rawls' Theory of Justice—I," p. 148)

For his part, Rawls seems (oddly) unconcerned by this kind of charge: "It [the procedure of reflective equilibrium] is, if you wish, a kind of psychology" ("The Independence of Moral Theory," p. 9). Of course, proponents of these versions of the MI will claim that they are concerned with what Williamson calls "states of the world," but their explicit focus on our considered judgments or commonsense beliefs, as well as the lack of any good reason to see such judgments or beliefs as tied to these states, tends to undermine this claim (see Williamson, *The Philosophy of Philosophy*, p. 211). I call—somewhat paradoxically—the doxography that is constitutive of these versions of the MI, their focus on what we happen to think, the antiquarianism of the present.

This is where the irony comes in. Often, the MI is presented as a refreshingly direct way to do philosophy, unimpeded by such non-philosophical "distractions" as trying to understand a past philosopher on his or her own terms. Employing the MI to achieve philosophical results is seen as decidedly philosophical in a way that, often, engagement with historical figures in philosophy is not. But now—in light of this second charge of taming—it turns out that in following certain versions of the MI one is less engaged with the facts that philosophy is concerned with than one might have thought. Further, and crucially, one is often less engaged with these facts than one is when one grapples with and struggles to understand on its own terms the thought of a philosopher who is him or herself more directly engaged with these facts instead of merely or primarily with his or her own (or anyone else's) opinions or intuitions. Thus, in engaging with, say, Hume, Leibniz, Spinoza, Sextus Empiricus, Parmenides, and many others—precisely because these philosophers tend not to dwell on their common sense beliefs but on reality itself—one is more likely to be doing philosophy directly than one is when one explores the contours of one's own (or Kripke's or Lewis' or Thomas Nagel's) intuitions about this or that matter. Engaging with certain historical figures in philosophy can thus be a way of doing philosophy in a less tamed fashion than is engaging with the latest journal articles that are trapped behind the veil of intuitions. In other words, in some cases, the study of the history of philosophy is a way of doing philosophy that is more philosophical than are certain current, relatively a-historical approaches to philosophy, approaches guided more completely by the MI. In this way, relatively a-historical approaches to philosophy are often relatively a-philosophical, and precisely this is one of the conclusions concerning the relation of philosophy to the study of its history that we reached (by different means) in chapter 7.

Of course, avoiding this turn inward and focusing directly on the facts without relying on appeals to intuitions as evidence may not be as easy as Williamson and other opponents of the MI sometimes make it out to be. It may be, then, that—as I've skeptically said—we have no principled starting points either in our intuitions or somewhere else. But then—as I've also skeptically said—so much the worse for us.

Is It Good?—Taming, Quine, and Revision

I will introduce the third challenge to the MI by focusing on the MRE in particular. I will briefly indicate how this challenge applies also to other versions of the MI such as Bealer's.

Begin with the point that the MRE is a method of bringing intuitions or considered judgments and principles into a process of, to use Goodman's phrase, "mutual adjustment." No particular intuition and no particular principle is treated as sacrosanct. Principles are not by themselves in a position to override intuitions, nor are intuitions by themselves able to overturn a principle that conflicts with those intuitions. Rather, there is an interplay at work, a "familiar give and take," as Sider puts it.[26] And we must adjust principles and intuitions to come up with the most coherent overall system, a system that does the best job of accommodating intuitions and also offers the most illuminating explanatory principles. But precisely because of what may seem to be its greatest virtue—its judicious balancing of intuitions and principles—the MRE faces another significant challenge. The flexible interplay between principles and intuitions means that when there is some kind of conflict between them, no one way of resolving the conflict is dictated. In the face of a conflict between an intuition and a principle, one can hold onto the intuition *come what may*, as long as one is willing to make requisite changes in the principles that one accepts and perhaps to modify, as well, certain other intuitions. Alternatively, in the face of this conflict, one can hold onto the principle *come what may* and revise or reconstrue or simply reject the offending intuition and make whatever other adjustments are required in the intuitions and principles one accepts. The general point is that because of the apparently welcome flexibility of the MRE, there is—in the case of a conflict between intuitions and principles—significant latitude: no one outcome is dictated either by the principles or by the intuitions or by the two together. This means that, for any line that one draws between intuitions and principles or between the claims that are kept and those that are rejected or modified, there are other such lines that one could equally well draw within a coherent system of principles and intuitions.

Given this multiplicity of incompatible ways of drawing the line, whatever line we draw is going to be arbitrary and unprincipled because there is no adequate basis for drawing that line as opposed to another. Drawing whichever

---

[26] Sider, *Four-Dimensionalism*, p. xvi.

line we draw is, in that respect, inexplicable. Or—to put the point another way—the line, the *relation*, between the principles and intuitions that we accept and those that we do not accept is ungrounded and inexplicable. And this inexplicability derives from something essential to the MRE: its flexible give-and-take between intuitions and principles.

This commitment on the part of the MRE to inexplicable distinctions of a certain kind is yet another instance of the taming of philosophy. In requiring that we arbitrarily choose one way of drawing the line between intuitions and principles as opposed to some other way, the MRE shuts us off from these other ways of gaining access to the facts that interest us as philosophers. The method thus necessitates an arbitrary and ungrounded limitation on philosophical perspectives. Such a limitation is constitutive of the phenomenon of the taming of philosophy as I have characterized it.

One way to make the significance of this charge of taming felt is to articulate the strong analogy between this criticism of the MRE and Quine's best argument against the analytic/synthetic distinction in "Two Dogmas of Empiricism," an argument I've already outlined in chapter 6, in the section "In Lieu of Aquinas: Quine and Davidson."

Here, again, is a skeletal version of this Quinean argument. Assume that there is a distinction between analytic statements which are true solely by virtue of their meaning and are not dependent for their truth on extra-conceptual facts about the world, facts that we have access to (if at all) only by virtue of experience. This is a distinction between statements we must hold onto (as long as we understand the statement) and statements that are subject to revision or rejection in light of facts about the world that are independent of the concepts contained in the statement itself. Any such distinction is arbitrary and illegitimate, Quine says, for, as he affirms, no statement is immune to revision, no statement is one that we must hold onto come what may. Any statement is such that it may be revised as long as one is willing to make the requisite changes in the system of other statements one accepts. Similarly, any statement is one we may hold onto come what may as long as we are willing to make requisite changes elsewhere in in our web of belief. As we saw in chapter 6, Quine puts the point this way:

> [I]t becomes folly to seek a boundary between synthetic statements, which hold contingently on experience, and analytic statements, which hold come what may. Any statement can be held true come what may, if we make drastic enough adjustments elsewhere in the system. ("Two Dogmas," p. 43)

The worry here is over the very intelligibility of the purported distinction. Quine says as I noted in chapter 6:

> [W]e at present lack any tenable general suggestion, either rough and practical or remotely theoretic, as to what it is to be an analytic sentence. ("Carnap and Logical Truth," p. 129; see also Quine, "Truth by Convention," p. 105)

This basic style of argumentation has influenced similar proponents of (meaning) holism, such as Davidson and many others. As we have seen (chapter 6, section "In Lieu of Aquinas: Quine and Davidson"), Quine explicitly ties this kind of argument to the Principle of Sufficient Reason (PSR). For Quine, the analytic/synthetic distinction is to be rejected because it violates the PSR.

So much for Quine's reason for rejecting the analytic/synthetic distinction. Let's return to the MRE where, I believe, a similar line of argument applies. Just as any analytic/synthetic distinction is arbitrary and inexplicable and thus should, for Quine, be rejected, so too, in the interplay between intuitions and principles, any distinction between claims we keep and those we reject is arbitrary and inexplicable and, for that reason, should be rejected. Since the MRE requires drawing such an arbitrary distinction, this method should be rejected too. That is: we should stop trying to accommodate intuitions and principles in the flexible manner embraced by the MRE.[27]

So this criticism of the MRE, this third instance of taming, gets additional force from its similarity to Quine's best argument against the analytic/synthetic distinction. But, perhaps, you don't like Quine's argument against the analytic/synthetic distinction (even though it is often regarded as one of the high points of analytical philosophy). OK then, allow me to state my point about the MRE directly, without the help of Quine. The MRE requires arbitrary distinctions and inexplicable relations between claims we accept and those we reject. Such inexplicable relations are not to be tolerated because

---

[27] This is not to say that Quine rejects the MRE. In this connection, it is interesting to note that Rawls explicitly ties the MRE to Quine's holism and the rejection of the analytic/synthetic distinction; see Rawls, *A Theory of Justice*, p. 579n33. Like Rawls, Quine may think that, in holistically adjusting our theory in the way MRE requires, we are avoiding the pitfalls of the analytic/synthetic distinction. But because such holistic adjustment is arbitrary in precisely the same way that the analytic/synthetic distinction is arbitrary and because Quine rejects the analytic/synthetic distinction on this basis, he should not endorse the MRE either. I think that a similar worry about arbitrariness threatens the coherence of Quine's Neurathian image of repairing one's ship while one is on that ship. Which repairs one undertakes may be arbitrary. See Quine, "Identity, Ostension, Hypostasis," p, 79.

these inexplicable relations constitute a failure of the MRE to carry out its inquiries non-arbitrarily, and this seems unacceptable. As I said in chapter 8 in the case of metaphysics: one should not make moves in one's metaphysical system arbitrarily. Similarly, and more generally, one should not make moves in one's philosophical system arbitrarily. Thus, embracing such arbitrary relations between claims we accept and those we do not constitutes an illegitimate narrowing of philosophy's perspective on the world, another instance of the taming of philosophy. It is the very flexibility of the MRE—the very point which earns this method its august status—that leads to this objection to that method.

Other versions, such as Bealer's, of the MI likewise appeal to fallible intuitions, and so these versions also would be faced with issues of arbitrariness in deciding which intuitions to modify or reject.

Of course, as before, rejecting the MRE (or, more generally, rejecting versions of the MI committed to fallible intuitions, in some sense of "intuition") and proceeding in a non-arbitrary fashion may not be possible. And, again as before, perhaps damned if you do, and damned if you don't. And, again as before and again skeptically, perhaps so much the worse for us.

Stepping back from the three charges of taming, we can see that they all turn on the unpleasant fact that each version of the MI relies on arbitrary and inexplicable *relations*. (Coming from me, this identification of relations as the culprit shouldn't be at all surprising.) Thus, the first charge of taming is that proponents of the MI have no non-arbitrary starting points or focal points and so they can draw no principled distinction between claims that they accept as starting points or focal points and those that they do not. This kind of taming is bound up with, as I explained, an objectionable conservatism on the part of the MI. Thus, the *relation* between claims that are accepted and claims that are not is arbitrary and inexplicable.

The second charge of taming was the charge that certain proponents of the MI treat as evidence for whatever conclusion they reach the fact that we have such-and-such intuitions or certain special attitudes toward particular cases or principles. This focus on us and on our psychology is, I claim, arbitrary because no principled reason is given for thinking that our responses should have primacy. Because of this unprincipled focus on us, we can see the proponents of the MI as committed yet again to ungrounded and inexplicable relations: for the proponents of these forms of the MI, there is no principled reason to treat intuitive claims as particularly worthy of respect, and so again there is an arbitrary line between the claims the proponents of these forms of the MI treat as valuable and those that they do not. The *relation* between the two classes of claims is arbitrary and inexplicable.

Similarly, with the third charge of taming, we pointed out that there are unintelligible relations at play because the *relation* between the claims one revises and the claims one does not is arbitrary and inexplicable, for the proponent of the MI.

Because of the centrality of the notion of inexplicable relations in the key objections to the MI, it seems that the fact that the MI is committed to unintelligible relations is the basic criticism of the MI. I criticized the MI in chapter 7 for presupposing realism which itself is committed to an unintelligible relation of distinction between one's beliefs and the facts or the world. This chapter—up to this point—can be seen as an elaboration of and a generalization of that criticism of the MI. Thus, this commitment to unintelligible relations is the chief reason for my negative answer to the first guiding question I raised concerning the MI earlier in this chapter: "Is it good?"

It is interesting that, although these arguments in criticism of the MI so far in this chapter focus on problems with inexplicable relations, these arguments don't—at least not explicitly—turn on a general rejection of all relations as unintelligible. A full-blown Bradleyan rejection of all relations is not (yet) needed. But I will now show that, in the answer to the historical question "Why Now?" about the recent dominance of the MI, the general Bradleyan rejection of relations in deeply implicated.

Why Now?

As I know from long experience (and, I venture to say, as you know too), pointing out and even demonstrating philosophical problems with a certain position usually does little to move philosophers in the grip of their intuitions. So, despite my arguments so far in this chapter against the MI, I will in this second part of my critique of the MI take a different tack and, as is my wont, "go historical." I will dig deeper into the sources at the turn of the twentieth century regarding the aversion among analytical philosophers, in particular, to counterintuitive views.

I noted earlier that the MI gained or regained prominence about one hundred years ago with the rise of so-called analytical philosophy, and so one question I raised was this: why did the MI become so prominent with the rise of analytical philosophy and why does it continue to be prominent? A full answer to this question must contain many strands which I cannot hope to explore here. But let me isolate one particularly revealing strand that invokes some of the themes of intelligibility that I have already relied on in my (negative) answer to the question, "Is it good?"[28]

The story I am about to tell begins on a familiar note: analytical philosophy, as we have come to know it, came into prominence in part because of Russell's and Moore's revolt against the idealism of Bradley and others, an idealism that was, at the turn of the twentieth century, the dominant philosophical movement at least in the English-speaking world. Now (as an irreverent supporter of Bradley might ask) why were Russell and Moore revolting? To see why, we need to look more closely at the idealism Russell and Moore sought to—and eventually did—knock off philosophy's pedestal. As Russell and Moore saw, a certain doctrine about relations lay at the heart of Bradley's idealism, and it was their rejection of this doctrine that lay at the heart of their new approach to philosophy. Thus Bradley, Russell, and Moore all shared this insight (as Russell put it):

> The question of relations is one of the most important that arise in philosophy, as most other issues turn on it: monism and pluralism, . . . idealism and realism in some of their forms, perhaps the very existence of philosophy as a subject distinct from science and possessing a method of its own. (Russell, "Logical Atomism," p. 333)

As we have seen, the doctrine Bradley advanced and the others challenged was that relations are not real: relations between things—including relations of distinction—are, in some sense, merely apparent. And so, for Bradley, multiplicity is merely apparent, there are no distinctions. Bradley's denial of the reality of relations thus quickly leads to a view that might, as I have explained, be misleadingly be called radical monism.

In denying the reality of relations, Bradley and other idealists were denying, in particular, that there is any relation of distinction between things and thoughts about those things. This lack of a distinction between thoughts and objects of thought is characteristic of one form of idealism, and so Bradley's denial of relations also led to a kind of idealism. Russell and Moore

---

[28] Dutilh Novaes and Geerdink, "The Dissonant Origins of Analytic Philosophy," tell an alternative and powerful story that focuses not, as mine does, on the MI's source in the tolerance of unintelligible relations, but rather on the MI and the value accorded to the method of analysis.

282   THE PARMENIDEAN ASCENT

thus were exercised both about Bradley's idealism and about his monism, but as Russell notes, "I think Moore was most concerned with the rejection of idealism, while I was most interested in the rejection of monism" (Russell, *My Philosophical Development*, p. 54).

Russell and Moore sometimes mischaracterized Bradley's thesis as the claim that all relations are internal and as merely a denial of external relations, i.e. of relations that are independent of the natures of the relata. Bradley does sometimes focus on external relations in his critique of relations, but, as we saw in chapter 3, his critique is as much a challenge to the notion of relationality as such: both internal and external relations come under attack. I will continue to speak of Bradley's attack in these more general terms.

Why does Bradley reject the reality of relations? As we have explained particularly in chapters 3 and 10, Bradley rejects relations because they are unintelligible, because they violate the PSR. In insisting that relations be explicable and should be rejected because they are not explicable, Bradley articulates a claim that is a general version of Quine's more specific rejection of relations of distinction between analytic and synthetic statements. Indeed, it's worth noting that Bradley—more than fifty years before Quine's "Two Dogmas"—argued against the analytic/synthetic distinction for reasons that are continuous with his reasons for the rejection of relations.[29] But the key point for the historical story that I am telling now is that Russell and Moore also saw Bradley's argument against relations (and thus his argument for monism and idealism) as turning on the PSR.

Russell is explicit on this point. He points out correctly (in *My Philosophical Development*, p. 58 and "The Monistic Theory of Truth," pp. 164–65) that Bradley's regress argument depends on the rejection of brute or inexplicable relations and on the PSR (or, as Russell calls it just as Quine does, "the Law of Sufficient Reason"). Seeing Bradley's use of the principle as the source of Bradley's monism and idealism, Russell attacks this principle. He flatly rejects the PSR and embraces inexplicable relations. Russell says (correctly, I believe) that Bradley's view on relations

> seems to rest upon some law of sufficient reason, some desire to show that every truth is "necessary." I am inclined to think that a large part of my disagreement with Mr. Bradley turns on a disagreement as to the notion of "necessity." I do not myself admit necessity and possibility as fundamental

---

[29] See Bradley, *Philosophy of Logic*, p. 185.

notions: it appears to me that fundamentally truths are merely true in fact, and that the search for a "sufficient reason" is mistaken. ("Some Explanations in Reply to Mr. Bradley," p. 374)

Given the fundamentality of Russell's rejection of the non-reality of relations to his critique of Bradleyan monism and idealism, and thus given its fundamentality to his role in the formation of analytical philosophy, it is no exaggeration to say that Russell's rejection of the PSR made possible his role as one of the founding theorists of analytical philosophy.

The same is true of Moore's role as a generator of analytical philosophy. Moore, too, sees Bradley's denial of the reality of relations as fundamental to Bradley's system, and he goes after Bradley at precisely that point. Moore obviously has no problem with ungrounded or inexplicable relations. In his early, landmark essay "The Nature of Judgement" (1899), an essay that, as Russell acknowledges was a major influence on Russell, Moore makes his acceptance of ungrounded relations clear in the context of his treatment of the relations between a thinker and concepts or possible objects of thought. Moore points out, in effect, that this relation is an external relation: "It is indifferent to their [concepts'] nature whether anybody thinks them or not" ("The Nature of Judgment," p. 4).

The general claim that there may be external relations, relations not grounded in the natures of the relata (or in anything else) emerges more clearly in Moore's 1919 paper "External and Internal Relations." That relations hold is, Moore says, often a mere matter of fact:

> It seems quite obvious that in the case of many relational properties which things have, the fact that they have them is *a mere matter of fact*. ("External and Internal Relations," p. 88, emphasis in original; see also p. 99)

In these passages, Moore's commitment to the rejection of the PSR is apparent and so is his commitment to ungrounded or inexplicable relations. And these commitments help form the basis of Moore's attack on Bradleyanism and help form the basis of Moore's contribution to the rise of analytical philosophy.

Fair enough, you might say, but so what? What does all this neat stuff about Russell's and Moore's fundamental commitment to the inexplicability of at least some relations and to the falsity of the PSR have to do with the prominence of the MI in philosophy as we know it today?

First, note that Moore is, in a way, the patron saint of the MI. The beliefs that Moore shows deference to are, above all, beliefs in the form of the dictates of so-called common sense. Thus, Moore says in another landmark essay "A Defence of Common Sense" (1925): "the 'Common Sense view of the world' is, in certain fundamental features, *wholly* true" (p. 118). For Moore, commonsense beliefs must be accommodated: "to speak with contempt of those 'Common Sense beliefs' which I have mentioned is quite certainly the height of absurdity" (p. 119).[30] Moore thus espouses a version of the MI in which commonsense beliefs (about cases in particular) are accorded primacy, and principles that go against commonsense beliefs have no legitimate role to play.[31]

Russell also is a fan of the commonsense version of the MI, though his endorsement is a more nuanced one that gives deference to science as well.[32] Although Russell supports his rejection of monism "on empirical grounds" informed by science ("Logical Atomism," pp. 338–39), we also find Russell explicitly rejecting the PSR and monism in part on the basis of something like common sense. Thus, he rejects the PSR by appealing to ways of defining necessity that "account for its common uses" ("Some Explanations in Reply to Mr. Bradley," p. 374), and in a classic statement of the MI, he says, "Pluralism is the view of science and common sense and is *therefore* to be accepted if the arguments against it are not conclusive."[33]

So Moore and Russell adhere to the MI and, in different ways, defer to common sense.

By contrast, Bradley is no fan of common sense and is much more willing than either Moore or Russell to go against our intuitions. Thus, we find Bradley acknowledging that the acceptance of external relations is a deliverance of common sense:

> At first sight obviously such external relations seem possible and even existing. They seem given to us . . . in change of spatial position and gain also in comparison. That you do not alter what you compare or rearrange in space seems to Common Sense quite obvious, and that on the other side

---

[30] Recall Kit Fine's Moorean comments quoted at the beginning of chapter 7.
[31] See also Moore's equally influential essay "Proof of an External World."
[32] Dutilh Novaes and Geerdink, "The Dissonant Origins of Analytic Philosophy," stress this and other differences between Russell's and Moore's commitments to a commonsense methodology.
[33] *An Outline of Philosophy*, p. 264, my emphasis; see also Russell, "The Philosophy of Logical Atomism," p. 178, and *Our Knowledge of the External World*, p. 65.

there are as obvious difficulties does not occur to Common Sense at all. (Bradley, *Appearance and Reality*, p. 514)

In rejecting external relations, as he does, Bradley is thus explicitly going against common sense. In a striking expression of non-deference to common sense, Bradley says:

I am not to be moved here by the charge of an insult offered to Common Sense. For not only in speculation, but in life, we must all be ready to affront that which somewhere, perhaps, in the name of Common Sense may claim our respect.... Common Sense taken ... at its worst, is in its essence a one-sidedness, which we must not be afraid to mark as stupid or even, perhaps, to denounce as immoral. (Bradley, "Relations," p. 640)

Although inveighing against common sense in these ways doesn't by itself mean that Bradley rejects the MI in general, he certainly comes closer to doing so than do either Russell or Moore.

I should note that Bradley's obvious disdain here for philosophy based on common sense opens up the possibility of seeing him as a fundamentally non-conservative thinker, in contrast to the usual interpretation of Bradley as a conservative and even as a reactionary. Peter Nicholson also offers a reading of Bradley as non-conservative at least when it comes to moral and political philosophy. (See Nicholson, *The Political Philosophy of the British Idealists*, chapter 1, section 8.)

OK then, Russell and Moore embrace a version of the MI, and Bradley seems more or less hostile to the MI. But, again, so what? What bearing does this interesting difference have on the other interesting difference, lately noted, between Bradley, on the one hand, and Russell and Moore, on the other, viz. the difference whereby Russell and Moore accept inexplicable relations and Bradley does not? To answer this question, recall that, as I have argued, inexplicable relations are fundamental to the MI (in any version). Further, as I have also argued, the key objections to the MI stem from this very commitment to inexplicable relations. In this light, we can see that once Russell and Moore—in their youthful, headlong effort to avoid Bradleyan idealism and monism—rushed to embrace inexplicable relations, the way was paved for them to adopt some version of the MI. Not only was the commitment to inexplicable relations necessary for adopting the MI, but it was also practically sufficient in this context for adopting the MI. Given that

Bradley's metaphysical views were, as we have just seen, bound up with his methodology which was in tension with the MI, it follows that in attending to Bradley's metaphysics it was only natural for Russell and Moore to address themselves to methodological matters. In particular, once Russell and Moore focused on the interaction between principles and intuitions, once inexplicable relations were allowed on the table, and once the major objections to the MI were thus off the table, there was, if I may put it this way, no reason for Russell and Moore *not* to adopt the MI, and so they did. In this context, in which, among other things, they succumbed to the allure of inexplicable relations, the MI was indeed almost inevitable.

And not only was it almost inevitable, it became so thoroughly ingrained among philosophers who followed in the footsteps of Russell and Moore that the problems with the MI did not even show up on the radar screen of most philosophers in the soon-to-be-dominant analytic tradition. Thus, as we saw, certain contemporary philosophers such as Pryor and Kelly channel Moore and praise philosophical conservatism without any apparent pangs of conscience. Indeed, we find more and more philosophers—right up until the present—pursuing philosophy behind what I have called the veil of intuition. For these philosophers who feel the now almost instinctive aversion to Bradleyan monism—an aversion that is more or less part of the collective unconscious (or collective conscious) of analytical philosophers—some version of the MI is completely natural, and any apparent alternative is, in effect, unthinkable.

In this light, it is not surprising that many contemporary philosophers who reject something like Bradleyan monism are explicitly fans of the MI.[34] In this light also, we can begin to see that philosophers, such as Quine, who promote (perhaps unknowingly) Bradley-esque arguments concerning relations are, like Bradley himself, less in line with the MI than most contemporary philosophers. Because of this Bradleyan connection, such philosophers may stand outside the analytic tradition in an important respect. Thus, Quine's Bradley-esque argument in "Two Dogmas"—in addition to being seen often as a high point of analytical philosophy—may also be, in fact, the beginning of the end of analytical philosophy, for it has influentially embodied a kind of argumentation that runs counter to the presuppositions on which analytical

---

[34] For example, Lewis—a proponent of the MI—is an atomist who rejects any form of monism. Schaffer—also a proponent of the MI—endorses, as we have seen, a form of monism but rejects the much more radical form to be found in Bradley. See Schaffer, "Monism: The Priority of the Whole."

philosophy was founded and which have, for better or worse, dominated much of philosophy ever since.

To be clear: my claim is not that Quine in "Two Dogmas" and philosophers such as Davidson who argue in this vein were directly influenced by Bradley. At the time of "Two Dogmas," practically no one—except perhaps Richard Wollheim—was reading Bradley any more. Nor am I saying that Quine and others explicitly rejected the MI. Rather, my claim is that the similarity between Quine's argument and Bradley's reveals Quine (and others) to be out of step both with the MI and with an originating force of analytical philosophy.

So we have at least a partial answer to the second guiding question: Why now? Why has the MI been so popular over the last one hundred years or so? The answer—or an answer—is that the rejection of Bradleyan monism required the acceptance of inexplicable relations which paved the way for the adoption of the MI. And, as we saw, we also have an answer to the first guiding question: Is it good? Is the MI a good method for philosophical inquiry? The answer I offered is that this method is highly problematic because, in several ways, the pursuit of the MI embroils its practitioners in inexplicable relations, relations of a kind that Quinean and Bradleyan arguments have taught us to be wary of and, more generally, inexplicable relations that seem to make the pursuit of philosophy more arbitrary than we might have expected or would have desired.

Indeed, we can now see that the story I have told in answer to the "Why Now?" question only strengthens the negative answer I gave to the "Is it Good?" question earlier in this chapter. For this narrative has revealed that a large part of the basis for the early analytic embrace of the MI derives from the rejection of the PSR as it is used in the Bradleyan argument against relations and thus in the Bradleyan argument for monism and idealism. And it is crucial to note that, although Russell and Moore explicitly or implicitly deny the PSR as it appears in Bradley's argument, they do so without offering any effective argument for that rejection.

I'm not aware of any place where Moore argues against the PSR instead of just question-beggingly, in this context, assuming its falsity. Russell does have more to say about his rejection of the PSR as the PSR is used in the cosmological argument for the existence of God.[35] However, there he focuses on the claim that the world has a cause, a claim which he regards as meaningless,

---

[35] See his famous debate with Copleston in Hick, *The Existence of God*, pp. 167–78. I am indebted to Alex Silverman for calling this exchange to my attention.

but he does not offer there an argument against the use of the PSR in the Bradleyan argument against relations.

Russell takes up a Bradleyan argument in "The Monistic Theory of Truth" (also in *My Philosophical Development*, chapter 5) when he addresses an argument against relations by Bradley's disciple Harold Joachim in Joachim's *The Nature of Truth*. Here Russell doesn't argue directly against the use of the PSR in the regress argument, and he instead focuses his critique on Joachim's and Bradley's claim—as Russell sees it—that all relations are internal. Yet, as we have mentioned a number of times, Bradley's conclusion is *not* that all relations are internal; rather, for Bradley, the conclusion is that all relations—internal and external—are to be rejected. Russell has simply misconstrued Bradley's position here.[36] Thus, Russell again has failed to engage directly with the core of Bradley's position and thus with the way Bradley employs the PSR to reach the conclusion he actually reaches. In this light, Russell's rejection of the use of the PSR in Bradley's argument is ineffectual and perhaps even question-begging.

And here it is worth keeping in mind that, in contrast to the lack of a good argument in Russell and Moore against the use of the PSR by Bradley, positive (and, of course, controversial) arguments *for* (an unrestricted version of) the PSR are available as I have stressed at the end of chapter 10, in the section "An Untenable Position for PSR-Tamers" and in my paper, "PSR."

Since Bradley's argument is explicitly dependent on a use of the PSR, and since Moore and Russell deny this use of the PSR without effective argument and perhaps even without a non-question-begging argument, Moore and Russell can be seen as simply having no good argument against Bradley. Yes, Moore's and Russell's arguments may have been rhetorically more effective in gaining adherents than Bradley's arguments couched, as they are, in leaden and often impenetrable prose, but in the end Moore's and Russell's arguments are, at best, dialectically ineffective, and so—as far as the attack of Moore and Russell is concerned—Bradley's argument and his position remain unscathed. Thus, the movement toward the MI at the origin of analytical philosophy is a movement conceived in sin—the sin of begging the question against or at least failing to properly address the argument of the far less elegant Bradley. This story—this *genealogy*—unmasks the suspect origins of the dominance of the MI and thus may add significant weight to the philosophical misgivings about the MI expressed earlier in this chapter.

---

[36] I advance no interpretation of Joachim's views here.

And with the MI thus neutralized or at least weakened, the way is clear for a different and more favorable perspective on the Parmenidean Ascent. As we have seen, the Parmenidean Ascent embodies such deeply implausible claims as the rejection of relations (including relations of distinction) and all the implausible claims that follow from this rejection. The fact that the Parmenidean Ascent may involve us in such implausibility and counterintuitiveness is now—with the multifarious challenges to the MI that I have presented—no longer to be regarded as a threat to the Parmenidean Ascent.

A Threefold Suggestion

Of course, the tendency to get sucked back not only into the MI, but also into the pursuit (discussed in chapter 10) of a limited PSR, and into the striving to endow our words and sentences with relational metaphysical significance is strong. And we must always be vigilant.[37] To help us make progress on our Parmenidean journey and to avoid setbacks, in the face of these non-Parmenidean urges, I would like to make the following threefold suggestion.

First, take explanatory demands seriously and let them be your guide. That is, explore without prejudice the implications of—including the skeptical implications of—explanatory demands. In other words, give full rein, as I have tried to do, to the PSR. Where it leads may be surprising, good, and troubling all at the same time.

Second, explore the history of philosophy, especially the history of philosophy before the iron curtain of the MI came down on philosophy. By disregarding intuition and taking seriously explanatory demands that were taken seriously when philosophers' vision was less clouded by the veil of intuitions, we will be helping to prepare the way for the Parmenidean Ascent.

Finally, throughout all these endeavors, don't run from skepticism and, in particular, don't, in desperation, do ultimately incoherent things in order to avoid a skepticism that you might initially find unattractive. Instead, take skepticism and its insights seriously, even up to the point of welcoming the self-undermining that extreme skepticism can bring.

These recommendations are, unsurprisingly, recommendations to do precisely the kind of thing that I have been doing throughout this

---

[37] Eternal vigilance is the price of philosophy.

book: examining various areas of philosophy with an eye to explanatory demands, with a deep appreciation of the study of the history of philosophy as a way of doing philosophy, and with a healthy respect for the power of skeptical methods and outcomes. This power is a power to free our words and sentences, to free philosophy, and to free ourselves from the scourge of unintelligible relations.

And to the extent that we realize this freedom, not only do we make the Parmenidean Ascent, but we also, realize a philosophy untamed.

12
Tractatus Parmenideo-Philosophicus[1]

---

[1] This chapter is an imperfect attempt to exhibit the freedom from relational metaphysical explanation that I advocate. This chapter was conceived before Tyron Goldschmidt's interesting and only superficially similar work, "A Demonstration of the Causal Power of Absences," appeared. The negative point Goldschmidt's paper expresses is not something that my chapter conveys. For invaluable advice concerning earlier versions of this chapter, I am indebted to many friends and colleagues, including the fellow travelers on a memorable late-night mini-bus ride (replete with glowing axles) to Jerusalem in May 2013.

13
The Parmenidean Ascent

I have often thought it ironic that the writings of Parmenides—one of the most famous monists in the history of philosophy—are available to us only in the form of

Bibliography

The following abbreviations are used in this book.

A   Gottfried Leibniz. *Sämtliche Schriften und Briefe*. Deutsche Akademie der Wissenschaften, Darmstadt, Leipzig, and Berlin: Berlin Academy, 1923–.

AG   Gottfried Leibniz. *Philosophical Essays*. Roger Ariew and Daniel Garber (trans.). Indianapolis: Hackett, 1989.

AT   René Descartes. *Oeuvres de Descartes*. Charles Adam and Paul Tannery (eds.). Paris: J. Vrin, 1964–1976.

CSM1 and CSM2 René Descartes, *The Philosophical Writings of Descartes*, vols. 1 and 2. John Cottingham, Robert Stoothoff, and Dugald Murdoch (eds. and trans.). Cambridge: Cambridge University Press, 1984, 1985.

CSMK   René Descartes. *The Philosophical Writings of Descartes*, vol. 3. John Cottingham, Robert Stoothoff, Dugald Murdoch, and Anthony Kenny (eds. and trans.). Cambridge: Cambridge University Press, 1991.

Adams, Robert. *Leibniz: Determinist, Theist, Idealist*. New York: Oxford University Press, 1994.
———. "Primitive Thisness and Primitive Identity." *Journal of Philosophy* 76 (1979): 5–26.
Aguilar, Jesus H. and Andrei Buckareff (eds.). *Causing Human Actions: New Perspectives on the Causal Theory of Action*. Cambridge, Mass.: MIT Press, 2010.
Alexander, Joshua, Ronald Mallon, and Jonathan M. Weinberg. "Accentuate the Negative." *Review of Philosophy and Psychology* 1 (2010): 297–314.
Amijee, Fatema. "Explaining Contingent Facts." *Philosophical Studies*, forthcoming.
———. "Relativism about Fundamentality." Unpublished manuscript.
———. "The Rationalist Foundations of Hume's Dictum." Unpublished manuscript.
Anscombe, G. E. M. *Causality and Determination*. Cambridge: Cambridge University Press, 1971.
———. "Chisholm on Action." In Geach and Gormally (eds.), *Human Life, Action and Ethics*, pp. 77–87.
———. *Human Life, Action and Ethics: Essays by G. E. M. Anscombe*, Mary Geach and Luke Gormally (eds.). Exeter: Imprint Academic, 2005.

———. *Intention*. Cambridge, Mass.: Harvard University Press, 2000 (originally published 1957).
———. "Practical Inference." In Geach and Gormally (eds.), *Human Life, Action and Ethics*, pp. 109–47.
Aquinas, St. Thomas. *Corpus Thomisticum*. www.corpusthomisticum.org (website containing original language versions of Aquinas' texts).
———. *The Summa Contra Gentiles of St. Thomas Aquinas*. Literally translated by the English Dominican Fathers from the latest Leonine edition, first book. London: Burns, Oates, and Washbourne, 1924.
———. *The Summa Theologica*. New York: Benziger Bros edition, 1947.
———. *Truth [De Veritate]*, vol. 1. Translated from the definitive Leonine text by Robert W. Mulligan, S. J. Chicago: Henry Regnery, 1952.
Aristotle. *The Basic Works of Aristotle*. Richard McKeon (ed.). New York: The Modern Library, 2001.
Armstrong, David. *A Combinatorial Theory of Possibility*. Cambridge: Cambridge University Press, 1989.
———. *A World of States of Affairs*. Cambridge: Cambridge University Press, 1997.
Audi, Paul. "Toward a Theory of the in-Virtue-of Relation." *Journal of Philosophy* 109 (2012): 685–711.
Ayers, Michael. "The Ideas of Power and Substance in Locke's Philosophy." In I. C. Tipton (ed.), *Locke on Human Understanding*. Oxford: Oxford University Press, 1977, pp. 77–104.
Ayers, Michael. *Locke: Epistemology and Ontology*, vol. 2. London: Routledge, 1991.
Barnes, Jonathan. *The Presocratic Philosophers*, vol. 1. London: Routledge, 1982.
Bealer, George. "The Incoherence of Empiricism." *Aristotelian Society*, supplementary vol. 66 (1992): 99–138.
———. "Intuition and the Autonomy of Philosophy." In DePaul and Ramsey (eds.), *Rethinking Intuition*, pp. 201–39.
———. "Modal Epistemology and the Rationalist Renaissance." In Gendler and Hawthorne (eds.), *Conceivability and Possibility*, pp. 71–125.
Bengson, John. "The Intellectual Given." *Mind* 124 (2015): 707–60.
Bennett, Jonathan. *A Study of Spinoza's Ethics*. Indianapolis: Hackett, 1984.
———. "Substratum." *History of Philosophy Quarterly* 4 (1987): 197–215.
Bennett, Karen. "By Our Bootstraps." *Philosophical Perspectives* 25 (2011): 27–41.
———. "Construction Area (No Hard Hat Required)." *Philosophical Studies* 154 (2011): 79–104.
———. *Making Things Up*. Oxford: Oxford University Press, 2017.
Bishop, John. *Natural Agency: An Essay on the Causal Theory of Action*. Cambridge: Cambridge University Press, 1989.
Bishop, Michael A. "Why the Generality Problem Is Everybody's Problem." *Philosophical Studies* 151 (2010): 285–98.
Black, Max. "The Identity of Indiscernibles." *Mind* 61 (1952): 153–64.
Bliss, Ricki. "Metaphysical Grounding." In Edward N. Zalta (ed.), *Stanford Encyclopedia of Philosophy*, online resource.
Boehm, Omri. *Kant's Critique of Spinoza*. New York: Oxford University Press, 2014.
———. "The Principle of Sufficient Reason, the Ontological Argument and the Is/Ought Distinction." *European Journal of Philosophy* 24 (2016): 556–79.
Bradley, Francis Herbert. *Appearance and Reality*. Oxford: Clarendon Press, 1968.

———. *Essays on Truth and Reality*. Oxford: Clarendon Press, 1914.
———. *The Principles of Logic*, vol. 1, 2nd edition. London: Oxford University Press, 1922.
———. "Relations." In Bradley, *Collected Essays*, vol. 2. Oxford: Clarendon Press, 1935, pp. 628–76.
Brampton, C. Kenneth. "Nominalism and the Law of Parsimony." *The Modern Schoolman* 41 (1964): 273–81.
Bratman, Michael. "Hierarchy, Circularity, and Double Reduction." In Bratman, *Structures of Agency: Essays*, pp. 68–88.
———. "Rational and Social Agency: Reflections and Replies." In Vargas and Yaffe (eds.), *Rational and Social Agency*, pp. 294–344.
———. "Reflection, Planning, and Temporally Extended Agency." *Philosophical Review* 109 (2000): 35–61.
———. *Structures of Agency: Essays*. New York: Oxford University Press, 2007.
———. "Two Problems about Human Agency." In Bratman, *Structures of Agency: Essays*, pp. 90–105.
Brewer, Bill. *Perception and Reason*. Oxford: Clarendon Press, 1999.
Broackes, Justin. "Substance." *Proceedings of the Aristotelian Society* 106 (2006): 133–68.
Cameron, Ross. "Truthmakers and Ontological Commitment: Or, How to Deal with Complex Objects and Mathematical Ontology without Getting into Trouble." *Philosophical Studies* 140 (2008): 1–18.
Campbell, Charles A. *Scepticism and Construction*. London: George Allen and Unwin, 1931.
Candlish, Stewart. *The Russell/Bradley Dispute and Its Significance for Twentieth-Century Philosophy*. New York: Palgrave MacMillan, 2007.
Cappelen, Herman. *Philosophy Without Intuitions*. Oxford: Oxford University Press, 2012.
Carriero, John. "Substance and Ends in Leibniz." In Paul Hoffman, David Owen, and Gideon Yaffe (eds.), *Contemporary Perspectives on Early Modern Philosophy: Essays in Honor of Vere Chappell*. Peterborough, Ontario: Broadview, 2008, pp. 115–40.
Cartwright, Richard. "Some Remarks on Essentialism." In Cartwright, *Philosophical Essays*. Cambridge, Mass.: MIT Press, 1987, pp. 149–59.
Cassam, Quassim. "Can the Concept of Knowledge be Analysed?" In Greenough and Pritchard (eds.), *Williamson on Knowledge*, pp. 12–30.
Clarke, Desmond. *Descartes's Theory of Mind*. Oxford: Oxford University Press, 2003.
Clarke, Timothy. *Aristotle and the Eleatic One*. Oxford: Oxford University Press, 2019.
Cohen, S. Mark. "Aristotle's Metaphysics." In Edward N. Zalta (ed.), *Stanford Encyclopedia of Philosophy*, online resource.
Cohen, Stewart. "How to Be a Fallibilist." *Philosophical Perspectives* 2 (1986): 91–123.
Comesaña, Juan. "A Well-Founded Solution to the Generality Problem." *Philosophical Studies* 129 (2006): 27–47.
Conee, Earl and Fred Feldman, "The Generality Problem for Reliabilism." *Philosophical Studies* 89 (1998): 1–29.
Correia, Fabrice and Benjamin Schnieder (eds.). *Metaphysical Grounding: Understanding the Structure of Reality*. Cambridge: Cambridge University Press, 2012.
Coxon, A. H. *The Fragments of Parmenides: A Critical Text with Introduction and Translation, the Ancient Testimonia, and a Commentary*, revised and expanded edition. Las Vegas: Parmenides, 2009.
Cummins, Robert. "Reflection on Reflective Equilibrium." In DePaul and Ramsey (eds.), *Rethinking Intuition*, pp. 113–27.

Curd, Patricia. *The Legacy of Parmenides: Eleatic Monism and Later Pre-Socratic Thought.* Princeton: Princeton University Press, 1998.

Daly, Chris. "Scepticism about Grounding." In Correia and Schnieder (eds.), *Metaphysical Grounding*, pp. 81-100.

D'Ambrosio, Justin. "Monogamy: Or How to Make a Commitment to Only One Thing and Stick with It." Unpublished manuscript.

Dancy, Jonathan, "Moral Particularism." In Edward N. Zalta (ed.), *Stanford Encyclopedia of Philosophy*, online resource.

Dasgupta, Shamik. "Metaphysical Rationalism." *Nous* 50 (2016): 379-418.

Davidson, Donald. "Actions, Reasons, and Causes." *Journal of Philosophy* 60 (1963): 685-700.

———. "Actions, Reasons, and Causes." In Davidson, *Essays on Actions and Events*, pp. 3-19.

———. "A Coherence Theory of Truth and Knowledge." In Ernest Lepore (ed.), *Truth and Interpretation: Perspectives on the Philosophy of Donald Davidson*. Oxford: Basil Blackwell, 1986, 307-19.

———. *Essays on Actions and Events*. Oxford: Oxford University Press, 1980.

———. "Freedom to Act." In Davidson, *Essays on Actions and Events*, pp. 63-81.

———. *Inquiries into Truth and Interpretation*. Oxford: Clarendon Press, 1984.

———. "Introduction." In Davidson, *Inquiries into Truth and Interpretation*, xiii-xx.

———. "Problems in the Explanation of Action." In Davidson, *Problems of Rationality*. Oxford: Clarendon Press, 2004, pp. 101-16.

———. "Reply to Foster." In Davidson, *Inquiries into Truth and Interpretation*, pp. 171-79.

———. "Truth and Meaning." In Davidson, *Inquiries into Truth and Interpretation*, pp. 17-36.

———. "On the Very Idea of a Conceptual Scheme." In Davidson, *Inquiries into Truth and Interpretation*, pp. 183-98.

Della Rocca, Michael. "Descartes, the Cartesian Circle, and Epistemology without God." *Philosophy and Phenomenological Research* 70 (2005): 1-33.

———. "The Elusiveness of the One and the Many in Spinoza: Substance, Attribute, and Mode." In Jack Stetter and Charles Ramond (eds.), *Spinoza in Twenty-First Century American and French Philosophy*. London: Bloomsbury, 2019, pp. 59-86.

———. "Essentialism vs. Essentialism." In Tamar Gendler and John Hawthorne (eds.), *Conceivability and Possibility.*, pp. 223-52.

———. "The Identity of Indiscernibles and the Articulability of Concepts." *Linguistics and Philosophical Investigations* 7 (2008): 29-36.

———. "Interpreting Spinoza: The Real Is the Rational." *Journal of the History of Philosophy* 53 (2015): 523-35.

———. "Parmenides' Insight and the Possibility of Logic." Unpublished manuscript.

———. "Perseverance, Power, and Eternity: Purely Positive Essence in Spinoza." Unpublished manuscript.

———. "Playing with Fire: Hume, Rationalism, and a Little Bit of Spinoza." In Della Rocca, *The Oxford Handbook of Spinoza*. New York: Oxford University Press, 2017, pp. 434-63.

———. "Primitive Persistence and the Impasse between Three-Dimensionalism and Four-Dimensionalism." *Journal of Philosophy* 108 (2011): 591-616.

———. "PSR." *Philosophers' Imprint* 10 (2010): 1-13.

———. "Rationalism, Idealism, Monism, and Beyond." In Eckart Förster and Yitzhak Melamed (eds.), *Spinoza and German Idealism*. Cambridge: Cambridge University Press, 2012, pp. 7–26.
———. "Razing Structures to the Ground." *Analytical Philosophy* 55 (2014): 276–94.
———. *Spinoza*, 2nd edition. London: Routledge, forthcoming.
———. "The Taming of Philosophy." In Mogens Laerke, Eric Schliesser, and Justin Smith (eds.), *Philosophy and Its History*. Oxford: Oxford University Press, 2013, pp. 188–208.
———. "Two Spheres, Twenty Spheres, and the Identity of Indiscernibles." *Pacific Philosophical Quarterly* 86 (2005): 480–92.
———. "Violations of the Principle of Sufficient Reason (in Leibniz and Spinoza)." In Correia and Schnieder (eds.), *Metaphysical Grounding*, pp. 139–64.
DePaul, Michael and William Ramsey (eds.). *Rethinking Intuition: The Psychology of Intuition and Its Role in Philosophical Inquiry*. Lanham, Md.: Rowman and Littlefield, 1998.
———. "Why Bother with Reflective Equilibrium?" In DePaul and Ramsey (eds.), *Rethinking Intuition*, pp. 293–309.
DeRose, Keith. *The Appearance of Ignorance: Knowledge, Skepticism, and Context*, vol. 2. Oxford: Oxford University Press, 2017.
———. *The Case for Contextualism: Knowledge, Skepticism, and Context*, vol. 1. Oxford: Clarendon Press, 2009.
———. "Solving the Skeptical Problem." *Philosophical Review* 104 (1995): 1–52.
deRosset, Louis. "Getting Priority Straight." *Philosophical Studies* 149 (2010): 73–97.
———. "Grounding Explanations." *Philosophers' Imprint* 13 (2013): 1–26.
Descartes, René. *Oeuvres de Descartes*. Charles Adam and Paul Tannery (eds.). Paris: J. Vrin, 1964–1976. (Abbreviated: AT)
———. *The Philosophical Writings of Descartes*, vols. 1 and 2. John Cottingham, Robert Stoothoff, and Dugald Murdoch (eds. and trans.). Cambridge: Cambridge University Press, 1984, 1985. (Abbreviated: CSM1 and CSM2)
———. *The Philosophical Writings of Descartes*, vol. 3. John Cottingham, Robert Stoothoff, Dugald Murdoch, and Anthony Kenny (eds. and trans.). Cambridge: Cambridge University Press, 1991. (Abbreviated: CSMK).
Descombes, Vincent. *Le Complément de Sujet: Enquête sur le fait d'agir de soi-même*. Paris: Gallimard, 2004.
———. *The Institutions of Meaning: A Defense of Anthropological Holism*. Cambridge, Mass.: Harvard University Press, 2014.
Devitt, Michael and Kim Sterelny. *Language and Reality: An Introduction to the Philosophy of Language*, 2nd edition. Cambridge, Mass.: MIT Press, 1999.
Diamond, Cora. *The Realistic Spirit: Wittgenstein, Philosophy, and the Mind*. Cambridge, Mass.: MIT Press, 1991.
Diamond, Cora and James Conant, "On Reading the *Tractatus* Resolutely: Reply to Meredith Williams and Peter Sullivan." In Max Kölbel and Bernhard Weiss (eds.), *Wittgenstein's Lasting Significance*. New York: Routledge, 2004, pp. 46–99.
Di Bella, Stefano. "Leibniz's Theory of Conditions: A Framework for Ontological Dependence." *The Leibniz Review* 15 (2005): 67–93.
Diels, Hermann and Walther Kranz (eds.). *Die Fragmente der Vorsokratiker*, 6th revised edition, 3 vols. Berlin: Weidmann, 1952 (first edition, 1903).
Dretske, Fred I. *Knowledge and the Flow of Information*. Cambridge, Mass.: MIT Press, 1981.

―――. "The Pragmatic Dimension of Knowledge." *Philosophical Studies* 40 (1981): 363–78.

Dummett, Michael. "Can Analytical Philosophy Be Systematic and Ought It to Be?" In Dummett, *Truth and Other Enigmas*. Cambridge, Mass.: Harvard University Press, 1978, pp. 437–58.

―――. *Frege: Philosophy of Language*. London: Duckworth, 1973.

―――. *Origins of Analytical Philosophy*. Cambridge, Mass.: Harvard University Press 1993.

Dutilh Novaes, Catarina and Leon Geerdink. "The Dissonant Origins of Analytic Philosophy." In Sandra Lapointe and Christopher Pincock (eds.), *Innovations in the History of Analytic Philosophy*. London: Palgrave Macmillan, 2017, pp. 69–102.

Elgin, Catherine. *Considered Judgment*. Princeton: Princeton University Press, 1996.

Elgin, Samuel. "Merely Partial Definition and the Analysis of Knowledge." *Synthese* (forthcoming).

Fantl, Jeremy and Matthew McGrath. "Evidence, Pragmatics, and Justification." *Philosophical Review* 111 (2002): 67–94.

Field, Hartry. "Deflationist Views of Meaning and Content." *Mind* 103 (1994): 249–85.

Fine, Kit. "Essence and Modality." *Philosophical Perspectives* 8 (1994): 1–16.

―――. "A Guide to Ground." In Correia and Schnieder (eds.), *Metaphysical Grounding*, pp. 37–80.

―――. Interview with *3am Magazine* (2012). https://316am.site123.me/articles/metaphysical-kit?c=end-times-archive.

―――. "Ontological Dependence." *Proceedings of the Aristotelian Society* NS 95 (1995): 269–90.

―――. "The Question of Realism." *Philosophers' Imprint* 1 (2001): 1–30.

―――. "Senses of Essence." In Walter Sinott-Armstrong, Diana Raffman, and Nicholas Asher (eds.), *Modality, Morality, and Belief: Essays in Honor of Ruth Barcan Marcus*. Cambridge: Cambridge University Press. 1995, pp. 53–73.

―――. "Some Puzzles of Ground." *Notre Dame Journal of Formal Logic* 51 (2010): 97–118.

―――. "The Study of Ontology." *Nous* 25 (1991): 263–94.

Fiocco, M. Oreste. "Each Thing Is Fundamental: Against Hylomorphism and Hierarchical Structure." *American Philosophical Quarterly* 56 (2019): 289–301.

Fodor, Jerry. "Fodor's Guide to Mental Representation: The Intelligent Auntie's Vade-Mecum." *Mind* 94 (1985): 76–100.

Ford, Anton. "Action and Generality." In Ford, Hornsby, and Stoutland (eds.), *Essays on Anscombe's Intention*, pp. 76–104.

Ford, Anton, Jennifer Hornsby, and Frederick Stoutland. *Essays on Anscombe's Intention*. Cambridge, Mass.: Harvard University Press, 2011.

Foster, John. "Meaning and Truth Theory." In Gareth Evans and John McDowell (eds.), *Truth and Meaning*. Oxford: Clarendon Press, 1976, pp. 1–32.

Frankfurt, Harry. "The Faintest Passion." In Frankfurt, *Necessity, Volition, and Love*. Cambridge: Cambridge University Press, 1999, pp. 95–107.

―――. "Identification and Externality." In Frankfurt, *The Importance of What We Care About*, pp. 58–68.

―――. "Identification and Wholeheartedness." In Frankfurt, *The Importance of What We Care About*, pp. 159–78.

―――. *The Importance of What We Care About*. New York: Cambridge University Press, 1988.

---. "The Problem of Action." In Frankfurt, *The Importance of What We Care About*, pp. 69–79.
Franks, Paul. *All or Nothing: Systematicity, Transcendental Arguments, and Skepticism in German Idealism*. Cambridge, Mass.: Harvard University Press, 2005.
Furth, Montgomery. "Elements of Eleatic Ontology." *Journal of the History of Philosophy* 6 (1968): 111–32.
Gallop, David (trans.). *Parmenides of Elea: Fragments*. Toronto: University of Toronto Press, 1984.
Garber, Daniel. *Descartes's Metaphysical Physics*. Chicago: University of Chicago Press, 1992.
———. *Leibniz: Body, Substance, Monad*. New York: Oxford University Press, 2009.
Gaskin, Richard. *The Unity of the Proposition*. Oxford: Oxford University Press, 2008.
Gendler, Tamar and John Hawthorne (eds.). *Conceivability and Possibility*. New York: Oxford University Press, 2002.
Gettier, Edmund L. "Is Knowledge Justified True Belief?" *Analysis* 23 (1963): 121–23.
Gilson, Étienne. "De la critique des forms substantielles au doute méthodique." In *Études sur le Rôle de la Pensée Médiévale dans la Formation du Système Cartésien*, 4th edition. Paris: J. Vrin, 1975, pp. 141–90.
———. *The Philosophy of Saint Thomas Aquinas*. St. Louis: B. Herder Book, 1941.
Glanzberg, Michael. "Truth." In Edward N. Zalta (ed.), *Stanford Encyclopedia of Philosophy*, online resource.
Goff, Philip (ed.). *Spinoza on Monism*. Basingstoke, Hampshire: Palgrave Macmillan, 2012.
Goldfarb, Warren. "Metaphysics and Nonsense." *Journal of Philosophical Research* 22 (1997): 57–73.
———. "*Das überwinden*: Anti-Metaphysical Readings of the *Tractatus*." In Rupert Read and Matthew A. Lavery (eds.), *Beyond the Tractatus Wars: The New Wittgenstein Debate*. New York: Routledge, 2011, pp. 6–21.
Goldman, Alvin I. "A Causal Theory of Knowing." *Journal of Philosophy* 64 (1967): 357–72.
———. "Discrimination and Perceptual Knowledge." *Journal of Philosophy* 73 (1976): 777–91.
———. *Epistemology and Cognition*. Cambridge, Mass.: Harvard University Press, 1986.
———. "Philosophical Intuitions: Their Target, Their Source, and Their Epistemic Status." *Grazer Philosophische Studien* 74 (2007): 1–26.
Goldschmidt, Tyron. "A Demonstration of the Causal Power of Absences." *Dialectica* 70 (2016): 85.
Goodman, Nelson. *Fact, Fiction, and Forecast*, 4th edition. Cambridge, Mass.: Harvard University Press, 1983.
Greenough, Patrick and Duncan Pritchard (eds.). *Williamson on Knowledge*. Oxford: Oxford University Press, 2009.
Gregory, Andrew. "Parmenides, Cosmology, and Sufficient Reason." *Apeiron* 47 (2014): 16–47.
Grice, H. P. "The Causal Theory of Perception." *Proceedings of the Aristotelian Society*, supplementary vol. 35 (1961): 121–52.
———. "Meaning." *Philosophical Review* 66 (1957): 377–88.
———. "Meaning Revisited." In N. V. Smith (ed.), *Mutual Knowledge*. New York: Academic Press, 1982, pp. 222–43.
———. "Method in Philosophical Psychology (From the Banal to the Bizarre)." *Proceedings and Addresses of the American Philosophical Association* 48 (1975): 23–53.

Guthrie, W. K. C. *A History of Greek Philosophy*, vol. 2. Cambridge: Cambridge University Press, 1965.

Hacker, P. M. S. "Was He Trying to Whistle It?" In Alice Crary and Rupert Read (eds.), *The New Wittgenstein*. London: Routledge, 2000, pp. 353–89.

Han, Sungil. "Identity, Dependence, and the Problem of Alienation." Ph.D. Dissertation. Yale University, 2013.

Hare, R. M. "Rawls' Theory of Justice—I." *Philosophical Quarterly* 23 (1973): 144–55.

Harman, Gilbert. "Skepticism and Foundations." In Steven Luper (ed.), *The Skeptics: Contemporary Essays*. Hampshire, England: Ashgate, 2003, pp. 1–11.

———. "Three Trends in Moral and Political Philosophy." *Journal of Value Inquiry* 37 (2003): 415–25.

Hawthorne, John. *Knowledge and Lotteries*. Oxford: Clarendon Press, 2004.

Hendricks, Vincent F. and John Symons. *Formal Philosophy: Aim, Scope, Direction*. Automatic Press: 2005.

Henninger, Mark. *Relations: Medieval Theories 1250-1325*. Oxford: Clarendon Press, 1989.

Hick, John. *The Existence of God: Readings Selected, Edited, and Furnished with an Introductory Essay*. New York: Macmillan, 1964.

Hoffman, Joshua and Gary S. Rosenkranz. *Substance: Its Nature and Existence*. London: Routledge, 1997.

Hofweber, Thomas. "Ambitious, Yet Modest, Metaphysics." In David J. Chalmers, David Manley, and Ryan Wasserman (eds.), *Metametaphysics: New Essays on the Foundations of Ontology*. Oxford: Oxford University Press, 2009, pp. 260–89.

Hogan, Desmond. "Metaphysical Motives of Kant's Analytic-Synthetic Distinction." *Journal of the History of Philosophy* 51 (2013): 267–307.

Hooker, Brad and Margaret Little (eds.). *Moral Particularism*. Oxford: Clarendon Press, 2000.

Horgan, Terence and Matjaž Potrč. *Austere Realism: Contextual Semantics Meets Minimal Ontology*. Cambridge, Mass.: MIT Press, 2008.

———. "Existence Monism Trumps Priority Monism." In Goff (ed.), *Spinoza's Monism*, pp. 51–76.

Hornsby, Jennifer. "The Standard Story of Action: An Exchange (2)." In Aguilar and Buckareff (eds.), *Causing Human Actions,* pp. 57–68.

Horwich, Paul. *Meaning*. Oxford: Clarendon Press, 1999.

Hume, David. *An Enquiry Concerning Human Understanding*. Tom L. Beauchamp (ed.). Oxford: Oxford University Press, 1999.

———. *A Treatise of Human Nature*. David Fate Norton and Mary J. Norton (eds.). Oxford: Oxford University Press, 2000.

Hutchison, Keith. "Dormitive Virtues, Scholastic Qualities, and the New Philosophies." *History of Science* 29 (1991): 245–78.

Hylton, Peter. *Russell, Idealism, and the Emergence of Analytic Philosophy*. Oxford: Clarendon Press, 1990.

Ichikawa, Jonathan and Matthias Steup. "The Analysis of Knowledge." In Edward N. Zalta (ed.), *Stanford Encyclopedia of Philosophy*, online resource.

Jenkins, C. S. I. "Intuition, 'Intuition,' Concepts and the *A Priori*." In Anthony Robert Booth and Darrell P. Rowbottom (eds.), *Intuitions*. Oxford: Oxford University Press, 2014, pp. 91–115.

Joachim, Harold H. *The Nature of Truth*. Oxford: Clarendon Press, 1906.

Jolley, Nicholas. *Locke: His Philosophical Thought*. Oxford: Oxford University Press, 1999.
Kahn, Charles. *Essays on Being*. Oxford: Oxford University Press, 2009.
Kagan, Shelly. "Thinking about Cases." *Social Philosophy and Policy* 18 (2001): 44-63.
Kant, Immanuel. *Critique of Pure Reason*. Paul Guyer and Allen Wood (eds. and trans.). Cambridge: Cambridge University Press, 1999.
———. "On a Discovery Whereby Any New Critique of Pure Reason Is to Be Made Superfluous by an Older One." In Kant, *Theoretical Philosophy after 1781*, Henry Allison and Peter Heath (eds.). Cambridge: Cambridge University Press, 2002, pp. 271-336.
Kelly, Thomas. "Common Sense as Evidence: Against Revisionary Ontology and Skepticism." *Midwest Studies in Philosophy* 32 (2008): 53-78.
———. "Moorean Facts and Belief Revision, or Can the Skeptic Win?" *Philosophical Perspectives* 19 (2005): 179-209.
Kenny, Anthony. *Aquinas on Being*. Oxford: Clarendon Press, 2002.
Kim, Jaegwon. "The Nonreductivist's Troubles with Mental Causation." In Kim, *Supervenience and Mind: Selected Philosophical Essays*. Cambridge: Cambridge University Press, 1993, pp. 336-57.
Kimhi, Irad. *Thinking and Being*. Cambridge, Mass.: Harvard University Press, 2018.
Kirk, G. S., J. E. Raven, and M. Schofield. *The Presocratic Philosophers: A Critical History with a Selection of Texts*. Cambridge: Cambridge University Press, 1984.
Kornblith, Hilary. "Naturalism and Intuitions." *Grazer Philosophische Studien* 74 (2007): 27-49.
Korsgaard, Christine. "The Normative Constitution of Agency." In Vargas and Yaffe (eds.), *Rational and Social Agency*, pp. 190-214.
———. "Personal Identity and the Unity of Agency." *Philosophy and Public Affairs* 18 (1989): 102-31.
———. *Self-Constitution: Agency, Identity, and Integrity*. New York: Oxford University Press, 2009.
Kripke, Saul. *Naming and Necessity*. Cambridge, Mass.: Harvard University Press, 1980.
———. *Wittgenstein on Rules and Private Language*. Cambridge, Mass.: Harvard University Press, 1982.
Laks, André and Glenn W. Most (eds. and trans.). *Early Greek Philosophy: Western Greek Thinkers*, part 2. Cambridge, Mass.: Harvard University Press, 2016.
Lavin, Douglas. "Must There Be Basic Action?" *Nous* 47 (2013): 273-301.
Leibniz, Gottfried. *Confessio Philosophi: Papers Concerning the Problem of Evil, 1671-1678*. Robert C. Sleigh, Jr. (ed. and trans.), with contributions from Brandon Look and James Stam. New Haven: Yale University Press, 2005.
———. *Discourse on Metaphysics*. In Leibniz, *Philosophical Essays*, Ariew and Garber (trans.), pp. 35-68.
———. *The Labyrinth of the Continuum: Writings on the Continuum Problem, 1672-1686*. Richard T. W. Arthur (trans. and ed.). New Haven: Yale University Press, 2001.
———. *Leibniz's "New System" and Associated Contemporary Texts*. Roger Woolhouse and Richard Francks (trans. and eds.). Oxford: Clarendon Press, 1997.
———. *Monadology*. In Leibniz, *Philosophical Essays*, Ariew and Garber (trans.), pp. 213-25.
———. *New Essays on Human Understanding*. Peter Remnant and Jonathan Bennett (trans. and eds.). Cambridge: Cambridge University Press, 1981.
———. *Philosophical Papers and Letters*, 2nd edition. Leroy Loemker (ed. and trans.) Dordrecht: Reidel, 1969.

———. *Philosophical Essays*. Roger Ariew and Daniel Garber (trans.). Indianapolis: Hackett, 1989. (Abbreviated: AG)

———. *Philosophical Writings*. Mary Morris and G. H. R. Parkinson (trans.). London: Dent, 1973.

———. *Die Philosophischen Schriften Von Gottfried Wilhelm Leibniz*, 7 vols. Carl Gerhardt (ed.). Berlin: Weidmann, 1875–1890.

———. *Sämtliche Schriften und Briefe*. Deutsche Akademie der Wissenschaften, Darmstadt, Leipzig, and Berlin: Berlin Academy, 1923–. (Abbreviated: A)

———. *De Summa Rerum: Metaphysical Papers, 1675–1676*. G. H. R. Parkinson (ed. and trans.). New Haven: Yale University Press, 1992.

———. *Textes Inédits*. Gaston Grua (ed.). Paris: Presses Universitaires de France, 1948.

———. *Theodicy: Essays on the Goodness of God, the Freedom of Man, and the Origin of Evil*. E. M. Huggard (trans.). LaSalle, Ill.: Open Court, 1985.

———. *Die Werke von Leibniz Reihe I: Historisch-politische und Staatswissenschaftliche Schriften*, vol. 9. Onno Klopp (ed.). Hannover: Klindworth, 1873.

Leisinger, Matthew. "Leibniz's Response to Primitive Persistence." Unpublished manuscript.

Levey, Samuel. "The Paradox of Sufficient Reason." *Philosophical Review* 125 (2016): 397–430.

———. "On Unity: Leibniz-Arnauld Revisited." *Philosophical Topics* 31 (2003): 245–75.

Levy, Yair. "Intentional Action First." *Australasian Journal of Philosophy* 91 (2013): 705–18.

Lewis, David. "Against Structural Universals." *Australasian Journal of Philosophy* 65 (1986): 25–46.

———. *Counterfactuals*. Cambridge, Mass.: Harvard University Press, 1973.

———. "Counterparts of Persons and their Bodies." *Journal of Philosophy* 68 (1971): 203–11.

———. "Elusive Knowledge." In Lewis, *Papers in Metaphysics and Epistemology*, pp. 418–45.

———. "How to Define Theoretical Terms." In Lewis, *Philosophical Papers*, pp. 78–95.

———. "Introduction." In Lewis, *Philosophical Papers*, pp. ix–xii.

———. "Mad Pain and Martian Pain." In Lewis, *Philosophical Papers*, pp. 122–30.

———. "New Work for a Theory of Universals." In Lewis, *Papers in Metaphysics and Epistemology*, pp. 8–55.

———. *Papers in Metaphysics and Epistemology*. Cambridge: Cambridge University Press, 1999.

———. *Philosophical Papers*, vol. 1. New York: Oxford University Press, 1983.

———. *On the Plurality of Worlds*. Oxford: Blackwell, 1986.

———. "Putnam's Paradox." In Lewis, *Papers in Metaphysics and Epistemology*, pp. 56–77.

———. "Tensing the Copula." *Mind* 111 (2002): 1–14.

Lewis, David and Rae Langton. "Defining Intrinsicness." In Lewis, *Papers in Metaphysics and Epistemology*, pp. 116–32.

Litland, Jon Erling. "On Some Counterexamples to the Transitivity of Grounding." *Essays in Philosophy* 14:1, Article 3 (2013).

Locke, John. *An Essay Concerning Human Understanding*. Peter H. Nidditch (ed.). Oxford: Clarendon Press, 1975.

———. *The Works of John Locke*, vol. 4. Aalen: Scientia Verlag, 1963. (Original edition: London: Tegg, 1823).

Long, A. A. "The Principles of Parmenides' Cosmogony." *Phronesis* 8 (1963): 90–107.

Longuenesse, Béatrice. "Kant's Deconstruction of the Principle of Sufficient Reason." *Harvard Review of Philosophy* 9 (2001): 67–87.

Look, Brandon. "Grounding the Principle of Sufficient Reason: Leibnizian Rationalism versus the Humean Challenge." In Carlos Fraenkel, Dario Perinetti, and Justin Smith (eds.), *The Rationalists: Between Tradition and Revolution*. Heidelberg: Springer, 2011, pp. 201–19.

Lovejoy, Arthur O. *The Great Chain of Being: A Study in the History of an Idea*. Cambridge, Mass.: Harvard University Press, 1936.

Lowe, E. J. "Ontological Dependence." In Edward N. Zalta (ed.), *Stanford Encyclopedia of Philosophy*, online resource.

———. *The Possibility of Metaphysics: Substance, Identity, and Time*. Oxford: Clarendon Press, 1998.

Ludwig, Kirk. "The Epistemology of Thought Experiments: First Person Versus Third Person Approaches." *Midwest Studies in Philosophy* 31 (2007): 128–59.

MacFarlane, John. *Assessment Sensitivity: Relative Truth and Its Applications*. Oxford: Oxford University Press, 2014.

Malebranche, Nicolas. *The Search after Truth*. Thomas M. Lennon and Paul J. Olscamp (trans. and eds.). New York: Cambridge University Press, 1997.

Matson, Wallace I. *Grand Theories and Everyday Beliefs: Science, Philosophy, and Their Histories*. New York: Oxford University Press, 2011.

Maurer, Armand. "Method in Ockham's Nominalism." *Monist* 61 (1978): 426–43.

———. "Ockham's Razor and Chatton's Anti-Razor." *Mediaeval Studies* 46 (1984): 463–75.

Maurin, Anna-Sofia. "Bradley's Regress." *Philosophy Compass* 7 (2012): 794–807.

McCann, Edwin. "Locke on Substance." In Lex Newman (ed.), *The Cambridge Companion to Locke's "Essay Concerning Human Understanding."* Cambridge: Cambridge University Press, 2007, pp. 157–91.

McDaniel, Kris. *The Fragmentation of Being*. Oxford: Oxford University Press, 2017.

McMahan, Jeff. "Moral Intuition." In H. LaFollette (ed.), *Blackwell Guide to Ethical Theory*. Malden, Mass.: Blackwell, 2000, pp. 92–110.

Melamed, Yitzhak, and Martin Lin. "The Principle of Sufficient Reason." In Edward N. Zalta (ed.), *Stanford Encyclopedia of Philosophy*, online resource.

Mercer, Christia. "The Contextualist Revolution in Early Modern Philosophy." *Journal of the History of Philosophy* 57 (2019): 529–48.

Millikan, Ruth. "Truth, Hoverflies, and the Kripke-Wittgenstein Paradox." *Philosophical Review* 99 (1990): 323–53.

Miracchi, Lisa. "Epistemic Agency and the Generality Problem." *Philosophical Topics* 45 (2017): 107–20.

Moore, G. E. "A Defence of Common Sense." In Moore, *Selected Writings*, pp. 106–33.

———. "External and Internal Relations." In Moore, *Selected Writings*, pp. 79–105.

———. "The Nature of Judgement." In Moore, *Selected Writings*, pp. 1–19.

———. "Proof of an External World." In Moore, *Selected Writings*, pp. 147–70.

———. *Selected Writings*. Thomas Baldwin (ed.). London: Routledge, 1993.

Mourelatos, Alexander P. D. *The Route of Parmenides*, revised and expanded edition. Las Vegas: Parmenides, 2008.

———. "Some Alternatives in Interpreting Parmenides." *Monist* 62 (1979): 3–14.

Mourelatos, Alexander P. D. and Massimo Pulpito, "Parmenides and the Principle of Sufficient Reason." In Massimo Pulpito and Pilar Spangenberg (eds.), *Ways to*

Think: Essays in Honour of Néstor-Luis Cordero. Bologna: Diogene Multimedia, 2018, pp. 121–41.

Mugnai, Massimo. "Leibniz and 'Bradley's Regress.'" *The Leibniz Review* 20 (2010): 1–12.

———. *Leibniz' Theory of Relations*. Stuttgart: F. Steiner, 1992.

Mühlebach, Deborah. "Reflective Equilibrium as an Ameliorative Framework in Feminist Epistemology." *Hypatia* 31 (2016): 874–89.

Nagel, Jennifer. *Knowledge: A Very Short Introduction*. Oxford: Oxford University Press, 2014.

Nehamas, Alexander. "On Parmenides' Three Ways of Inquiry." *Deucalion* 33/34 (1981): 97–111.

———. "Parmenidean Being/Heraclitean Fire." In Victor Caston and Daniel Graham (eds.), *Presocratic Philosophy: Essays in Honour of Alexander Mourelatos*. Hants: Ashgate, 2002, pp. 45–64.

Nicholson, Peter P. *The Political Philosophy of the British Idealists: Selected Studies*. Cambridge: Cambridge University Press, 1990.

Normore, Calvin. "Buridan's Ontology." In James Bogen and J. E. McGuire (eds.), *How Things Are*. Dordrecht: Reidel, 1985, pp. 189–204.

Nozick, Robert. *Philosophical Explanations*. Cambridge, Mass.: Harvard University Press, 1981.

Ott, Walter. *Causation and Laws of Nature in Early Modern Philosophy*. Oxford: Oxford University Press, 2009.

Owen, G. E. L. "Eleatic Questions." *Classical Quarterly* N.S. 10 (1960): 84–102.

———. "Plato and Parmenides on the Timeless Present." *Monist* 50 (1966): 317–40.

Palmer, John. (2012), "Parmenides." In Edward N. Zalta (ed.), *Stanford Encyclopedia of Philosophy*, online resource.

———. *Parmenides and Presocratic Philosophy*. Oxford: Oxford University Press, 2009.

Parsons, Charles. "Platonism and Mathematical Intuition in Kurt Gödel's Thought." *Bulletin of Symbolic Logic* 1 (1995): 44–74.

Paul, L. A. "Metaphysics as Modeling: The Handmaiden's Tale." *Philosophical Studies* 160 (2012): 1–29.

Paul, Sarah. "Deviant Formal Causation." *Journal of Ethics and Social Philosophy* 5 (2011): 1–23.

Peacocke, Christopher. "Deviant Causal Chains." *Midwest Studies Philosophy* 4 (1979): 123–55.

———. *Holistic Explanation: Action, Space, Interpretation*. Oxford: Clarendon Press, 1979.

Phemister, Pauline. *Leibniz and the Natural World*. Dordrecht: Springer, 2005.

Plato. *Theaetetus*. In Plato, *Complete Works*, John Cooper (ed.). Indianapolis: Hackett, 1997, pp. 157–234.

Priest, Graham. *One: Being an Investigation into the Unity of Reality and of Its Parts, Including the Singular Object Which Is Nothingness*. Oxford: Oxford University Press, 2014.

Pruss, Alexander. *The Principle of Sufficient Reason: A Reassessment*. Cambridge: Cambridge University Press, 2010.

Pryor, James. "The Skeptic and the Dogmatist." *Nous* 34 (2000): 517–49.

Putnam, Hilary. "The Meaning of 'Meaning.'" In Putnam, *Mind, Language and Reality: Philosophical Papers*, vol. 2. Cambridge: Cambridge University Press, 1975, pp. 215–71.

———. "Models and Reality." *Journal of Symbolic Logic* 45 (1980): 464–82.
Quine, W. V. O. "Carnap and Logical Truth." In Quine, *The Ways of Paradox and Other Essays*, pp. 107–32.
———. "Five Milestones of Empiricism." In *Theories and Things*, pp. 67–72.
———. *From a Logical Point of View*, 2nd edition revised. Cambridge, Mass.: Harvard University Press, 1980.
———. "Identity, Ostension, Hypostasis." In Quine, *From a Logical Point of View*, pp. 65–79.
———. *Pursuit of Truth*, revised edition. Cambridge, Mass.: Harvard University Press, 1992.
———. "Reference and Modality." In Quine, *From a Logical Point of View*, pp. 139–59.
———. "Reply to Professor Marcus." In Quine, *The Ways of Paradox and Other Essays*, pp. 177–84.
———. "Responses." In Quine, *Theories and Things*, pp. 173–86.
———. *Theories and Things*. Cambridge, Mass.: Harvard University Press, 1986.
———. "Three Grades of Modal Involvement." In Quine, *The Ways of Paradox and Other Essays*, pp. 158–76.
———. "Three Indeterminacies." In Robert B. Barrett and Roger F. Gibson (eds.), *Perspectives on Quine*. Oxford: Blackwell, 1990, pp. 1–16.
———. "Truth by Convention." In Quine, *The Ways of Paradox and Other Essays*, pp. 77–106.
———. "Two Dogmas of Empiricism." In Quine, *From a Logical Point of View*, pp. 20–46.
———. "Two Dogmas in Retrospect." *Canadian Journal of Philosophy* 21 (1991): 265–74.
———. *The Ways of Paradox and Other Essays*, revised and enlarged edition. Cambridge, Mass: Harvard University Press, 1976.
Railton, Peter. "How to Engage Reason: The Problem of Regress." In *Reason and Value: Themes from the Philosophy of Joseph Raz*. Oxford: Oxford University Press, 2004, pp. 176–201.
———. "Normative Guidance." In Russ Schafer-Landau (ed.), *Oxford Studies in Metaethics* 1 (2006), pp. 3–33.
Rapp, Christoph. "Zeno and the Eleatic Anti-Pluralism." In M. M. Sassi (ed.), *The Construction of Philosophical Discourse in the Age of the Presocratics*. Pisa: Edizioni della Scuola Normale Superiore, 2006, pp. 161–82.
Raven, Michael. "Is Ground a Strict Partial Order?" *American Philosophical Quarterly* 50 (2013): 193–201.
Rawls, John. "The Independence of Moral Theory." *Proceedings and Addresses of the American Philosophical Association* 48 (1974–75): 5–22.
———. *Justice as Fairness: A Restatement*. Cambridge, Mass.: Harvard University Press, 2001.
———. "Outline of a Decision Procedure for Ethics." *Philosophical Review* 60 (1951): 177–97.
———. *A Theory of Justice*. Cambridge, Mass.: Harvard University Press, 1971.
Rinard, Susanna. "Why Philosophy Can Overturn Common Sense." In Tamar Szabo Gendler and John Hawthorne (eds.), *Oxford Studies in Epistemology* 4 (2013), pp. 185–213.
Rodriguez-Pereyra, Gonzalo. *Leibniz's Principle of Identity of Indiscernibles*. New York: Oxford University Press, 2014.
———. "Why Truthmakers." *Philosophy Compass* 1 (2006): 186–200.

Rorty, Richard. *Philosophy and the Mirror of Nature.* Princeton: Princeton University Press, 1980.
Rosen, Gideon. "Metaphysical Dependence: Grounding and Reduction." In Bob Hale and Aviv Hoffman (eds.), *Modality: Metaphysics, Logic, and Epistemology.* Oxford: Oxford University Press, 2010, pp. 109–36.
Rovane, Carol. *The Bounds of Agency: An Essay in Revisionary Metaphysics.* Princeton: Princeton University Press, 1998.
———. "From a Rational Point of View." *Philosophical Topics* 30 (2002): 209–35.
———. "Self-Constitution, Reductionism, and Their Moral Significance." Forthcoming.
———. "What Sets the Boundaries of Our Responsibility." Forthcoming.
Rozemond, Marleen. *Descartes' Dualism.* Cambridge, Mass.: Harvard University Press, 1998.
———. "Distinction, Separability, and Corporeal Substance in Descartes." *Midwest Studies in Philosophy* 35 (2011): 240–58.
Russell, Bertrand. *A History of Western Philosophy.* New York: Simon and Schuster, 1945.
———. *Logic and Knowledge.* Robert C. Marsh (ed.). New York: George Allen and Unwin, 1956.
———. "Logical Atomism." In Russell, *Logic and Knowledge*, pp. 321–43.
———. "The Monistic Theory of Truth." In Russell, *Philosophical Essays.* London: Longmans, Green, 1910, pp. 150–69.
———. *My Philosophical Development.* London: George Allen and Unwin, 1956.
———. *Our Knowledge of the External World as a Field for Scientific Method in Philosophy.* Chicago: Open Court, 1915.
———. *An Outline of Philosophy.* London: George Allen and Unwin, 1927.
———. "The Philosophy of Logical Atomism." In Russell, *Logic and Knowledge*, pp. 175–281.
———. "Some Explanations in Reply to Mr. Bradley." *Mind* 19 (1910): 373–78.
Rutherford, Donald. *Leibniz and the Rational Order of Nature.* Cambridge: Cambridge University Press, 1995.
Sattler, Barbara. *The Concept of Motion in Ancient Greek Thought: Foundations in Logic, Method, and Mathematics.* Cambridge: Cambridge University Press, forthcoming.
Scanlon, T. M. "Rawls on Justification." In Samuel Freeman (ed.), *The Cambridge Companion to Rawls.* Cambridge: Cambridge University Press, 2003, pp. 139–67.
Schaffer, Jonathan. "Contrastive Knowledge." In Tamar Szabo Gendler and John Hawthorne (eds.), *Oxford Studies in Epistemology* 1 (2005), pp. 235–71.
———. "From Nihilism to Monism." *Australasian Journal of Philosophy* 85:2 (2007): 175–91.
———. "Grounding, Transitivity, and Constrastivity." In Correia and Schnieder (eds.), *Metaphysical Grounding*, pp. 122–38.
———. "Monism." In Edward N. Zalta (ed.), *Stanford Encyclopedia of Philosophy*, online resource.
———. "Monism: The Priority of the Whole." *Philosophical Review* 119 (2010): 31–76.
———. "On What Grounds What." In David J. Chalmers, David Manley, and Ryan Wasserman (eds.), *Metametaphysics: New Essays on the Foundations of Ontology.* Oxford: Oxford University Press, 2009, pp. 347–83.
———. "What Not to Multiply Without Necessity." *Australasian Journal of Philosophy* 93 (2015): 644–64.
———. "Why the World Has Parts: Reply to Horgan and Potrč." In Goff (ed.), *Spinoza on Monism*, pp. 77–91.

Schapiro, Tamar. "Kant's Approach to the Theory of Agency." In Ruth Chang and Kurt Sylvan (eds.), *The Routledge Handbook of Practical Reason*. Forthcoming.
———. "Three Conceptions of Action in Moral Theory." *Nous* 35 (2001): 93–117.
Schechtman, Anat. "Substance and Independence in Descartes." *Philosophical Review* 125 (2016): 155–204.
Schmaltz, Tad. "Descartes on the Metaphysics of the Material World." *Philosophical Review* 127 (2018): 1–40.
———. *The Metaphysics of the Material World: Suárez, Descartes, Spinoza*. Oxford: Oxford University Press, 2019.
Searle, John. *Intentionality*. New York: Cambridge University Press, 1983.
———. *The Rediscovery of the Mind*. Cambridge, Mass.: MIT Press, 1992.
Sedley, David. "Parmenides and Melissus." In A. A. Long (ed.), *The Cambridge Companion to Early Greek Philosophy*. Cambridge: Cambridge University Press, 1999, pp. 113–33.
Sehon, Scott. "Deviant Causal Chains and the Irreducibility of Teleological Explanation." *Pacific Philosophical Quarterly* 78 (1997): 195–213.
———. *Teleological Realism*. Cambridge, Mass.: MIT Press, 2005.
Setiya, Kieran. *Reasons Without Rationalism*. Princeton: Princeton University Press, 2007.
Sextus Empiricus. *Against the Logicians with an English*. R. G. Bury (trans.). Cambridge, Mass.: Harvard University Press, 1935.
———. *Against the Logicians*. Richard Bett (trans. and ed.). New York: Cambridge University Press, 2005.
Shields, Christopher. *Aristotle*, 2nd edition. London: Routledge, 2014.
Sider, Theodore. *Four-Dimensionalism: An Ontology of Persistence and Time*. Oxford: Clarendon Press, 2001.
———. *Writing the Book of the World*. Oxford: Clarendon Press, 2011.
Singer, Peter. "Sidgwick and Reflective Equilibrium." *Monist* 58 (1974): 490–517.
Sleigh, Robert C. *Leibniz and Arnauld: A Commentary on Their Correspondence*. New Haven: Yale University Press, 1990.
Smith, Michael. "Four Objections to the Standard Story of Action (and Four Replies)." *Philosophical Issues* 22 (2012): 387–401.
———. "The Standard Story of Action: An Exchange (1)." In Aguilar and Buckareff, *Causing Human Actions*, pp. 45–55.
Soames, Scott. "Truth and Meaning: In Perspective." *Midwest Studies in Philosophy* 32 (2008): 1–19.
———. *What Is Meaning?* Princeton: Princeton University Press, 2010.
Sober, Elliott. *Ockham's Razors: A User's Manual*. Cambridge: Cambridge University Press, 2015.
Sosa, Ernest. *Reflective Knowledge: Apt Belief and Reflective Knowledge*, vol. 2. Oxford: Clarendon Press, 2009.
Speaks, Jeff. "Theories of Meaning." In Edward N. Zalta (ed.), *Stanford Encyclopedia of Philosophy*, online resource.
———. "Truth Theories, Translation Manuals, and Theories of Meaning." *Linguistics and Philosophy* 29 (2006): 487–505.
Spinoza, Benedict de. *Ethics*. In Edwin Curley (ed. and trans.), *A Spinoza Reader*. Princeton: Princeton University Press, 1994.
Stanley, Jason. *Knowledge and Practical Interests*. Oxford: Clarendon Press, 2005.
Stine, Gail. "Skepticism, Relevant Alternatives, and Deductive Closure." *Philosophical Studies* 29 (1976): 249–61.

Stoljar, Daniel and Nic Damnjanovic. "Deflationary Theories of Truth." In Edward N. Zalta (ed.), *Stanford Encyclopedia of Philosophy*, online resource.

Stoutland, Fred. "Introduction: Anscombe's Intention in Context." In Ford, Hornsby, Stoutland (eds.), *Essays on Anscombe's Intention*, pp. 1–22.

Stroud, Barry. "Epistemological Reflection on Knowledge of the External World." In Stroud, *Understanding Human Knowledge*, pp. 122–38.

———. "Introduction." In Stroud, *Understanding Human Knowledge*, pp. ix–xx.

———. "Scepticism and the Possibility of Knowledge." In Stroud, *Understanding Human Knowledge*, pp. 1–8.

———. *Understanding Human Knowledge*. Oxford: Oxford University Press, 2002.

Symons, John. "Intuition and Philosophical Methodology." *Axiomathes* 18 (2008): 67–89.

Thompson, Michael. *Life and Action: Elementary Structures of Practice and Thought*. Cambridge, Mass.: Harvard University Press, 2008.

Thomson, Judith Jarvis. "How It Was." In Steven M. Cahn (ed.), *Portraits of American Philosophy*. Lanham, Md.: Rowman and Littlefield, 2013, pp. 47–62.

Tor, Shaul. *Mortal and Divine in Early Greek Epistemology: A Study of Hesiod, Xenophanes and Parmenides*. Cambridge: Cambridge University Press, 2017.

Unger, Peter. "Minimizing Arbitrariness: Toward a Metaphysics of Infinitely Many Isolated Concrete Worlds." *Midwest Studies in Philosophy* 9 (1984): 29–51.

Vallicella, William. "Relations, Monism, and the Vindication of Bradley's Regress." *Dialectica* 56 (2002): 3–35.

van Inwagen, Peter. *An Essay on Free Will*. Oxford: Clarendon Press, 1983.

———. *Metaphysics*, 3rd edition. Boulder, Colo.: Westview Press, 2009.

Vargas, Manuel and Gideon Yaffe (eds.). *Rational and Social Agency: The Philosophy of Michael Bratman*. New York: Oxford University Press, 2014.

Velleman, J. David. *How We Get Along*. Cambridge: Cambridge University Press, 2009.

———. "Introduction." In Velleman, *The Possibility of Practical Reason*, pp. 1–31.

———. *The Possibility of Practical Reason*. Ann Arbor: University of Michigan Library, 2000.

———. "What Happens When Someone Acts?" In Velleman, *The Possibility of Practical Reason*, pp. 122–43.

Vogel, Jonathan. "The New Relevant Alternatives Theory." *Philosophical Perspectives* 13 (1999): 155–80.

Vogler, Candace. *Reasonably Vicious*. Cambridge, Mass.: Harvard University Press, 2009.

Walker, Ralph C. S. *The Coherence Theory of Truth*. New York: Routledge, 1989.

Weatherson, Brian. "What Good Are Counterexamples?" *Philosophical Studies* 115 (2003): 1–31.

Watkins, Eric. *Kant and the Metaphysics of Causality*. Cambridge: Cambridge University Press, 2005.

Wedin, Michael V. *Aristotle's Theory of Substance: The Categories and Metaphysics Zeta*. Oxford: Oxford University Press, 2000.

———. *Parmenides' Grand Deduction: A Logical Reconstruction of the Way of Truth*. Oxford: Oxford University Press, 2014.

Weinberg, Jonathan. "How to Challenge Intuitions Empirically Without Risking Skepticism." *Midwest Studies in Philosophy* 31 (2007): 318–43.

Weinberg, Jonathan M., Stephen Crowley, Chad Gonnerman, Ian Vandewalker, and Stacey Swain. *Essays in Philosophy* 13 (2012): 256–83.

Weinberg, Julius. *Abstraction, Relation, Induction: Three Essays in the History of Thought.* Madison and Milwaukee: University of Wisconsin Press, 1965.
Williams, Bernard. *Descartes: The Project of Pure Enquiry.* Harmondsworth, Middlesex: Penguin Books, 1978.
Williamson, Timothy. *Knowledge and Its Limits.* Oxford: Oxford University Press, 2000.
———. *The Philosophy of Philosophy.* Oxford: Blackwell, 2007.
Wilson, Jessica. "Essence and Dependence." In Mircea Dumitru (ed.), *Metaphysics, Meaning, and Modality: Themes from Kit Fine.* Oxford: Oxford University Press, forthcoming.
Wittgenstein, Ludwig. *Tractatus Logico-Philosophicus.* Brian McGuiness and David Pears (trans.). London: Routledge, 1974.
———. *Tractatus Logico-Philosophicus.* C. K. Ogden (trans.). Oxford: Routledge, 1922.
Wollheim, Richard. *F. H. Bradley.* Harmondsworth: Penguin, 1969.
Wood, William. "Thomas Aquinas on the Claim That God Is Truth." *Journal of the History of Philosophy* 51 (2013): 21–47.

Index

For the benefit of digital users, indexed terms that span two pages (e.g., 52–53) may, on occasion, appear on only one of those pages.

acrophobia, 23, 82
action, xv–xvi, xvii, 83–111, 139
    building-block views, 88, 89–90, 105
    causes of, 85–99
    reasons for, 84–86
Adams, Robert, 48n.31, 189–90n.10, 236, 237–38, 238n.19
Agrippan Trilemma, 77, 137
Alexander, Joshua, 266n.12
Amijee, Fatema, 216n.42, 228–29n.1, 244n.24, 248n.29
analytical philosophy, xviii, 74, 182–96, 198–99, 226–27, 260–62, 278–79, 280–90
Anaximander, 9
Anaximenes, 9
Anscombe, G.E.M., 84–85, 86, 98–102, 105, 106, 107, 108, 109–10, 141n.34, 263–64n.4
Aquinas, St. Thomas, 82, 110–11, 143–44, 170, 177–78, 180–81, 218
Aristotle, xiii, 24, 25–40, 41–42, 47, 50, 52, 54–55, 59–60, 71–72, 77–78, 79–80, 82, 100–1, 141n.34
    Categories, 25–26, 27, 28–29, 35–36, 40, 41
    form/matter distinction, 30, 39
    Metaphysics, 26–29
Armstrong, David, 63, 247–48n.27
Arnauld, Antoine, 51
Audi, Paul, 198–99n.5, 199, 202n.16, 203n.22, 206n.30
Ayers, Michael, 54–55n.37

bang-for-the-buck principle, 204–5, 209, 210, 214–16
bankruptcy, xxiin.7

Barnes, Jonathan, 5n.10, 14n.17
Baumgarten, Alexander, 230
Bealer, George, 185–86, 186n.6, 263, 264n.5, 266, 270–71, 272–73, 276, 279
Beatles, White Album, *passim*
being, xv–xvi, 12–16, 22–23, 78, 81–82, 83, 240. *See also* substance
Bengson, John, 185–86, 186n.6, 263, 270n.21, 272
Bennett, Jonathan, 53n.35, 54–55n.37, 228–29
Bennett, Karen, 63, 65n.7, 198–99n.5, 199–200n.9
Berkeley, George, 267–68
Berstler, Sam, 241n.21
Bishop, John, 90–91
Bishop, Michael A., 125n.21
Black, Max, 189n.9
Bliss, Ricki, 199–200
Boehm, Omri, 232–33
Bradley, F.H., xvi, 21–22, 65n.7, 67–68, 73–77, 109, 141, 142, 145, 168, 180, 199–200, 221–22, 230, 235–36, 245, 249, 251, 261–62, 280, 281–88
Bratman, Michael, 96–97, 105n.19, 109
Brewer, Bill, 125n.21
Broackes, Justin, 25n.1
Buridan, Jean, 76–77n.26, 210, 211, 227–28

Campbell, Charles A., 74n.20
Candlish, Stewart, 74n.20, 75n.22
Cappelen, Herman, 186n.6, 186–87
Carriero, John, 49n.33
Carroll, Lewis, 171n.23
Cartwright, Richard, 201n.12

Cassam, Quassim, 132n.27, 137n.30
Clarke, Desmond, 32n.10
Clarke, Timothy, xiv, xvn.4, 16n.20
Cohen, S. Mark, 28, 29
Cohen, Stewart, 127–28
Comesaña, Juan, 125n.21
common sense, 80–81, 159–60, 162, 185–87, 188, 189–90, 260, 261–62, 263, 265, 266–71, 272, 275, 284–85
Conant, James, 99–100n.16, 221n.1
Conee, Earl, 125n.21
conservatism, xxii, 81, 224, 260–61, 267–72, 279, 285, 286
Copleston, Frederick, 287–88n.35
Coxon, A.H., xvn.3
Crowley, Stephen, 186n.6
Cummins, Robert, 270–71n.23
Curd, Patricia, 9n.14, 10, 14n.17

Daly, Chris, 198–99n.4, 199n.8
D'Ambrosio, Justin, 207–8
Damnjanovic, Nic, 176–77n.26, 177–78
Dancy, Jonathan, 263–64n.3
Dasgupta, Shamik, xx–xxi, 228, 233–34, 235–36, 243–44, 245, 255, 257, 258–59
Davidson, Donald, xvii–xviii, 84–90, 95, 99–101, 103, 105, 108, 109–10, 148, 162–65, 166, 167–68, 172, 173–76, 183, 278
  "Actions, Reasons, and Causes," 85–86, 87–88
  "On the Very Idea of a Conceptual Scheme," 173–76
Della Rocca, Michael, xxii–xxiiin.8, xxiii, 21–22n.22, 21–22n.23, 47n.29, 65n.6, 76–77n.25, 119n.14, 159n.11, 171n.22, 189–90n.10, 193n.13, 198–99n.3, 201n.15, 206n.31, 215–16n.41, 225n.9, 230n.2, 248n.29, 257–58
DePaul, Michael, 264n.6
DeRose, Keith, 113–14, 121–22n.18, 124–26, 127–28, 140, 142
deRosset, Louis, 65n.7, 203n.22
Descartes, René, 25, 30–33, 35–41, 42, 47, 50, 52, 54–55, 59–60, 61–62, 64–65, 71, 72, 77–78, 79–80, 80n.31, 82, 186n.6
Descombes, Vincent, 154–56, 166, 172–73

Deviant causal chains, 86–99, 150–51
Devitt, Michael, 147
Diamond, Cora, 221n.1
Di Bella, Stefano, 239n.20
Diehls, Hermann, xvn.3
discreteness, 187–88, 189, 190, 191, 192, 193, 194
distinctions, xiv–xvi, xxi, 10, 16, 78–82, 169–70, 182–83, 194, 195, 216–18, 220–23, 224–25, 226, 243, 249–50, 251–52, 255, 257, 258
Don't mistake the fact that you don't like my conclusions, xxi–xxii, 226
dormitive virtue, 32–34, 73, 100–1, 107, 137
Dretske, Fred, 121–26, 140
du Châtelet, Émilie, 230
Dummett, Michael, 172–73, 183, 190–91, 192
Dutilh Novaes, Catarina, 185–86n.5, 268n.16, 280–81n.28, 284n.32

Elgin, Samuel, 138n.31
essence, constitutive vs. consequential, 65–67, 250
essentialist facts, 233–34, 244, 255–56
experimental philosophy, 266
explanation, xii–9, 54, 113, 197–218, 219, 220, 222–24, 227–28, 233–34, 244–45, 246, 250–51, 252–54, 256, 258, 259, 260–61
explanatory circle, 32–34, 47–48, 55–58, 60, 61, 67, 68–69, 71, 73, 75, 92, 95, 97–98, 101–2, 106–7, 109, 117, 119, 120, 134, 135, 136, 137, 138, 140, 155, 166, 247, 251, 257
explanatory demand, xviii–xx, 26–30, 35–36, 47, 52, 53–54, 61, 81–82, 83–105, 112–16, 123, 127, 130–31, 132–34, 137–40, 145–48, 149–50, 153, 154–57, 158, 159, 160, 161–62, 163, 164–65, 166, 167–68, 169, 176–77, 178–79, 180, 195, 197, 199–200, 217, 219, 227–28, 255, 258, 289–90

Fantl, Jeremy, 130–31n.24, 131–32n.25
Faulkner, William, 196
feature, not a bug, 5–6, 221–22, 222n.4
Feeney, Thomas, 49n.32

INDEX 313

Feldman, Fred, 125n.21
Field, Hartry, 156n.7, 157n.9
Fine, Kit, xx–xxi, 62–63n.3, 65–67, 69n.15, 184, 185–86, 189–90, 198–99, 199n.7, 203n.20, 228, 233–34, 233–34n.13, 246n.25, 284n.30
Fiocco, M. Oreste, 199–200n.10
Fitzgerald, F. Scott, 192
Fodor, Jerry, 150–51
Ford, Anton, 83–84
Foster, John, 164
fragments, xiii, 36–37, 223, 292
Frankfurt, Harry, 86–88, 92–94, 95, 96, 99–100, 109–10, 263
Franks, Paul, 77n.27
Frege, Gottlob, 190, 192
functionalism, 149–52, 167
Furth, Montgomery, xiv, 5–6, 15n.19

Gallop, David, xvn.3
Garber, Daniel, 36n.16, 50–52
Gaskin, Richard, 65n.7, 76–77n.26
Geerdink, Leon, 185–86n.5, 268n.16, 280–81n.28, 284n.32
Gettier, Edmund L., 116–17, 120, 263
Gilson, Étienne, 32–33n.11, 82n.33, 110–11n.21
God, 19, 39–40, 82, 110–11, 143, 170, 180–81, 218, 231–32
Goldfarb, Warren, 221n.1
Goldman, Alvin, 117n.11, 120, 124–25, 126–27, 140, 142, 186n.7
Goldschmidt, Tyron, 291n.1
Gonnerman, Chad, 186n.6
Goodman, Nelson, 265, 272, 276
great resistance, xxii, 226, 260
Gregory, Andrew, 4–5, 14n.17, 14–15n.18
Grice, H.P., 149–52, 158, 164–65, 166–67
ground, xviii–xix, 60–82, 197–200, 202–14, 216–18. *See also* explanation
   as sentential operator, 69–71, 198

Hacker, P.M.S., 221n.1
Han, Sungil, 247–48n.29
Hare, R.M., 270–71n.22, 274
Harman, Gilbert, 268n.16
Hawthorne, John, 130–31n.24
Heide, Dai, 47–48n.30
Henninger, Mark, 76–77n.26

Heraclitus, 9
history of philosophy, xiii–xiv, xviii, 25, 182–96, 275, 289
   and isolationism, 192–93
   and philosophy, 195–96
Hoffman, Joshua, 40n.23
Hofweber, Thomas, 198–99n.4
Hogan, Desmond, 231–32n.7, 232–33n.9, 252–53n.30
holism, xvii–xviii, 170–76, 194–95, 278
Homer, 12–13
Horgan, Terence, 3n.4, 79n.29, 207–8
Hornsby, Jennifer, 89n.7, 99
Horwich, Paul, 146–47, 156–58, 176–77n.26
how, 15, 28, 29, 35–36, 39–40, 42, 55, 72–74, 73n.18, 88–89, 123, 134–35, 141, 155, 159
Hume, David, 21–22, 230, 233, 245, 246–48, 257–58, 261–62, 275
Humean supervenience, 187–88
Hutchison, Keith, 32–33n.11
Hylton, Peter, 74n.20, 75n.22

Ichikawa, Jonathan, 141n.33
intuition, xxii, 66–67, 80–81, 110, 132, 159–60, 162, 199, 216–17
   fallibility of, 186, 188, 266
   method of, 184–88, 189–90, 193, 194, 201–2, 227, 260–90
   veil of, 274, 275, 286, 289
Inwood, Brad, 16n.20

Jenkins, C.S.I., 185–86n.4, 186n.6
Jetsons, The 34n.13
Joachim, Harold, 288
John Wayne moment, 34–36, 38–40, 47, 52, 64–65, 73, 90, 97–98, 118–20, 130, 131–32, 134, 138, 164–65, 168
Jorati, Julia, 49–50

Kagan, Shelly, 264n.5
Kahn, Charles, xvn.4
Kant, Immanuel, xx–xxi, 102–3, 105–6, 184, 228, 230–33, 234, 235–36, 243–44, 245, 250–54, 255, 257, 258–59, 260
Kelly, Thomas, 186n.7, 264n.6, 269–70, 286

Kenaan, Hagi, 224n.8
Kim, Jaegwon, 206–7n.32
Kimhi, Irad, 221
Kirk, G.S, xvn.3, 14n.17
knowledge, xv–, 91–92, 99–100, 112–44
   building-block views, 115–33, 138–39, 141, 142–43
   contextualist theories of, 113–14, 120–21, 124–25, 126–32
   invariantist theories of, 120–23, 124–25, 126–27, 130–32
   knowledge-first views, 99–100, 115–16, 132–39, 140, 141, 142–43
Kornblith, Hilary, 186n.6
Korsgaard, Christine, 102–4, 105n.20, 109–10
Kovacs, David, 132n.26
Kranz, Walther, xvn.3
Kripke, Saul, 95n.13, 158–61, 166, 167–68, 275

ladder, xix–xx, 5–7, 220–21, 222–23
Laks, André, xvn.3
Langton, Rae, 161–62n.15
Lavin, Douglas, 86–87n.4, 99
Leibniz, Gottfried, xx–xxi, 19, 25, 30–32, 35–39, 40–52, 54–55, 59–60, 63, 64–65, 65n.6, 71, 72, 76–78, 79–80, 82, 141n.34, 202–3n.17, 203, 230, 236–43, 247–48, 255–56, 275
Leisinger, Matthew, 46n.28
Leiter, Brian, 185n.2
Levey, Samuel, 228–29n.1
Levy, Yair, 99–100n.15
Lewis, David, 65n.6, 113n.8, 121–22n.18, 125–26n.22, 127, 128–29, 131–32, 135n.28, 149–50n.2, 161–62, 166, 167–68, 185–86, 186n.6, 187–88, 201n.11, 230, 263, 265, 266–67, 268, 272, 275, 286–87n.34
Lin, Martin, 232–33n.8
Locke, John, 25, 52–57, 59–60, 64–65, 72, 79–80, 82, 141n.34
Long, A.A., 4–5n.8
Longuenesse, Béatrice, 252–53
Look, Brandon, 237–38n.18
Lovejoy, Arthur O., 234–35
Lowe, E.J., 39, 40, 72, 77–78
Ludwig, Kirk, 186n.6

MacFarlane, John, 121n.16
Malebranche, Nicolas, 32–33
Mallon, Ronald, 266n.12
mass noun, 78, 109–10, 143, 170, 172n.24, 180, 218, 240
Matar, Anat, 191n.12
Matson, Wallace, 23n.24
Maurer, Armand, 202–3n.17
Maurin, Anna-Sofia, 62n.2
McCann, Edwin, 54, 54–55n.37
McCartney, Paul, 125
McDaniel, Kris, 78n.28
McGrath, Matthew, 130–31n.24, 131–32n.25
McMahan, Jeff, 264n.5
MDR, xxiii, 63
meaning, xv–xviii, 145–81, 182–83, 187–88, 190, 193–95
   causal theories of, 158–60
Melamed, Yitzhak, 21–22n.23, 232–33n.8
Mele, Alfred, 92n.10
Melissus, 7–8n.13
method of intuition. *See* intuition
Millikan, Ruth, 161n.13
Miracchi, Lisa, 125n.21
Molière moment, 33–35, 39–40, 47, 52, 71–72, 100–1, 107, 137–38, 168
monism, xiii–xv, xx–xxi, 1–23, 81–82, 195, 223, 281–82, 283, 285–87
   of action, 107–11
   of being, 78–82, 240
   existence, 3, 21–22, 79, 143
   of explanation, 216–18
   of goodness, 224
   of knowledge, 114, 142–44
   of meaning, 169–76, 179–80, 194–95
   non-strict, 1, 10–13, 17, 19–21, 81–82n.32
   priority, 3, 21–22, 79, 143, 234, 235–36, 256–57
   Radical (RM), 235–36, 240–45, 247–49, 250, 251, 254–57, 281
   strict, 1–2, 3–13, 17, 19–23, 81–82n.32
   of truth, 176–81
Moore, G.E., 188, 190, 260–61, 263, 267–68, 272, 281–82, 283–88
Most, Glenn, xvn.3
Mourelatos, Alexander, xiv, xvn.3, 5, 8–9, 21–22n.23, 38n.18
   and speculative predication, 9–13, 14n.17, 14–15n.18, 16n.20, 16

INDEX

Mugnai, Massimo, 76–77n.25
Mühlebach, Deborah, 270n.19

Nagel, Jennifer, 112, 117–18, 120n.15, 125n.21
Nagel, Thomas, 275
negation, 10–13, 17–21
Nehamas, Alexander, 9n.14
Nicholson, Peter, 285
Nietzsche, Friedrich, 261–62
non-being, 1, 5–6, 10–16, 22–23, 64–65, 73, 77, 81–82, 220, 222–23
Normore, Calvin, 76–77n.26
Nozick, Robert, 113, 121–22n.17, 122–23

Ockham's Razor, xviii, 69, 201–16
Ontological akrasia, 210, 211
Ott, Walter, 32–33n.11
Owen, G.E.L., xiv, 4, 5–6, 14n.17

Palmer, John, 7–8, 21n.21
paradox. *See* self-undermining
   maw of, 197
Parmenidean Ascent. *See* monism
Parmenides, xiii–xvi, xix, 1–23, 25, 29, 35–36, 38, 38n.18, 64–65, 73, 76, 77, 81–82n.32, 109, 220, 221–23, 227–28, 230, 235–36, 245, 261–62, 275, 292
   cosmology of, 1–2, 3–5
   journey of, xv–xvi
Paul, L.A., 268n.16
Paul, Sarah, 95, 99n.14, 100–1n.17, 109
Peacocke, Christopher, 90–92, 123
Phemister, Pauline, 36n.17
Plato, xiii, 27–28, 35–36, 95n.13, 117–18
Portč, Matjaž, 3n.4, 79n.29, 207–8
Priest, Graham, 73n.18
principle of charity, 7–8, 260
principle of sufficient reason (PSR), xiv, 12–23, 29, 61, 74, 201, 228–59, 278, 282–83, 287–88, 289
Pryor, James, 268, 286
PSR. *See* principle of sufficient reason
Pulpito, Massimo, 14n.17, 14–15n.18
Putnam, Hilary, 158–61, 166

Quine, Willard van Orman, xvii–xviii, 65n.7, 170–74, 176, 183, 198–200, 201–2, 213–14, 215–16, 277–79, 286–87

Railton, Peter, 97–98, 109
Ramsification, 135, 150
Rapp, Christoph, 9n.14
rationalism, xiv–xv, xx–xxi, 73–74, 227–28
Raven, J.E, xvn.3, 14n.17
Raven, Michael, 67n.1
Rawls, John, 265–67, 270–71, 272–75, 278n.27
realism, xvii–xviii, 183–84, 187–88, 189, 193–94, 226
reference magnetism, 160–62, 167–68
reflective equilibrium, 264–66, 267, 270–71, 273–75, 276–79
regress, 18–19, 36–38, 39–40, 57–58, 60, 61, 64–65, 66, 67, 68–69, 71, 73, 74–75, 76, 92, 97, 101–2, 107, 109, 118–20, 132, 136, 137, 140, 142, 146n.1, 155, 166, 168, 171n.23, 246–47, 248–50, 251–52, 253, 254–55, 257, 282, 288
relations, xvi, 59–82, 188–89, 198, 216–18, 219–25, 226, 245–47, 249–50, 251–55, 257, 258–59, 260–61, 275, 276–77, 278–80, 281–83, 284–90
   action-making, 108–10
   internal vs. external, 60, 71, 75, 86–87, 89–90, 98–100, 105–6, 108, 109–10, 169, 188–89, 194, 282, 283, 284–85, 288
   knowledge-making, 139–44
   meaning-making, 159, 165–68
   not free-floating, 61–62, 66, 73–74, 246, 247, 249–50, 254
   as objects, 67–69
   and relational facts, 68–71
   substance-making, 59–65, 71–73
relevant alternatives, 91–92, 120–32
Rinard, Susanna, 270–71n.24
Rodriguez-Pereyra, Gonzalo, 199–200n.9
Rorty, Richard, 223–24n.7
Rosen, Gideon, 198–99, 199–200n.9
Rosenkranz, Gary S., 40n.23
Rovane, Carol, 102–3, 104, 105n.20, 109–10
Rozemond, Marleen, 40
Russell, Bertrand, xiv, 21–22, 187–88, 190, 191–92, 230, 247, 249, 260–61, 281–83, 284–86, 287–88
Rutherford, Donald, 43n.27, 44, 48–50

Sattler, Barbara, xiv, 4–5, 13n.16, 14n.17, 15n.19
Scanlon, Thomas, 270n.19
Schaffer, Jonathan, xx–xxi, 3, 3n.4, 65n.8, 67n.11, 76n.24, 129–30, 143, 198–99n.1, 5, 199–200n.9, 202–8, 209, 211–13, 214–16, 234, 235–36, 244–45, 257, 266n.11, 286–87n.34
Schapiro, Tamar, 102–3, 104, 105, 109–10
Schechtman, Anat, 40n.24
Schmaltz, Tad, 36n.17
Schmid, Stefan, 49n.32
Schofield, Malcolm xvn.3, 14n.17
Searle, John, 147–48, 153–54, 158, 166–67, 169
Sedley, David, 4–5n.8, 14n.17
see the world aright, xiv–xv, xix, 22–23, 79–80, 82, 180, 220–21, 223–25
Sehon, Scott, 92n.10
self-undermining, xviii–xix, 5–7, 196, 197, 219–25, 226, 258, 289
Setiya, Kieran, 83–84, 95, 109
Sextus Empiricus, 5–6, 223–24n.7, 261–62, 275
Shields, Christopher, 28
Sider, Ted, 69n.16, 161–62n.14, 183–84, 266, 267–68, 272, 276
Silverman, Alex, 287–88n.35
Singer, Peter, 269n.17
Skepticism, xvii, 73, 76, 77, 122, 222, 260–61, 266–67, 271–72, 275, 279, 289–90
Sleigh, Robert, 38n.20
Smith, Michael, 89n.7, 90–91
Soames, Scott, 147, 152–53, 158, 164n.19, 166–67, 169
Sober, Elliott, 202–3n.17
so much the worse for us, 271, 275, 279
Sosa, Ernest, 117, 119n.14
Speaks, Jeff, 147, 149, 156–57n.8, 164n.19
sphere, well-rounded, 14–15
Spinoza, Benedict, xxii–xxiii, 21–22, 30–31, 66, 80n.31, 186n.6, 190, 230, 261–62, 275, and *passim*
Stanley, Jason, 113, 115, 116n.9, 130–32, 140, 142
Steup, Matthias, 141n.33

Stine, Gail, 128
Stoljar, Daniel, 176–77n.26, 177–78
Stoutland, Fred, 100
Strawson, P.F., 268n.16
Stroud, Barry, 112
substance, xv–xvii, 24–58, 59–82, 139. *See also* being
  and complete concepts, 42–43, 45, 48–49, 72
  and force, 49–50, 72
  parts of, 36–39, 59–60
  subject of predication, 25–27, 40, 41
  unity of, 26, 29–31, 32–33, 36–39, 41–42, 44–45, 49–52, 72
substantial forms, 30–36, 38–39, 40, 42, 43–45, 48–49, 50–52
substratum, 53–54
Symons, John, 268n.15

Taming of Philosophy, 260–90
taming of the PSR, xx–xxi, 227–28, 229–31, 233–36, 242, 243–45, 250–52, 255–59, 260
Tarski, Alfred, 162–63, 173–74
Thales, 9
Thompson, Michael, 85n.2
Thomson, Judith Jarvis, 185–86
Tor, Shaul, xvn.4
truth, xvii–xviii, 162–65, 174, 176–81

Unger, Peter, 230n.3

vagueness, 12–13
Vallicella, William, 65n.6
van Cleve, James, 61n.1
Vandewalker, Ian, 186n.6
van Inwagen, Peter, 75, 228–29n.1
Velleman, J. David, 83–84, 93–95, 96, 97, 99–100, 109–10
Vogel, Jonathan, 128n.23
Vogler, Candace, 99

Watkins, Eric, 252–53n.30
Weatherson, Brian, 186n.6
Wedin, Michael, xiv, 6n.11, 14n.17, 27, 29, 30, 35
Weinberg, Jonathan, 186n.6, 266n.12

Weinberg, Julius, 76–77n.26
Williams, Bernard, 183, 184
Williamson, Timothy, 99–100, 113, 115–16, 132–38, 140, 141, 142, 170–71, 272–73, 274–75
Wilson, Jessica, 62–63n.3, 198–99n.4
Wittgenstein, Ludwig, xiv–xv, xix–xx, 5–7, 102, 156, 187–88, 220–21, 258
Wolff, Christian, 230
Wollheim, Richard, 65n.7, 287